IFIP Advances in Information and Communication Technology

574

Editor-in-Chief

Kai Rannenberg, Goethe University Frankfurt, Germany

IFIP – The International Federation for Information Processing

IFIP was founded in 1960 under the auspices of UNESCO, following the first World Computer Congress held in Paris the previous year. A federation for societies working in information processing, IFIP's aim is two-fold: to support information processing in the countries of its members and to encourage technology transfer to developing nations. As its mission statement clearly states:

IFIP is the global non-profit federation of societies of ICT professionals that aims at achieving a worldwide professional and socially responsible development and application of information and communication technologies.

IFIP is a non-profit-making organization, run almost solely by 2500 volunteers. It operates through a number of technical committees and working groups, which organize events and publications. IFIP's events range from large international open conferences to working conferences and local seminars.

The flagship event is the IFIP World Computer Congress, at which both invited and contributed papers are presented. Contributed papers are rigorously refereed and the rejection rate is high.

As with the Congress, participation in the open conferences is open to all and papers may be invited or submitted. Again, submitted papers are stringently refereed.

The working conferences are structured differently. They are usually run by a working group and attendance is generally smaller and occasionally by invitation only. Their purpose is to create an atmosphere conducive to innovation and development. Refereeing is also rigorous and papers are subjected to extensive group discussion.

Publications arising from IFIP events vary. The papers presented at the IFIP World Computer Congress and at open conferences are published as conference proceedings, while the results of the working conferences are often published as collections of selected and edited papers.

IFIP distinguishes three types of institutional membership: Country Representative Members, Members at Large, and Associate Members. The type of organization that can apply for membership is a wide variety and includes national or international societies of individual computer scientists/ICT professionals, associations or federations of such societies, government institutions/government related organizations, national or international research institutes or consortia, universities, academies of sciences, companies, national or international associations or federations of companies.

More information about this series at http://www.springer.com/series/6102

Augusto Casaca · Srinivas Katkoori ·
Sandip Ray · Leon Strous (Eds.)

Internet of Things

A Confluence of Many Disciplines

Second IFIP International Cross-Domain Conference, IFIPIoT 2019
Tampa, FL, USA, October 31 – November 1, 2019
Revised Selected Papers

 Springer

Editors
Augusto Casaca ⓘ
INESC-ID/INOV
Lisbon, Portugal

Srinivas Katkoori ⓘ
University of South Florida
Tampa, FL, USA

Sandip Ray ⓘ
University of Florida
Gainesville, FL, USA

Leon Strous
De Nederlandsche Bank
Amsterdam, The Netherlands

ISSN 1868-4238   ISSN 1868-422X (electronic)
IFIP Advances in Information and Communication Technology
ISBN 978-3-030-43607-0   ISBN 978-3-030-43605-6 (eBook)
https://doi.org/10.1007/978-3-030-43605-6

This Springer imprint is published by the registered company Springer Nature Switzerland AG
The registered company address is: Gewerbestrasse 11, 6330 Cham, Switzerland

Preface

"To connect the unconnected," is the overarching goal of Internet of Things (IoT), an ongoing technology transition. It has great promise to revolutionize the way humans will live on this planet. IoT technology has vast scope and touches every aspect of human life, such as, healthcare, transportation, city living, work life, sustainability, etc. The IFIP Domain Committee on IoT organized the Second IFIP Internet of Things (IoT) conference in Tampa, Florida, which took place during October 31 – November 1, 2019.

The IoT Technical Program Committee consisted of 34 members from 13 countries who considered 22 submissions for the second edition of this conference. Each paper was on average refereed by three reviewers, using the single-blind review principle. In total, 11 papers were selected for presentation resulting in an acceptance rate of 50%. This book contains the revised versions of the refereed papers presented at the conference. The papers were selected on the basis of originality, quality, and relevance to the topic. As expected, the peer-reviewed papers covered a wide array of topics such as self-driving cars, smart buildings, e-health, patient self-monitoring, irrigation management, hybrid context reasoning, hardware security, social-science discourse on IoT research, and edge node processing requirements. The attendees coming from such diverse disciplines had great interaction during the presentation of the technical papers.

Besides peer-reviewed papers, the conference featured 12 invited talks from leading researchers and thought leaders in the IoT space. The invited talks covered topics such as energy constrained inference on distributed IoT edge nodes, adiabatic and low energy IoT edge computing, AI and IoT Security, AI and communications, V2X communication security, edge devices for foolproof detection of fall of adults, IoT security hands-on laboratory, IoT curriculum design of first Bachelor's degree in IoT in the USA, and smart grid. This book includes eight papers from invited speakers. The table of contents indicates which papers were invited talks.

The conference featured two keynote speakers. The first keynote was given by Prof. Marilyn Wolf, Chair of Computer Science and Engineering Department at University of Nebraska-Lincoln, USA. Prof. Wolf's talk entitled "The Case of Edge Intelligence" presented and motivated with various IoT application scenario examples the need for machine learning (ML) on the edge and how ML can be implemented on the edge. The second keynote was given by Prof. Swarup Bhunia, Director of Warren B. Nelms Institute for the Connected World, University of Florida, USA. Prof. Bhunia presented the IoT vision of the Nelms Institute as well as ongoing research on global problems related to critical safety, security, and sustainability.

A panel entitled "AI and IoT" was held and moderated by Mr. Leon Strous. It had three panelists, namely, Prof. Swarup Bhunia (University of Florida, USA), Prof. Kwang-Cheng Chen (University of South Florida, USA), and Mr. Pete Nicoletti (Cybraics, USA). The panel started with the question "Are we intelligent enough to optimize the potential of IoT or do we need AI" and touched upon various topics such as the need for AI in the IoT, how AI can play a critical role in IoT security, etc.

A PhD student forum was held with the intent of providing feedback by the IoT experts in the conference audience to the doctoral students working in the IoT space. A total of 13 PhD posters were presented by students from five universities and three countries. The student research topics included IoT security, IoT edge processor design, smart transportation, light-weight cryptography for IoT communications, Internet of Medical Things (IoMT), smart grid, edge device for automatic stress detection and control, etc.

Both the panel outcome and the PhD posters are not included in this book but we emphasize that these were valuable parts of the program that generated good discussions.

We thank the authors, the Program Committee, and the participants for their hard work and contributions and look forward to their continued involvement.

We feel that all the contributions make the book a rich volume in the IFIP AICT series and we trust and hope that the reader will be inspired by it.

January 2020

Augusto Casaca
Srinivas Katkoori
Sandip Ray
Leon Strous

Organization

General Co-chairs

Srinivas Katkoori   University of South Florida, USA
Leon Strous   De Nederlandsche Bank, The Netherlands

Program Co-chairs

Augusto Casaca   INESC-ID/INOV, Portugal
Sandip Ray   University of Florida, USA

Finance Chair

Mehran Mozaffari Kermani   University of South Florida, USA

Publicity Chairs

Robert Karam   University of South Florida, USA
Jose Neuman de Souza   Federal University of Ceara, Brazil
Simon Perrault   Singapore University Technology and Design, Singapore
Ricardo Reis   Federal University of Rio Grande do Sul, Brazil
Damien Sauveron   Université de Limoges, France

Local Arrangements Chairs

Hao Zheng   University of South Florida, USA
Yier Jin   University of Florida, USA

Web Chair

Omkar Dokur   University of South Florida, USA

Technical Program Committee

Kechar Bouabdellah   University of Oran 1 Ahmed Ben Bella, Algeria
Luis Camarinha-Matos*   Nova University of Lisbon, Portugal
Augusto Casaca*   INESC-ID/INOV, Portugal
Rekha Govindaraj   Apple, Inc., USA
Miria Grisot   IFI, University of Oslo, Norway
Robert Karam   University of South Florida, USA
Srinivas Katkoori*   University of South Florida, USA

Arianit Kurti	Linnaeus University, Sweden
Maryline Laurent	Institut Mines-Télécom, France
Tiziana Margaria	University of Limerick, Ireland
Peter Marwedel	Technical University Dortmund, Germany
Maristella Matera	Politecnico di Milano, Italy
Mehran Mozaffari Kermani	University of South Florida, USA
Jose Neuman de Souza*	Federal University of Ceará, Brazil
Mario Nunes	INOV, USA
Fabio Paterno*	CNR-ISTI, Italy
Sreehari Rao Patri	National Institute of Technology Warangal, India
Shilpa Pendyala	Intel, USA
Simon Perrault	Singapore University of Technology and Design, Singapore
Joachim Posegga	University of Passau, Germany
Ricardo Rabelo	Federal University of Santa Catarina, Brazil
Franz Rammig	University of Paderborn, Germany
Sandip Ray	University of Florida, USA
Rajsaktish Sankaranarayanan	Intel, USA
Carmen Santoro	ISTI-CNR, Italy
Damien Sauveron*	Université de Limoges, France
Davide Rew Spano	ISTI-CNR, Italy
Leon Strous*	De Nederlandsche Bank, The Netherlands
Himanshu Thapliyal	University of Kentucky, USA
Jean-Yves Tigli	Université Côte d'Azur, CNRS, France
Ulrika Westergren*	Umeå University, Sweden
Marco Winckler*	University Paul Sabatier, France
Hao Zheng	University of South Florida, USA

Additional Reviewer

| Muhammad Yasin | Université de Limoges, France |

*are also members of the IFIP Domain Committee IoT

Contents

IoT Applications

Architecting Systems-of-Systems of Self-driving Cars for Platooning
on the Internet-of-Vehicles with SosADL...................... 3
    Flavio Oquendo

Energy Efficiency in Smart Buildings: An IoT-Based Air Conditioning
Control System.. 21
    Felipe Rocha, Lucas Cristiano Dantas, Luís Felipe Santos,
    Samela Ferreira, Bruna Soares, Alan Fernandes, Everton Cavalcante,
    and Thais Batista

Toward Blockchain Technology in IoT Applications:
An Analysis for E-health Applications......................... 36
    Maurício Moreira Neto, Emanuel Ferreira Coutinho,
    Leonardo Oliveira Moreira, and José Neuman de Souza

Context Reasoning and Situational Awareness

I^2VSM Approach: Self-monitoring of Patients Exploring Situational
Awareness in IoT 53
    Rogério Albandes, Roger Machado, Jorge Barbosa,
    and Adenauer Yamin

An IoT Proposal for the Irrigation Management Exploring
Context Awareness.. 71
    Rogério Albandes, Roger Machado, João L. B. Lopes, Jorge Barbosa,
    and Adenauer Yamin

An IoT Architecture to Provide Hybrid Context Reasoning 86
    Roger Machado, Ricardo Almeida, Rogério Albandes,
    Ana Marilza Pernas, and Adenauer Yamin

IoT Security

REDEM: Real-Time Detection and Mitigation of Communication Attacks
in Connected Autonomous Vehicle Applications (Invited) 105
    Srivalli Boddupalli and Sandip Ray

Trust in IoT Devices: A Logic Encryption Perspective................. 123
    Yasaswy Kasarabada, David Luria, and Ranga Vemuri

Latent Space Modeling for Cloning Encrypted PUF-Based Authentication . . .   142
   Vishalini Laguduva Ramnath, Sathyanarayanan N. Aakur,
   and Srinivas Katkoori

Lightweight Countermeasure to Differential-Plaintext Attacks
on Permutation Ciphers   159
   Matthew Lewandowski and Srinivas Katkoori

Smart and Low Power IoT

Challenges in the Design of Integrated Systems for IoT (Invited)   179
   Ricardo Reis

Mixed Precision Quantization Scheme for Re-configurable ReRAM
Crossbars Targeting Different Energy Harvesting Scenarios (Invited)   197
   Md Fahim Faysal Khan, Nicholas Anton Jao, Changchi Shuai, Keni Qiu,
   Mehrdad Mahdavi, and Vijaykrishnan Narayanan

Smart Network Architectures

Toward Holistic Integration of Computing and Wireless Networking
(Invited)   219
   Kwang-Cheng Chen, Yingze Wang, Zixiang Nie, and Qimei Cui

The Thing About the Internet of Things: Scoping the Social Science
Discourse in IoT Research   235
   Viktor Mähler

Evaluating Edge Processing Requirements in Next Generation
IoT Network Architectures   252
   Brooks Olney, Shakil Mahmud, and Robert Karam

Smart System Design and IoT Education

Good-Eye: A Combined Computer-Vision and Physiological-Sensor Based
Device for Full-Proof Prediction and Detection of Fall of Adults (Invited) . . .   273
   Laavanya Rachakonda, Akshay Sharma, Saraju P. Mohanty,
   and Elias Kougianos

Building a Low-Cost and State-of-the-Art IoT Security
Hands-On Laboratory (Invited)   289
   Bryan Pearson, Lan Luo, Cliff Zou, Jacob Crain, Yier Jin,
   and Xinwen Fu

Curriculum Design Requirements and Challenges for the First Bachelor's
Degree on IoT in the US (Invited)   307
   Kemal Akkaya

IoT in Smart Grid: Energy Management Opportunities
and Security Challenges (Invited) 319
    *Motahareh Pourbehzadi, Taher Niknam, Abdollah Kavousi-Fard,
    and Yasin Yilmaz*

Author Index 329

IoT Applications

Architecting Systems-of-Systems
of Self-driving Cars for Platooning
on the Internet-of-Vehicles with SosADL

Flavio Oquendo$^{(\boxtimes)}$ (iD)

IRISA – UMR CNRS 6074, Univ. Bretagne Sud, Vannes, France
flavio.oquendo@irisa.fr

Abstract. A Software-intensive System-of-Systems (SoS) is architecturally designed to exhibit emergent behavior from the interactions among independent constituent systems. With the upcoming generation of self-driving vehicles, an important case of emergent behavior is vehicle platooning. In a platoon, a group of vehicles (which is dynamically formed) safely travel closely together like in a convoy. It requires, on the one hand, that each vehicle in the platoon control its velocity and the relative distance to the vehicle in front of it for avoiding rear collision and, on the other hand, that vehicles coordinate for enabling other vehicles to dynamically join or leave the platoon. This paper investigates the mediated approach for architecting a platooning of self-driving vehicles, with SosADL, a novel SoS Architecture Description Language (ADL) enhanced with broadcasting for the Internet-of-Vehicles (IoV). In particular, it demonstrates how architectural mediators expressed with broadcast constructs of *SosADL for IoV* supports platooning architecture descriptions through an excerpt of a real application for architecting platoons of Unmanned Ground Vehicles (UGVs). This novel approach is supported by an integrated toolset for SoS architects.

Keywords: Software architecture · Self-driving vehicle platooning · Internet-of-Vehicles (IoV) · Systems-of-Systems (SoS) · Broadcasting · SosADL

1 Introduction

Definitely, a key facet of the design of any software-intensive system, being a single system or a System-of-Systems (SoS) [19], is its software architecture, i.e. the fundamental organization of the system embodied in its constituents, their relationships to each other, and to the environment, and the principles guiding its design and evolution, as defined by ISO/IEC/IEEE 42010 [12].

In the case of single systems, the software architecture is described in terms of components, connectors binding together these components, and their configurations [20]. The resultant system behavior is said to be aggregative, for instance, like the behavior of a car that is the result of the sum of the behaviors of its components (e.g. the moving behavior of a car is the resultant of the engine that applies a torque on the wheels turning them forward, the wheels push backwards on the road surface and, in reaction, the road surface pushes back in a forward direction).

A. Casaca et al. (Eds.): IFIPIoT 2019, IFIP AICT 574, pp. 3–20, 2020.
https://doi.org/10.1007/978-3-030-43605-6_1

Differently, in the case of SoSs, the software architecture is described in terms of constituent systems, mediators for enabling interaction among the constituents, and their coalitions [27]. The resultant system behavior is said to be emergent [16], like the behavior of a platoon of cars which results from the interactions of its constituent cars.

In a platoon, a group of vehicles (which is dynamically formed) safely travel closely together like in a convoy [13]. It requires, on the one hand, that each vehicle in the platoon controls its velocity and the relative distance to the vehicle in front of it for avoiding rear collision and, on the other hand, that vehicles coordinate for enabling other vehicles to dynamically join or leave the platoon.

Note that a car is not designed to have the platooning behavior, this emergent behavior "appears" as the result of the interactions among multiple cars. Nevertheless, the car needs to have the capabilities required for participating in platoons.

Nowadays, the Internet-of-Things (IoT) enables the engineering of SoSs, which are opportunistically constructed for achieving specified missions in specific operational environments [10, 38]. In particular, in the subset of IoT where "things" are predominantly connected vehicles (i.e. mobile "things"), the so-called Internet-of-Vehicles (IoV) [14], the challenge is to coordinate different vehicles for performing together, through emergent behavior, traffic-related missions, especially platooning. In the IoV, in a platoon, two or more self-driving vehicles are connected together in convoy using automated driving support and, possibly, wireless connectivity.

There are two main kinds of platoons of self-driving vehicles [41]: (i) platoons of stand-alone self-driving cars: they are formed and managed based only on the local sensing and actuating capabilities of each self-driving car for controlling its velocity and the relative distance to the vehicle in front of it; (ii) platoons of connected self-driving cars: they are formed and managed based, on the one hand, on the local sensing and actuating capabilities of each self-driving car and, on the other hand, on inter-vehicle communication for coordinating movements with neighboring vehicles.

Conceiving Software Architecture Description Languages (ADLs) has been the subject of intensive research in the last 25 years resulting in the definition of several ADLs for modeling initially static architectures, then dynamic architectures of (often large) single systems, and presently evolutionary architectures of SoSs [20]. However, none of the existing ADLs has the expressive power to describe the evolutionary architecture of opportunistic SoSs on the Internet-of-Vehicles [27, 36], which requires for a car to dynamically discover which other cars are in its neighborhood as well as to dynamically create a communication channel with a specific car for coordinating maneuvers while driving, such as in platoons and in crossroads.

The corresponding challenge in the architectural design of SoSs on IoV is to conceive concepts and mechanisms for describing how an SoS architecture is able to create, on the fly, and maintain emergent behaviors from connected vehicles, where the actual vehicles are not known at design time.

To fill this gap, we have enhanced SosADL [25, 32], a novel ADL specially conceived for formally describing the architecture of software-intensive SoSs, based on supervenience principles [31], with novel features for supporting SoS architecture description on the IoV, i.e. broadcast for discovering vehicles in the neighborhood and unicast for communicating over a communication channel with a specific vehicle.

SosADL for IoV brings contributions beyond the state-of-the-art to the formalization of SoS architectures exposing emergent behaviors relying on connected self-driving vehicles.

The remainder of this paper is organized as follows. Section 2 refines the notion of IoV and of vehicle platooning on the IoV. Section 3 presents how SosADL was enhanced to meet the needs of the IoV, issuing the novel *SosADL for IoV*. Section 4 introduces a field study encompassing vehicle platooning on the IoV and demonstrates how the enhanced SosADL is applied to IoV, through an excerpt of a real application, focusing on the platooning of a fleet of self-driving vehicles. In Sect. 5, we outline the implemented toolset for *SosADL for IoV*. In Sect. 6, we present the validation of *SosADL for IoV*. In Sect. 7, we compare *SosADL for IoV* with related work. To conclude, we summarize, in Sect. 8, the main contributions of this paper and outline ongoing and future work.

2 Internet-of-Vehicles and Vehicle Platooning

Let us introduce the notion of Internet-of-Vehicles and its underlying network technology, i.e. the VANET (Vehicular Ad-hoc Network).

VANETs apply the principles of Mobile Ad-hoc Networks (MANETs), i.e. the spontaneous creation of a wireless network for data exchange, to the domain of vehicles. They enable thereby the creation of the IoV, relying on both V2V communication between cars and V2I between cars and the roadside infrastructure (and more broadly on V2X, i.e. vehicle-to-everything).

Especially, VANET provides a short-range communication technology that enables vehicles to exchange information several times per second, about position, speed, acceleration, and braking. Vehicles equipped with VANET are thereby able to identify possible risks within ca. 300 m and take automatic collision-avoidance actions or alert their drivers, possibly assisted by fog/cloud computing accessed via infrastructure.

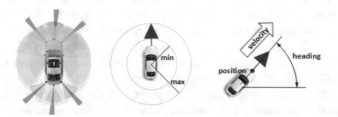

Fig. 1. Self-driving vehicles: wireless connectivity and automated driving support

As depicted in Fig. 1 (left), the upcoming generation of self-driving vehicles provides sensors, including radars and lidars, for sensing information from the environment and from other cars, processing this information, feeding it to drivers as well as communicating it to other cars, the infrastructure and, in general, with any "thing".

As also depicted in Fig. 1 (middle), there are two critical zones around a vehicle: the minimal safe separation from other vehicles and in general for any kind of obstacle and the maximal separation (the perception range of the sensors and V2V communication enabling to coordinate with other cars and possibly the infrastructure). Note that the relative distance between two vehicles is determined using a radar or lidar (light detection and ranging sensor, usually with rotating laser beams; it measures the distance to a neighboring vehicle by illuminating that vehicle with pulsed laser light and measuring the reflected pulses).

As furthermore depicted in Fig. 1 (right), self-driving vehicles are equipped with Global Positioning System (GPS) for positioning and controlling heading and speed determining its direction and velocity. These data are generally transmitted via VANETs to the neighboring vehicles and the infrastructure. In addition to computing real time position in terms of GPS coordinates, a connected vehicle may also share the GPS coordinate with other vehicles.

VANETs make possible to set up and maintain vehicle platoons, as depicted in Fig. 2. Each vehicle communicates with some other vehicles in the platoon, in particular the ones closest in front of and behind it, but also via multihop routing to others. In a platoon, there is a "leader" vehicle that controls the speed and heading of the platoon, which drives to the destination, and "follower" vehicles (with matched acceleration and braking) that respond to the leading vehicle movements. Note that a "leader" may be explicitly or opportunistically determined.

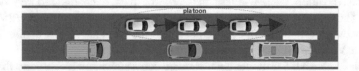

Fig. 2. Vehicles in platoon: one leader and many followers

Platooning is the process of cars autonomously following a leader to form a road convoy. It requires that each vehicle in the platoon control its velocity and the relative distance to the vehicle in front of it, and possibly also to the one behind of it. For supporting maneuvers, with vehicles joining/leaving the platoon, VANETs are used.

Vehicle platooning has several advantages: reduced risk of accidents, greater fuel economy due to reduced air resistance, higher efficiency of the vehicles and increased capacity of the highways. However, this comes with challenging issues to be considered: rear collision must be avoided in case of emergency braking, each vehicle in the platoon must have stable dynamics, and the platoon as whole must have string stability (i.e. if a deviation occurs w.r.t. the desired distance between the virtual leader and the first follower, this error should decrease towards the rear of the platoon and not the opposite). Vehicles coordinate using multi-hop routing in VANETs to ensure the string stability of the whole platoon.

By considering self-driving vehicles, it is possible to create a vehicle platoon that can travel autonomously. The platoon of vehicles travels in general on a single lane by using a longitudinal coordination strategy for each vehicle, as well as considers cases in which a vehicle has to join or leave the platoon, involving the lateral coordination of the vehicle. The platoons may also need to change lane.

3 Enhancing SosADL for the Internet-of-Vehicles

SosADL was conceived to overcome limitations of existing ADLs by providing the expressive power to describe the architectural concerns of software-intensive SoSs [29], and in particular to enable the description of emergent behaviors [30].

The core architectural concepts are the one of *system* to represent the constituents, the one of *mediator* to represent the enforced interactions among constituents, and the one of *coalition* to represent their formation as an SoS.

In SosADL, SoS architectures are represented in abstract terms (as the concrete systems which will become constituents of the SoS are not necessarily known at design-time; for instance, in vehicle platoon, the SoS architect does not know at design-time which vehicles will participate in a platoon).

Afterwards, the defined abstract architecture will be evolutionarily concretized at run-time, by identifying and incorporating concrete constituent systems; for instance, in the case of a platoon, cars which become platoonmates are discovered at run-time (see [9] for details on the automated synthesis of concrete SoS architectures from SosADL descriptions).

3.1 Extending SosADL with Digital Twins of "Things"

For extending SosADL for the IoV, we first extended SosADL for the IoT in general [32]. For achieving this aim, we investigated what are the architectural abstractions suitable for architecting SoS on the IoT.

There are indeed different notions and reference architectures for developing software-intensive systems, in particular cyber-physical systems, on the IoT.

Among them, the notion of digital twin (proposed in [7] and extended for IoT [5]) fits well the needs for coupling the physical and virtual worlds in terms of "things", as required in software-intensive SoSs on IoT.

A digital twin provides a virtual replica (in the edge, fog or the cloud) of its physical counterpart which is virtually indistinguishable from its physical twin (in the sense that it dynamically replicates the behavior and properties of the physical twin as well as enriches the replica with additional information about the physical counterpart). It is in fact a dynamic digital representation of its physical counterpart. Dynamic in the sense that the physical asset and its digital twin are connected during their whole lifecycle.

In general, the digital twin monitors the physical twin through data provided by sensors on the IoT as well as information coming from domain experts to maintain a utility replica of the physical asset. It acts back on the physical twin through actuators on IoT.

In the Internet-of-Vehicles, the digital twin of each self-driving vehicle will inspect the physical vehicle (the physical twin), which provides all the data to the digital twin.

Therefore, to enable the architectural description of enhanced IoT applications, SosADL was extended with constructs for expressing digital twins (for details, see [33]).

3.2   Constructs for Autonomous Constituent Systems in SosADL

SosADL was firstly conceived for describing SoS architectures which involve SoSs composed of autonomous systems, i.e. where constituents are systems that behave according to only its own capabilities, sensing and actuating in its local environment.

The key point to be addressed was the one of partial information, as no constituent system of the SoS has complete knowledge, each one having only partial knowledge according to the information it can perceive in its local environment.

Therefore, for handling partial knowledge in SoS architectural design and particularly in the description of the designed SoS architecture, SosADL was conceived to enable the representation of partial information as well as to reason on this partial information to influence the behavior of the SoS. By the decentralized nature of SoSs, these representation and reasoning mechanisms are expressed from the viewpoint of each constituent system and mediators enabling their interactions and thereby influencing individual behaviors as well as the raising of emergent behaviors.

For defining the formal semantics of SosADL handling partial information, we evaluated different behavior calculi developed for modeling complex systems and identified several forms of the π-Calculus [21], however none of them complied with the SoS requirements for architectural behavior description [27].

We have therefore designed a novel π-Calculus for SoS [28], which extended the original π-Calculus with mediated constraints, where mediation is achieved by constraining interactions, and where constrained interactions raise emergent behaviors [2]. More precisely, the π-Calculus for SoS generalizes the original π-Calculus with the notion of computing with partial information based on the concurrent constraint paradigm and in particular on the principles of constraint-based calculi [23].

Formally based on the π-Calculus for SoS, SosADL provides: (i) a **tell** construct for adding a constraint to the local environment; (ii) an **ask** construct for querying if a constraint can be inferred from the local environment.

These constructs enable each constituent system to behave according to the constraints imposed by other constituent systems sharing the same local environment.

Intuitively speaking, based on π-Calculus for SoS, in SosADL a constituent can publicly **tell** to the environment about the pieces of information that it knows, while maintaining private information internally. A constituent can also **ask** information from the environment that influences on its own behavior.

The communication between composed constituent systems is supported by unicast connections: (i) a **send** construct for synchronously sending a value over a connection to another constituent system; (ii) a **receive** construct for synchronously receiving a value over a connection from another constituent system.

Relying on the π-Calculus for SoS, the formal operational semantics of SosADL was defined by means of a formal transition system, expressed by labelled transition rules. For details on the formal semantics of SosADL in terms of π-Calculus for SoS, see [28].

If SosADL demonstrated to be a suitable formal ADL for SoSs, able to describe the SoS architectures of flocks of autonomous drones and platoons of autonomous self-driving cars, it is not able to support the description of SoS architectures based on wireless network communications in addition to sensing/actuating capabilities.

3.3   Extending SosADL with Constructs for Connected Constituent Systems

In this paper, we extend SosADL for describing SoS architectures which involve SoSs composed of communicating autonomous systems, i.e. where SoS constituents are connected systems to wireless local area networks, supporting in particular Vehicle-to-Vehicle (V2V) data exchange through VANETs, that behave in coordination with its own neighboring constituents in partially shared environments.

For extending SosADL for IoV, the key points to be addressed were: (i) delimiting the wireless communication range (the communication is limited to constituent systems in the neighborhood, that is determined by the maximum wireless communication range of the V2V radio technology); (ii) discovering which are the other constituent systems that are within the V2V communication range; (iii) getting specific V2V communication channels to interact with relevant neighbors.

Therefore, for handling communication supported by wireless local area networks in SoS architectural design and particularly in the description of the designed SoS architecture, SosADL was enhanced to address each one of these three points.

First, it was extended to enable to physically sense which are the neighboring constituent systems within a given radius. For instance, in the case of autonomous cars, it senses which are the other cars in front of it and behind of it in the same road lane as well as in adjacent lanes using a lidar.

Formally, we have extended SosADL with a new construct for expressing neighborhood of mobile constituents. The notion of neighborhood is given by extending digital twins accessing physical properties, i.e. every digital twin of a "thing" is able to inform about (a subset of) physical properties of its physical counterpart. These properties are available in all digital twins through built-in constraints in SosADL for IoT.

Thereby, a physical twin can **tell** about its physical properties and the digital twin can apply the **ask** construct for getting each physical property of the related physical twin: (i) **ask range for** *thing* to get the maximum V2V communication range in *meter* (the radius) of the *thing* in question; (ii) **ask neighborhood within** *range* **for** *thing* to get the set of "things" in the neighborhood of the *thing* in question; (iii) **ask [local] coordinate for** *thing* to get the coordinate of the *thing* in question (the coordinate is given in global or local coordinate systems, the default being global coordinate in terms of GPS). All physical properties are given in *SI* unit (the International System of Units) and all these *SI* datatypes are equipped with operations for manipulation and conversion.

Second, SosADL was extended to enable to communicate with all neighbors of a "thing" using *broadcasting*, supporting one-to-many communication and its opposite *collect* concept, which supports many-to-one communication.

Hereafter, we will focus on *broadcasting*, which provides the essential concept for supporting SoS architectures on the IoV. Broadcasting is the mechanism of transferring a message from a sender to all receivers, simultaneously, within the communication range. It is worth highlighting that, as demonstrated in [4], *broadcast* cannot be encoded with *unicast* and thereby is needed as a primitive concept in an ADL for IoV.

For expressing broadcast, we extend SosADL with two constructs: **talk** and **listen**.

The **talk** construct is expressed as **via** *connection* [**within** *range*] **talk** *data*, meaning that *connection* is used to transmit *data* to all "things" that are within the given *range*. In case *range* is not specified, it is by default the maximum communication range. Thereby data will be transmitted to all "things" in the **neighborhood**.

The **listen** construct is expressed as **via** *connection* [**within** *range*] **listen** *placeholder*, meaning that *connection* is used to receive *data* in the *placeholder* talked by all "things" that are within the given *range*. In case *range* is not specified, it is by default the maximum communication range. Thereby data transmitted from all "things" in the **neighborhood**, can be listened.

4 SoS Architecture Description for UGV-Based Platooning

To demonstrate how *SosADL for IoV* can be applied to architecturally describe SoS architectures on the IoV, we will present hereafter an excerpt of an SoS architecture description that we have designed in a cooperative project with stakeholders of the city of Sao Carlos as part of a pilot for a Flood Monitoring and Emergency Response SoS [26], focusing on the platooning of Unmanned Ground Vehicles (UGVs).

UGVs are self-driving (driverless) vehicles equipped with V2V wireless technology, supporting on-the-fly creation of VANETs. They are usually used for applications where it is inconvenient, dangerous, or impossible to have a human operator present.

In this pilot SoS, the UGV-based Emergency Response SoS is formed by UGVs deployed from different city councils in the metropolitan area of Sao Carlos and neighbor municipalities. Several fleets of UGVs can be activated by the gateway of the WSN-based Urban River Monitoring SoS for accomplishing disaster relief missions and search and rescue operations. UGVs drive autonomously using built-in GPS to the inundated area identified by drones.

The acquired UGVs are fully autonomous, able to self-navigate in GPS-enabled environments as well as to detect and avoid obstacles. They in particular provide a *follow* mode enabling wireless tethering to another UGV. In this mode, it reacts to its frontrunner movements and direction while having the mission route saved for autonomous execution. The *follow* mode is used by the autopilot of a UGV, when it is participating in a platoon for following the UGV that is in front of it.

Let us now focus on the supervenient emergent behavior of the UGV-based Emergency Response SoS to create and maintain platoons of UGVs through self-organization during the journey to the destination. More specifically, we will concentrate on the maneuvers for a UGV to join an ongoing platoon, where the maneuvers are coordinated between the UGV joining the platoon and UGVs that are already in the platoon using wireless communication on VANETs.

Hereafter, we will demonstrate how to apply *SosADL for IoV* to describe the SoS architecture of UGV platooning as well as explain the operational semantics of the resulting SoS architecture description during the join maneuver of a UGV into a platoon.

In the formalization with *SosADL for IoV*, we will first describe the digital twin mediators enforcing the join maneuver required for a UGV to join a platoon (we will not present the digital twins of the UGVs due to page limit). Next, we will describe the abstract architecture of the SoS on the IoV as a whole in terms of a digital coalition.

Let us now declare, in *SosADL for IoV*, the *Platooning* mediator which will support the platooning as well as the join maneuver of a UGV in the vehicle platoon.

As shown in **Listing 1**, *Platooning* is described as a digital mediator: we declare the duties of the mediated UGV and the behavior abstractions that can be applied during the mediation, i.e. **abstraction** *Leading_platoon(…)* declares the behavior abstraction for leading the platoon; **abstraction** *Following_platoonmate(…)* declares the behavior abstraction for following the in-front platoonmate in the platoon; and **abstraction** *Steering_to_join_platoon(…)* declares the behavior abstraction for joining the platoon. The declared main behavior for self-driving the UGV is **behavior** *Self_Driving(…)*.

```
//use the predefined library for the Internet-of-Vehicles (IoV)
with IoV
//declare the self-driving vehicle mediator for platooning
digital mediator Platooning(min:Distance) is {
 //declare the duty to support the join maneuver into platoons
 duty join is {
  //declare a broadcast channel for communicating with platoonmates
  connection request_ch is broadcast{connection[connection[Thing]]}
 }
 duty control is {
  //declare connections for steering the mediated UGV
  connection align_x_start is out{…}
  connection align_x_end is in{…}
  connection align_y_start is out{…}
  connection align_y_end is in{…}
  connection keep_x_distance is out{…}
  connection keep_y_distance is out{…}
 }
 //declare the behavior abstraction for leading the UGV platoon
 abstraction Leading_platoon(…) is {…}
 //declare the behavior abstraction for following in the UGV platoon
 abstraction Following_platoonmate(…) is {…}
 //declare the behavior abstraction for joining into the UGV platoon
 abstraction Steering_to_join_platoon(…) is {…}
 //declare the main behavior for self-driving the UGV
 behavior Self_Driving(…) is {…}
}
```

Listing 1. Digital mediator declaration for platoonmates in *SosADL for IoV*

Based on the declaration of UGVs as systems (not shown for brevity) and of the digital mediator, presented in **Listing 1**, let us now declare the *PlatooningSoS* architecture (presented in **Listing 2**). It describes which are the digital twins of the constituent systems that can participate in the SoS, the digital mediators that can be created and managed for coordinating the constituent systems via their digital twins and the digital coalitions that can be formed to achieve the SoS emergent behavior of platooning. As declared in the platoon coalition, by creating concretions, a digital mediator will be synthesized for each digital twin of a UGV that participates in the fleet of UGVs.

```
//use UGV system abstraction and Platooning mediator abstraction
  with IoV,UGV,Platooning
  architecture PlatooningSoS(min:Distance) is {
   coalition platoon is compose{
    fleet is sequence{UGV()}
    platooning is sequence{Platooning(min)}
   } binding {
      forall {ugv in fleet suchthat
        exists{one steer in platooning suchthat
          unify one{steer::join} to one{ugv::join}
          unify one{steer::control} to one{ugv::control}}}}
  }
```

Listing 2. Platooning SoS architecture declaration in *SosADL for IoV*

Let us now describe, in **Listing 2**, the SoS architecture enabling the platooning emergent behavior as well as maneuvers in the platoon.

The SoS architecture description, shown in **Listing 2**, comprises the declaration of a sequence of digital twins of constituent systems complying with the system abstraction of *UGV* and a sequence of digital mediators conforming with the mediator abstraction of *Platooning* (as declared in **Listing 1**).

Based on the digital twins of these systems and mediator abstractions, the digital coalition for creating emergent behavior is declared, named *platoon*, as shown in **Listing 2**. In particular, the digital coalition of UGVs is described as a sequence of digital twins of UGVs where each digital twin has an associated steering digital mediator created in the digital coalition, with the specified minimum separation distance (*min*) as parameter. The emergent behavior of the digital coalition, *platoon*, is giving by the macro-scale behavior created by supervenience from the mediating micro-behaviors, according to each situation.

Let us now declare the digital mediating behavior, described in **Listing 3**. For the sake of space, we will focus on the general case of the join maneuver somewhere in the middle of the vehicle platoon. In this case, a vehicle that is not in the platoon, i.e. the joining UGV, broadcasts a joining request to the platoonmates expressing its intention to join the platoon. One of the concerned platoonmates, which listened the broadcast, contact back the joining UGV to accept the request and send the information required for the UGV to join the platoon. The agreed platoonmate increases the space in front of it until enough space has been created, i.e. at least two times the min separation distance plus the size of the joining UGV, and in parallel the joining UGV aligns longitudinally itself between the agreed platoonmate and the platoonmate in front of it. Then, the joining UGV aligns laterally itself by changing its road lane to the same as the platoon. Once it merges into the platoon, being completely aligned in the lane of the platoon, it keeps driving forward while keeping a safe distance to the platoonmate in front of it. It becomes a regular platoonmate, and its autopilot (an adaptive cruise controller) takes the command (it automatically steers to maintain the platoon, regulating its distance to the platoonmate in front of it). Note that along the join maneuver, the joining UGV as well as the platoonmates drive forward with respect to the road geometry.

```
//behavior abstraction of the mediator for UGV to join the platoon
abstraction Steering_to_join_platoon(min:Distance) is {
  repeat {
    //ask the "thing" handle of the joining UGV itself
    value ugv is ask itself
    //ask the max V2V communication range of the joining UGV itself
    value ugv_range is ask ugv for range
    //request to join the platoon talking to its neighbors in platoon
    behavior Requesting_to_join(min,ugv,ugv_range)
  }
  //broadcast intention to join platoon and then wait for responses
  abstraction Requesting_to_join(min:Distance,ugv:Thing,
    ugv_range:Distance) is {
    //ask the vehicle size in the x axis of the joining UGV itself
    value ugv_size_in_x is ask ugv for size_in_x
    //declare unicast channel of channel for communicating with mate
    restrict ugv_request_ch:connection[connection[Thing]]
    //broadcast the unicast ch of ch for all neighboring platoonmates
    via join::request_ch within ugv_range talk ugv_request_ch
    replicate {//wait for the responses from neighboring platoonmates
      //receive the unicast channel from the platoonmate which agreed
      via ugv_request_ch receive platoonmate_ch:connection[Thing]
      //receive the "thing" handle of the platoonmate which agreed
      via platoonmate_ch receive platoonmate:Thing
      //receive the "thing" handle of its in-front platoonmate
      via platoonmate_ch receive frontmate:Thing
      //align in x,y the joining ugv between platoonmate and frontmate
      behavior Aligning_to_join(min,ugv_size_in_x,ugv,platoonmate,
        frontmate) }
  }
  //maneuver to align the mediated UGV for joining the platoon
  abstraction Aligning_to_join(min:Distance,ugv_size_in_x:Distance,
    ugv:Thing,platoonmate:Thing,frontmate:Thing) is {
    via control::align_x_start send [min,ugv_size_in_x,
      ugv,platoonmate,frontmate]
    via control::align_x_end receive ugv_in_x_coordinate:Coordinate
    via control::align_y_start send [ugv,platoonmate,frontmate]
    via control::align_y_end receive ugv_in_y_coordinate:Coordinate
    //once inside, follow the UGV in front of it, i.e. its frontmate
    behavior Following_platoonmate(min,ugv,front_mate)
  }
  abstraction Following_platoonmate(min:Distance,ugv:Thing,
    frontmate:Thing) is {
    choose {
      //once aligned, the joining UGV behave as a platoonmate
      via control::keep_x_distance send min
      behavior Following_platoonmate(min,ugv,frontmate)
      //in case, the UGV as platoonmate will support others joining
    or replicate { via join::request_ch listen ugv_request_ch:
                   connection[connection[Thing]]
        restrict platoonmate_ch:connection[Thing]
        via ugv_request_ch send platoonmate_ch
        via platoonmate_ch send ugv
        via platoonmate_ch send frontmate
        via platoonmate_ch receive joining_frontmate
      behavior Following_platoonmate(min,ugv,frontmate) } }
  }
}
```

Listing 3. Digital mediator behavior for platoonmates in *SosADL for IoV*

It is by the application of the mediating behaviors, described in **Listing 3**, commanding the digitally mediated UGVs, that a UGV, when approaching a platoon, will perform the maneuver to join the platoon. It will stepwise behave to get closer to the neighboring UGVs in the platoon and then join the platoon. For an external observer, at the macro-scale level, a UGV somewhere in the middle of the platoon will create a space in front of it allowing the joining UGV to safely come into the platoon, while avoiding collision. The safe space is of at least two times the minimum separation distance plus the size of the UGV joining the platoon.

It is worth noting that the maneuver for joining the platoon is coordinated by the digital twins of the UGVs. Each UGV is not aware of the rest of the platoon, except for its own neighbors, generally composed of the platoonmates in front of and behind itself. For instance, a UGV in the platoon is not aware of the size of the platoon, i.e. of how many members has the platoon.

From the abstract SoS architecture described in **Listing 1**, **Listing 2**, and **Listing 3**, different concrete SoS architectures of platoons may be created based on the identified UGVs for each particular operational environment. These platoons, through the mediated platooning behavior, support the maneuvers for other UGVs joining the platoon dynamically. For instance, as mentioned, in the case of the UGV-based Emergence Response SoS of the Monjolinho river, the fleet of identified UGVs are located at different municipalities along the river. They are then commanded to drive and reach an area with high risk of flooding for an emergency response mission (triggered by the monitoring of the urban river). From each departing point, the UGVs will leave to the destination zone in platoons (economizing on fuel) and, along the way, other UGVs will join the running platoons for forming larger ones. Once in destination, they will dissolve the platooning SoSs adopted in the navigation mission to reach the destination point and then adopt another SoS architecture for the search and rescue mission.

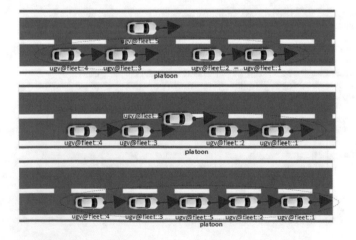

Fig. 3. Snapshots of the mediated maneuver of a UGV joining a platoon

For illustrating the platooning mediation in the support of the maneuvers for a UGV joining a platoon, let us now suppose that a UGV enters the roadway and, at some point, drives in a contiguous lane of another where there is a platoon, as shown in Fig. 3 (top). This approaching UGV can join the platoon by the application of the *Steering_to_join(...)* mediated behavior declared in **Listing 3**.

First the joining UGV broadcast its intention to join the platoon, then get a response from a member of the platoon, a platoonmate, which creates the space needed for the insertion of the joining UGV in front of it. The joining UGV will then align longitudinally to be closer to that platoonmate. When the gap appears between the near UGVs, i.e. in this case between ugv@fleet::3 and ugv@fleet::2 as shown in Fig. 3 (middle), the joining UGV, in this case ugv@fleet::5, initiates the maneuver to align laterally, as shown in Fig. 3. Smoothly, the ugv@fleet::5 maneuvers to come into the platoon, as shown in Fig. 3 (from top to bottom).

Note that other maneuvers are supported in the field study (not shown for reason of space): UGVs leaving a platoon, a platoon split in smaller platoons, and different platoons merging together to form larger ones.

5   SosADL Implementation

We have developed an SoS Architecture Development Environment, named *SosADL Studio* [34], for supporting the architecture-centric formal development of SoSs using SosADL (from missions to SoS architectures [39], and their validation/verification), while providing guarantees of correctness of the elaborated SoS architectures [35].

This toolset is constructed as plugins in Eclipse (http://eclipse.org/). It provides a model-driven architecture development environment where the SosADL meta-model is defined in EMF/Ecore (http://eclipse.org/modeling/emf/), with the textual concrete syntax expressed in Xtext (http://eclipse.org/Xtext/), the graphical concrete syntax developed in Sirius (http://eclipse.org/sirius/), and the type checker implemented in Xtend (http://www.eclipse.org/xtend/), after having being proved using the Coq proof assistant (http://coq.inria.fr/).

By applying model-to-model transformations, SoS architecture descriptions are transformed and converted to input languages of analysis tools, including UPPAAL (http://www.uppaal.org/) for extensive model checking, DEVS (http://www.ms4systems.com/) for simulation, and PLASMA (http://project.inria.fr/plasma-lab/) for statistical model checking.

The constraint solving mechanism implemented to support the **tell** and **ask** constructs are based on the Kodkod SAT-solver (http://alloy.mit.edu/kodkod/).

Of particular interest for validating SoS emergent behavior is the automated generation of concrete SoS architectures, by automated transformation from SosADL to DEVS, and the subsequent simulation in DEVS enabling to observe and tune the described emergent behavior of an SoS [6].

For supporting verification of SoS architectures, we have conceived a novel logic, named DynBLTL [37], for expressing correctness properties of evolving architectures as well as verifying these properties by model checking [3].

The *SosADL Studio for IoV* extends the core *SosADL Studio* with enhancements to the ADL, incorporating in particular the new constructs for *broadcast* (i.e. *talk* and *listen*), and their implementation in the toolchain, as well as *collect*. The different concrete syntaxes, the abstract syntax in terms of the meta-model, the type checker as well as the model-to-model transformations were extended accordingly.

In addition to these domain independent tools, the resulting *SosADL Studio for IoV* was extended with VEINS, https://veins.car2x.org/, which provides an open source framework for running vehicular network simulations, including inter-vehicular communication with VANETs.

The implemented toolchain in *SosADL Studio for IoV* provides the ability to validate and verify the studied SoS architectures on the IoV very early in the SoS lifecycle with respect to its correctness properties, in particular regarding emergent behaviors.

6   SosADL Validation for the IoV by Controlled Experiment

For validating *SosADL for IoV* and its supporting toolchain, *SosADL Studio for IoV*, we carried out a field study of a real SoS for Flood Monitoring and Emergency Response and studied its concretization in the Monjolinho river, which crosses the city of Sao Carlos (see [26] for more details on the description of the field study).

The mission of the designed SoS is to monitor potential floods and to handle related emergencies. The SoS stakeholder is the DAEE (Sao Paulo's Water and Electricity Department), a government organization of the State of Sao Paulo, Brazil, responsible for managing water resources, including flood monitoring of urban rivers. This SoS also involves as stakeholders the different city councils crossed by the Monjolinho river, the policy and fire departments of the city of Sao Carlos that own UAVs (drones) and have UGVs (self-driving vehicles) equipped with VANET. Also involved are the hospitals of the city of Sao Carlos (they have ambulances equipped with VANETs).

The aim of this field study developed conjointly with USP was to assess the fitness for purpose and the usefulness of, on the one hand, SosADL as a formal SoS architectural language, and on the other hand, of SosADL Studio as an SoS architecture development environment to support the architectural description and analysis of real SoSs.

In addition to IoT in general, to validate that the expressive power of SosADL for IoT copes with the needs of IoT, we carried out a controlled experiment for addressing IoV in particular through its challenging case of vehicle platooning, which involves ad-hoc networking and physical mobility. The controlled experiment was designed as a subset of the field study of the Flood Monitoring and Emergency Response SoS applied to the Monjolinho river in the city of Sao Carlos, as cited.

Overall, the result of the assessment based on the controlled experiment concluded that *SosADL for IoV* enables descriptions of SoS architectures on the IoV which were not possible to be described with core SosADL or even its customized *SosADL for IoT*.

The reason is that SosADL and *SosADL for IoT* (for stationary "things") are based only on unicast communication constructs, i.e. *send/receive*, while *SosADL for IoV* (for mobile "things") was extended with *broadcast* constructs. Formally speaking, the *broadcast* constructs were demonstrated to be not encodable with the *unicast* ones [4].

Intuitively, it means that the behaviors expressed in the maneuver for joining platoons cannot be specified in languages providing only unicast *send/receive* constructs, which is today the case of all existing ADLs [36].

7 Related Work

Related work on the description of behaviors shaped by software architectures is of two kinds: aggregative behavior in single systems architecture [15, 36] and emergent behavior in SoS architectures [8]. SoS architectures on the IoV imply the need to describe emergent behaviors drawn from the interaction of mobile "things".

Let us first analyze related work on emergent behavior related to SoS, of which the key ones are proposed by Wachholder and Stary [40] and Motus et al. [22].

Wachholder and Stary [40] presents an attempt for describing emergent behavior in SoSs. The proposed approach is based on Bigraphs and focuses on the modeling of both the structure and the structural dynamics of an SoS. It, however, does not address the behavioral aspects of emergent behavior, limiting the solution to the configuration and re-configuration features. The proposed solution is limited only to concrete (one-of-a-kind) SoS architectures and limited only to the endogenous approach for modeling emergent behavior in SoS. These limitations restrict the expressiveness of the proposed approach, which does not cope with the needs for architecting SoS on IoV.

Motus et al. [22] address the importance of mediating interactions among constituent systems to achieve emergent behavior. In particular, it proposes a middleware based on mediated interaction. That work is complementary to ours in the sense that SoS architectures described with SosADL can be deployed in the proposed middleware.

Let us now analyze how emergent behavior has been specifically addressed for designing platoons as SoSs. This issue has been tackled by two related works: Kumar et al. [17] and Labrado et al. [18].

Kumar et al. [17] proposed a modeling approach based on Bond Graph Theory for describing a platoon of autonomous vehicles. The proposed solution is limited to the physical model of the vehicle platoon, as well as can only be applied to a concrete (one-of-a-kind) SoS based on endogenous modeling. Its role is mainly for supervision purposes. This work is complementary to ours in the sense that SoS architectures described with SosADL for IoV can be refined to bound graph models to study the physical properties of the architected SoS platooning. It however does not address the digital counterpart.

Labrado et al. [18] proposed a testbed for simulating SoSs based on physical robots connected to a cloud. Platoon is one of the supported kinds of SoS. Again, this work is complementary to ours in the sense that SoS architectures described with SosADL for IoV can be refined to concrete implementations that can then be simulated using the proposed simulation framework. Again, it does not address the digital counterpart.

Let us now analyze related work on aggregative behavior exposed by single systems. The description of single systems architecture as based on three notions: component, connector, and configuration. The notion of connector as a first-class entity in architecture description has been proposed two decades ago [1]. Connectors were firstly designed as static entities, that never changed during run-time, then as dynamic entities changing dynamically at run-time to support dynamic architectures [24]. More recently the automatic synthesis of connectors during design-time was proposed [11].

The notion of mediator proposed in SosADL, which provides the basis for exogenously describing SoS architectures, generalizes the notion of connector. In particular, SosADL advances the current state-of-the-art on synthesized connectors at design-time in single systems architecture exposing aggregative behavior by providing the novel concept of mediator, based on synthesized mediators at run-time, on demand, in SoS architectures exposing emergent behavior. In addition, *SosADL for IoV* encompasses mediators supporting broadcast communication, which cannot be expressed on languages based only on unicast connectors, which is the case of all existing ADLs.

Overall, currently, other ADLs are not expressive enough to be able to describe SoS architectures on the IoV such as in vehicular platooning with dynamic join/leave. *SosADL for IoV* is therefore the first ADL designed for meeting the needs of IoV, while based on a formal calculus enabling to formally express correctness properties as well as to verify these properties through automated tools, in particular statistical model checkers.

8   Conclusion and Future Work

This paper presented the novel concepts and constructs of *SosADL for IoV*, extending the core SosADL, while generalizing SosADL for IoT to both stationary and mobile "things". In particular, it demonstrated how architectural mediators expressed with *SosADL for IoV* support SoS architecture descriptions on the IoV through an excerpt of a real application for architecting a UGV-based platooning enabling dynamic maneuvers, e.g. joining/leaving, focusing on the join maneuver. It provides the first formal SoS architectural description of connected autonomous vehicles supporting dynamic maneuvers, all others being only limited to the architectural formation of SoS platooning.

The formal foundation of *SosADL for IoV* extends the π-Calculus enhanced with concurrent constraints, the π-Calculus for SoS, bringing contributions beyond the state-of-the-art by providing the first full formal ADL having the expressive power for describing emergent behavior in software-intensive SoS architectures on the IoV, in particular IoV-connected vehicle platooning with dynamic maneuvers, grounded on its constraint solving mechanism, mobile unicast, and now broadcast communication.

SosADL has been applied in several case studies and pilots where the suitability of the language and the supporting toolchain has been validated, including *SosADL for IoV* for SoS applications in smart-cities.

On-going and future work is mainly related with the application of *SosADL for IoV* to real-scale projects on the Internet-of-Vehicles. They include joint work with IBM for applying SosADL to architect smart-farms on the IoT in general and IoV in particular, and with SEGULA for applying *SosADL for IoV* to architect SoSs in the navy domain, based on 5G. Description of SoS architectures on the IoV, and their validation and verification using the *SosADL for IoV* toolchain, are main threads of these pilot projects.

References

1. Allen, R., Garlan, D.: A formal basis for architectural connection. ACM TOSEM **6**(3), 213–249 (1997)
2. Blachowicz, J.: The constraint interpretation of physical emergence. J. Gen. Philos. Sci. **44**, 21–40 (2013). https://doi.org/10.1007/s10838-013-9207-7
3. Cavalcante, E., Quilbeuf, J., Traonouez, L.-M., Oquendo, F., Batista, T., Legay, A.: Statistical model checking of dynamic software architectures. In: Tekinerdogan, B., Zdun, U., Babar, A. (eds.) ECSA 2016. LNCS, vol. 9839, pp. 185–200. Springer, Cham (2016). https://doi.org/10.1007/978-3-319-48992-6_14
4. Ene, C., Muntean, T.: Expressiveness of point-to-point versus broadcast communications. In: Ciobanu, G., Păun, G. (eds.) FCT 1999. LNCS, vol. 1684, pp. 258–268. Springer, Heidelberg (1999). https://doi.org/10.1007/3-540-48321-7_21
5. Tao, F., Zhang, M., Nee, A.Y.C.: Digital Twin Driven Smart Manufacturing. Academic Press, Cambridge (2019)
6. Graciano Neto, V.V., et al.: ASAS: an approach to support simulation of smart systems. In: 51st HICSS, Waikoloa, Hawaii, USA, January 2018
7. Grieves, M.: Virtually Perfect: Driving Innovative and Lean Products through Product Lifecycle Management. Space Coast Press, Cocoa Beach (2011)
8. Guessi, M., Graciano, V.V., Bianchi, T., Felizardo, K.R., Oquendo, F., Nakagawa, E.Y.: A systematic literature review on the description of software architectures for systems-of-systems. In: 30th ACM SAC, Salamanca, Spain, April 2015
9. Guessi, M., Oquendo, F., Nakagawa, E.Y.: Checking the architectural feasibility of systems-of-systems using formal descriptions. In: 11th IEEE SoSE, Kongsberg, Norway, June 2016
10. INCOSE, SE Vision 2025 (2014). www.incose.org/AboutSE/sevision
11. Inverardi, P., Tivoli, M.: Automatic synthesis of modular connectors via composition of protocol mediation patterns. In: 35th ACM/IEEE ICSE, May 2013
12. ISO/IEC/IEEE 42010:2011: Systems and Software Engineering – Architecture Description, December 2011
13. Jia, D., Lu, K., Wang, J., Zhang, X., Shen, X.: A survey on platoon-based vehicular cyber-physical systems. IEEE Commun. Surv. Tutor. **18**(1), 263–284 (2016)
14. Kaiwartya, O., et al.: Internet of vehicles: motivation, layered architecture, network model, challenges, and future aspects. IEEE Access **4**, 5356–5373 (2016)
15. Klein, J., van Vliet, H.: A systematic review of system-of-systems architecture rescarch. In: 9th ACM QoSA, Vancouver, Canada, June 2013
16. Kopetz, H., Höftberger, O., Frömel, B., Brancati, F., Bondavalli, A.: Towards an understanding of emergence in systems-of-systems. In: 10th IEEE SoSE, San Antonio, Texas, USA, May 2015
17. Kumar, P., Merzouki, R., Bouamama, B.O., Koubeissi, A.: Bond graph modeling of a class of system-of-systems. In: 10th IEEE SoSE, San Antonio, Texas, USA, May 2015
18. Labrado, J.D., Erol, B.A., Ortiz, J., Benavidez, P., Jamshidi, M., Champion, B.: Proposed testbed for the modeling and control of a system of autonomous vehicles. In: 11th IEEE SoSE, Kongsberg, Norway, June 2016
19. Maier, M.W.: Architecting principles for systems-of-systems. Syst. Eng. J. **1**(4), 267–284 (1998)
20. Malavolta, I., et al.: Architectural Languages Today: The Up-to-Date List of ADLs, 7 April 2019. http://www.di.univaq.it/malavolta/al/
21. Milner, R.: Communicating and Mobile Systems: The π-Calculus. Cambridge University Press, Cambridge (1999)

22. Motus, L., Preden, J.S., Meriste, M., Pahtma, R.: Self-aware architecture to support partial control of emergent behavior. In: 7th IEEE SoSE, Genoa, Italy, July 2012
23. Olarte, C., Rueda, C., Valencia, F.D.: Models and emerging trends of concurrent constraint programming. Int. J. Constr. **18**(4), 535–578 (2013). https://doi.org/10.1007/s10601-013-9145-3
24. Oquendo, F.: π-ADL: an architecture description language based on the higher-order typed π-Calculus for specifying dynamic and mobile software architectures. ACM SEN **29**(3), 1–14 (2004)
25. Oquendo, F.: Formally describing the software architecture of systems-of-systems with SosADL. In: 11th IEEE SoSE, Kongsberg, Norway, June 2016
26. Oquendo, F.: Case study on formally describing the architecture of a software-intensive system-of-systems with SosADL. In: 15th IEEE SMC, Budapest, Hungary, October 2016
27. Oquendo, F.: Software architecture challenges and emerging research in software-intensive systems-of-systems. In: Tekinerdogan, B., Zdun, U., Babar, A. (eds.) ECSA 2016. LNCS, vol. 9839, pp. 3–21. Springer, Cham (2016). https://doi.org/10.1007/978-3-319-48992-6_1
28. Oquendo, F.: The π-Calculus for SoS: novel π-Calculus for the formal modeling of software-intensive systems-of-systems. In: Communicating Process Architectures (CPA 2016), August 2016
29. Oquendo, F.: Formally describing the architectural behavior of software-intensive systems-of-systems with SosADL. In: 21st IEEE ICECCS, Dubai, UAE, November 2016
30. Oquendo, F.: Architecturally describing the emergent behavior of software-intensive system-of-systems with SosADL. In: 12th IEEE SoSE, Waikoloa, Hawaii, USA, June 2017
31. Oquendo, F.: On the emergent behavior oxymoron of system-of-systems architecture description. In: 13th IEEE SoSE, Paris, France, June 2018
32. Oquendo, F.: Formally describing self-organizing architectures for systems-of-systems on the internet-of-things. In: Cuesta, C.E., Garlan, D., Pérez, J. (eds.) ECSA 2018. LNCS, vol. 11048, pp. 20–36. Springer, Cham (2018). https://doi.org/10.1007/978-3-030-00761-4_2
33. Oquendo, F.: Dealing with uncertainty in software architecture on the internet-of-things with digital twins. In: Misra, S., et al. (eds.) ICCSA 2019. LNCS, vol. 11619, pp. 770–786. Springer, Cham (2019). https://doi.org/10.1007/978-3-030-24289-3_57
34. Oquendo, F., Buisson, J., Leroux, E., Moguérou, G., Quilbeuf, J.: The SosADL studio: an architecture development environment for software-intensive systems-of-systems. In: SiSoS 2016, Copenhagen, DK. ACM, November 2016
35. Oquendo, F., Buisson, J., Leroux, E., Moguérou, G.: A formal approach for architecting software-intensive systems-of-systems with guarantees. In: 13th IEEE SoSE, Paris, France, June 2018
36. Ozkaya, M.: The analysis of architectural languages for the needs of practitioners. Softw. Pract. Exp. **48**, 985–1018 (2018)
37. Quilbeuf, J., Cavalcante, E., Traonouez, L.-M., Oquendo, F., Batista, T., Legay, A.: A logic for the statistical model checking of dynamic software architectures. In: Margaria, T., Steffen, B. (eds.) ISoLA 2016. LNCS, vol. 9952, pp. 806–820. Springer, Cham (2016). https://doi.org/10.1007/978-3-319-47166-2_56
38. Roca, D., Nemirovsky, D., Nemirovsky, M., Milito, R., Valero, M.: Emergent behaviors in the internet-of-things: the ultimate ultra-large-scale system. IEEE Micro **36**(6), 36–44 (2016)
39. Silva, E., Cavalcante, E., Batista, T., Oquendo, F.: Bridging missions and architecture in software-intensive systems-of-systems. In: 21st IEEE ICECCS, Dubai, UAE, November 2016
40. Wachholder, D., Stary, C.: Enabling emergent behavior in systems-of-systems through bigraph-based modeling. In: 10th IEEE SoSE, San Antonio, Texas, USA, May 2015
41. Wang, Z., Wu, G., Barth, M.J.: A review on cooperative adaptive cruise control (CACC) systems: architectures, controls, and applications. In: Intelligent Transportation Systems (ITSC 2018), Maui, HI, USA (2018)

Energy Efficiency in Smart Buildings: An IoT-Based Air Conditioning Control System

Felipe Rocha, Lucas Cristiano Dantas, Luís Felipe Santos, Samela Ferreira, Bruna Soares, Alan Fernandes, Everton Cavalcante$^{(\boxtimes)}$ (iD), and Thais Batista (iD)

DIMAp, Federal University of Rio Grande do Norte, Natal, Brazil
felipebarbalho.95@gmail.com, lucascristiano27@gmail.com,
santosfluis19@gmail.com, samelabrunaferreira@hotmail.com,
brunasdcosta@gmail.com, alan.fernandes63@gmail.com,
everton@dimap.ufrn.br, thaisbatista@gmail.com

Abstract. The misuse of high-power electrical appliances such as air conditioners in both commercial and residential buildings has contributed to the inefficient use of energy resources. To face this scenario, smart buildings focus on minimizing energy consumption while improving the experience and productivity of users in these environments. Aiming at optimizing the use of air conditioners towards energy efficiency, this work presents *Smart Place*, an Internet of Things (IoT)-based ambient management system for automatically controlling those equipments. In this system, sensors and video cameras collect data regarding temperature, humidity, and presence of people in monitored spaces. These data are parameters for performing interventions on air conditioners in order to avoid keeping them turned on when the environment is not being used. The system also provides a Web interface for managing devices and monitored environments as well as it is integrated to the FIWARE platform as underlying middleware. This paper describes *Smart Place*, its architecture, and its operation at the Federal University of Rio Grande do Norte (UFRN), Natal, Brazil. The paper also discusses the benefits resulted from the automatic intervention performed by *Smart Place*, which has been able to save 61.8% in energy consumption compared to the traditional manual control in a set of classrooms.

Keywords: Energy efficiency · Smart building · Internet of Things · Air conditioning · Smart campus

1 Introduction

Commercial and residential buildings account for about 60% of the world's electricity consumption [3]. In USA, about 40% of energy is consumed by buildings [4] whereas this amount was 20% in China by 2015, but it has been growing

A. Casaca et al. (Eds.): IFIPIoT 2019, IFIP AICT 574, pp. 21–35, 2020.
https://doi.org/10.1007/978-3-030-43605-6_2

fast in the last decade [11]. This is an alarming situation as most of the world's energy matrix is made up of non-renewable sources, such as coal, oil, and natural gas, which have a negative impact on the Earth.

In Brazil, a survey conducted by the Brazilian Association of Energy Conservation Service Companies revealed a waste of electricity equal to 143.6 million GWh between 2014 and 2016, which is equivalent to more than US$ 16 billion. One of the main reasons for this situation is the outdated industrial machinery, lamps, and home appliances in buildings and homes.

Air conditioners particularly contribute to high energy consumption due to intensive use resulted from the climatic conditions observed in tropical countries (such as Brazil) during most part of the year, as well as the great diffusion of these types of equipment in both commercial and academic buildings. This situation worsens when these devices are misused or used in unsupervised ways, e.g. when they remain turned on for several hours in environments that are not in use. Even if a building is designed and built in an ecologically, energy efficiently way, a significant portion of energy can be wasted if there is no energy management or it is inadequately performed during the operation of the building [11].

As a response to this scenario, modern ways to reduce energy consumption have been proposed through the development of environmental monitoring and control systems, without compromising quality of life and economic development. This leads to the concept of smart buildings, which refer to buildings able to minimize energy consumption and improve the experience and productivity of users in these environments [8]. Smart buildings are related to the Internet of Things (IoT) paradigm, which envisions a myriad of physical objects embedded with sensors and actuators connected by wireless networks and communicating through the Internet. Besides the interconnection with each other and with other physical and/or virtual resources, these smart objects can perform several processes, capture environmental variables, and react to external stimuli.

Aiming to contribute to energy efficiency in university rooms, this work presents *Smart Place*, an environment management system to automatically control air conditioners while avoiding waste of electricity and providing greater comfort to people in such environments. *Smart Place* consists of hardware to control air conditioners based on data collected by motion, temperature, and humidity sensors, as well as video cameras. The system is integrated with FIWARE [2], an European initiative intended to provide an interoperable middleware platform made up of several generic components to leverage the development of smart cities, IoT, and Future Internet applications. Furthermore, *Smart Place* has a Web platform for managing devices and monitored environments. The system is part of the smart campus solutions developed under the Smart Metropolis Project at the Federal University of Rio Grande do Norte (UFRN), Natal, Brazil, being currently deployed at fifteen rooms and laboratories in the university.

The remainder of this paper is structured as follows. Section 2 briefly discusses related work. Section 3 introduces *Smart Place* and its operation in terms of hardware, software, and integration with the FIWARE platform. Section 4 describes some of the results from the deployment of *Smart Place* in different locations and its contribution to existing solutions. Finally, Sect. 5 brings some concluding remarks.

2   Related Work

The existing literature reports a significant number of studies aiming to use control systems to make environments smarter, reduce the waste of energy, and provide more comfort to their users. This section describes five of these studies and relates them to the proposal presented in this paper. All of them were retrieved from the IEEEXplore electronic database, which is one of the most used publication sources in Computing and Engineering. We have prioritized work published in the last two years and selected the studies that have presented energy saving as goal, a hardware prototype, and means of accessing collected data.

The home automation system proposed by Havard et al. [5] aims to avoid waste of energy and increase the level of security of residential or commercial leases by monitoring environmental variables related to temperature, humidity, lighting, etc. The prototype of the unit responsible for gauging these data is composed of an ESP32 device and a BME680 sensor to measure temperature, pressure, humidity, and presence of gas. To send the obtained data, a network based on the LoRaWAN protocol is used due to its long range and low energy consumption. All measured data are stored into a database within the Amazon Web Services cloud service. Data are used in an application that analyzes them and performs actions such as decreasing or increasing the temperature of the air conditioner, switching on or off the lighting of an environment, informing the resident if there is a gas leakage, etc.

Malche and Maheshwary [6] proposed a smart domestic system to be implemented in smart cities in India. This system is based on the FLIP IoT platform, whose architecture encompasses four layers, namely (i) devices, (ii) gateway, (iii) cloud, and (iv) client application. The device layer is composed of an Arduino Nano controller, a Wi-Fi/Bluetooth communication module, sensors, and actuators. The gateway layer consists of a local processing unit that uses Raspberry Pi 3. The cloud layer integrates a Mosquitto MQTT broker, a MongoDB database, and a Node.js system to process data and create services for the client application layer. The client application layer provides control and monitoring through a dashboard. The FLIP device is connected to sensors, lights, air conditioners, cameras, and door and window systems. The system can also send notifications to users, as well as control lights and air conditioners based on temperature and humidity levels of the environment.

Medina and Manera [7] developed a project to automatically control air conditioners through a wireless sensor and actuator network based on the DigiMesh protocol. The system consists of a central unit that controls all air conditioners connected to the network, an actuator module, and a temperature monitoring module. The central control unit configures the days and hours at which the devices will be turned on or off, as well as it performs diagnoses of them. The temperature monitoring module is responsible for collecting data about the local temperature and humidity. The actuator module receives messages from the central control unit indicating if the current operating time of the air conditioner is within the working period, besides a message from the temperature monitor informing the most suitable temperature for that operation. The PIR sensor detects motion and the actuator sends an infrared signal to the air conditioner, turning it on at the last temperature set. Once it is turned on, the temperature of the device will be constantly adjusted according to the external temperature and air humidity.

Nguyen-ANH and Le-Trung [9] proposed RFL-IoT, a framework for reconfiguring IoT systems with focus on intelligent context management based on fuzzy logic. The RFL-IoT architecture is structured in three layers, (i) physical, (ii) middleware, and (iii) application. The physical layer is composed of an ESP8266 device and sensors that capture humidity and temperature data from the environment, which are sent to the middleware layer via the MQTT protocol. The middleware layer is responsible for persisting and publishing data collected by the physical layer, where the fuzzy logic is placed to use collected data towards deciding about the reconfiguration of the device. Such a reconfiguration concerns resetting the device controller firmware, thus modifying its internal behavior. At the application layer, administrators can view collected data at real-time and the time to reconfigure the device and make changes to the reconfiguration rules. The authors reported a significant reduction regarding the use of electricity and the cost and time for reconfiguring a device.

To reduce the energy consumption of homes and buildings, Song et al. [10] developed a smart air conditioning control system composed of a smart meter to control air conditioners, a gateway, and a server. The system uses the ZigBee protocol to perform communication between the gateway and the control devices. The smart meter consists of temperature and humidity sensors, an infrared emitter and receiver used to control the air conditioner and receive information from the gateway, an electrical switch, a power meter that detects the energy consumption of the air conditioner at real-time, and a ZigBee module. This device receives control information from the gateway to turn the air conditioner on or off and to increase or decrease the temperature of the device. Next, it sends an infrared signal to the air conditioner based on the received commands. The server receives temperature and power consumption information from the gateway and it analyzes these data to make control decisions. These decisions will compose a strategy for energy usage to avoid overconsumption.

The aforementioned works bring interesting concepts in the studied context, all of them aiming to save energy and concerning means of displaying data for management or monitoring in a graphical user interface. Table 1 presents a comparison of the works regarding the issues discussed in this paper.

As presented in Table 1, most works do not encompass important issues inherent to the environment automation scenario and application of IoT concepts. The use of an IoT middleware platform is important because it abstracts away the specificities of the integrated physical devices, provides the system with

Table 1. Important issues addressed by related work

Issues	[5]	[6]	[7]	[9]	[10]
Is an IoT middleware platform used?		X		X	
Is the proposal applied to rooms/buildings?	X	X	X	X	X
Is there a graphical user interface?		X		X	X
Does the proposal control air conditioners?	X	X	X	X	X
Do the devices fit different deployment environments?		X	X	X	X

greater interoperability regarding other solutions, and contributes to ease application development, but most of the works neglects this issue. The Malche and Maheshwary [6] and Nguyen-ANH and Le-Trung's [9] works are the only ones that use a middleware platform, but the former does not use a platform that allows customizing the solution, whereas the latter uses a platform that was proposed in the authors' previous works. Regarding the other issues, the proposals of Havard et al. [5] and Medina and Manera [7] do not have a graphical user interface, thus hampering setup and monitoring by an end-user. In particular, Havard et al. [5] did not also concern adapting the prototype to different scenarios. All these issues were considered in the development of *Smart Place* and they will be discussed in Sect. 4.

3   Smart Place

Smart Place was designed to automatically control air conditioning devices and keep them turned on upon detecting the presence of people in the monitored environment or when it is expected to be used within fifteen minutes after the detection of no occupants in the room. If these conditions are not met, then the device must be turned off. This is due to the fact that frequently turning the air conditioner on and off can result in greater energy consumption and reduce its service life. *Smart Place* is inserted into the context of a set of applications developed to create a smart campus at the Federal University of Rio Grande do Norte (UFRN), Natal, Brazil.

The system is composed of: (i) a *hardware device*, which is responsible for collecting data related to the environment and sending commands to air conditioning devices; (ii) a *middleware platform*, which provides services such as context management, devices management, and data persistence; and (iii) a *Web platform* capable of accessing persisted data from devices and making them available for system's users through querying interfaces. These elements are illustrated in Fig. 1 and detailed in Sects. 3.1 to 3.3

3.1   Hardware Devices

The hardware device is a component aimed to monitor and control air conditioners. This component is composed of a Raspberry Pi microcomputer that (i)

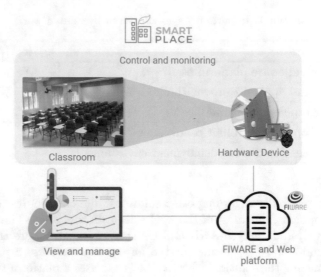

Fig. 1. Overview of *Smart Place*.

acts on the air conditioners by sending infrared signals and (ii) manages data measured by different sensors plugged on the microcomputer to measure environmental variables such as motion, temperature, and humidity, as well as a camera for image capturing. Raspberry Pi also runs the decision algorithm that decides about the actuation action according to data received from sensors and the camera. Both measurements coming from sensors and the camera as well as decisions about acting on the air conditioning devices are forwarded to the underlying middleware platform.

Figure 2 shows a customized 3D-printed structure to host the hardware device with sensors, actuators, and camera, all attached to Raspberry Pi. The hardware device must be deployed in positions that allow for better monitoring the room and actuation on air conditioners. The infrared signal must reach all air conditioners and the camera should have the widest range of vision. The camera should also preferentially have a frontal view of occupants to achieve greater accuracy in counting people.

To support the decision process, the device is configured to access a third-party system, e.g., a system that registers the scheduled use for the rooms. Data from this system are locally saved in the Raspberry Pi to offline use until the end of the current academic term, when they will be updated. If the presence sensor detects motion in the room, then images provided by the camera are not used for deciding about the activation of the air conditioner.

Algorithm 1 depicts the procedure for controlling air conditioners based on both data gathered from sensors and images from camera. To turn on/off an air conditioner, the Raspberry Pi's local system is programmed to execute a set of actions based on the periodic verification of the motion sensor and the camera. When the sensor detects motion, the room management service is queried to

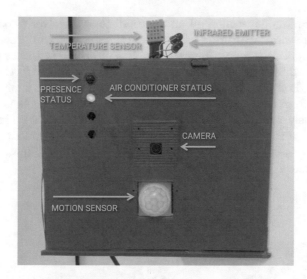

Fig. 2. Hardware device deployed in a room.

verify whether an activity is scheduled for that time. If yes, then the system turns on the air conditioner. Otherwise, if no movement is detected or there is no scheduled activity, the system checks the images from the camera to verify people presence in the room. In case of confirming people presence, the air conditioner is also activated. The difference between these two methods is due to the precision of the motion sensor and the camera. As the motion sensor is more error-prone than the camera, a more rigid methodology is adopted: data from camera are used to double check the presence when no movement is indicated by the motion sensor or when there is a movement in a the room that is not scheduled to have an activity.

Algorithm 1. Air conditioner control algorithm

```
1  while true do
2  |   if air conditioner is turned off then
3  |   |   if (has motion and room is scheduled) or camera detected people then
4  |   |   |   turn air conditioner on;
5  |   |   |   save last presence time;
6  |   |   end
7  |   else
8  |   |   if has motion or camera detected people then
9  |   |   |   save last presence time;
10 |   |   else
11 |   |   |   turn air conditioner off;
12 |   |   end
13 |   end
14 end
```

The decision about turning off an air conditioner involves frequently verifying the motion sensor, capturing images from the camera, and processing images every three seconds for monitoring the amount of people in the monitored environment. After fifteen minutes without motion and no people in the images, the device is turned off. To regulate the temperature, the system analyzes each new measurement from the temperature sensor to verify if it is $\pm 1\,^{\circ}\text{C}$ when compared to the previously configured value (normally $23\,^{\circ}\text{C} \equiv 73.4\,^{\circ}\text{F}$). If the temperature is outside that threshold, then the system sends a signal to the device to adjust the temperature. Figure 3 depicts the communication flows involving the hardware device.

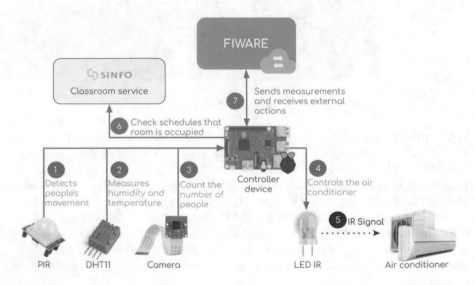

Fig. 3. Hardware measurement and actuation flow.

The environments at which the system may be deployed are very heterogeneous. Hence, an essential system requirement is complying with the plurality of characteristics of these environments. Some characteristics that may vary in each deployment environment are different amounts and models of air conditioners, different room sizes, and the need of using the camera. Such a heterogeneity is handled through a configuration file for each room deployment, which specifies the elements that the device will use. This file is loaded and interpreted at the beginning of the device execution. This strategy allows using a unique base code to different air conditioners and a flexible implementation to control each room.

As rooms may have different sizes or may be divided into (sub)spaces, it would be hard for a single device to monitor the observed environment variables and act on more than one air conditioner in the same room. Therefore, a device distribution strategy needs to be used in the environment. Multiple hardware devices are deployed at the room while maintaining the status of a single device to the system. This happens through the distribution of control units as agents with different roles in different locations of the monitored environment. In this configuration, an agent assumes the role of *master* and the others become *slaves*. Slaves are simpler microcontrollers, which are connected only to the temperature, motion, and humidity sensors to reduce the system's overall implementation cost. Figure 4 shows an example of how organizing devices as master and slaves to control the air conditioners in a room.

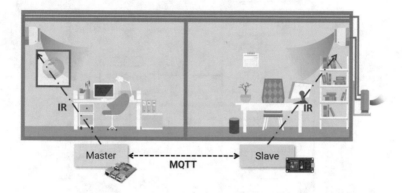

Fig. 4. Devices distributed in a master-slave organization.

The communication among agents is wireless, using the MQTT protocol (the master acts as an MQTT broker). Slaves report to the master whenever there are changes in the monitored environment. The master is responsible for deciding about turning on/off or updating the temperature of the air conditioner in each space within the room.

3.2 Middleware

As middleware infrastructure, *Smart Place* uses the European platform FIWARE, which was chosen due to the fact of being a generic, open-source solution, as well as providing many reusable, interoperable components to ease system development in different application domains, the so-called *Generic Enablers* (GEs). FIWARE encompasses GEs for different purposes, such as context entity management, device management, historical data storage, entity event processing, security, creation of dashboards, etc.

Some FIWARE GEs are indispensable to develop IoT-based applications, which involves an interaction among physical devices and the need of integrating applications to share data and entities related to the application domain. Three FIWARE GEs are used in *Smart Place*, namely *Orion Context Broker*, *IoT Agent*, and *Cygnus*. Orion Context Broker is responsible for managing context entities and subscriptions of parties interested in its state changes. The IoT Agent is responsible for device management and communication among devices that use distinct communication protocols. Cygnus binds state changes events to databases that are responsible for storing these event data.

Figure 5 illustrates the FIWARE elements that are the main bridge between hardware devices and the Web platform. The Web platform receives and processes user requests for triggering actions or querying stored data regarding events and devices' data.

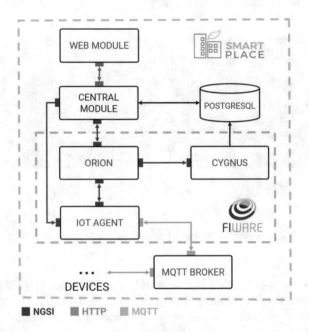

Fig. 5. Communication with FIWARE GEs within *Smart Place*.

The hardware device uses the MQTT protocol to send the monitored variables (temperature, humidity, presence, number of people) to an MQTT broker instance, Mosquitto [1]. Data are then forwarded from the MQTT broker to the FIWARE IoT Agent, at which working devices are registered. Deployments of FIWARE GEs may contain multiple IoT Agents, each one supporting a different set of IoT communication protocols. This allows employing protocols different from MQTT to be used in hardware devices to communicate with the platform.

Once the device registered at the IoT Agent (associated with the physical device) receives a new measurement from the physical counterpart, the measurement is sent to the entity that represents and stores the attributes of the device at Orion Context Broker. The value of the attribute associated with the sent measurement is updated. Next, an entity update notification is sent to all components subscribed to receive notifications about data changes on the entity. Some of these subscribed components are Cygnus and the RESTful API of the *Smart Place* Web component, in which the event will be processed and sent to the Web client application to update the exhibition of device data.

3.3   Web Platform

The *Smart Place* Web platform provides services to configure entities and devices on FIWARE GEs, access historical data, and monitor application events. By using the Web platform, users can manage monitored environments and receive alerts regarding the occurrence of unexpected behaviors. The Web platform also displays data charts in a condensed way to allow for a better analysis on the available information. Users can set parameters to the system execution and trigger commands that are sent to devices, such as turning an air conditioner on or off, setting the desired room temperature, etc.

The architecture of the *Smart Place* Web platform is shown in Fig. 6. It is composed of: (i) a *Central Module*, which integrates services and modules related to authorization, notification, control, entities and devices configuration, actuation, and measurements access; (ii) a *Persistence Module* for storing the structure of entities registered at Orion Context Broker for system reconfiguration purposes after an eventual reboot; (iii) an *Alert Module* to receive context information and send notifications in case of problems, e.g., the absence of data from a device deployed at a room; and (iv) a *Web Module* that provides a graphical Web interface for executing user operations through requests to the RESTful API of the Central Module.

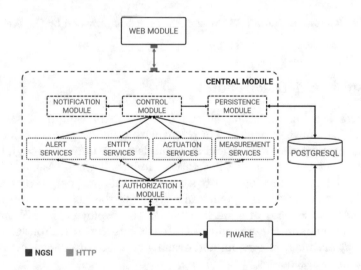

Fig. 6. Internal architecture of *Smart Place* Web component.

The graphical user interface provided by the Web module enables users to invoke operations such as creating, editing, removing, and visualizing entities related to buildings, rooms, sensors, and air conditioners. Moreover, users can visualize measurements obtained from devices deployed at rooms, the actuation made on devices, and energy consumption statistics. Figure 7 shows a visualization of one of the monitored rooms with information such as the number of air conditioners in the room, how many of them are turned on, the number of people in the room, and the current temperature.

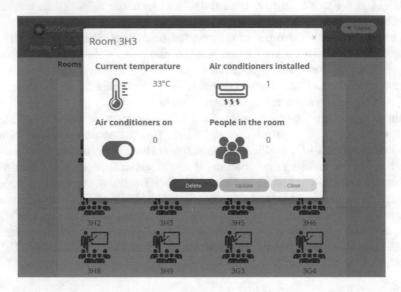

Fig. 7. Visualization of Room 3H3 through the interface provided by the Web module.

4   Results and Discussion

Smart Place has been running at the UFRN's main campus since January 2019 with fifteen devices deployed in rooms with different purposes, including a research laboratory, classrooms, and an administrative office. Through the analysis of data sent by devices to the Central Module, it was possible to evaluate the impact of *Smart Place* on energy saving. For this purpose, we carried out a study with a set of seven classrooms in a sector of the university during workdays (Monday to Friday) of a week. Prior to the deployment of *Smart Place*, the air conditioners in these rooms operated uninterruptedly from 6:50 a.m. to 10:40 p.m. at morning, afternoon, and evening classes. Air conditioners are usually off during weekends.

Figure 8 shows a comparison regarding the number of hours that each monitored air conditioner was kept turned on in each room during the analyzed week. The chart compares the actuation of *Smart Place* with the manual intervention, without the system. With the manual intervention, these devices would be kept turned on for approximately 79 h during the week, more than 15 h per day on average. On the other hand, the automatic control of *Smart Place* resulted in a reduction of the usage time to 42 h in the observed week, 8.4 h per day on average. This represents an approximate reduction of 46.8% of the total time in which air conditioners are kept turn on in comparison to the manual operation.

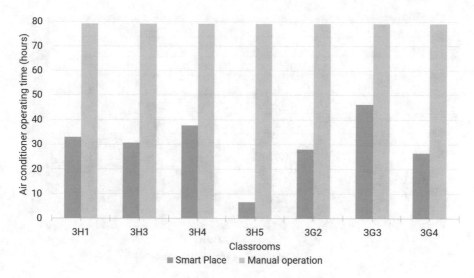

Fig. 8. Results on the number of operating hours comparing the manual intervention with the one performed by *Smart Place*.

Information about device power was obtained through the Brazilian National Energy Conservation Label (ENCE), which provides information about energy consumption and it is a guarantee of the Brazilian National Institute of Metrology, Quality, and Technology (INMETRO) that the equipment has passed a series of safety, energy efficiency, and operation tests. Figure 9 shows results on energy consumption of air conditioners deployed at the rooms with and without *Smart Place* intervention for the same period.

As shown in Fig. 9, the total amount of used energy was approximately equal to 780.8 kWh with the *Smart Place* intervention. In the scenario without the use of *Smart Place*, the total consumption was equal to 2037.75 kWh. Therefore, it is possible to observe a total energy saving of 1256.95 kWh provided by the intervention of *Smart Place* during one week for the set of rooms in the study, being equivalent to a reduction of 61.68% in the consumption. By analyzing the two previous charts, it is noteworthy that the energy consumption is lower in comparison to others, even though the air conditioner has been used for a longer period. This disparity is due to the fact that some types of air conditioner have higher power and hence they consume more energy than others.

With respect to related work (see Sect. 2), *Smart Place* covers all of the issues presented in Table 1. The system uses FIWARE as a middleware platform, which ensures an accessible, interoperable layer for other applications that need to consume data available at *Smart Place* through the FIWARE components embedded into the system. In addition, *Smart Place* has proven to be applicable to rooms with different characteristics. This is possible by the description of device configurations according to the requirements of the deployment site and the operation mode in a master-slave distributed scheme for environments with

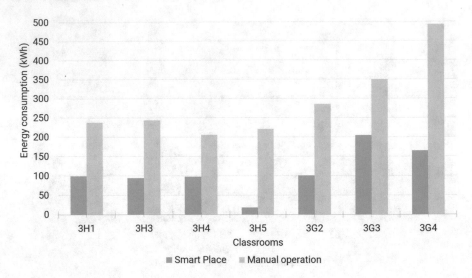

Fig. 9. Results on the energy consumption comparing the manual intervention with the one performed by *Smart Place*.

larger dimensions. The graphical user interface provided by the system also eases controlling and visualizing data of all monitored environments.

5   Concluding Remarks

This paper introduced *Smart Place*, an environment management system that automatically controls indoor air conditioners aiming to contribute to reduce energy waste. The system integrates: (i) a hardware device to collect data regarding temperature, humidity, and presence of people in monitored places, as well as perform interventions in air conditioners; (ii) a middleware platform that provides services such as context management, device logging, and data persistence; and (iii) a Web platform that accesses data provided by hardware devices and makes them available for control and visualization purposes, besides detecting any abnormality. *Smart Place* is currently monitoring classrooms and laboratories at the UFRN's main campus in Natal, Brazil. By analyzing the use of different rooms in the university with and without the use of *Smart Place* during one week, it was possible to observe a significant reduction in energy consumption, with an average reduction of 46.8% on the air conditioners working time and 61.8% on energy consumption.

As future work, we intend to evaluate the accuracy of the software executed in the devices regarding the decision to turn the air conditioner on/off according to the occupancy of the monitored place. Another evaluation will assess the real impact of the adoption of *Smart Place* in reducing energy consumption through directly monitoring the electrical network, thus allowing for determining how much consumption has been saved and the impact in terms of cost reduction.

Regarding software, the system will be subjected to a performance experimental study aimed to assess the impact of monitoring a large number of devices simultaneously delivering data to the Central Module and the effect of this operation load on Quality of Service (QoS) and Quality of Experience (QoE) requirements.

Acknowledgments. This research is supported by (i) UFRN/IMD/Smart Metropolis Project, (ii) INES 2.0, FACEPE grant APQ-0399-1.03/17, CAPES grant 88887.136410/2017-00, and CNPq grant 465614/2014-0; and (iii) CNPq grant 308274/2016-4 for Thais Batista.

References

1. Eclipse Mosquitto^{TM}: An open source MQTT broker. https://mosquitto.org/
2. FIWARE. https://www.fiware.org/
3. Araya, D.B., Grolinger, K., ElYamany, H.F., Capretz, M.A., Bitsuamlak, G.: An ensemble learning framework for anomaly detection in building energy consumption. Energy Build. **144**, 191–206 (2017). https://doi.org/10.1016/j.enbuild.2017. 02.058
4. Chen, Y., Wen, J.: A whole building fault detection using weather based pattern matching and feature based PCA method. In: 2017 IEEE International Conference on Big Data (Big Data), pp. 4050–4057. IEEE (2017). https://doi.org/10.1109/ BigData.2017.8258421
5. Havard, N., McGrath, S., Flanagan, C., MacNamee, C.: Smart building based on Internet of Things technology. In: Proceedings of the 12th International Conference on Sensing Technology (ICST), pp. 278–281. IEEE (2018). https://doi.org/ 10.1109/ICSensT.2018.8603575
6. Malche, T., Maheshwary, P.: Internet of things (IoT) for building smart home system. In: Proceedings of the 2017 International Conference on I-SMAC (IoT in Social, Mobile, Analytics and Cloud) (I-SMAC), pp. 65–70. IEEE (2017). https:// doi.org/10.1109/I-SMAC.2017.8058258
7. Medina, B.E., Manera, L.T.: Retrofit of air conditioning systems through an wireless sensor and actuator network: an IoT-based application for smart buildings. In: Proceedings of the 14th IEEE International Conference on Networking, Sensing and Control (ICNSC), pp. 49–53. IEEE (2017). https://doi.org/10.1109/ICNSC. 2017.8000066
8. Moreno, M.V., et al.: Big data: the key to energy efficiency in smart buildings. Soft Comput. **20**(5), 1749–1762 (2016). https://doi.org/10.1007/s00500-015-1679-4
9. Nguyen-ANH, T., Le-Trung, Q.: RFL-IoT: an IoT reconfiguration framework applied fuzzy logic for context management. In: Proceedings of the 2019 IEEE-RIVF International Conference on Computing and Communication Technologies (RIVF), pp. 1–6. IEEE (2019). https://doi.org/10.1109/RIVF.2019.8713619
10. Song, W., Feng, N., Tian, Y., Fong, S.: An IoT-based smart controlling system of air conditioner for high energy efficiency. In: Proceedings of the 2017 IEEE International Conference on Internet of Things (iThings) and IEEE Green Computing and Communications (GreenCom) and IEEE Cyber, Physical and Social Computing (CPSCom) and IEEE Smart Data (SmartData), pp. 442–449. IEEE (2017). https://doi.org/10.1109/iThings-GreenCom-CPSCom-SmartData.2017.72
11. Zhu, J., Shen, Y., Song, Z., Zhou, D., Zhang, Z., Kusiak, A.: Data-driven building load profiling and energy management. Sustain. Cities Soc. (2019). https://doi. org/10.1016/j.scs.2019.101587

Toward Blockchain Technology in IoT Applications: An Analysis for E-health Applications

Maurício Moreira Neto[1,2,5](✉), Emanuel Ferreira Coutinho[1,2,3](✉),
Leonardo Oliveira Moreira[1,2,4](✉), and José Neuman de Souza[2,5](✉)

[1] IBITURUNA - Research Group of Cloud Computing and Systems, Fortaleza, Brazil
[2] Federal University of Ceará (UFC), Fortaleza, Ceará, Brazil
maumneto@alu.ufc.br, {emanuel.coutinho,neuman}@ufc.br
[3] Graduate Program in Computer Science (PCOMP), Quixadá, Brazil
[4] Virtual University Institute (UFC-VIRTUAL), Fortaleza, Brazil
leoomoreira@virtual.ufc.br
[5] Master and Doctorate in Computer Science (MDCC), Fortaleza, Brazil

Abstract. Research involving Blockchain technology has been growing due to its decentralization and immutability characteristics. Several applications from the most varied areas can benefit from the Blockchain, such as finance, logistics, and others. Internet of Things (IoT) is a new paradigm that has emerged to provide services to users through intelligent objects arranged in the day-to-day and provided various research, for example, smart buildings, smart cities, precision agriculture, and E-health. E-health applications can be considered as a set of computational solutions focused on the health area. This paper aims to study the introduction of Blockchain technology in an E-health approach. A Blockchain tool was used in conjunction with an E-health database and evaluated its performance. The results indicated that the transaction validation times are favorable for the characteristics of an E-health application.

Keywords: Blockchain · E-health · Internet of Things · Performance analysis

1 Introduction

Due to advances in microelectronics and wireless communication, it has been possible to develop small mobile devices that have the computational power to

This work was partially supported by Universal MCTI/CNPq 28/2018 (426701/2018-6).

This work is partially supported by São Paulo Research Foundation – FAPESP, through grant number 2015/24144-7.

capture data and retransmit them to other devices in order to generate information, thus providing services to users [6,16]. These devices may contain one or more sensors to monitor the status of a given individual, and from that data generate useful information for the user. These advances provided the rise of the Internet of Things (IoT).

IoT is an emerging paradigm that has combined several technologies. IoT interconnects various physical devices present in daily life, and that has the computational power to capture data, providing services to users. These physical devices are called smart objects. IoT covers a wide variety of different types of applications, such as education, transportation, agriculture, health, among others [1,6].

E-health applications are a set of health-related computing solutions that use the internet to provide their services [15]. These applications can range from monitoring a patient's physiological data to the medication management system in a hospital infrastructure [11]. One of the main challenges of E-health is the security and privacy of the data captured or manipulated by these applications. E-health application data are considered sensitive because it can present information about the disease and the treatment of a particular patient [11,15]. That means unauthorized persons should not access it.

A Blockchain consists of a set of data composed of a chain of data packets (blocks) where a block comprises multiple transactions [17]. Blockchain is extended by each additional block and thus represents a complete general record of the transaction history. The network using cryptographic mechanisms can validate these blocks [17].

Blockchain is known to be the technology used to create Bitcoin. However, due to its characteristics, it is possible to use it in several other applications. Currently, there are studies on the use of Blockchain technology in applications that need its features. IoT can be cited as one of those applications that fit with the use of Blockchain. Conoscenti et al. described some uses of blockchain with IoT, such as the use of blockchain to exchange data collected by IoT device sensors and other goods and to store and manage data collected by IoT devices, decentralized and private-by-design fashion [7].

Many IoT applications require information storage that can be auditable and have a history of data changes, such as E-health applications. Blockchain technology can provide several advantages to E-health applications. Advantages like immutability, audacity, security, and others are part of Blockchain technology.

This paper aims to present research on the introduction of Blockchain technology in an E-health approach. An E-health application architecture is proposed with the insertion of a Blockchain, based on the [15] model. In order to reach the proposed goal, a Blockchain experiment was carried out in conjunction with an E-health database. The BigchainDB is a distributed Blockchain database.

The performance of Blockchain is analyzed with the data provided by the used E-health application. We discussed the possibility of the integration of Blockchain in several types of E-health applications.

The rest of this paper is divided into the following sections: in Sect. 2 a brief background is presented on IoT, E-health, and Blockchain technologies, respectively. In Sect. 3 shows the work related to the proposal of this work. Section 4 details our approach to using Blockchain technology in an E-health application. Subsequently, in Sect. 5, the experimental design is described. Section 5 presents the detail about the experiments. Section 6 presents the results and discussions derived from the experiments conducted. Finally, in the Sect. 7 the conclusions are presented.

2   Background

2.1   Internet of Things and E-health

Internet of Things (IoT) has been an emerging paradigm in recent years. Advances in wireless technologies, embedded systems, and sensing have led to the emergence of this new paradigm [16]. IoT is a set of computational devices that can monitor and transmit data from an environment over the Internet, providing services and information to users [6,16]. These devices are called smart-objects and can exchange data and information from the monitored environment with each other [6,9].

Smart objects are usually limited in computing power and do not have the same level of protection as personal computers and smartphones. This feature of smart objects makes it necessary to research efficient and low computational techniques for access control and data privacy in IoT applications.

IoT has provided the creation of applications in various sectors such as transportation, industry 4.0, education, health, and smart-* applications[1].

According to the Healthcare Information and Management Systems Society (HIMSS), E-health is a set of the application of the Internet and other technologies related to the health sector to improve access, efficiency, and effectiveness of quality clinical processes. It also aims to improve the business processes used by healthcare organizations, professionals, patients, and consumers to improve patients' health status.

E-health includes several dimensions:

- Delivery of relevant information to health partners;
- Provision of essential delivery services (example: medicines);
- Ease of interaction between health professionals and patients;
- Ease of integration of business processes related to the health sector;
- Local and remote access to health information;
- Remote monitoring of patients;
- Support for employers and employees, payers and suppliers.

---

[1] Smart-* application are applications that offer services based on monitoring, e.g., smart-cities.

In this context, the overall objective is to improve the health status of patients, as well as to provide more efficient services, avoiding possible complications. Electronic Health Records (EHRs) are an evolving concept defined as a longitudinal collection of electronic health information about individual patients and populations [10].

Initially, the EHR is a mechanism for integrating health care information currently collected into printed and electronic medical records to improve the quality of care. These records consist of a series of patient data such as complaints, laboratory tests, medicines used, procedures performed, and various other information. With the possession of the data of the registry, it is possible to carry out instant analyzes, identifying relations between the existing data.

In general, delivery of E-health services related to remote monitoring of vital signs consists of collecting signals on a mobile or wearable device, transmitting the raw or pre-processed signals to a server, storing them, processing them, and them to the end-user. Also, depending on the usage scenario, the remote monitoring process may involve voice and video consultation of the end-users.

However, these data are considered sensitive data since they should not be accessed and should not be modified by unauthorized persons. Blockchain technology can provide these essential features for E-health applications.

2.2   Blockchain

Blockchain is a block sequence, which contains the complete record of transactions as a public book, indicating the order in which the transactions occurred [5]. Figure 1 shows a Blockchain in which the newly validated block points to the immediately preceding block generated. That is, each block in the chair confirms the integrity of the previous and the way back to the first block, called the genesis block.

A Blockchain consists of a set of data composed by a chair of data packets (blocks) where a block comprises multiple transactions [17]. Blockchain is extended by each additional block and thus represents a complete general record of the transaction history. The network using cryptographic mechanisms can validate these blocks [17]. In addition to transactions, each block contains a timestamp (date and time), the hash value of the previous block (parent), and a random number used to check the hash named Nonce. This concept ensures the integrity of the entire Blockchain up to the first block (genesis block).

The hash values are unique, preventing fraud from being performed on the system since changes to a block in the chain would immediately change its hash value [17].

The block can be added to the chain if most of the network nodes agree through a consensus mechanism on the validity of the transactions in a block and on the validity of the block itself. Therefore, new transactions are not automatically added to the record.

The consensus process ensures that these transactions are stored in a block for some time before being transferred to the ledger (for example, in Bitcoin[2] is 10 min). After this process, the Blockchain information can no longer be changed.

In the Bitcoin, the blocks are created by the so-called "miners", who are rewarded with Bitcoins for the validation of the blocks. The Bitcoin example illustrates that Blockchain's principle can change not only the process of money-making transactions. Using encryption, people around the world can trust each other, and transfer different types of assets, point to point on the internet.

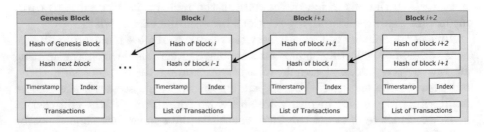

Fig. 1. Example of blocks in the Blockchain [17,21].

All Blockchain implementations are based on virtual currency [18]. The basic types of records kept by the book are transactions related to the creation of new coins (only made by miners), as well as the transfer of currency from one user to another. That is, in addition to these simple transactions, many Blockchains allow distributed books to store smart contracts.

A smart contract is an autonomous application with pre-defined inputs and outputs that can be performed by a miner in a deterministic manner [18]. Any user can invoke a smart contract, the result of which is logged as a transaction in the distributed log book. That is, the user can use Blockchain technology in other contexts. Blockchain becomes an exciting technology in the health area due to its inherent characteristics.

A smart contract can also be viewed as a collection of codes and data (functions and states) that are implemented through transactions [20]. It should be emphasized that an intelligent contract should generate a similar result in all nodes that perform the same contract, maintaining cohesion. However, not all Blockchain networks allow the use of smart contracts [20]. There are several possibilities of use for smart contracts, such as calculations, information storage, automation of financial assets, among others [13].

3   Related Work

In this section, it is present selected papers that involved IoT, E-health applications, and Blockchain.

---

[2] Cryptocurrency using Blockchain technology.

The paper proposed by Metter presented an account of initial points of use of Blockchain in E-health applications [14]. The work was focused on the management of medical care, user-oriented research, and pharmaceutical falsification in the pharmaceutical sector. Medical treatment processes usually involve more than one health care specialist and need access to information from their patients. Blockchain technology enables transparent access for those interested in patient care information. This ability to track the interaction between patient and physician is fundamental to correct treatment.

In the paper of Liu et al. proposed a Blockchain architecture focusing on E-health applications called Advanced BlockChain (ABC) [12]. This proposed architecture is described as a reliable and secure solution for medical record exchanges. This work presented some fundamentals of E-health and Blockchain, considered the following elements of the architecture: Blockchain and E-health protocols, inter-domain adaptations, certification authorities and security operations, regulatory compliance, additional value E-health systems [12]. With computational logic to be incorporated into E-Health's blockchains, personalized medicine is enabled by the complete and consistent data blocks available to all service providers involved [12]. The Advanced BlockChain mechanism enables security audits, regulatory compliance reports, billing updates, lab results alerts, and medication events.

Rifi et al. presented problems for E-health, and Blockchain could help develop a safe and scalable medical solution. They paid attention to the data exchange security and the low computational power of the sensors [19]. Patients, doctors, and hospitals are connected to a Blockchain, which provides privacy and security of medical data. These data can come from patient-connected sensors or the hospital infrastructure, and the data generated can trigger smart contracts that will notify interested parties. As sensors generally have low computational power, gateways can be used for this function, and thus enjoy an IoT environment with Blockchain.

The work proposed by Freitas and Rolim presented a framework called Demochain to assist in the development of hybrid Blockchains platforms in the context of IoT [8]. The lack of standardization of IoT devices due to their different areas of operation makes it difficult to implement a Blockchain network customized for IoT. Therefore, the proposed framework aims to create Blockchain hybrid networks [8]. This framework can offer combination options of different levels in Blockchain architecture and functionalities, varying protocols and encryptions. This framework provides the creation of IoT applications from various areas.

It possible to observe from the works cited that there are several proposals for E-health applications and, because the data is sensitive, privatization and security become a challenge in this category of applications. E-health applications can have several aspects that, consequently, manipulate different data types. However, because the manipulated data present relevant information about the patient, it is necessary to use a security mechanism and data privatization. Also, retrieving the history of data changes in E-health applications is essential for applications that manipulate medical protuberances.

Blockchain's technology provides a history of all the transactions that have been performed through the ledger, i.e., it is possible to analyze which changes were made to a given file. It is also possible to insert data anonymization algorithms into a Blockchain, preventing unauthorized users from satisfactorily extracting the data.

Our application aims to evaluate the possibility of using Blockchain technology in IoT applications, particularly in the E-health application. It is possible to evaluate the insertion of Blockchain in an application that requires a low latency through code execution time and transaction validation metrics.

4   Description of Our Approach

The purpose of this article is to study the use of Blockchain technology in an E-health approach. A distributed Blockchain database tool was tested with the MHEALTH dataset used by Moreira Neto et al. proposal architecture. We intend to analyze the possibility of the use of the Blockchain database in conjunction with the E-health approach.

The proposal of Moreira Neto et al. presents a three-layer architecture in which: (i) the first layer is the perception layer that is composed of smart objects; (ii) a network layer that is responsible for managing, routing, and identifying network technologies used in the application; and (iii) an application layer that is responsible for providing services to users. In this architecture, we can see that each layer offers a service to the top layer. Figure 2 presents the three-layer architecture proposed by Moreira Neto et al.

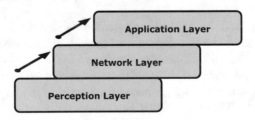

Fig. 2. Three layer architecture [15].

The application proposed by [15] is divided into three parts. The first part of the approach is the collection of users' physiological data through wearable devices. The communication of these devices is done using a communication protocol of low cost (i.e., Bluetooth Low Energy - BLE). This physiological information is made available by the mobile application. The mobile app presents the physiological data of the user and the feedback of the responsible health professional.

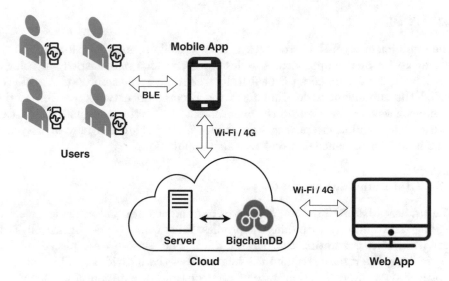

Fig. 3. Architecture of the application of Moreira et al. with the introduction of a Blockchain module.

The second part is responsible for sending the captured data for processing and storage in the cloud. Information inferences are made from the data stored in the cloud. It is possible to create information historical about the behavior of the patient's physiological data through inference. The data is sent to the healthcare professional through a web application. The web application is the third part and it is responsible for receiving the information processed in the cloud and presented to the health professional through visualizations.

Figure 3 presents our proposed architecture. Our approach is to evaluate the introduction of the Blockchain module into the E-health architecture. This module can be added to a remote server that is located in a public or private cloud.

By capturing the patients' physiological data through wearable devices, these data are routed to the mobile application. The mobile application receives this data and presents it to the user through views, as well as it sends the data to the server to be processed and stored. The server will process the data and generate information through statistical inferences. Blockchain will store this information and send it to the healthcare professional through the web application.

5 Experimental Design

As previously reported, the goal of the paper is to evaluate the use of Blockchain technology in an IoT application. Therefore, to use the BigchainDB tool together with the E-health database to analyze tool performance. This section details the materials and evaluation methods applied for the proposed application.

5.1   Goals

The experiment's goals are to check if it is possible to insert a Blockchain tool into an IoT-E-health approach. A series of experiments were carried out using a Blockchain database and an E-health dataset to achieve the proposed goal. We scaled the number of nodes that form the Blockchain network, as well as the number of sent transactions in the experiments. Using these evaluations, we can verify if the validation and execution times of the algorithm may or may not impact the performance of a real E-health application.

5.2   Materials and Methods

The dataset MHEALTH [2–4] has body movement data and vital sign recordings on ten volunteers with different profiles. Each volunteer performed physical activities, thus generating the dataset data. The sensors were placed on the pelvic floor, the right wrist, and the left ankle of the individuals. These sensors captured data of acceleration, rate of rotation, and orientation of the magnetic field. The sensor positioned on the breastplate captured the 2-lead ECG measurements, which can be used for essential cardiac monitoring and can detect arrhythmias. Data extracted from the dataset was preprocessed and sent to the Blockchain network in the form of JSON[3] files. Each sent JSON file corresponds to a transaction with the default shown below:

- {'heartBeats': Double, 'speed': Double, 'acelerometerX': Double, 'acelerometerY': Double, 'acelerometerZ': Double, 'indexData': Integer}

We used the BigchainDB[4], which is a Blockchain database that offers Blockchain characteristics such as decentralization and immutability. BigchainDB also allows deploying scalable IoT applications and artificial intelligence. It was created six Virtual Machines (VM) with 1 GB of primary memory and 20 GB secondary memory, similar to Amazon t2.micro. The operating system used was Ubuntu 18.04-LTS. These virtual machines were virtualized from a server with processor: Intel(R) Xeon(R) E5645 @2.40 GHz.

The experiment consists of varying the number of transactions, observing the validation times of transactions, and the average number of blocks created by execution. The same experiment is performed for a Blockchain network with two, four, and six virtual machines. Table 1 presents a set of performed experiments.

---

[3] Available at https://www.json.org/. Accessed: 12 July 2019.
[4] Available at https://www.bigchaindb.com/. Accessed: 12 July 2019.

Table 1. Experimental design.

	Experiment I	Experiment II	Experiment III
	Number of transaction		
2 VM	100	150	200
4 VM	100	150	200
6 VM	100	150	200

Legend: VM = Virtual Machine.

We execute three different scenarios based on the number of transactions, each executed five times, that is, 5×100 transactions, 5×150 transactions and 5×200 transactions.

5.3 Metrics

The metrics that were used to evaluate the viability of using the Blockchain tool in an E-health application are presented below:

- Execution time of the algorithm;
- Validation time of the Transactions;
- Number of blocks created.

Also, it was extracted statistical data analysis from the validation times of the transactions, considering that it is the most important metric because it is directly responsible for Blockchain's performance.

The execution time of the algorithm is the time that the algorithm takes to send the transactions to BigchainDB. This metric is strongly related to the send mode of transaction. BigchainDB has three send modes: commit mode, asynchronous mode, and synchronous mode. In our experiment, we used the synchronous mode; that is, the processing to send transactions only finished after the storage confirmation return. The synchronous mode may provide a longer delay than asynchronous mode by waiting for block storage confirmation. However, the synchronous mode guarantee that the block has been properly inserted into the Blockchain.

The validation time of transactions is the time when all transactions were successfully stored in Blockchain. This metric is also related to the sending mode. The sending mode can impact the time of validation.

Finally, the number of created blocks is directly related to the block creation time parameter. Each block has a timeout for closing the block, i.e., all transactions sent by the end of that time will be stored in the block. All subsequent transactions will be stored in the next block, and so on.

6   Experiments and Results

Figures 4(a) and (b) present, respectively, the median and the mean of the validation times of the transactions of each performed experiment. We choose the median validation times because it is the more reliable metric due to the low influence on the values derived from the outliers data.

Table 2. Validation times of the transactions.

	2 Nodes			4 Nodes			6 Nodes		
	Mean	Median	SD	Mean	Median	SD	Mean	Median	SD
100 Transaction	0.46	0.46	0.026	0.54	0.54	0.026	0.61	0.60	0.025
150 Transactions	0.51	0.51	0.026	0.48	0.57	0.027	0.45	0.62	0.028
200 Transactions	0.69	0.57	0.033	0.75	0.75	0.034	0.86	0.85	0.034

Legend: SD = Standard Deviation. *The collected times are in the order of seconds.

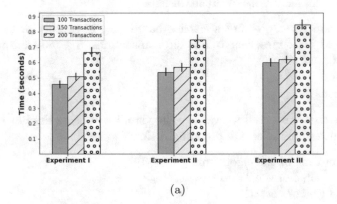

(a)

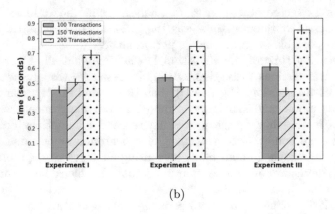

(b)

Fig. 4. (a) Median transaction times and (b) Average transaction times.

It was observed the occurrence of outliers during the experiments. These outliers come from the creation of empty blocks. When an empty block occurs, it means that the timeout has been reached, so the counted time of this block is high and it becomes an outlier about other blocks. These outliers have a high impact on the mean values of the validation times but have little impact on the values of the medians. Table 2 presents the mean, median and standard deviation data of the conducted experiments.

It can be seen from Fig. 4(a) that transaction validation times grow according to the increase in the number of transactions sent to the Blockchain network. We also observed this feature when analyzing Fig. 5, which presents the execution times of the algorithm for sending the transactions. There was a positive correlation between the number of transactions and the execution time of the algorithm.

Another point observed is the growth of the time of the about the number of nodes in the Blockchain network, as can be seen in Fig. 5 and Table 3. The validation time of the blocks grows as more nodes compose the Blockchain network, and this happens due to the intense communication between the nodes during the validation stage of the transactions. During the consensus that will validate the transaction, it occurs intense exchange information between the nodes of the Blockchain network until the moment the block is created and stored in the cash book of each node.

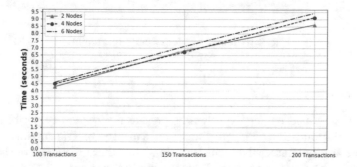

Fig. 5. Executions times of the algorithm.

Table 3. Execution times of the algorithm.

	2 Nodes	4 Nodes	6 Nodes
100 Transactions	4.3 s	4.5 s	4.6 s
150 Transactions	6.8 s	6.7 s	7.1 s
200 Transactions	8.6 s	9.1 s	7.4 s

Figure 6 shows the number of blocks created by experiments. Each experiment adds two nodes in the Blockchain network to a network of a maximum of 6 nodes. It can be observed that as we increase the number of transactions, consequently, there is an increase in the number of blocks. It is also possible to observe the occurrence of empty blocks in each set of blocks. These empty blocks occur due to the block creation timeout. Each block has a timeout parameter that, when reached, causes the block to be generated empty. Transactions that come after this timeout are stored in the next block and so on. There is a low occurrence of empty blocks in each experiment because the BigchainDB consensus algorithm took a few seconds to validate the transactions stored in the blocks.

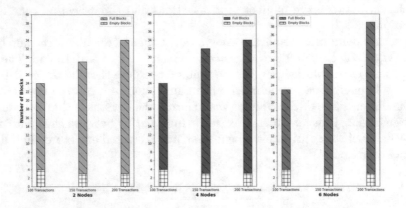

Fig. 6. Number of blocks per experiment.

6.1   Discussion

The results obtained by the experiments present a satisfactory performance for an E-health application. The medians and averages of transaction validation times were approximate, which characterizes that there were few outliers. Outliers causing the average to grow from the median were found to be caused by the generation of empty blocks during the storage of transactions in Blockchain blocks.

Transaction validation time has increased as the number of transactions sent to Blockchain has increased, which may impact the performance of an E-health system. However, the order of transaction validation time remained in seconds until the maximum value of transactions sent by the conducted experiments. Another interesting aspect that was analyzed is the relation between the validation times and the number of nodes in the Blockchain network. It has been noted that the average time on a block node network with few nodes is less than the average time on a network with many nodes. This factor can be justified by the intense exchange of information between the nodes that make up the network during the consensus stage.

Finally, it was observed the execution time of Blockchain's transaction submission algorithm. The execution time had a linear growth with the number of transactions sent, as observed in Fig. 5. This feature is due to the executed transaction submission mode, which expects a return with a confirmation of the validation of the submitted transactions.

7   Conclusion

This paper proposed research for the use of Blockchain technology in E-health applications. An E-health application architecture was created using the Blockchain database. Experiments were performed using the BigchainDB tool together with the M-HEALTH database to evaluate the possibility of using a Blockchain tool in an E-health application. The results presented validation times in the order of seconds and the creation of a few empty blocks, which allows a satisfactory performance to introduce the tool in an E-health approach architecture.

As future work, we intend to use other Blockchain tools and compare them to mitigate the performance of each, showing which tool best fits E-health applications. We intend to analyze the recovery time of information that is stored in a Blockchain and evaluated the possibility of introducing privacy techniques in Blockchain.

References

1. Al-Fuqaha, A., Guizani, M., Mohammadi, M., Aledhari, M., Ayyash, M.: Internet of things: a survey on enabling technologies, protocols, and applications. IEEE Commun. Surv. Tutor. **17**(4), 2347–2376 (2015). https://doi.org/10.1109/COMST. 2015.2444095
2. Banos, O., et al.: mHealthDroid: a novel framework for agile development of mobile health applications. In: Pecchia, L., Chen, L.L., Nugent, C., Bravo, J. (eds.) IWAAL 2014. LNCS, vol. 8868, pp. 91–98. Springer, Cham (2014). https://doi.org/10.1007/ 978-3-319-13105-4_14
3. Banos, O., Garcia, R., Saez, A.: UCI machine learning repository: mhealth dataset data set (2018). http://archive.ics.uci.edu/ml/datasets/mhealth+dataset
4. Banos, O., et al.: Design, implementation and validation of a novel open framework for agile development of mobile health applications. BioMed. Eng. OnLine **14**(2), S6 (2015). https://doi.org/10.1186/1475-925X-14-S2-S6
5. Bhaskar, N.D., Chuen, D.L.K.: Bitcoin mining technology, chap. 3. In: Chuen, D.L.K. (ed.) Handbook of Digital Currency, pp. 45–65. Academic Press, San Diego (2015). https://doi.org/10.1016/B978-0-12-802117-0.00003-5. https://www. sciencedirect.com/science/article/pii/B9780128021170000035
6. Choudhary, G., Jain, A.K.: Internet of things: a survey on architecture, technologies, protocols and challenges. In: 2016 International Conference on Recent Advances and Innovations in Engineering (ICRAIE), pp. 1–8 (2016). https://doi. org/10.1109/ICRAIE.2016.7939537
7. Conoscenti, M., Vetrò, A., De Martin, J.C.: Blockchain for the internet of things: a systematic literature review. In: 2016 IEEE/ACS 13th International Conference of Computer Systems and Applications (AICCSA), pp. 1–6 (2016). https://doi.org/ 10.1109/AICCSA.2016.7945805
8. Freita, L.W., Rolim, C.O.: Demochain - framework destinado a criação de redes blockchain híbridas para dispositivos iot. In: II Workshop Blockchain (Wblockchain) (2019)
9. Gharaibeh, A., et al.: Smart cities: a survey on data management, security, and enabling technologies. IEEE Commun. Surv. Tutor. **19**(4), 2456–2501 (2017). https://doi.org/10.1109/COMST.2017.2736886

10. Gunter, T.D., Terry, N.P.: The emergence of national electronic health record architectures in the United States and Australia: models, costs, and questions. J. Med. Internet Res. **7**(1), e3 (2005). https://doi.org/10.2196/jmir.7.1.e3

11. Liu, W., Park, E.K., Zhu, S.S., Krieger, U.: Smart and connected e-health R & D platform. In: 2015 17th International Conference on E-health Networking, Application Services (HealthCom), pp. 677–679 (2015). https://doi.org/10.1109/HealthCom.2015.7454591

12. Liu, W., Zhu, S.S., Mundie, T., Krieger, U.: Advanced block-chain architecture for e-health systems. In: 2017 IEEE 19th International Conference on e-Health Networking, Applications and Services (Healthcom), pp. 1–6 (2017). https://doi.org/10.1109/HealthCom.2017.8210847

13. Mell, P., Kelsey, J., Shook, J.: Cryptocurrency smart contracts for distributed consensus of public randomness. In: Spirakis, P., Tsigas, P. (eds.) SSS 2017. LNCS, vol. 10616, pp. 410–425. Springer, Cham (2017). https://doi.org/10.1007/978-3-319-69084-1_31

14. Mettler, M.: Blockchain technology in healthcare: the revolution starts here. In: 2016 IEEE 18th International Conference on e-Health Networking, Applications and Services (Healthcom), pp. 1–3 (2016). https://doi.org/10.1109/HealthCom.2016.7749510

15. Neto, M.M., Coutinho, E.F., Moreira, L.O., de Souza, J.N., Agoulmine, N.: A proposal for monitoring people of health risk group using IoT technologies. In: 2018 IEEE 20th International Conference on e-Health Networking, Applications and Services (Healthcom), pp. 1–6 (2018). https://doi.org/10.1109/HealthCom.2018.8531196

16. Neto, M.M., Coutinho, E.F., Oliveira, R.M., Moreira, L.O., Souza, J.N.: ASP: an IoT approach to help sedentary people. In: 6th International Workshop on ADVANCEs in ICT Infrastructures and Services (ADVANCE) (2018)

17. Nofer, M., Gomber, P., Hinz, O., Schiereck, D.: Blockchain. Bus. Inf. Syst. Eng. **59**(3), 183–187 (2017). https://doi.org/10.1007/s12599-017-0467-3

18. Polyzos, G.C., Fotiou, N.: Blockchain-assisted information distribution for the internet of things. In: 2017 IEEE International Conference on Information Reuse and Integration (IRI), pp. 75–78 (2017). https://doi.org/10.1109/IRI.2017.83

19. Rifi, N., Rachkidi, E., Agoulmine, N., Taher, N.C.: Towards using blockchain technology for ehealth data access management. In: 2017 Fourth International Conference on Advances in Biomedical Engineering (ICABME), pp. 1–4 (2017). https://doi.org/10.1109/ICABME.2017.8167555

20. Yaga, D., Mell, P.: NISTIR 8202: blockchain technology overview, chap. 1, pp. 1–68. National Institute of Standards and Technology (2018). https://doi.org/10.6028/NIST.IR.8202

21. Zheng, Z., Xie, S., Dai, H.N., Chen, X., Wang, H.: Blockchain challenges and opportunities: a survey. Int. J. Web Grid Serv. (IJWGS) **14**, 352–375 (2017)

Context Reasoning and Situational Awareness

I²VSM Approach: Self-monitoring of Patients Exploring Situational Awareness in IoT

Rogério Albandes[1]([✉])(iD), Roger Machado[2](iD), Jorge Barbosa[3](iD),
and Adenauer Yamin[1,2](iD)

[1] Catholic University of Pelotas, Pelotas, Brazil
rogerio.albandes@sou.ucpel.edu.br, adenauer.yamin@ucpel.edu.br
[2] Federal University of Pelotas, Pelotas, Brazil
rdsmachado@inf.ufpel.edu.br
[3] Universidade do Vale do Rio dos Sinos, São Leopoldo, Brazil
jbarbosa@unisinos.br

Abstract. Mobility has become a daily practice of physicians, so it is possible that they remain periods of time without contact with the teams that support them in the treatment of patients. Longer periods between communications can cause delays in performing procedures, drug prescribing, etc. Considering this scenario, this work has as objective the conception an approach, called I²VSM, exploring IoT features and integrating: (i) a platform for acquisition of vital signs, (ii) an environment for contextual processing, which through customizable rules builds the Situational Awareness of the patients; and (iii) a textual and graphic display interface for these signals. As a source of vital signs, the MIMIC-III database is being used, which has been widely accepted by the international community for this purpose. In turn, for the evaluation of I²VSM together with health professionals, we explored the Technology Acceptance Model (TAM), obtaining promising results.

Keywords: Internet of Things · Situational Awareness · Vital signs

1 Introduction

Considering that mobility is a common practice in the everyday life of physicians, which implies in transit through different environments (hospitals, clinics, ambulatory, etc.), it is possible that they remain periods of time without contact with the nursing teams that support them in the treatment of patients [6].

In turn, studies have indicated that the frequency in the communication between physicians and other health professionals in hospitals is an important

This study was financed in part by the Coordenação de Aperfeiçoamento de Pessoal de Nível Superior - Brasil (CAPES) - Finance Code 001 and Fundação de Amparo à Pesquisa do Rio Grande do Sul (FAPERGS) - PqG.

aspect in the treatment of hospitalized patients. Longer periods between communication can lead to delays in performing procedures, drug prescribing, etc., which contributes to a possible increase in the period of hospitalization [30].

The premise pursued in this paper is to explore Internet of Things (IoT) resources, both for the acquisition of information about patients and to perform an interoperation with the medical community whenever necessary. This interoperation will be coordinated by automated procedures, governed by mechanisms for Situational Awareness.

Situational Awareness refers to a model in which the computational system is able to verify the aspects which are of its interest and, when necessary, to react to its changes by triggering relevant procedures. This approach materializes IoT premises, in which there is an autonomous communication between intelligent objects, used by health professionals, cooperating for the advancement of their different activities [25].

According to [31], for the construction of Situational Awareness in distributed environments, as in the case of the present proposal, some challenges must be addressed: (i) context acquisition from heterogeneous and distributed sources; (ii) processing of contextual data acquired; and (iii) the respective actions directed at the devices and individuals involved.

Considering this scenario, this paper aims at the conception of an approach, called I^2VSM (Interactive and IoT-based Vital Signs Monitor), which integrates: (i) a platform for acquiring vital signs; (ii) an environment for contextual processing, which through customizable rules builds the patients' Situational Awareness, and, when necessary, sends notifications to the health professionals involved; and (iii) a textual and graphical display interface of these signals, which can be accessed remotely.

To do so, the software architecture of the EXEHDA middleware, particularly its subsystem dedicated to contextual processing, will be explored in the conception of the I^2VSM approach, which will be used in the inference of the patients' situation.

It is expected that the I^2VSM allows physicians to remotely anticipate diagnoses and the consequent prescribing of procedures. In addition, it is understood that the research in progress has the potential to contribute to the reduction of hospitalization time.

This paper is organized into seven sections. The second section presents theoretical concepts considered interesting when reviewing the literature related to the proposal. In the third section, the related works are discussed. In the fourth section, the EXEHDA middleware is introduced and highlight its main functionalities involved in obtaining the Situational Awareness. The fifth section presents the I^2VSM approach, addressing its main characteristics. In the sixth section, the prototyping and tests for the I^2VSM approach are discussed. Finally, the final section presents the final considerations and future work.

2 Scope

In this section are presented concepts judged relevant when reviewing the literature in relation to the developed proposal.

2.1 Situational Awareness

Situational Awareness consists of perception and comprehension of one or more contextual information and projection of their status in the future [10,11]. The definition of contextual information was proposed by Dey [8], which defines context as any information that can be used to characterize the situation of an entity.

In order to obtain situational awareness, three levels can be defined [24]:

Perception: involves the processes of monitoring, detection, and recognition that leads to realizing the value of multiple situational elements. These elements could be the temperature registered by a sensor, alerts reported by intrusion detection systems, events recorded in files as well as their current states: time, place, conditions, forms, and actions;

Comprehension: consists of the synthesis and correlation of disconnected elements identified in the level of perception through different strategies, for example, based on knowledge or anomalies. This level requires the integration of these pieces of information to understand how could impact on the situation of the computational environment;

Projection: responsible for the ability to avoid occurrences of unwanted situations, through the comprehension of the elements of the current system. Achieved by the knowledge of the situation, the dynamism of the elements and the comprehension of the situation.

2.2 Vital Signs

Vital signs are medical signs that indicate the status of the vital (life-sustaining) functions of the human body. These measures are taken to help assess a person's overall health, provide clues to possible illness, and show progress towards recovery. Among vital signs, the following are considering the main ones:

- **Temperature:** it represents the equilibrium between the produced heat and the lost heat, also known as thermoregulation [23];
- **Pulse:** it is defined as the palpable rhythmic expansion of an artery produced by the increase in the volume of blood introduced into the vessel by the contraction and relaxation of the heart [34];
- **Blood pressure:** refers to the pressure exerted by the blood against the arterial wall. It is influenced by cardiac index, peripheral vascular resistance, blood volume and viscosity, and elasticity of the vessel wall [26];

- **Respiratory frequency:** is the designation given to the number of completed respiratory cycles in a specific time interval, more often being expressed in breaths per minute. The respiratory rate is an important data in the observation of the patient and its precise measurement is fundamental for its evaluation [13];
- **Heart rate:** is the velocity of the cardiac cycle, blood flow, and blood pressure that occur from the beginning of a heartbeat to the next heartbeat, divided into two periods. Relaxation period called the diastole, in which the heart distends when it receives the blood, and contraction period named systole, in which the heart ejects the blood [22]. It is measured by the number of heart contractions per minute and may vary according to the physical needs of the body [32]. It is usually equal to or close to the arterial pulse measured at any peripheral point of the body;
- **Pulse Oximetry:** is the measurement of oxygen saturation of the blood, which is the percentage of oxygen being transported in the blood circulation. Pulse oximetry is a non-invasive method to monitor the oxygen saturation of a person (SO2). Although the reading of SpO2 (peripheral oxygen saturation) is not always identical to the most desirable reading of SaO2 (arterial oxygen saturation) of the arterial blood gas, both are sufficiently correlated so that the safe, convenient, noninvasive and inexpensive method of pulse oximetry is a valuable option for measuring oxygen saturation in clinical use [21];
- **AVPU Scale:** the AVPU Scale (an acronym for "alert, voice, pain, unresponsive") is a system with which health professionals can measure patients' level of consciousness [16]. The AVPU scale has four possible outcomes for analysis and subsequent recording. The evaluator should always work from the best (A) to the worst (U) to avoid unnecessary testing in clearly conscious patients. The four possible outcomes are [4]: (A) Alert - the patient is alert, able to communicate and responsive; (V) Verbal - the patient does not respond until you speak to him; (P) Pain - the patient only responds when you apply a painful stimulus (such as pinching the trapezius muscle); and (U) No response - the patient is unconscious.

2.3   Tracking and Monitoring Scoring Systems

There are systems called Track-and-trigger scores, and these systems calculate a score that reflects the health status of a patient regarding his or her vital signs. Several scoring systems are used internationally [3], such as the Early Warning Score (EWS) [5], the Modified Early Warning Score (MEWS) [35] and the VitalPAC Early Warning Score (VIEWS) [28]. In addition, some hospitals introduced their own prior warning scores, such as the Chelsea Early Warning Score (CEWS), introduced by the Chelsea and Westminster Hospital in the United Kingdom [2].

Among these systems, one of the most used is the EWS, which is based on vital signs of respiratory rate, oxygen saturation, temperature, arterial pressure, pulse/heart rate and AVPU response [5]. The value ranges were established in

Table 1. EWS computation

EWS sinal vital score	3	2	1	0	1	2	3
SpO2	<85	85–95	90–92	>92			
Temperature		>38,5	38–38,9	36–37,9	35–35,9	34–34,9	<34
Systolic blood pressure		<34		100–199	80–99	70–79	<70
Heart rate	>129	110–129	100–109	50–99	40–49	30–39	<30
Respiratory rate	>35	31–35	21–30	9–20			
AVPU				Alert	Verbal	Pain	No response

each vital signal (see Table 1) and a value was adopted for each one. Thus, the EWS calculation consists of the sum of the scores of each Vital Sign.

2.4 Medical Information Mart for Intensive Care (MIMIC)

The MIMIC, currently in version III, is a relational database containing data on patients who remained in intensive care units at Beth Israel Deaconess Medical Center (Boston, Massachusetts, USA), which comprehends more than 58,000 hospital admissions of 38,645 adults and 7,875 newborns [14]. Data range from June 2001 to October 2012, including vital signs, medications, laboratory measurements, observations and annotations by care providers, fluid balance, procedure codes, diagnostic codes, image reports, hospitalization time, survival data, among others.

The MIMIC-III database is notable for the following reasons: (i) it is the only database of critical care on open access. The open nature of the data allows the clinical studies to be reproduced and improved upon, which otherwise would not be possible; (ii) its data set covers more than one area, with detailed information on the individual care of each patient; and (iii) the data analysis is unrestricted, which allows both clinical research and its use in education.

3 Related Works

During the research effort, several approaches related to the remote monitoring of patients were identified, among which five papers were selected. For its selection the work should contemplate the following aspects: (i) monitor vital signs; (ii) support remote operations of both sensors and actuation (sending of alerts, etc.); and (iii) consider the use of Situational Awareness.

The work of [12] presents a model that automates the collection, delivery, and processing of vital patient data with the help of an edge device and the Docker container [37]. According to the author, health monitoring and IoT-based emergency response applications require a shorter latency and delay when exchanging information. Information is exchanged between the edge server, the cloud, and the user's device, which directly affects performance. To reach the goal proposed in the paper, a Raspberry Pi is used as the edge device to optimize the process of data analysis of the sensors, thus it is possible to work with low bandwidth, low latency and with congested networks.

In the paper of [9], the SM-IoT platform is proposed, an IoT-based platform for intelligent and personalized health care for patients and caregivers. The objective of this platform is to improve the remote monitoring of the patient and to promote health services. The SM-IoT platform is capable of collecting data from heterogeneous information sources, integrating them using a flexible semantic web, storing them in the cloud for later analysis, visualizing these data with friendly interfaces and facilitate their sharing, taking into account their aspect of privacy.

In the work of [15], a distributed, autonomous, flexible and low-cost hospital automation system is proposed. It consists of servers and sensors that can be easily configured. An Intel Galileo board with an integrated Wi-Fi card acts as a web server, allowing access to authorized people on the same LAN using a personal computer, or remotely via Wi-Fi or 3G/4G using a smartphone. The system benefits not only patients receiving more efficient treatment, but also physicians who can expedite their efforts to serve a larger number of patients. The main idea of this system is continuous monitoring of patients and an instrument control via the internet.

The proposal of [1] presents a generic Health-IoT framework that contains a Clinical Decision Support Systems (CDSS), to provide a self-adequate health monitoring system personalized for the elderly in the home environment. The framework is focused primarily on support sensors, the communication means, secure and reliable data communication, cloud-based storage, and remote data access. CDSS is used to provide a personal report on the health status of individuals based on the daily observation of vital signs. A set of predetermined rules is used to classify individual health parameters and Case-Based Reasoning (CBR) is applied to generate the general state of health of a user.

In [20], the EcoHealth (Health Care Devices Ecosystem) is presented, a middleware platform that integrates heterogeneous body sensors to allow remote monitoring of patients and improvement of medical diagnostics. Its main objective is to integrate information obtained from these heterogeneous sensors for the purposes of monitoring, processing, visualization and storage of such data, as well as notification and acting concerning the current conditions of the patients and their vital signs. The EcoHealth project is based on several well-established Web technologies (HTTP, REST and EEML) with the aim of standardizing and simplifying the development of applications in the context of IoT, thus minimizing compatibility and interoperability problems between manufacturers, proprietary protocols and data formats.

Among the main differences in I^2VSM is the use of the Early Warranty Score (EWS), which is a recognized international standard for Vital Signs Tracking and Monitoring, which has been used in non-automated approaches and is not included in the related work.

Another particularity of I²VSM is the use of a middleware, which is only employed by one related work [20]. For the treatment of the challenge of providing support for the Situational Awareness to the IoT applications, it is worth highlighting the use of middleware, which is inserted between computing infrastructures and applications [27]. The middlewares, through high-level interfaces, allow the interoperability of different IoT devices, providing, among other functionalities, a standardized means for access to the resources available in them.

4   EXEHDA Middleware

EXEHDA consists of a service-centric, service-oriented middleware that aims to create and manage a widely distributed computing environment, as well as to promote the execution of applications on it. The middleware has been explored on research fronts that address IoT challenges [33].

EXEHDA has an organization composed of a set of execution cells, as can be observed in Fig. 1. Each cell, regarding the provision of Situational Awareness, is composed by a Context Server (CS), and by several Edge Servers (ES) and/or Gateways.

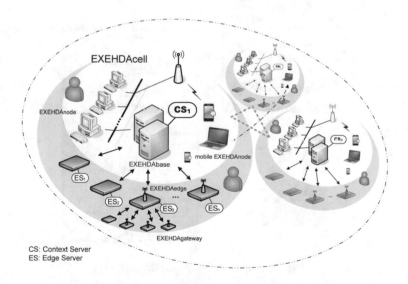

Fig. 1. IoT environment managed by EXEHDA

The gateways collect contextual information from physical or logical sensors and are intended to treat the heterogeneity of the various types of sensors, in both hardware and protocol aspects, and to transfer the collected in a standardized way to the Edge Servers. In EXEHDA, the Gateways are implemented on a specific embedded hardware for the purpose of interoperating with the sensors and actuators.

In EXEHDA, the processing of the contextual information is distributed, being the Edge Server responsible for one part, and the Context Server with another (see Fig. 1).

The data received by the various Edge Servers are transmitted to the Context Server that manages and performs the contextual processing and storing steps. The Context Server can combine data from Edge Servers with historical information, which is stored in the Context Information Repository. A broader discussion of the different functionalities of both Gateway and Edge Servers is available in [33], and in turn, an evaluation of the different potentialities of the Context Server can be found in [19].

5   I²VSM: Conception and Functionalities

The software architecture designed for the I²VSM approach is presented in Fig. 2, below. During this section, the functionalities of the different modules are treated and their operational profiles are discussed.

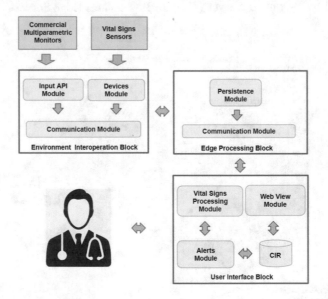

Fig. 2. I²VSM software architecture

5.1   Environment Interoperation Block

The Environmental Interoperation Block is constituted by the API Input Module, Devices Module, and Communication Module. This I²VSM block operates on a native EXEHDA middleware gateway.

The API Input Module includes the input of vital signals from commercial parametric monitors and has a RESTful API that allows any manufacturer to make their data available to the I²VSM. The Device Module is responsible for receiving information from vital-signal sensors by means of an ESP32, having a Python program that collects the data coming from the sensors. In turn, the Communication Module is responsible for transferring/receiving information and commands from the Vital Signs Processing Block.

5.2   Edge Processing Block

Two modules form the Edge Processing Block, which is instantiated on the EXEHDA Edge Server. The Communication Module, which is responsible for interoperating with the User Interface Block; this functionality is instantiated in the Edge Server Interoperation Module of EXEHDA. And the Persistence Module, which aims to perform a temporary persistence if the Internet connection with the User Interface Block is lost. This feature is instantiated on the EXEHDA's Edge Server Persistence Module.

5.3   User Interface Block

The User Interface Block is constituted by the Vital Signs Processing Module, Web Visualization Module, Alerts Module, and the Contextual Information Repository, operating on an EXEHDA middleware Context Server.

Vital Signs Processing Module

Processing takes place in the Vital Signs Processing Module, where the data is received and standardized according to the internal pattern of the system. After standardized, these data will pass through the set of rules that will define the EWS indexes. Afterward, it is processed by the Medical Individual Rules Pattern (MIRP), which is a set of rules defined by the physician, individuated for each patient. In this module, all the rules related to the triggering of alerts, based on the collected vital signs, are treated. The following integrate the set of rules: (i) rules defined by the user, that will meet their specifics based on their professional experience or their specialty's particularities; (ii) rules based on international standards.

The EWS score is used by default by the I²VSM for the generation of alerts. Triggers and alerts are different for each hospital, and I²VSM allows the EWS score to be defined and allows the physician to define their own triggers and corresponding alerts. The triggers used by the Norfolk and Norwich University Hospital, or NNUH, will be used as a base. According to the NNUH, physicians should be called for a review when the EWS score is equal to or higher than 5, and if greater than or equal to 6 the physician needs to attend to the patient immediately (within 30 min).

The physician user of I²VSM can configure its rules templates using their own definitions, established pattern rules, or a hybrid set of rules - which makes

Fig. 3. I²VSM template register screen

the configuration of their personalized alerts flexible. The configuration of custom rules (see Fig. 3) has an intuitive interface, called the Template Register, where the physician defines which vital signs will be used, their values, relational operators (equal, different, higher, lower, higher or equal, lesser or equal) and the logical operators (and, or) to concatenate the different vital signs. With this, the practitioner creates a template for each situation of his or her specialty. This template gets a name and will be stored for later use on any patient.

Alerts Module

In this proposal, the role of alerts is preponderant, considering the characteristics of health professionals' activities regarding mobility and long periods without the possibility of answering telephone calls. Alerts will be issued to the team responsible for the patient according to the set of rules and/or internationally accepted indicators. From a literature review, it was observed that it is internationally accepted the use of 2 services of alert sending that use the Internet as a medium: (i) PushOver and (ii) Telegram. And, if the Internet or the hospital's local network is inoperative, the Short Message Service (SMS) service of the GSM (Global System for Mobile Communications) network will be used.

Pushover: it is a paid service – the cost is greatly reduced and the payment is made only once – of instant notifications for tablets and cell phones, which can be generated from a variety of sources. In more detail, Pushover is a platform for sending and receiving push notifications. On the server side, there is an HTTP API for receiving the requests, and on the opposing one an application where the professional receives the alert and stores them for offline visualization [29].

To consume the Pushover API, the python-pushover[1] library is used. Listing 1.1 shows an example of sending alerts in the Python language, using the python-pushover library.

```
1    from pushover import Client
2
3    client = Client("<user-key>", api_token="<api-token>")
4    client.send_message("Patient Xxxx, Yyyy - EWS > 5",
5                        title="I2VSM")
```

Listing 1.1. Python code for sending messages via Pushover

Telegram: it is a fast, simple and free messaging application. It functions as SMS and email combined, and can send photos, videos, and files of any kind. It provides an API where alerts can be sent to the medical team [36].

Telegram main characteristics are: (i) the messages are strongly encrypted and can self-destruct; (ii) Telegram allows the access of the messages from several devices; (iii) Telegram servers are scattered around the world for security and speed; (iv) has free open for all API and protocol; and (v) is free of charge, without ads or a subscription fee. This service allows the physician to respond to the alert, thus notifying the hospital that they received the message and, if he or she wishes, to send procedures for the staff to perform until their arrival.

Listing 1.2 shows an example of sending an alert using the Telethon-aio library[2].

```
1    from telethon import TelegramClient, events, sync
2
3    client=TelegramClient('<session-name>', '<api-id>',
4                          '<api-hash>')
5    client.start()
6    client.send_message('<username>',
7                        'Patient Xxxx, Yyyy - EWS > 5')
```

Listing 1.2. Python code for sending messages via Telegram

---

[1] https://pypi.org/project/python-pushover.
[2] https://pypi.org/project/Telethon-aio/.

SMS Gateway: service designed to provide alerts using the cellular telephone network, as there may be a lack of internet connectivity, either due to a problem in the backbone or even in the internal network of the hospital.

The SMS Gateway service of the I2 VSM architecture employs the embedded ESP32 NodeMCU. Also used is the SIM800L, a Quad-Band GSM/G-PRS transceiver (GSM 850, EGSM 900, DCS 1800 and PCS 1900), which works on the 850 MHz, 900 MHz, 1800 MHz and 1900 MHz frequencies, and accepts a micro-SIM card, allowing any microcontroller or microprocessor with a Universal Asynchronous Receiver/Transmitter (UART) port to communicate over the GSM network of its choice. The SIM card (subscriber identity module) is a smart card-type printed circuit used to identify, control, and store data from GSM technology cellphones. It usually stores data such as subscriber information, schedules, configurations, contracted services, SMS and other information.

To use the ESP32 with SIM800L, it was necessary to use the original MicroPython variant[3], called MicroPython Loboris[4]. Originally developed for ESP32 that have a pseudo-static random-access memory (PSRAM), these can be used in any ESP32. The choice by this variation of MicroPython was made on account of containing a native library for access to the SIM800L. The communication between the ESP32 and the SIM800L is based on its General Purpose Input/Output (GPIO). Table 2 shows the GPIOs used in communication between the two chips.

Table 2. GPIOS

ESP 32	SIM 800L
GPIO 2 (TX)	RX
GPIO 4 (RX)	TX
GND	GND

Using the Loboris MicroPython native library, the alerts are sent through the code shown in Listing 1.3

```
1   import gsm
2   gsm.start(tx=2, rx=4)
3   gsm.atcmd('ATI4')
4   gsm.atcmd('ATI4',printable=True)
5   gsm.atcmd("AT+CMGF=1",printable=True)
6   gsm.atcmd('AT+CMGS="+<telephone-number>"',
7            timeout=1000,response='> ',
8            cmddata='Patient Xxxx, Yyyy - EWS > 5 \x1a'
             ,
9            printable=True)
```

Listing 1.3. Python code for sending alerts via GSM

---

[3] https://micropython.org/.

[4] https://github.com/loboris/MicroPython_ESP32_psRAM_LoBo.

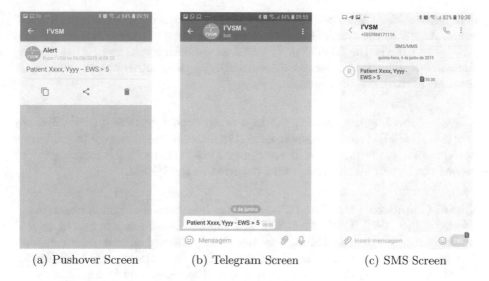

| (a) Pushover Screen | (b) Telegram Screen | (c) SMS Screen |

Fig. 4. Example of alerts sent by I²VSM

Figure 4 shows examples of alerts received using the three services provided by I²VSM.

Web Visualization Module

The Web Visualization Module is responsible for all the I²VSM's visual interface. Their functions go from the login routines to the patient dashboard views and screens that show important data.

The Web Visualization Module was divided into smaller components, as shown in Fig. 5. These are Authentication, Logs, Data Storage, Web Front End, Cloud Connector, and Administration and Configuration.

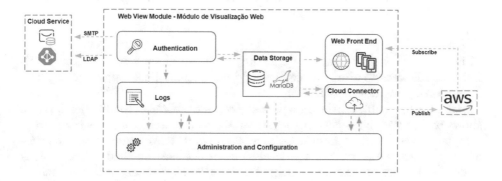

Fig. 5. Architecture of the Web Visualization Module

Authentication: this component is responsible for the authentication of I^2VSM users. Access to the system occurs in 3 ways: (i) Using a password stored in the database; (ii) via the SMTP protocol of an e-mail server; and (iii) using the Lightweight Directory Access Protocol (LDAP) protocol to obtain credentials from an Active Directory domain.

Logs: in the Log component, the logs of all events occurring in I^2VSM are written. As I^2VSM stores sensitive data [17], a method is necessary to track user activities for audit purposes, if necessary. Thus, this module was designed to record the logs of all the events that occurred in the I^2VSM.

Cloud Connector: the Cloud Connector module connects to the Amazon cloud service called AWS IOT[5]. AWS IOT is a suite of cloud services geared to IoT applications. I^2VSM publishes data from the "Environmental Interoperation Block" in the AWS IOT. The Cloud Connector component uses AWS service variables to process data, make analyzes, and generate charts for dashboards used for better visualization by the user.

Web Front End: the Web Front End component is responsible for the user interface. In this component are all the screens that will make the interaction between the final users and the I^2VSM. They contain the registration of medical templates screen, patients' registration screen, histories of vital signs history screen, among others. This component is also responsible for consuming the AWS API via the MQTT protocol, whose data will be used in dashboard assemblies.

Administration and Configuration: in the Administration and Configuration component, all the parameters necessary for the I^2VSM to function are inserted. In this component are established the users' credentials and their access levels. It also has screens for registering variables used at run times, which avoids changes in the source code at every exchange of hosting server, for example.

CIR

It is the Context Information Repository that we already used in the EXE-HDA middleware to store the contextual information. This repository explores a relational database model.

CIR is responsible for the data persistence that the Web Visualization Module shows to users. In this repository are stored the contextual data of the users, their templates, visualization interfaces, as well as the I^2VSM configuration parameters. Besides, we also store the vital signs of the patients and the situations identified by the processing of the rules. Relational database easiness such as views, stored procedures, and triggers are used to make access to data faster and more reliable.

---

[5] https://aws.amazon.com/pt/iot/.

6   I²VSM: Evaluation

In Brazilian hospitals, it is common practice to measure vital signs when the nurses change their shift, which occurs every 6 h. In the MIMIC-III database, the collections are carried out every 15 min. In order to adapt the database to the reality of the proposal, data outside these values were excluded: 00 h 00 min, 06 h 00 min, 12 h 00 min and 18 h 00 min. Data that is not in the EWS indicator was also suppressed from the table containing the measurements performed on the patients (CHARTEVENTS). In it, there were 5,131 possible measurements per patient, from which only Temperature, SpO2, Manual BP [Systolic], Heart Rate and Respiratory Rate were maintained - which are necessary for the indicators used; with these changes, the total number of registers went from 330,712,483 to 43,332,281.

In order to evaluate the functioning of the Vital Signs Processing Module, the MIMIC-III was adapted to the Brazilian reality and to the scope of this work, and the following alerts were configured: (i) EWS index is greater than 5 (called a yellow alert); (ii) EWS index is equal to or greater than 6 (called a red alert); and (iii) Alert configured by the physician, increase in heart rate, associated with fever. 1,000 patients were processed, generating 45 yellow alerts, 30 red alerts and 12 alerts with the parameters configured by the physician.

Table 3. TAM questionnaire responded by physicians

Construct	Affirmative
Perceived ease of use	1 - I consider the use of the I2VSM clear and objective
	2 - Interacting with this proposal does not require much mental effort
	3 - I find the proposal easy to use
Perceived utility	4 - The use of I2VSM would improve my daily performance
	5 - Using this technology would increase my productivity
	6 - The use of this technology would make me more efficient

In turn, the Technology Acceptance Model (TAM), a model proposed by [7], was used to evaluate health professionals. This questionnaire has the advantage of being specific for information technology and has a strong theoretical basis, in addition to broad empirical support. The model suggests that when users are introduced to a new technology, several factors influence their decision on how and when they will use it, notably: (i) Perceived Usefulness (PU) - and the degree to which a person believes that using a particular system would increase their performance at work; and (ii) Perceived Ease of Use (PEOU) - and the degree to which a person believes that using a particular system would be free of effort [7]. As such, a questionnaire was elaborated whose questions are shown in Table 3 using the Likert scale [18]: Strongly disagree; Partially disagree; Indifferent; Partially agree; and Fully agree.

In this stage of conception of I^2VSM, the evaluation questionnaire developed was applied to 10 physicians from 3 hospitals in the city of Pelotas-RS, Brazil, presenting to them a demonstration of the I^2VSM, with the alerts being generated from the MIMIC-III, using the EWS and also the parameters configured by them, which brought them closer to the real operation of the proposal. The applied questionnaire is presented in Table 3, and Table 4 shows the Likert Scale [18] resulting from the evaluation. The performed analysis indicates a promising result for the continuity of I^2VSM.

Table 4. Results of perceived usability and ease of use assessment (TAM)

Question	Strongly disagree	Partially disagree	Indifferent	Partially agree	Fully agree
1	0,00%	0,00%	0,00%	20,00%	80,00%
2	0,00%	0,00%	0,00%	10,00%	90,00%
3	0,00%	0,00%	10,00%	20,00%	70,00%
4	0,00%	0,00%	0,00%	10,00%	90,00%
5	0,00%	0,00%	20,00%	10,00%	70,00%
6	0,00%	0,00%	0,00%	0,00%	100,00%

7   Final Considerations

The I^2VSM acquires the vital signs data of hospitalized patients, through commercial multiparametric monitors and via individual sensors. The acquired data are processed by rules that will define the EWS score, as well as by rules defined by the medical team. Based on the processing of these rules, alerts are generated so that the physicians are notified of events occurring with their patients. With the I^2VSM, it is possible to anticipate diagnoses and procedures by the medical team, making possible a reduction in the hospitalization time. The results obtained from the physicians regarding the evaluation of perceived Utility and Ease of Use (TAM) are promising and point to the continuation of I^2VSM research, as an approach that employs the EXEHDA middleware in providing approaches to health care. Among the expected future work is the development of a native application for smartphones, and the construction of an API for integrating with the hospitals' legacy systems.

References

1. Ahmed, M.U.: An intelligent healthcare service to monitor vital signs in daily life - a case study on health-IoT. Int. J. Eng. Res. Appl. (IJERA) **7**(3), 43–55 (2017)

2. Austen, C., Patterson, C., Poots, A., Green, S., Weldring, T., Bell, D.: Using a local early warning scoring system as a model for the introduction of a national system. Acute Med. **11**(2), 66–73 (2012)
3. Bleyer, A.J., et al.: Longitudinal analysis of one million vital signs in patients in an academic medical center. Resuscitation **82**(11), 1387–1392 (2011)
4. Brunker, C., Harris, R.: How accurate is the AVPU scale in detecting neurological impairment when used by general ward nurses? An evaluation study using simulation and a questionnaire. Intensive Crit. Care Nurs. **31**(2), 69–75 (2015)
5. Audit Commission, et al.: Critical to Success: The Place of Efficient and Effective Critical Care Services Within the Acute Hospital. Audit Commission, London (1999)
6. Costa Dias, E.: Condições de trabalho e saúde dos médicos: uma questão negligenciada e um desafio para a associação nacional de medicina do trabalho. Rev. bras. med. trab **13**(2), 60–68 (2015)
7. Davis, F.D., Bagozzi, R.P., Warshaw, P.R.: User acceptance of computer technology: a comparison of two theoretical models. Manag. Sci. **35**(8), 982–1003 (1989)
8. Dey, A.K.: Understanding and using context. Pers. Ubiquit. Comput. **5**(1), 4–7 (2001). https://doi.org/10.1007/s007790170019
9. Dridi, A., Sassi, S., Faiz, S.: A smart IoT platform for personalized healthcare monitoring using semantic technologies. In: 2017 IEEE 29th International Conference on Tools with Artificial Intelligence (ICTAI), pp. 1198–1203. IEEE (2017)
10. Endsley, M.: Designing for Situation Awareness: An Approach to User-Centered Design, 2nd edn. CRC Press, Boca Raton (2016). https://books.google.com.br/books?id=eRPBkapAsggC
11. Evesti, A., Kanstrén, T., Frantti, T.: Cybersecurity situational awareness taxonomy. In: 2017 International Conference on Cyber Situational Awareness, Data Analytics and Assessment (Cyber SA), pp. 1–8, June 2017. https://doi.org/10.1109/CyberSA.2017.8073386
12. Jaiswal, K., Sobhanayak, S., Turuk, A.K., Bibhudatta, S.L., Mohanta, B.K., Jena, D.: An IoT-cloud based smart healthcare monitoring system using container based virtual environment in edge device. In: 2018 International Conference on Emerging Trends and Innovations in Engineering and Technological Research (ICETIETR), pp. 1–7. IEEE (2018)
13. Jevon, P.: How to ensure patient observations lead to prompt identification of tachypnoea. Nurs. Times **106**(2), 12–14 (2010)
14. Johnson, A.E., et al.: MIMIC-III, a freely accessible critical care database. Sci. Data **3**, 160035 (2016)
15. Karthikeyan, S., Devi, K.V., Valarmathi, K.: Internet of Things: hospice appliances monitoring and control system. In: 2015 Online International Conference on Green Engineering and Technologies (IC-GET), pp. 1–6. IEEE (2015)
16. Kelly, C.A., Upex, A., Bateman, D.N.: Comparison of consciousness level assessment in the poisoned patient using the alert/verbal/painful/unresponsive scale and the glasgow coma scale. Ann. Emerg. Med. **44**(2), 108–113 (2004)
17. Kruse, R.L., Ewigman, B.G., Tremblay, G.C.: The zipper: a method for using personal identifiers to link data while preserving confidentiality. Child Abuse Neglect **25**(9), 1241–1248 (2001)
18. Likert, R.: A Technique for the Measurement of Attitudes. Archives of Psychology (1932)
19. Lopes, J.L., et al.: A middleware architecture for dynamic adaptation in ubiquitous computing. J. Univ. Comput. Sci. **20**(9), 1327–1351 (2014)

20. Maia, P., Baffa, A., Cavalcante, E., Delicato, F.C., Batista, T., Pires, P.F.: Uma plataforma de middleware para integração de dispositivos e desenvolvimento de aplicações em e-health. In: Anais do XXXIII SBRC, pp. 361–374 (2015)
21. Millikan, G.A.: The oximeter, an instrument for measuring continuously the oxygen saturation of arterial blood in man. Rev. Sci. Instrum. **13**(10), 434–444 (1942)
22. Obrist, P.A., Black, A., Brener, J., DiCara, L.V.: Cardiovascular Psychophysiology: Current Issues in Response Mechanisms, Biofeedback and Methodology. Routledge, Abingdon (2017)
23. Oey, C., Moh, S.: A survey on temperature-aware routing protocols in wireless body sensor networks. Sensors **13**(8), 9860–9877 (2013)
24. Onwubiko, C.: Situational Awareness in Computer Network Defense: Principles, Methods and Applications. IGI Global, Hershey (2012)
25. Perera, C., Zaslavsky, A., Christen, P., Georgakopoulos, D.: Context aware computing for the Internet of Things: a survey. Commun. Surv. Tutor. **16**(1), 414–454 (2014). https://doi.org/10.1109/SURV.2013.042313.00197
26. Perry, A., Potter, P.: Clinical Nursing Skills & Techniques. Mosby (2002). https://books.google.com.br/books?id=OAZtAAAAMAAJ
27. Pires, P.F., Cavalcante, E., Barros, T., Delicato, F.C., Batista, T., Costa, B.: A platform for integrating physical devices in the Internet of Things. In: Proceedings of the 12th IEEE International Conference on Embedded and Ubiquitous Computing, pp. 234–241 (2014)
28. Plate, J.D., Peelen, L.M., Leenen, L.P., Hietbrink, F.: Validation of the VitalPAC early warning score at the intermediate care unit. World J. Crit. Care Med. **7**(3), 39 (2018)
29. Pushover (2019). https://pushover.net/. Accessed 15 Feb 2019
30. Rufino, G.P., Gurgel, M.G., Pontes, T.D.C., Freire, E.: Avaliação de fatores determinantes do tempo de internação em clínica médica. Revista Brasileira Clínica Médica **10**(4), 291–297 (2012)
31. Sezer, O.B., Dogdu, E., Ozbayoglu, A.M.: Context-aware computing, learning, and big data in Internet of Things: a survey. IEEE Internet Things J. **5**(1), 1–27 (2018)
32. Shaffer, F., Ginsberg, J.: An overview of heart rate variability metrics and norms. Front. Public Health **5**, 258 (2017)
33. Souza, R., Lopes, J., Geyer, C., Cardozo, A., Yamin, A., Barbosa, J.: An architecture for IoT management targeted to context awareness of ubiquitous applications. J. Univ. Comput. Sci. **24**(10), 1452–1471 (2018)
34. Stedman, T.L.: Stedman's Medical Dictionary for the Health Professions and Nursing. Lippincott Williams & Wilkins, Baltimore (2005)
35. Subbe, C., Kruger, M., Rutherford, P., Gemmel, L.: Validation of a modified early warning score in medical admissions. QJM **94**(10), 521–526 (2001)
36. Telegram (2019). https://telegram.org/. Accessed 15 Feb 2019
37. Turnbull, J.: The Docker Book: Containerization is the New Virtualization (2014)

An IoT Proposal for the Irrigation Management Exploring Context Awareness

Rogério Albandes[1][✉][iD], Roger Machado[2][iD], João L. B. Lopes[3][iD],
Jorge Barbosa[4][iD], and Adenauer Yamin[1,2][iD]

[1] Catholic University of Pelotas, Pelotas, Brazil
rogerio.albandes@sou.ucpel.edu.br, adenauer.yamin@ucpel.edu.br
[2] Federal University of Pelotas, Pelotas, Brazil
rdsmachado@inf.ufpel.edu.br
[3] Federal Institute Sul-Rio-Grandense, Pelotas, Brazil
joaolopes@cavf.ifsul.edu.br
[4] Universidade do Vale do Rio dos Sinos, São Leopoldo, Brazil
jbarbosa@unisinos.br

Abstract. With the changes in technologies and the rapid consumption of natural resources by humans, it is vital to implement smart irrigation techniques to overcome the scarcity of water resources shortly. The amount of fresh water existing on the planet, the use for irrigation corresponds to about 70% of all water consumed in the world, Inadequate water management creates a number of problems, such as lower productivity, lower quality fruits, environmental damage, soil erosion and reduced soil air, which has been motivating the evaluation of alternatives for water supply agricultural crops. One solution that can be exploited is IoT, helping to achieve optimum water-resource utilization. Considering this scenario, this article presents the EXEHDA-SF proposal, which aims to explore IoT solutions and Context Awareness in the decision-making process, with the perspective of minimizing socioenvironmental impacts. For the evaluation of EXEHDA-SF, as an irrigation alternative, without the use of physical sensors, a prototype was developed that integrates open source IoT technologies with the EXEHDA middleware and explores a meteorological forecasting service. The results achieved were considered promising, reaching a success rate of approximately 94% regarding the irrigation decision.

Keywords: Internet of Things · Context Awareness · Watering automatic control · EXEHDA middleware

This study was financed in part by the Coordenação de Aperfeiçoamento de Pessoal de Nível Superior - Brasil (CAPES) - Finance Code 001 and Fundação de Amparo à Pesquisa do Rio Grande do Sul (FAPERGS) - PqG.

1   Introduction

Water is considered the most important resource for maintaining life on Earth. Of the amount of fresh water existing on the planet, the use for irrigation corresponds to about 70% of all water consumed in the world. With the need to produce food and knowing the limitation of agriculture, producers seek measures that will allow them to produce more, being irrigation one of them [9].

The design of an irrigation system can be evaluated through several performance indicators, considering the scope of this article, it is possible to highlight its operational efficiency and the costs associated with the water consumed. Inadequate water management creates a number of problems, such as lower productivity, lower quality fruits, environmental damage, soil erosion and reduced soil air, which translates into a high socio-environmental impact. In this sense, the literature has pointed out that the use of irrigation systems has been harmed by inadequate decisions regarding the moment of irrigation [24].

In 2016, the total water demand for irrigation in Brazil was 969 thousand liters per second throughout the year, amount that according to the National Water Agency (ANA[1]), corresponded to 46.2% of all clean water used in Brazil in the period [5].

Excessive use of clean water resources around the globe has generated a need for its use in a smarter way. One solution that can be exploited is IoT, in which the solutions are based on the application specific sensors' data acquisition and intelligent processing.

IoT based smart irrigation management systems can help in achieving optimum water-resource utilization in the precision farming landscape [18]. Besides, we highlight the use of Context Awareness to support the irrigation decision, providing adaptable services. Context Awareness becomes an essential approach in IoT systems to select the most appropriated decision according to the contextual information that is relevant to the user or to change operational parameters of services in execution [29].

The operations of context-aware systems involve a significant amount of context information that needs to be: continuously collected; efficiently interpreted; quickly processed; disseminated to interested applications; stored in context repositories [3,28]. Therefore, to minimize the development efforts, in the literature, we can found approaches exploring middlewares.

The middlewares use can reduce the complexity of context-aware applications development by providing support for context acquisition, modeling, storage, and processing, among other aspects. The use of middleware can reduce the developer's attention from context-related concerns, allowing them to focus on defining business rules and developing application-specific functionalities [20,25].

Being motivated for this scenario, this article discusses a proposal of a system of Smart Farming (SF) based on IoT concepts, called EXEHDA-SF (Execution Environment for Highly Distributed Applications-Smart Farming). This

---

[1] http://www3.ana.gov.br/.

proposal explores Context Awareness to decide the need for irrigation, aiming to water reduction. Besides, our proposal uses EXEHDA middleware [21] under development in the G3PD/UCPEL (Parallel and Distributed Processing Research Group).

The proposal uses as a data source, the information provided by a weather forecasting service. Thus, EXEHDA-SF explores a logical sensor, without the use of physical sensors, minimizing installation, calibration, and maintenance efforts.

EXEHDA-SF was evaluated through a case study that explored prototyping of the proposal considering the software architecture of the EXEHDA middleware. In this case study, the EXEHDA-SF monitoring the climatic conditions of the region of Pelotas city, obtained from a public service of the forecast, and based on these data it evaluates the need for irrigation. The obtained results were very promising, reaching high levels of correctness when deciding to irrigation or not.

This article is organized in six sections. Section 2 discusses the context awareness design and the characteristics of the EXEHDA middleware. In the third section some related papers are discussed. Section 4 exhibits the proposal EXEHDA-SF, showing its main functions. In the fifth section the prototyping of the proposal is discussed, being addressed the hardware and software used and the evaluation that was done. Finally, the sixth section presents the final considerations and future work.

2   Background

This section introduces the main concepts associated with context awareness and EXEHDA middleware, highlighting the principal features explored in the EXEHDA-SF.

2.1   Context Awareness

Context is any information that can be used to characterize the situation of an entity (person, place, or object) considered relevant to the interaction between user and application, including the user and the application [8,16]. Context Awareness is the ability of a system to use context to provide relevant information and services to the user [8,17].

Some motivations for application of Context Awareness in computational systems are: assisting in the understanding of reality; facilitate the adaptation of systems; contribute to the process of transforming data into information; support the comprehension of events; help identify situations of interest.

Figure 1 presents a vision of the process involved to obtain context awareness, in which we can see that the construction of a context-aware system occurs mainly through four steps [20,25]:

- acquisition: refers to the process of monitoring and capturing contextual information. This step aims at abstracting from context-aware applications the

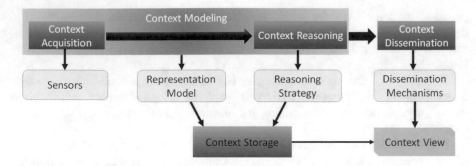

Fig. 1. Steps involved to obtain the context awareness.

complexity of data collection, enabling the reuse of sensors and the separation between obtaining and using contextual information [1];

- modeling: refers to the process of designing a model of real-world entities, their properties, the state of their environment and situations. The purpose of creating a context model is to provide a uniform, machine processable context representation scheme, facilitating context sharing and interoperability between different applications. The uniformity of the model between acquisition, reasoning, and utilization of context information is considered vital [17];
- distribution: refers to the step that allows the injection of context into the context-aware application and its delivery to all entities that have expressed any form of interest in this data [3];
- reasoning: can be defined as a method of deducing new knowledge, and better understanding, based on the available context [4]. It can also be explained as a process of providing knowledge deduction from a set of contexts [12].

In addition to the four steps that can be viewed at the top of the Fig. 1, we highlighted storage and view layers. Context storage is responsible for storing the acquired context data as well as for the contextual information that was inferred by the reasoning step. Context view provides data visualization methods in a way that facilitates access from the context-aware applications to captured data and detected situations.

Regarding the reasoning step, in the literature can be found different strategies for context reasoning, which have advantages and disadvantages considering the distinct domains of application [30]. Among these strategies, we highlight the rule-based, which is the most used strategy to perform the context reasoning in IoT applications [25].

2.2 EXEHDA Middleware

EXEHDA is a middleware designed to manage distributed, mobile, and context-aware applications, available from anywhere, anytime. The EXEHDA includes in its structure a core and services loaded on demand. The G3PD has explored the middleware on research fronts that consider the IoT challenges [31]. The main services provided are organized into subsystems related to Ubiquitous Access, Communication, Distributed Execution, Context Recognition, and Adaptation [2].

The IoT environment provided by EXEHDA is formed by multi-institutional equipment, being composite of user devices and equipment for infrastructure supporting. Each device is instantiated by their respective execution profile in the middleware, which implies on the need to adopt a cellular organizational management in this environment, aimed at ensuring the autonomy of the institutions involved [21].

Figure 2 shows an IoT environment managed by EXEHDA, wherein each cell, related to the provision of Context Awareness, is formed by a server Context Server, and by various Edge Servers and/or Gateways.

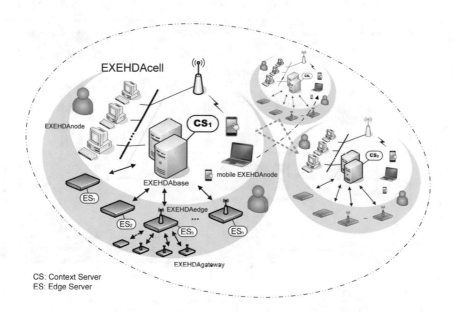

Fig. 2. IoT environment provided by EXEHDA

The gateways collect contextual information from physical or logical sensors, and have the purpose of treating the heterogeneity of the various types of sensors, in aspects of both hardware and protocol; transfer the collected information in a standard way to the Edge Servers.

In EXEHDA the processing of contextual information is distributed, remaining a part with the Edge Server, and another with the Context Server (see Fig. 3). The data received by the several Edge Servers are transmitted to the Context Server that manages them, and performs the storage and contextual processing steps. Context Server can combine the data from the Edge Servers with historical information, which are recorded in the Context Information Repository. A broader discussion about the different functionalities of both the Gateway and the Edge Servers is available in [31]. On the other hand, an approach of the different capabilities of the Context Server can be found in [21].

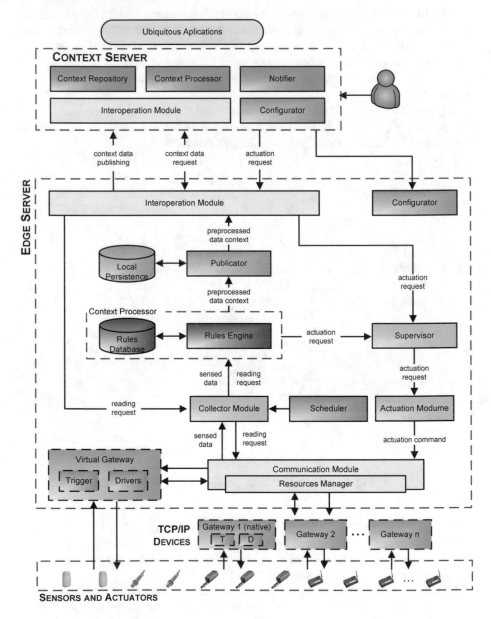

Fig. 3. Software architecture of EXEHDA to provide Context Awareness

3   Related Work

This section discusses papers related to the proposal EXEHDA-SF. A review of the literature was carried out, with the criteria for selection of the papers being its modernity and the use of methodologies associated with SF and IoT.

In paper [11] an intelligent irrigation architecture based on IoT is proposed, along with a hybrid approach based on machine learning to predict soil moisture. The proposed algorithm uses sensor data from the recent past and predicted meteorological data for soil moisture forecast for the following days.

The work [13] shows an automatic water supply system for agriculture using data from 2 sensors (soil moisture and light intensity). In addition, notifications are sent to the farm manager if there is a lack of water, and the interaction between the system and the manager is possible through the exchange of short message service (SMS) messages.

In the paper [18] a cloud-based framework and IoT are proposed to implement an intelligent irrigation system that preserves harvest during unforeseen rains, increases groundwater levels with a competent mechanism and reuses the excessive water generated during the rain for the irrigation of crops.

In the article [19] the linear regression algorithm is used, which helps in the prediction of the amount of water required for daily irrigation based on data provided by sensors scattered around the environment. The proposed system also reduces human and energy efforts. People can gain instant access to data through a mobile application.

The paper [6] uses field-scattered moisture sensors that are connected to a microprocessor (Arduino UNO). Whenever the humidity decreases below the plant wilting point, the sensors report to the system, which in turn triggers the irrigation pump, and when there is sufficient humidity, the shutdown command is sent.

Analyzing the five selected papers, among the several articles identified, it can be highlighted that EXEHDA-SF has two main differentials: (i) it does not use physical sensors, reducing installation, calibration and maintenance costs; and (ii) it explores Context Awareness in the decision of irrigation, considering as contextual variables the volume of recent previous precipitation, as well as the forecast of occurrence of precipitation in the following hours.

4   EXEHDA-SF: Organization and Functionalities

The organization of the software platform designed for EXEHDA-SF is presented in Fig. 4. After in this section, the functionalities of the different modules will be touched, and their operational profiles discussed.

4.1   Environment Interoperation Block

Environment Interoperation Block consists of the Forecast API Module, Communication Module and Actuator Module. This EXEHDA-SF block operates on a Native Gateway of middleware EXEHDA.

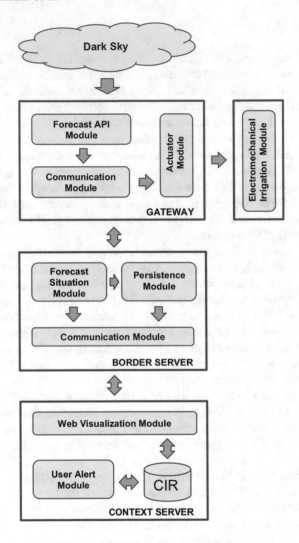

Fig. 4. EXEHDA-SF prototipation

Forecast API Module from the geographical coordinates of the city obtains the weather forecast data provided by the Dark Sky Service [7]. Its execution happens every hour, capturing the climatic data of the last 24 h, and in case it has rained, the volume of precipitated water is also captured. In addition, the climatological forecast is collected for the following 24 h, recording both the probability of occurrence of precipitation and the expected rainfall intensity. The Communication Module is responsible for transferring/receiving information and commands from the Edge Server. Finally, the Actuation Module manages the electromechanical device used to control the irrigation procedure.

4.2   Irrigation Control Block

Three modules form the Irrigation Control Block, which is instantiated on the EXEHDA Edge Server:

- Communication Module, which is responsible for interoperating with the User Interface Block, this functionality is instantiated in the Server Interoperation of the Edge Server;
- Persistence Module, which is intended to perform a temporary persistence if the Internet connection with the User Interface Block is lost. This functionality is instantiated on the Local Persistence module of the Edge Server;
- Forecast Situational Module, which is central to the EXEHDA-SF proposal, and is based on the Edge Server Rule Engine (see Fig. 3), and it has two main responsibilities that are detailed below.

Calculation of Probability of Precipitation (PoP)

It quantifies the possibility of precipitation occurrence in a given area over a specified period of time. The probability of precipitation (PoP) is defined by the product between two percentages:

- **C:** the confidence that precipitation will occur somewhere in the forecast area;
- **A:** the percentage of the area that will receive precipitation if it actually occurs.

Considering that there is 50% confidence (C) that a precipitation will occur and the expectation that measurable rain will occur around 80% of the area considered (A), the PoP will be 40%, that is, $PoP = C \times A$ (0.5×0.8) [14].

Algorithm for Irrigation Decision

In EXEHDA-SF the Irrigation Decision Algorithm is based on the moment of irrigation defined by the user and considers the rain data and its intensity, both from the previous 12 h and from the following 12 h. Based on the average values in the literature [15], the decision to irrigate at EXEHDA-SF will be considered as a 25 mm rainfall reference and as a 60% PoP.

The 25 mm reference for rainfall intensity is an international standard that consider the amount of rainwater that has accumulated in a given location over a period of time. In the International System of Units, the millimeter (mm) is used as the unit. A rainfall intensity of 1 m equals the accumulation of the volume of 1 liter (L) of rainwater over a surface area equal to 1 square meter [10]. An internationally accepted distribution is shown in Table 1.

As indicated in Fig. 5, if in the previous 12 h there was higher volume of precipitation than 25 mm, no irrigation will be triggered. Otherwise, the PoP will be considered for the next 12 h, if less than 60% it will be irrigated. If the PoP of the following 12 h is greater than 60% should be evaluated by the precipitation value; if less than 25 mm the irrigation must happen.

Table 1. Intensity of rain

Intensity (mm)	Description
<5 mm	Light rain
Between 5.1 mm and 25 mm	Moderate rain
Between 25.1 mm and 50 mm	Heavy rain
>50 mm	Violent rain

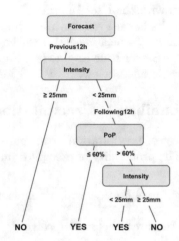

Fig. 5. Hierarchical decision structure

4.3   User Interface Block

User Interface Block was designed by exploring the functionality of the EXE-HDA Context Server (see Fig. 3). This EXEHDA-SF block, besides providing information to users through the Internet, also includes persistence and notification functions.

- CIR Module is implemented in the Context Information Repository. Particularly on the relational database functionalities. All information regarding irrigation decision making is stored;
- Web Visualization Module provides the user with information on weather forecasts and irrigation decisions. The user is allowed to have the history records, with the possibility of indicating the occurrence and totals considering a certain period of time;
- User Alert Module scans the functions of the Notifier, and sends alerts to users using a public message sending platform, in this case Telegram.

5   EXEHDA-SF: Prototyping and Results

This section presents the decisions regarding the choice of hardware/software technologies for the EXEHDA-SF prototyping. The fact that the technology is open-source was the basic criterion for its selection.

5.1   Hardware Adopted

Gateway in the EXEHDA-SF architecture explores the ESP32 NodeMCU module (see Fig. 6a). This module consists of an IoT-oriented System-on-a-chip (SOC), formed by a 32-bit Tensilica Xtensa dual core microprocessor with built-in support for the Wi-Fi network (802.11) and bluetooth version 4.2, and with a 16 Mb integrated flash memory [22]. Its choice is because it supports multi-threading programming in Python, and because it is an open source hardware with excellent cost-benefit relation.

Edge Server in EXEHDA-SF explores Raspberry PI III b (see Fig. 6b). The used model offers network connection and for its operation an operating system called Raspbian was installed, which is a variant of the Linux's Debian distribution. The different functionalities of the Edge Server were designed through the Python Programming Language [27].

As an electromechanical actuator to control the water flow, the Hunter PGV-101G valve was used, which is supplied at 24 V and offers a flow rate ranging from 0.7 to 150 l/min (see Fig. 6c). This valve is triggered by a solenoid, and its choice was a consequence of both its large use in irrigation projects and its ease of interfacing with different microcontroller platforms.

5.2   Software Frameworks Adopted

Besides the software platforms used in the other modules of the EXEHDA middleware that are discussed in [21,31], the following software artifacts stand out for the design of EXEHDA-SF:

- **MicroPython:** besides implementing a selection of the main Python language libraries, MicroPython includes specific features for use with microcontrollers. In the case of the EXEHDA-SF Gateway, the "machine" library stands out, which is used to access different hardware features such as input and output ports [23].
- **Picoweb:** also in the Gateway of EXEHDA-SF a webserver, named Picoweb [26], was installed, under which algorithms were developed to interpret REST commands sent via the GET command by the Edge Server, using the JSON notation. Based on these functionalities, the Communication Module has been designed, through which it is possible to implement performance commands, particularly the activation of the Hunter PGV-101G valve, which activates the irrigation.
- **Dark Sky API:** it is an API that provides hourly weather conditions for a given region [7]. In EXEHDA-SF the Dark Sky API behaves as the source of the contextual data used to infer a possible irrigation situation.

Fig. 6. Prototype developed for EXEHDA-SF evaluation

5.3   Evaluation

In order to evaluate the EXEHDA-SF, data about its operation were collected over a period of 90 days. Data generated at 6 am and 6 pm, on consecutive days, totaling 180 sensing procedures. The tests were carried out in the neighborhood Las Acacias in Pelotas, RS, which is part of the forecasting task offered by Dark Sky. Its API has coverage for areas with a radius of approximately 50 km. Table 2 shows the total errors that were observed. Precipitation volumes were estimated with the aid of a rain gauge.

In the universe of 180 decision making situations made by EXEHDA-SF, a total of 11 non confirmed cases by the observation of what actually occurred, which translates into a correctness rate of approximately 94%. These non confirmed cases happened due to errors in the forecast API. For example, inconsistent values regarding rain intensity of the previous 12 h, or incorrect predictions of probability of precipitation (PoP) and/or rain intensity of the following 12 h.

Table 2. Decision errors by EXEHDA-SF

Period of measurement	$\geq$25 mm	<25 mm
Previous 12 h	2	1
Following 12 h (PoP $\geq$ 60%)	4	2
Following 12 h (PoP < 60%)	1	1

6   Conclusions

The study and research effort related to the conception and development of EXEHDA-SF pointed out that the combined exploration of Context Awareness and the Internet of Things is a promising way for computational systems to adjust their behavior regarding modifications in their contexts of interest.

On the other hand, it can be observed that the middleware-based approach can reduce the complexity of the development of context-aware applications by providing support for the acquisition, modeling, storage and processing of the context, among other aspects. Thus, the use of middleware may release developers of context-related concerns, allowing them to focus on defining the operational rules and developing the application-specific functionality.

The high percentage of clean water used in irrigation, in the case of Brazil, 46.2% in 2016, highlights the importance of optimizing irrigation procedures for world agriculture, with the aim of improving their efficiency, contributing to the farmers who seek for alternatives that provide better use of water to meet their water requirements.

From this perspective, this paper presented the EXEHDA-SF proposal, which aims to explore the Context Awareness in decision making for irrigation, seeking to minimize socio-environmental impacts. EXEHDA-SF aims to explore the Context Awareness in decision making for irrigation, seeking to minimize socio-environmental impacts. In addition, the proposal does not employ physical sensors, thus reducing installation, calibration and maintenance costs. In EXEHDA-SF the decision to perform irrigation is based on rainfall data and its intensity, both from the previous 12 h and from the following 12 h.

The proposal EXEHDA-SF was evaluated based on data collected and information regarding its operation over a period of 90 days. In this evaluation, a success rate of 94% was obtained in the decision making, achieving promising results pointing to the continuity of the research. Among the expected future work is the expectation of observing the behavior of EXEHDA-SF throughout the 4 seasons of the year, as well as to use a machine learning algorithm to optimize the parameters used for the irrigation decision, including the difference in water consumption with the use of EXEHDA-SF.

References

1. Alegre, U., Augusto, J.C., Clark, T.: Engineering context-aware systems and applications. J. Syst. Softw. **117**(C), 55–83 (2016). https://doi.org/10.1016/j.jss.2016.02.010
2. Augustin, I., Yamin, A., Silva, L.: Building a smart environment at large-scale with a pervasive grid middleware. In: Grid Computing Research Progress, pp. 182–186. Nova Science Publishers, Inc. (2008)
3. Bellavista, P., Corradi, A., Fanelli, M., Foschini, L.: A survey of context data distribution for mobile ubiquitous systems. ACM Comput. Surv. **44**(4), 24:1–24:45 (2012). https://doi.org/10.1145/2333112.2333119
4. Bikakis, A., Patkos, T., Antoniou, G., Plexousakis, D.: A survey of semantics-based approaches for context reasoning in ambient intelligence. In: Mühlhäuser, M., Ferscha, A., Aitenbichler, E. (eds.) AmI 2007. CCIS, vol. 11, pp. 14–23. Springer, Heidelberg (2008). https://doi.org/10.1007/978-3-540-85379-4_3
5. Brasil: Governo do brasil (2018). http://www.brasil.gov.br/noticias/meio-ambiente/2018/03/. Último acesso 02 Dezembro 2018
6. Chavda, R., Kadam, T., Hattangadi, K., Vora, D.: Smart drip irrigation system using moisture sensors. In: ICSCET, pp. 1–4. IEEE (2018)
7. Darksky (2018). http://darksky.net/dev. Último acesso 2 Dezembro 2018
8. Dey, A.K.: Understanding and using context. Pers. Ubiquit. Comput. **5**(1), 4–7 (2001). https://doi.org/10.1007/s007790170019
9. Erthal, E.S., Berticilli, R.: Sustentabilidade: Agricultura irrigada e seus impactos ambientais. Ciência Tecnologia **2**(1), 64–74 (2018). http://revistaeletronica.unicruz.edu.br/index.php/CIENCIAETECNOLOGIA/article/view/6940
10. Glickman, T.S., Zenk, W.: Glossary of meteorology. American Meteorological Society (2000)
11. Goap, A., Sharma, D., Shukla, A., Rama Krishna, C.: An IoT based smart irrigation management system using machine learning and open source technologies. Comput. Electron. Agric. **155**, 41–49 (2018). https://linkinghub.elsevier.com/retrieve/pii/S0168169918306987
12. Guan, D., Yuan, W., Lee, S., Lee, Y.: Context selection and reasoning in ubiquitous computing. In: The 2007 International Conference on Intelligent Pervasive Computing (IPC 2007), pp. 184–187, October 2007. https://doi.org/10.1109/IPC.2007.102
13. Imteaj, A., Rahman, T., Hossain, M.K., Zaman, S.: IoT based autonomous percipient irrigation system using Raspberry Pi. In: 2016 19th International Conference on Computer and Information Technology (ICCIT), pp. 563–568. IEEE (2016)
14. Joslyn, S., Nadav-Greenberg, L., Nichols, R.M.: Probability of precipitation: assessment and enhancement of end-user understanding. Bull. Am. Meteorol. Soc. **90**(2), 185–194 (2009)
15. Kamienski, C., et al.: SWAMP: an IoT-based smart water management platform for precision irrigation in agriculture. In: 2018 Global Internet of Things Summit (GIoTS), pp. 1–6. IEEE (2018)
16. Khattak, A.M., et al.: Context representation and fusion: advancements and opportunities. Sensors **14**(6), 9628–9668 (2014). https://doi.org/10.3390/s140609628
17. Knappmeyer, M., Kiani, S., Reetz, E., Baker, N., Tonjes, R.: Survey of context provisioning middleware. IEEE Commun. Surv. Tutor. **15**(3), 1492–1519 (2013). https://doi.org/10.1109/SURV.2013.010413.00207

18. Koduru, S., Padala, V.G.D.P.R., Padala, P.: Smart irrigation system using cloud and Internet of Things. In: Krishna, C.R., Dutta, M., Kumar, R. (eds.) Proceedings of 2nd International Conference on Communication, Computing and Networking. LNNS, vol. 46, pp. 195–203. Springer, Singapore (2019). https://doi.org/10.1007/978-981-13-1217-5_20
19. Kumar, A., Surendra, A., Mohan, H., Valliappan, K.M., Kirthika, N.: Internet of Things based smart irrigation using regression algorithm. In: International Conference on Intelligent Computing, Instrumentation and Control Technologies (2017)
20. Li, X., Eckert, M., Martinez, J.F., Rubio, G.: Context aware middleware architectures: survey and challenges. Sensors 15(8), 20570 (2015). https://doi.org/10.3390/s150820570
21. Lopes, J.L., de Souza, R.S., Geyer, C., da Costa, C., Barbosa, J., Pernas, A.M., Yamin, A.: A middleware architecture for dynamic adaptation in ubiquitous computing. J. Univ. Comput. Sci. 20(9), 1327–1351 (2014)
22. Node MCU (2018). https://nodemcu.readthedocs.io/en/dev-esp32/. Último acesso 15 Dezembro 2018
23. Micropython (2018). https://micropython.org. Último acesso 2 Dezembro 2018
24. Penteado, S.R.: Manejo da Á gua e irrigação – em propriedades ecológicas. Via Orgânica (2010)
25. Perera, C., Zaslavsky, A., Christen, P., Georgakopoulos, D.: Context aware computing for the Internet of Things: a survey. IEEE Commun. Surv. Tutor. 16(1), 414–454 (2014). https://doi.org/10.1109/SURV.2013.042313.00197
26. Picoweb (2018). https://github.com/pfalcon/picoweb. Último acesso 3 Dezembro 2018
27. Raspberry (2018). https://www.raspberrypi.org/. Último acesso 15 Dezembro 2018
28. Sahu, C.G., Adane, D.S.: A survey on context-aware middleware. Int. J. Adv. Res. Comput. Commun. Eng. 4(5), 650–656 (2015). https://doi.org/10.17148/IJARCCE.2015.45138
29. Sánchez Guinea, A., Nain, G., Le Traon, Y.: A systematic review on the engineering of software for ubiquitous systems. J. Syst. Softw. 118(C), 251–276 (2016). https://doi.org/10.1016/j.jss.2016.05.024
30. Sezer, O.B., Dogdu, E., Ozbayoglu, A.M.: Context-aware computing, learning, and big data in Internet of Things: a survey. IEEE Internet Things J. 5(1), 1–27 (2018). https://doi.org/10.1109/JIOT.2017.2773600
31. Souza, R., Lopes, J., Geyer, C., Cardozo, A., Yamin, A., Barbosa, J.: An architecture for IoT management targeted to context awareness of ubiquitous applications. J. Univers. Comput. Sci. 24(10), 1452–1471 (2018)

An IoT Architecture to Provide Hybrid Context Reasoning

Roger Machado[1(✉)], Ricardo Almeida[1], Rogério Albandes[2],
Ana Marilza Pernas[1], and Adenauer Yamin[1,2]

[1] Federal University of Pelotas, Pelotas, Brazil
{rdsmachado,rbalmeida,marilza,adenauer}@inf.ufpel.edu.br
[2] Catholic University of Pelotas, Pelotas, Brazil
rogerio.albandes@sou.ucpel.edu.br

Abstract. Considering the dynamic nature of the modern computational infrastructures provided by IoT, applications need to be aware of the contextual data that interest them, to be able to operate with as little human intervention as possible. Thus, context awareness becomes a key concept to provide adaptive services in IoT environments. Context reasoning is one of the more critical steps to obtain context awareness. However, a context reasoning strategy that can be applied satisfactorily in different application domains has not yet been found. Because of this, hybrid strategies for context reasoning are gaining prominence. In the literature, some researchers explore hybrid proposals, but these proposals do not offer flexibility on the use of the reasoning strategies. In this research, we conceive hybrid reasoning based on compositional rules, enabling a dynamic composition of different strategies. Thus, the context-aware applications can choose among different reasoning strategies, those that are most appropriate depending on the contexts that will be treated. To validate our architecture, we design and test it on a scenario based on healthcare. The obtained results showed that our architecture allows the utilization of hybrid strategies for context reasoning, improving situations identification, and decision-making.

Keywords: Internet of Things · Context awareness · Hybrid context reasoning

1 Introduction

In the last twenty years, technology has advanced considerably, with the proliferation of connected devices of different computational capacities and on a

---

This study was financed in part by the Coordenação de Aperfeiçoamento de Pessoal de Nível Superior - Brasil (CAPES) - Finance Code 001 and Fundação de Amparo à Pesquisa do Rio Grande do Sul (FAPERGS) - PqG. Roger da Silva Machado is a FAPERGS/CAPES - BRAZIL Scholarship holder.

A. Casaca et al. (Eds.): IFIPIoT 2019, IFIP AICT 574, pp. 86–102, 2020.
https://doi.org/10.1007/978-3-030-43605-6_6

scale that will reach a total of 50 billion connected devices in 2020 [5]. IoT systems have become an important and even essential part of our daily lives. Smart homes are good examples of where such systems can be found. However, the development of IoT systems is a difficult task because it involves multiple areas of computing, such as software engineering, artificial intelligence, and distributed systems [21].

Due to the fast grown of IoT computing, an increasing number of contextual data is continuously generated from different sources, formats, or semantics which is needed to be evaluated together to identify situations of interest to context-aware applications [12].

In this aspect, context awareness becomes an essential approach for providing adaptive and autonomous services. It can be used, for example, to select the most appropriate services according to the context information that is relevant to the user or to change operational parameters of services in execution. Thus, context-aware applications must be able to adapt their changing behaviors reducing human intervention, introducing to this, several challenges to developers [10].

In order to build and execute context-aware applications, some features need to be provided, ranging from the acquisition of contextual information from heterogeneous and distributed sources, representation of this information, storage, processing, and reasoning for their use on decision-making [2].

Given the importance of the context reasoning to obtain the context awareness, diverse strategies for that have recently been proposed. However, they are not versatile enough to individually meet the reasoning requirements for different IoT applications. Thus, the need for a combination of different methods for context reasoning is identified by means the hybrid strategies [3,12].

Although several proposals on hybrid context reasoning are innovative, they are not able to deal with the dynamic needs from actual IoT demands. Thus, the goal of this work is the conception of an IoT software architecture, providing an approach to hybrid context reasoning. For this, we propose a compositional approach for context reasoning that enables the composition of different strategies. Consequently, the context-aware applications can choose among different reasoning strategy, and if they will be used individually or in combination, considering the contexts that will be treated. Considering this, we provide flexibility for the application to customize the context awareness provided, according to their demands.

The proposed compositional approach for context reasoning is an extension of the Context Recognition and Adaptation Subsystem of the EXEHDA middleware [14]. EXEHDA consists of a situation-aware middleware to IoT, which aims to create and manage a widely distributed computing system environment, as well as to promote the implementation of applications on it.

The remainder of this paper is organized as follows. Section 2 reviews some related works. We describe the compositional reasoning proposed in Sect. 3. In the fourth Section, we discuss the evaluation of the proposal, exploring a use case with the use of a dynamic strategy for context reasoning. Finally, the Fifth Section presents our conclusions and future work.

2   Related Work

In the literature, several papers explore hybrid strategies for context reasoning in IoT. To identify these papers, we performed a Systematic Literature Review (SLR) analyzing papers published between 2012 and 2017, more details can be found in [16]. SLR is a research methodology that foresees the execution of some procedures to generate a literature review in an area, to identify a set of papers that bring a precise prospection of the addressed state of the art [11]. With the execution of the SLR, we selected seven papers. In the following, we present aspects regarding reasoning strategy, as well as main functionalities about the seven works.

The paper [15] proposes a software architecture for context awareness called DynamiCC. The proposal focuses on the conception of a context model and a software architecture that allow the interpretation and the dynamic composition of the information acquired by sensors positioned in different locations of the ubiquitous environment. A hybrid strategy for reasoning was proposed to perform the processing of contextual information. DynamiCC uses semantic reasoning provided by the ontology, through axioms and rules to infer new knowledge based on the ontology instances. In addition to this, DynamiCC uses reasoning based on rules such as ECA (Event-Condition-Action), which performs the processing of contextual information provided by a relational model.

In [24] is proposed a software architecture called CASP (Context-Aware Service Platform). This platform has as main characteristics to be context-aware and deal with the aggregation and abstraction of context information using ontologies to represent them. CASP platform uses two reasoning strategies in the context processing stage, one based on ontological rules and the other in cases. The ontological rules represent general knowledge of the domain, while the cases capture specific knowledge. Ontological reasoning evaluates the rules provided and adds the inferred information to the knowledge base. Case-based reasoning recovers similar situations and uses the corresponding solutions to update the data in the knowledge base represented by the ontological model.

The paper [25] presents the architecture of a framework for hybrid reasoning developed for the CARA (Context-Aware Real-time Assistant) system. The authors use hybrid reasoning based on cases and fuzzy rules, making it more robust and adaptable to an environment subject to change. Case-based is used to detect conditional anomalies for residential automation, and the fuzzy rules to deal with exceptions, as well as case retrieval and adaptation of query-sensitive cases.

In [23] is proposed the software conception of a group recommendation system for concerts for groups of users. The prototype is context-aware and takes into account the user's location and timing when giving recommendations. In order to perform the reasoning of contextual data, the authors propose a hybrid strategy that implements two algorithms, which take advantage of the historical information of the users: a collaborative lineage algorithm (K-Nearest Neighbor) and a matrix-factorization algorithm. The algorithms can be used individually or in combination.

The paper [1] proposes software that individually classifies the retail products on a shop shelf. The authors propose two different hybrid strategies. The first combines SVMs (Support Vector Machines) with HMMs (Hidden Markov Models). In the second, the SVMs are combined with CRF (Conditional Random Fields) aiming to form a new context. Probabilistic models are trained by learning from context-free classifier errors (SVMs) and neighboring relationships between retail products.

In [19] is proposed a framework for a hybrid strategy for context reasoning for the Mining Minds, which offers personalized support for health and wellbeing. In order to perform the context reasoning, a new conjunctive approach is proposed, based on ontology and machine learning. The machine learning strategy supports the inference by classifying high-level contexts based on the data set instantiated in the ontology.

The paper [13] proposes a framework that uses a hybrid strategy for context reasoning to middleware SWARMs (Smart and Networking Underwater Robots in Cooperation Meshes). The approach consists of three reasoning: (i) ontology axioms to infer knowledge related to the classes contained in ontology; (ii) ontology rule that process the contextual data contained in the ontology, using SWRL (Semantic Web Rule Language) for the design of the rules; and (iii) Multi-Entity Bayesian Network, which consists of a logical system that integrates first-order logic with Bayesian probability theory.

Table 1 presents a comparative analysis of the seven papers selected. This analysis was based on the steps followed to obtain context awareness [12]: (i) types of sensors used in the acquisition step; (ii) models used to perform the context representation; (iii) model used to store the contextual data; and (iv) strategies to implement the context reasoning.

Based on Table 1, we can observe that, in the acquisition step, only two papers do not present how they collect contextual data. The remaining works have support to deal with different types of sensors, allowing the treatment of different applications.

Regarding the modeling step, we can see that four papers use the ontology-based model, mainly due to its semantic representation characteristic. It is worth mentioning that [15] proposed the use of hybrid modeling, combining ontological and relational models.

Issues related to contextual information storage are not discussed by the majority of the papers, although it is essential for context-aware applications. The work of [25] uses the markup scheme model XML (eXtensible Markup Language), mainly because it can be utilized to transmit information between different components. The work of [15] uses a relational model of storage, which is not considered a satisfactory model for the storage of data provided by the ontologies [4]. Besides, the work of [19] proposes the use of the triple model along with Jena TDB, being a more indicated model to perform the persistence of information provided by ontologies.

We believe that mechanisms with different characteristics are required for context storing since the current context-aware applications tend to deal with

Table 1. The comparison performed among related work.

Paper	Acquisition	Representation model	Storage model	Reasoning strategy
[15]	Sensor: Physical and Logical	Ontological and Relational	Ontological Rules and Rules	Relational
[24]	Sensor: Physical and Logical	Ontological	Information Not Available	Case-based and Ontological Rules
[25]	Sensor: Physical and Logical	Fuzzy	XML	Case-based and Fuzzy Rules
[23]	Information Not Available	Information Not Available	Information Not Available	Machine Learning (K-Nearest Neighbor and Matrix Factorization
[1]	Information Not Available	Information Not Available	Information Not Available	Machine Learning and Probabilistic Logic
[19]	Sensor: Physical and Logical	Ontological	Triple	Machine Learning and Ontological Axioms
[13]	Sensor: Physical and Logical	Ontological	Information Not Available	Ontological Axioms, Ontological Rules, and Probabilistic Logic

diverse types of data, semantic levels, among other aspects. In turn, the efficiency of these mechanisms is a significant aspect, considering the scalability of the volume of contextual data involved, and its constant updating or search.

Regarding context reasoning, despite using hybrid strategies, the solutions do not allow the application to choose a strategy that better fits their needs. Besides, we note the absence of an approach that enables the combination of the different strategies for context reasoning. In this research, we propose the creation of compositional reasoning that could increase the flexibility for the use of contextual data, facilitating the identification of interest situations. Moreover, with the development of this strategy, applications can choose whether these different reasoning strategies will be utilized individually or combined, depending on application demand and the contextual data treated.

3   Software Architecture Proposed

The differential of our proposal is to allow the applications to choose among the strategies offered to context reasoning. Thus, providing greater flexibility for the application to customize the context awareness provided, according to their demands. Figure 1 gives an overview of the proposal, where we can see the software components necessary to offer a dynamic strategy for context reasoning. The main features of these components are discussed below, highlighting the Reasoning Component focused on this paper.

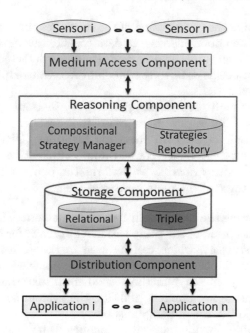

Fig. 1. Overview of proposal

In Fig. 1, Medium Access Component is responsible for sending and receiving information from the applications. It performs the context acquisition from distinct types of sensors, such as events about the use of operating system resources and log files internal to the system, and can receive contextual data from different devices. Moreover, it performs the configured actions based on the identified situations. These actions can be alerts by email, instant messaging service, or commands execution, which results in the nonfunctional adaptation of the environment at runtime.

Storage Component is formed by two storage models offering: (i) a relational model, which has a satisfactory behavior in many situations, being used to store the configuration necessary to perform compositional approach for context reasoning, providing an easy data access and facilitating it's modification if required; (ii) a triple model, which allows the manipulation of ontological data more efficiently compared to its manipulation in memory or using a relational model [20].

Distribution Component communicates with context-aware applications, being responsible for the configuration of the proposal, for receiving the requests made by the applications, and for the visualization of the stored contextual information.

In the middle of Fig. 1, the Reasoning Component has a module called Compositional Strategy Manager, which provides a dynamic strategy for context reasoning. Reasoning Component allows the applications to choose which strategy or strategies they want to use, being the Compositional Strategy Manager responsible for making the composition of the strategies that will be used to context reasoning. This component receives data collected from sensors of Medium Access Component, transmits the data and situations detected to Storage Component, and sends a notification to the Medium Access Component for the execution of determined actions.

In order to offer multiple reasoning strategies, Reasoning Component provides the Strategies Repository. Each reasoning strategy is cataloged in the repository with a unique Uniform Resource Identifier (URI). Thus, allowing access to a specific strategy that a context-aware application wishes to use.

Among the strategies available to perform the context reasoning, we can mention the use of three of the main strategies [18]:

- rules-based following the event-condition-action pattern. This strategy is used to allows the conception of the compositional approach for context reasoning;
- ontology-based strategy, which can be used in two forms, in the first, the internal axioms in the ontology are used to infer knowledge about the classes represented in the ontology. In the second form, external rules written in the SWRL language are applied, allowing the system to infer new context information exploring the ontology instances;
- supervised learning provides several techniques to be used. In the first step, this strategy uses a training set, where, in this set, the data are categorized [9]. After training, in the second step, exploring the learning acquired is possible to classify new context data.

The dynamic strategy is conceived based on compositional rules, allowing the use of different strategies for reasoning in a combined way. Each rule can contain three different methods: compositional rules, learning techniques, or ontology-based strategy. Each method is represented by marking tags, in which is used a specific tag for each one.

Marking tags begin with the "#" symbol followed by an identifier and a number, thus allowing to recognize the desired composite rule. When the tag has to be replaced by another compositional rule, the "M" identifier must be used. The identifier "A" will be replaced by a supervised learning strategy. Also, identifier "O" can be used to represent an ontology-based strategy.

In order to support the use of the dynamic reasoning strategy, we include specific tables in the relational database in the Storage Component. Figure 2 presents the ER (Entity Relationship) diagram that represents the compositional approach concepts and how it can be modeled to enables their conception.

As presented in Fig. 2, we create an entity to model the strategy used called "Reasoning". This entity contains the "id" attribute, responsible for identifying the rules, this attribute being the primary key of the table. Applications can identify which rule will be used by searching for "id" and "rule" attribute referring to the compositional rule that will be applied. Also, the "category" attribute is used to find out what kind of strategy will be used, whether it is learning or ontology-based.

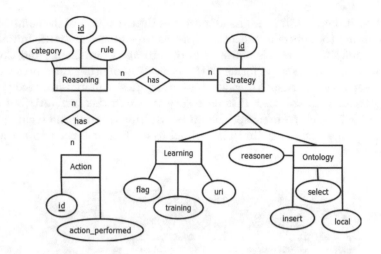

Fig. 2. ER diagram of compositional rules

Considering that, context reasoning can be composed of several strategies. Thus, we define a "Strategy" entity with the "id" attribute responsible for identifying strategies. In Fig. 2, the strategies based on supervised learning and ontologies are modeled in independent entities, being a specialization from "Strategy".

"Learning" entity has the "uri" attribute, which is responsible for identifying which learning technique should be used. Besides, this entity has the "training" attribute, which specifies which training set should be used to train the chosen learning technique. Also, "flag" attribute is designed to determine the need to perform the training of the selected technique, so when the training step is necessary, its value will be "1", otherwise "0".

"Ontology" entity has the "reasoner" attribute, which specifies which statement should be executed to perform the ontology's reasoning. The "select" and "insert" attributes refer to the SPARQL queries that must be executed to search the data present in the ontology and to insert the data into the triple model of Storage Component. Also, this entity has the "local" attribute, which specifies the location on the disk of the OWL description file of the ontology used.

In Fig. 2 the entity "Action" can also be visualized, which has the "id" attribute that is responsible for the identification of the actions, the value of this attribute is used in the compositional rule to identify which action will be performed. Besides, the entity has the "action_performed" attribute, which specifies the actions to be performed. These actions are transferred to Medium Access Component, which is responsible for carrying out the necessary action. The commands are represented in the compositional rules by the "#C" tag followed by an identifier, which is the "id" attribute of the "Action" table.

Compositional Strategy Manager performs the execution of the compositional rule according to a specific execution flow, as we can see in Fig. 3. Initially, the desired compositional rule is obtained in the Storage Component, and Compositional Strategy Manager performs the identification of other rules present in the initial compositional rule. After, strategy categories explored are recognized. If learning techniques are used, it is necessary to search the "uri" attribute. Also, it is identified which training set should be used for training the technique, and the value of the "flag" attribute is verified to confirm the need to execute the training step.

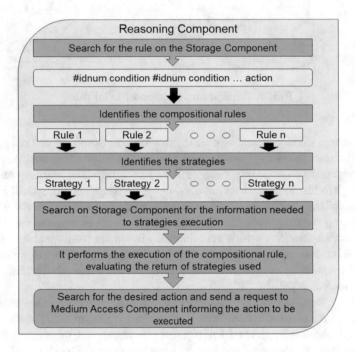

Fig. 3. Execution flow of compositional rule

If the use of ontology-based reasoning was detected, it is necessary to search for the "local" attribute, which contains the location on disk of the ontology, allowing it to be loaded. After that, the Compositional Strategy Manager identifies the mechanism of reasoner chosen, being represented by the "reasoner" attribute. Also, the Compositional Strategy Manager searches the "select" attribute representing the SPARQL query that must be run to fetch the instances that were inferred during the reasoner process. Lastly, the "insert" attribute representing the SPARQL query that will insert the new instances into the triple model of Storage Component is identified.

After the identification of the strategy used and their processing, the Compositional Strategy Manager identifies the command represented in the compositional rule and sends a notification of the need for action to the Medium Access Component.

4   Evaluation

Several evaluation methods are present in the literature, among them, this work highlights the scenario-based assessment, which is considered a mature alternative to be used in context-aware environments [17]. Scenario-based methods evaluate the ability of the software architecture to deal with the demands of a set of interest scenarios [22]. Thus, to evaluate our proposed architecture, we use a scenario-based method.

This scenario is based on work [6], where our architecture monitors the vital signs of patients in cardiac rehabilitation and generates early alerts with the use of scores. For this, we proposed a compositional rule combining a rule-based and supervised learning strategy with the use of regression techniques. Thus, making it possible to predict possible situations of a collapse of a patient and anticipate the activation of the rapid response teams to the action.

With the use of compositional rules, unlike other studies, it is possible to combine the scores generated by different vital signs. Moreover, even the rules used to produce the scores are customizable and can be adapted to distinct patterns of patient behavior. Table 2 shows the values analyzed, in this scenario, to generate the early alerts based on the vital signs obtained.

Table 2. Early alerts score.

Vital sign	1	2	3	0	1	2	3
Heart rate	–	≤40	41–50	51–100	101–110	111–129	≥130
O₂ saturation	<85	85–89	90–92	≥130	–	–	–

Figure 4 shows the compositional rule used in this scenario. We can see that the compositional rule is composed of two other rules, which are represented by #M1 and #M2, and they have conditionals to be evaluated, resulting in an action to be performed.

First, the Compositional Strategy Manager performs the identification of rules contained in the compositional rule. In this way, the rules M1 and M2 are identified, making it necessary to search for the rules described by the id with values 1 and 2 in the reasoning table, and the substitution of the tags that represent the rules in the compositional rule. After, Compositional Strategy Manager verifies if the rules have other rules represented by #M or if they have some tag #A referring to the learning technique or #O for ontology-based.

```
#M1
#M2
if((heart==2 and saturation==2) or (heart==3 or saturation==3)):
 #C1(name, "critical")
```

Fig. 4. Compositional rule used in evaluation scenario.

With the verification performed, the tags #A1 and #A2 are identified, making necessary find which techniques are present in the Learning table that have the ids with values 1 and 2. After the search, the Compositional Strategy Manager substitutes the tags by the URIs referring to the techniques. As learning strategies are used, the concatenation of the URI with the string "predict" is done, thus allowing to predict the data passed by parameter.

In Fig. 5 is shown the rule referring to tag #M1, which has the id field with value 1, which is used to treat the vital sign heart rate. Figure 6 shows the rule referring to tag #M2, with the id with value 2, which processes the data provided by the vital sign O_2 saturation.

```
If(#A1<130):
 heart=3
elif((#A1<=40) or (#A1>=111 and #A1<=129)):
 heart=2
elif(#A1>=41 and #A1<=50) or (#A1>=101 and #A1<=110):
 heart=1
elif(#A1>=51 and A1<=100):
 heart=0
```

Fig. 5. Rule that replaces the M1 tag.

```
If(#A2<85):
 saturation=3
elif(#A2>=85 and #A2<=89):
 saturation=2
elif(#A2>=90 and #A2<=92):
 saturation=1
elif(#A2>=93):
 saturation=0
```

Fig. 6. Rule that replaces the M2 tag.

Figure 7 shows the rule resulting from the substitution of tag #A1 by the learning technique chosen to perform the reasoning. Where can be visualized the choice of linear learning technique Lars[1]. This rule refers to the generation of alerts based on the data collected from the heart rate, creating the values of the score to be analyzed in the compositional rule.

```
if(lars.predict(d)<130):
  heart=3
elif((lars.predict(d)<=40) or (lars.predict(d)>=111 and lars.predict(d)<=129)):
  heart=2
elif((lars.predict(d)>=41 and lars.predict(d)<=50) or (lars.predict(d)>=101 and lars.predict(d)<=110)):
  heart=1
elif(lars.predict(d)>=51 and lars.predict(d)<=100):
  heart=0
```

Fig. 7. Rule with A1 tag replaced.

In Fig. 8 is shown the rule resulting from the substitution of the tag #A2 by the learning technique chosen to carry out the reasoning. Where can be visualized the choice of linear learning technique Lasso[2]. This rule refers to the generation of alerts based on the collected data of the O_2 saturation, creating the values of the score to be analyzed in the compositional rule.

```
If(lasso.predict(d)<85):
  saturation=3
elif(lasso.predict(d)>=85 and lasso.predict(d)<=89):
  saturation=2
elif(lasso.predict(d)>=90 and lasso.predict(d)<=92):
  saturation=1
elif(lasso.predict(d)>=93):
  saturation=0
```

Fig. 8. Rule with A2 tag replaced.

It is important to note that the same parameter is passed for the two reasoning techniques because, in this scenario is always predicted the next expected value for that signal. The values of vital signs are passed to each technique during the training phase, which in this scenario occurs with each new vital sign collection.

---

[1] http://scikit-learn.org/stable/modules/generated/sklearn.linear_model.Lars.html.
[2] http://scikit-learn.org/stable/modules/generated/sklearn.linear_model.Lasso.html.

Figure 9 presents the compositional rule that is applied in this scenario, where all markup tags have already been replaced, both by other rules and by learning techniques. Also, the action that should be executed, if the rule is evaluated as true, has already been inserted in the place of the #C1 tag. This action refers to sending a message by the instant message application to the responsible doctor, where the patient's name and the situation of critical prediction are passed on in the message.

```
If(lars.predict(d)<130):
   heart=3
elif((lars.predict(d)<=40) or (elif lars.predict(d)>=111 and lars.predict(d) <=129)):
   heart=2
elif((lars.predict(d)>=41 and lars.predict(d)<=50) or (elif lars.predict(d)>=101 and lars.predict(d)<=110)):
   heart=1
elif(lars.predict(d)>=51 and lars.predict(d)<=100):
   heart=0
if(lasso.predict(d)<85):
   saturation=3
elif(lasso.predict(d)>=85 and lasso.predict(d)<=89):
   saturation=2
elif(lasso.predict(d)>=90 and lasso.predict(d)<=92):
   saturation=1
elif(lasso.predict(d)>=93):
   saturation=0
if((heart==2 and saturation==2) or (heart==3 or saturation==3)):
   sender.send_msg(str(name), str('Critical'))
```

Fig. 9. Rule applied for alert generation.

In order to analyze the performance of learning techniques when predicting the next value of vital sign reading, it was decided to use measurements made available by the MIMIC database[3] (Multiparameter Intelligent Monitoring in Intensive Care). The MIMIC database includes data from more than 90 patients registered in an Intensive Care Unit (ICU), collected between 1992 and 1999, containing an average of 40 hours of physiological signal records [7].

Performance verification was based on the accuracy metric that is the proportion of instances predicted correctly. The use of this metric is justified by the fact that it is widely used to evaluate the quality of the results in several areas of artificial intelligence research with an emphasis on machine learning [8].

In this scenario, it is treated as a correctly classified instance, when the technique accurately predicts which score the future value of vital sign reading will have. In order to analyze the performance of the learning strategy, the prediction of the categories of the next vital sign value was performed using ten patients from the MIMIC database.

---

[3] https://www.physionet.org/physiobank/database/mimicdb/.

Table 3. Accuracy of strategy for heart rate.

Patient	0	1	2	3	Total
055	0.996	0.993	0.979	0.9	0.993
211	0.999	0.875	0.836	–	0.997
221	0.998	0.945	0.956	–	0.995
226	0.966	0.977	0.985	0.995	0.979
230	0.999	0.5	0.696	0.571	0.999
248	0.982	0.778	0.832	0.476	0.956
252	1	–	–	–	1
253	0.999	0.92	–	–	0.999
401	0.999	0.5	–	–	0.999
403	1	–	–	–	1

Table 4. Accuracy of strategy for O_2 saturation.

Patient	0	1	2	3	Total
055	0.999	0.848	0.0.907	0.972	0.999
211	0.998	0.989	0.936	0.971	0.996
221	1	–	–	–	1
226	0.998	0.988	0.989	0.993	0.996
230	0.997	0.98	0.989	0.992	0.995
248	0.999	0.950	0.666	0.957	0.999
252	0.998	0.987	0.985	0.991	0.995
253	0.998	0.993	0.978	0.984	0.996
401	0.997	0.989	0.99	0.868	0.993
403	0.996	0.995	0.99	0.951	0.995

Tables 3 and 4 shows the accuracy achieved by the learning techniques employed, both for heart rate and SO_2 saturation. Note that in some cells of the table is contained the character "– ", which represents that for that patient no instance of that category was analyzed.

As we can see in Tables 3 and 4, the performance of learning strategies was satisfactory, reaching more than 0.95 % of hits in the total number instances of each patient. Note that in some cases all the predictions were correct, and these cases happened for the patients that have all the instances of the same score category. The worst accuracy rates obtained were 0.5 %, where it can be analyzed that they are of categories that had few instances, and still, it is of cases that the vital signs change rapidly among the score categories.

5   Conclusion

In this paper, we considered the challenges faced by context-aware applications in IoT, dealing with an increasing number of contextual data from different sources, formats, or semantics. In order to process these contextual data, works present in literature have explored hybrid reasoning strategies. Although many papers propose a hybrid reasoning strategy, we can note the absence of an approach that enables the processing of context information from different reasoning strategies stands out.

Considering these challenges, the following contributions have been achieved with the development of this work: (i) the design of an IoT architecture that supports hybrid context reasoning; (ii) the proposal of a Reasoning Component that provides multiple reasoning strategies; (iii) the conception of a compositional approach for context reasoning that enables the use of different reasoning strategies in a dynamic form, allowing the strategies utilization both individually or in a combined way.

With the conception of the compositional approach for context reasoning, the context-awareness services of the EXEHDA middleware have been updated, and now the middleware can provide different reasoning strategies. Thus, increasing the flexibility of acquired contexts reasoning, improving the identification of situations of interest, and facilitating decision-making.

The proposal was evaluated through one scenario that explores the use of the compositional strategy for context reasoning on the scope of current relevance, which is context awareness in healthcare. In this scenario, the compositional strategy was applied to process the vital signs of heart rate and SO_2 saturation. We used two supervised learning techniques, and combine the results into a single compositional rule to identify risk situations with anticipation. With the use of compositional rules, we possibility the combination of scores of different vital signs, and the creation of rules customizable and adaptable to distinct patterns of patient behavior.

As future work, we highlight: (i) the interfaces developing using data visualization techniques to facilitate the interpretation of the stored contextual information and identified situations; (ii) explore the compositional strategy in different use cases, which can benefit from the features offers for context reasoning.

References

1. Baz, I., Yoruk, E., Cetin, M.: Context-aware hybrid classification system for fine-grained retail product recognition. In: 2016 IEEE 12th Image, Video, and Multidimensional Signal Processing Workshop, IVMSP 2016 (2016). https://doi.org/10.1109/IVMSPW.2016.7528213
2. Bellavista, P., Corradi, A., Fanelli, M., Foschini, L.: A survey of context data distribution for mobile ubiquitous systems. ACM Comput. Surv. **44**(4), 24:1–24:45 (2012). https://doi.org/10.1145/2333112.2333119
3. Bettini, C., et al.: A survey of context modelling and reasoning techniques. Pervasive Mob. Comput. **6**(2), 161–180 (2010). https://doi.org/10.1016/j.pmcj.2009.06.002

4. Can, O., Sezer, E., Bursa, O., Unalir, M.O.: Comparing relational and ontological triple stores in healthcare domain. Entropy **19**(1), 30 (2017)
5. United States. Federal Trade Commission: The Internet of Things: Privacy and Security in a Connected World. Federal Trade Commission staff reports, DIANE Publishing Company, USA (2015). https://books.google.com.br/books?id=alQ7rgEACAAJ
6. Dias, F.O.: Um Modelo Proativo de Antecipação de Ações de Times de Resposta Rápida Baseado em Análise Preditiva. Dissertação de mestrado em computação aplicada, Unisinos, São Leopoldo-RS (2017)
7. Goldberger, A.L., et al.: Physiobank, physiotoolkit, and physionet: Components of a new research resource for complex physiologic signals. Circulation **101**(23), e215–e220 (2000). Circulation Electronic Pages
8. Japkowicz, N., Shah, M.: Evaluating Learning Algorithms: A Classification Perspective. Cambridge University Press, New York (2011)
9. Khan, N., Alegre, U., Kramer, D., Augusto, J.C.: Is 'context-aware reasoning = case-based reasoning'? In: Brézillon, P., Turner, R., Penco, C. (eds.) CONTEXT 2017. LNCS (LNAI), vol. 10257, pp. 418–431. Springer, Cham (2017). https://doi.org/10.1007/978-3-319-57837-8_35
10. Khattak, A.M., et al.: Context representation and fusion: advancements and opportunities. Sensors **14**(6), 9628–9668 (2014). https://doi.org/10.3390/s140609628
11. Kitchenham, B., Charters, S.: Guidelines for performing systematic literature reviews in software engineering. Joint report, Keele University and Durham University, Durham (2007)
12. Li, X., Eckert, M., Martínez, J.F., Rubio, G.: Context aware middleware architectures: survey and challenges. Sensors **15**(8), 20570 (2015). https://doi.org/10.3390/s150820570. http://www.mdpi.com/1424-8220/15/8/20570
13. Li, X., Martínez, J.F., Rubio, G.: Towards a hybrid approach to context reasoning for underwater robots. Appl. Sci. **7**(2) (2017). https://doi.org/10.3390/app7020183
14. Lopes, J., et al.: A middleware architecture for dynamic adaptation in ubiquitous computing. J. Univers. Comput. Sci. **20**(9), 1327–1351 (2014). http://www.jucs.org/jucs_20_9/a_middleware_architecture_for
15. Lopes, J.L., et al.: A distributed architecture for dynamic contexts composition in ubicomp. In: 38th Latin America Conference on Informatics - CLEI 2012 - Conference Proceedings (2012). https://doi.org/10.1109/CLEI.2012.6427253
16. Machado, R., Almeida, R., Lopes, J., Pernas, A., Yamin, A.: Construção do estado da arte em estratégias híbridas para raciocínio de contexto: uma abordagem explorando revisão sistemática da literatura. In: SBCUP - 10° Simpósio Brasileiro de Computação Ubíqua e Pervasiva (2018)
17. Patidar, A., Suman, U.: A survey on software architecture evaluation methods. In: 2nd International Conference on Computing for Sustainable Global Development (INDIACom), pp. 967–972, March 2015
18. Perera, C., Zaslavsky, A., Christen, P., Georgakopoulos, D.: Context aware computing for the internet of things: a survey. IEEE Commun. Surv. Tutor. **16**(1), 414–454 (2014). https://doi.org/10.1109/SURV.2013.042313.00197
19. Razzaq, M.A., Amin, M.B., Lee, S.: An ontology-based hybrid approach for accurate context reasoning. In: 2017 19th Asia-Pacific Network Operations and Management Symposium (APNOMS), pp. 403–406, September 2017. https://doi.org/10.1109/APNOMS.2017.8094159
20. Rosa, F.L., Machado, R.S., Cavalheiro, G.G.H., Yamin, A.C., Pernas, A.M.: Análise de desempenho de sistemas de gerenciamento de dados em triplas com base no benchmark watdiv. WSCAD-WIC (2017)

21. Sánchez Guinea, A., Nain, G., Le Traon, Y.: A systematic review on the engineering of software for ubiquitous systems. J. Syst. Softw. **118**(C), 251–276 (2016). https://doi.org/10.1016/j.jss.2016.05.024
22. Shanmugapriya, P., Suresh, R.M.: Software architecture evaluation methods - a survey. Int. J. Comput. Appl. **49**(16), 19–26 (2012)
23. Smaaberg, S., Shabib, N., Krogstie, J.: A user-study on context-aware group recommendation for concerts. In: CEUR Workshop Proceedings - SP 2014: Social Personalisation Workshop (2014)
24. Strobbe, M., Van Laere, O., Dhoedt, B., De Turck, F., Demeester, P.: Hybrid reasoning technique for improving context-aware applications. Knowl. Inf. Syst. **31**(3), 581–616 (2012). https://doi.org/10.1007/s10115-011-0411-7
25. Yuan, B., Herbert, J.: Context-aware hybrid reasoning framework for pervasive healthcare. Pers. Ubiquit. Comput. **18**(4), 865–881 (2014). https://doi.org/10.1007/s00779-013-0696-5

IoT Security

REDEM: Real-Time Detection and Mitigation of Communication Attacks in Connected Autonomous Vehicle Applications

Srivalli Boddupalli[✉] and Sandip Ray

Department of Electrical and Computer Engineering,
University of Florida at Gainesville, Gainesville, USA
bodsrivalli12@ufl.edu, sandip@ece.ufl.edu

Abstract. Emergent vehicles will support a variety of connected applications, where a vehicle communicates with other vehicles or with the infrastructure to make a variety of decisions. Cooperative connected applications provide a critical foundational pillar for autonomous driving, and hold the promise of improving road safety, efficiency and environmental sustainability. However, they also induce a large and easily exploitable attack surface: an adversary can manipulate vehicular communications to subvert functionality of participating individual vehicles, cause catastrophic accidents, or bring down the transportation infrastructure. In this paper we outline a potential direction to address this critical problem through a resiliency framework, REDEM, based on machine learning. REDEM has several interesting features, including (1) smooth integration with the architecture of the underlying application, (2) ability to handle diverse communication attacks within the same underlying foundation, and (3) real-time detection and mitigation capability. We present the vision of REDEM, identify some key challenges to be addressed in its realization, and discuss the kind of evaluation/analysis necessary for its viability. We also present initial results from one instantiation of REDEM introducing resiliency in Cooperative Adaptive Cruise Control (CACC).

Keywords: Vehicular communication · Automotive security · Machine learning · Anomaly detection

1 Introduction

Recent years have seen rapid transformation of automotive systems from being primarily human-operated, electro-mechanical systems to complex electronic systems with hundreds of connected Electronic Control Units (ECUs), a variety of

This research has been partially supported by the National Science Foundation under Grant CNS-1908549.

A. Casaca et al. (Eds.): IFIPIoT 2019, IFIP AICT 574, pp. 105–122, 2020.
https://doi.org/10.1007/978-3-030-43605-6_7

sensors and actuators, several in-vehicle networks, several miles of cable, and several hundred megabytes of software code. Much of this transformation has been towards increasing autonomy, i.e., augmenting and replacing human functionality with electronics and software. Autonomous features hold the promise of dramatically increasing road safety, by reducing and eventually eliminating human errors [27]. However, an unfortunate effect of this trend is a corresponding increase in the vulnerability of these systems to a variety of cyber-attacks. Recent research has shown that it is possible,—even relatively straightforward,— to compromise a vehicle and get control over its driving function [11,21,25,26]. The trend towards increasing autonomy will only exacerbate this situation: the increasing dependence of critical vehicular operations on complex electronics and software will result in an increased attack surface as well as the increasing ability of an attacker to create catastrophic impact from a compromise. *Consequently, the proliferation or even adoption of autonomous vehicles critically depends on our ability to ensure that they perform securely, in a potentially adversarial environment.*

A critical feature of emergent autonomous vehicles is *connectivity*, i.e., the ability to communicate with other vehicles (V2V), with the infrastructure (V2I), and with other devices connected to the Internet (V2IoT). Vehicular communications, referred to as V2X, are performed through a variety of protocols, e.g., DSRC, and form a fundamental enabler for autonomous driving by enabling cooperative information sharing for streamlining traffic movement, improving road safety, and efficiently utilizing traffic and transportation infrastructure. V2X forms the foundation for critical applications like platooning [8], cooperative route management [12,14], intersection management [29], etc. Unfortunately, V2X is also a highly vulnerable feature that can be exploited by an adversary to disrupt traffic movement and cause catastrophic accidents. A key problem with V2X is that it obviates the need for an adversary to actually hack a vehicle: sending misleading or malformed V2X communications is often sufficient to disrupt the connected car ecosystem. For example, in platooning, an adversary may cause an accident simply by sending a misleading message with an acceleration directive while braking [1]. Unsurprisingly, in a recent survey by the world's second-largest reinsurer Munich Re, 55% of the surveyed corporate risk managers named security of vehicular communications as their top concern for autonomous vehicles [17]. Perhaps even more alarming, 64% of the companies surveyed mentioned that they were completely unprepared to address this threat.

In this paper, we present the vision of a potential approach to address this critical problem. Our proposed solution is REDEM (for "REal-time DEtection and Mitigation"), a novel resiliency architecture that can be integrated with a variety of cooperative autonomous applications to detect and mitigate communication attacks. A key component of REDEM is an anomaly detection system (ADS) based on machine learning to detect malicious V2X communications in real time. The central idea is to build models that can learn normal behavior corresponding to benign V2X communication and detect anomalous behavior in order to sense potentially malicious communication. On detecting an anomaly, REDEM performs real-time mitigation, also using machine learning to estimate the appropriate driving decisions. A unique feature of REDEM is its flexibility: the same infrastructure can address an elaborate set of adversaries in the connected car ecosystem, including man-in-the-middle (MITM), wormhole, Sybil, Denial-of-Service (DoS), etc. Furthermore, it accounts for the natural differences in communication patterns among a variety of driving scenarios, road conditions, etc. *This is in contrast to most related work on V2X security* [2,15,29] *that require detailed, continuous models of vehicular and adversarial functionalities.*

REDEM is early work in progress. We are currently realizing the REDEM vision in introducing resiliency to a specific but foundational connected car application, Cooperative Adaptive Cruise Control (CACC). We provide initial results on resilient CACC to demonstrate the viability of REDEM.

The remainder of the paper is organized as follows. Section 2 provides the relevant background on connected car applications and related research. In Sect. 3 we discuss challenges and design constraints involved in the development of resilient connected car applications, and REDEM's approach to addressing them. Sections 4 and 5 discuss REDEM's envisioned architecture and Sect. 6 discusses evaluation challenges. In Sect. 7 we present initial results from our current efforts on realizing REDEM on CACC. We conclude in Sect. 8.

2   Background and Related Work

2.1   Connected Car Applications and Security Challenges

We present a brief overview of a few connected car applications to explain the scope and spectrum of security challenges in V2X communications. The following are representative examples.

– *Platooning.* Platooning involves a group of autonomous vehicles (referred to as a string or platoon) traveling with relatively small headway distance and very small relative velocity [9]. The goal is to improve the operational efficiency of the transportation infrastructure by improving highway capacity. The vehicles must brake or accelerate simultaneously to ensure safety of the platoon and optimal usage of the highway infrastructure. In emergent, distributed platooning systems, a vehicle uses V2V messages to communicate its intent (e.g., to brake or accelerate), as well as its relative distance with its neighbor; every vehicle in the platoon accounts for this information to compute its course of action.
– *Smart Intersection Management.* This application is developed for smart cities, with the goal to enable smart and efficient control of (autonomous) vehicles approaching an isolated intersection. In this case, vehicles communicate with an intersection manager through V2I communications to notify estimated arrival time to the intersection. The intersection manager uses this information to schedule vehicles for crossing the intersection.

- *Cooperative Collision Detection.* The goal of this application is for vehicles approaching an intersection from directions to coordinate through V2V messages and avoid collision. Vehicles broadcast their speed, direction of motion, and position relative to the intersection. A vehicle $\mathcal{E}$ receiving this communication from other vehicles $\mathcal{T}$ computes its relative distance, angle, and speed and determines if a collision is possible. In recent CCD systems, vehicles communicate, in addition to their own information, data about other vehicles within their V2V communication range; each vehicle accounts for this additional information to increase precision of its calculation and facilitate fault tolerance in sensor measurements.
- *Dynamic Cooperative Route Management.* Augmenting dynamic routing strategies with Co-operative communication enables improved traffic management, faster recovery from an unforeseen disturbance in the traffic flow, better congestion control as well as improved safety of the vehicles [13]. The co-operative application is proven to be more efficient and accurate, than mapping services that rely purely on satellite imagery. In this application, vehicles constantly broadcast their mapping and localization and in turn utilize the information shared by other vehicles driving along the desired routes.

Clearly, viability of all the above applications critically depends on the trustworthiness of the V2V and V2I communications. A rogue vehicle participating in the application can send misleading, malicious, or confusing messages designed to cause accidents or disrupt the transportation infrastructure. Such messages can easily result in catastrophic accidents or disruption of the entire connected car infrastructure. Since vehicles are consumer items, an adversary can simply buy a car, hack its vehicular communication components, and use such a compromised vehicle to disrupt a connected car application. Correspondingly, adversarial activity in V2I application may entail a compromised or hacked infrastructural component, or one that is "confused" by a compromised vehicle participating in the application. Finally, it is not necessary for an adversary to actually compromise a vehicle: connected car applications are vulnerable to rogue intermediary agents performing man-in-the-middle (MITM) attack, Sybil attack, and many others. In traditional secure communications, such problems are addressed through strong message authentications; however, this requires computationally intensive algorithms which may not be practical with the limited computational resources of automotive ECUs under aggressive real-time requirements.

2.2 State of the Practice and Related Research

In today's industrial practice, detection of security vulnerabilities in connected car applications primarily entails manual *penetration testing*. Human validators with deep insight into the application, the implementation of the vehicular functionality, and potential vehicle responses to various V2X communication, conceive various adversarial scenarios with elaborate simulation models, physical prototype of vehicles, or field testing environments. Such methods obviously depend crucially on the insight of the experts. Furthermore, since elaborate prototypes of vehicular functionality are only available late in the design life-cycle, mitigation of security vulnerabilities identified precludes complex changes in the overall system architecture of individual vehicles; instead, workarounds are employed, including functionality reduction, patches, and point-fixes, which themselves may lead to further vulnerabilities and in-field attacks.

Given the importance of security in automotive systems, there has been significant research interest for security mechanisms to ensure resiliency of vehicular functionality. In related work, vehicle intrusion detection systems (IDS) are largely divided by the targets for security assurance. IDS for in-vehicle network considers intrusion and anomaly detection on CAN [10,20], while IDS for vehicular adhoc network (VANET) considers security of V2X communications [4,19]. These works do not consider security of V2X communications across connected car applications in a comprehensive framework considered in this work. In research on connected cars in particular, there have been works on security of platooning and cooperative adaptive cruise control [7]. Proposed approaches include a variety of techniques based on control theory to address targeted adversary models [16], and application-specific techniques assuming certain adversary properties such as rationality [23]. However, control-theoretic approaches require detailed models precisely specifying the adversary operation, machine learning techniques suffer from the unavailability of sufficient data for training the models, and rationality-based techniques need assumptions that may be violated by in-field adversaries. Furthermore, these works do not explore the viability of realizing the approaches with on-board computational resources.

There are also related machine learning research relevant to our work. Levi [22] provides a data abstraction approach that converts raw vehicle data to events that helps in filtering noise and reducing data dimensionality. For automotive systems, machine learning has been used for computer vision modules to improve on-board perception [30,32]. Tiwari [31] describes attack features that are undetectable at each time instance but can be detected from sequence data. There has also been related work on adversarial attacks on these systems [24,33].

3   REDEM Vision

3.1   Design Constraints

REDEM is an anomaly detection system (ADS) based on machine learning, that can be installed in autonomous vehicles involved in connected car applications; it will enable the vehicle (referred to as *ego vehicle*) to detect adversarial communications in real time, and perform mitigation. For such a system to be viable, it must satisfy the following requirements.

- *Basic Safety:* Any driving decision generated from an automated source must be *safe*, *i.e.*, should not increase the risk of accident. This applies particularly to any system that performs real-time mitigation in response to detected anomalies: road safety should not be compromised by the mitigating action irrespective of whether the response is to a message classified as anomalous as the result of a real attack or imprecision/inaccuracy in the detection algorithm.

- *Reusability/Extensibility:* Connected car applications are proliferating rapidly. Furthermore, new, previously unknown, attacks are being discovered every day in research as well as in practice. *It is critical for a viable ADS mechanism to be easily extensible for a variety of new adversarial operations.* Note that ADS approaches based on control theory depend on detailed mathematical models that precisely define the adversarial activity: solutions for Denial-of-Service (DoS) and data corruption attacks typically require different mathematical models and independent analysis. This makes it difficult to deploy such solutions to practical automotive applications.
- *Limited Computation:* Any solution integrated within an automotive system architecture must operate within the constraints imposed by that architecture and the real-time response requirements of connected car applications. Consequently, it must be realizable by smooth, disciplined extension of the system functionality without significant design overhaul. Furthermore, it must be possible to perform the computation with automotive ECUs in real time. This rules out any solution that requires installation of sophisticated, computation-intensive algorithms implemented within ECUs.
- *Small Data Problem and Machine Learning Attacks:* Any ADS system based on *machine learning* must additionally cope with two critical challenges. First, machine learning solutions targeted towards learning anomalies suffer from the so-called "small data" problem: assuming that the number of adversarial in-field examples is limited, there is only a small amount of field data exhibiting anomalous behavior. Furthermore, unlike traditional machine learning targets (*e.g.*, recommendation systems), it is generally impossible for security training sets to get progressively sophisticated through accumulation of years of anomaly data. Recent research has shown that it is also possible for an adversary to target the machine learning system itself [3,28], resulting in degradation in prediction accuracy that renders the system useless.

3.2   REDEM Approach and Viability

REDEM addresses the above constraints by exploiting a number of critical observations as described below.

- REDEM on-board Mitigator includes an explicit *Plausibility Checker* to determine whether the mitigation response can potentially compromise safety of the application (see Sect. 4). Consequently, *basic safety* is preserved by construction.
- *We address real-time requirements by separating the training of prediction models from on-road prediction.* The key observation is that the computation-intensive component of the machine learning solutions is in training predictor models to be used in the ADS; once the model is created, detection can be performed within the limited resources of automotive ECUs. Our system

includes a cloud-based methodology for training prediction models, while the on-board architecture is responsible for collecting data and performing real-time prediction.

- *We do not require detailed adversarial model beyond the assumption that the adversary affects V2X communications outlined in our threat model described in Sect.* 3.3. This makes the same approach applicable for diverse connected car applications, *e.g.*, we are applying the same framework for platooning, cooperative route management, and cooperative collision detection. Furthermore, our on-board architecture is designed to account for compatibility with automotive electronic system architectures from the ground up.

- *To address the small data problem, we observe that while the data concerning anomalous behavior is limited, data on normal behavior is typically plentiful.* Consequently, we train prediction algorithms to learn *normal behavior model* (NBM), *i.e.*, the normal (benign) pattern of V2X communications relevant to a connected vehicle application rather than the anomalous behavior; the on-board anomaly detector then operates by calculating the degree of deviation from NBM as a measure of anomaly. Furthermore, the NBM training uses data collected from *all* vehicles with the ADS architecture integrated, in addition to the ego vehicle.

- *We enable resilience against adversarial machine learning attacks by noting that such attacks require sustained, consistent deviation of predicted behavior from actual for a continued period of time.* Consequently, the system can be resilient to the *effects* of such attacks by appropriate choice of prediction parameters such that attacks on prediction system have no perceptible effect on the safety of the application beyond tolerable degradation in performance. Furthermore, the prediction parameters can be tuned to minimize the effects of adversarial machine learning attacks on performance.

3.3   Threat Model and Design Assumptions

We consider connected cooperative applications that make use of V2X communications to augment information obtained from sensors to make various on-road decisions. We assume that the application can still function in the absence of V2X by relying on sensory information alone, albeit with significantly lower efficiency. For example, in Cooperative Adaptive Cruise Control (CACC) [6], the ego vehicle in the absence of V2V messages from the leading car can fall back on Adaptive Cruise Control (ACC), where the basic functionality (*i.e.*, following the leading car at a safe distance) is maintained, albeit at a much higher time headway. One key goal of REDEM is to ensure resiliency while enabling targeted applications to enjoy the higher efficiency induced by V2X as much as possible.

Given our focus on V2X security, our threat model assumes that the attacker can tamper arbitrary V2X messages. This includes (1) message mutation, *i.e.*, arbitrary modification of a V2X message packet while in flight, resulting in either malformed communications or misleading/erroneous messages; (2) denial of delivery of a message packet to its receiver; (3) masquerading as a legitimate vehicular or infrastructure entity; and (4) fabrication and transmission of arbitrary new (legitimate or malformed) message packets. Note that the last component also covers flooding or jamming attacks. Our framework is also oblivious to the source of the attack: it can be a rogue car, a compromised transportation infrastructure component, a compromised V2X mechanism, or an intermediate networking component, *e.g.*, denial of message delivery is possible by compromising the software/hardware component of the ego vehicle or interfering with the communication protocol. We assume that our on-board ADS architecture *in the ego vehicle*, as well as the actuarial/control components it controls, are not compromised. We also assume the sensor data in the ego vehicle (*e.g.*, data captured through radar, LIDAR, camera, etc.) is not compromised. Note that there has been significant work on attacks to automotive sensors; nevertheless, in the context of our approach, assuming fidelity of sensor data is reasonable since it is unlikely that the same adversary can concurrently manipulate both sensor and V2X inputs. Finally, our infrastructure does not require real-time, on-road communication between the ego vehicle and cloud: transfer of trained models and on-road V2X data can be performed periodically offline when the vehicle is connected to secure communication channels.

4   REDEM On-board Architecture

We design the on-board architecture of REDEM with three goals: (1) reusability across different connected car applications, (2) compatibility with existing automotive system architecture, and (3) realizability within the limited computation resources of automotive ECUs. We assume the existence of a cloud-based infrastructure for NBM generation for the targeted applications (which will be considered in Sect. 5).

The key insight behind our on-board design is that the architecture of most connected car features follow a standard template with two major components, a *Decision Computation Module* and an *Actuarial Controller*. Given the sensory and V2X inputs pertaining to the application, the Decision Computation Module computes the desired actuarial actions of the vehicle, and the Actuarial Controller generates the control commands for the actuators. For CACC, [6], the V2X messages for any control cycle t are the intended acceleration/deceleration information $a_{\mathcal{L}}^t$ provided by the leading car $\mathcal{L}$, the sensory information is the distance $d_{\mathcal{E},\mathcal{L}}^t$ between $\mathcal{L}$ and the ego vehicle $\mathcal{E}$, the desired actuarial action is the corresponding response of the ego vehicle, *e.g.*, acceleration $a_{\mathcal{E}}^t$ computed as a function of $a_{\mathcal{L}}^t$ and $d_{\mathcal{E},\mathcal{L}}^t$, and the actuarial controller manipulates the motor output torque and braking pressure to achieve $a_{\mathcal{E}}^t$. REDEM augments this template with additional components to account for resilience of the ego vehicle to malicious V2X communications. Consequently, the same architecture would work on a variety of connected car features with little reconfiguration; and it will be compatible with the on-board system architecture for most emergent autonomous vehicles.

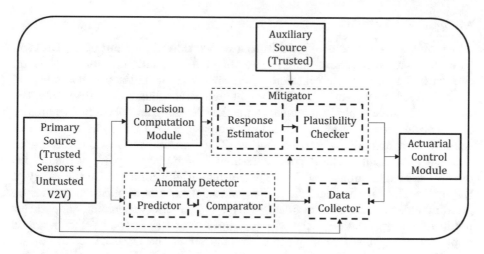

Fig. 1. REDEM on-board architecture. The subsystems bordered with dashed lines are components introduced by REDEM.

Figure 1 provides a high-level view of REDEM on-board architecture. Roughly, it introduces three additional system components (on top of the underlying connected application architecture).

1. *Anomaly Detector* is responsible for detecting suspicious V2X communications;
2. *Mitigator* is responsible for adjusting the actuarial action of the vehicle in response to a detected anomaly; and
3. *Data Collector* captures real-world on-road data for improving prediction accuracy of the anomaly detector and mitigator components.

The data from the *Data Collector* is periodically transferred to trusted cloud server to retrain the machine learning components in Anomaly Detector and Mitigator (*e.g.*, the Predictor and Response Estimator respectively). Recording real-world data in this manner facilitates curating a database of different communication anomalies, eventually improving anomaly detection. The roles of Anomaly Detector and Mitigator are described in more detail below.

Anomaly Detector

The Anomaly detection subsystem comprises of two components, Predictor and Comparator. The Predictor implements a machine learning model trained to learn normal behavior of the Decision Computation Module of a conventional application, as discussed in Sect. 5. The output of the Predictor is compared by the Comparator against the (real) output of the Decision Computation Module. A deviation beyond a pre-defined threshold is classified as an anomaly. If no anomaly is detected, the output of the Decision Computation Module is applied to the vehicle; otherwise, the Mitigator is triggered (see below).

Mitigator

When an anomaly is detected, the Mitigator overrides the output of the Decision Computation Module and computes a different decision that relies solely on the trusted source of information, *viz.*, sensors. It includes two components, Response Estimator and Plausibility Checker. Analogous to the Predictor, the Response Estimator also implements a machine learning model trained to predict the expected response of the Decision Computation Module, but it only uses sensory data in training and prediction. The Plausibility Checker determines whether the output of the Response Estimator, if applied in place of the output of the Decision Computation Module, can potentially compromise the safety of the application. If the check fails (*i.e.*, the safety of the application cannot be guaranteed), then the system falls back to a more conservative, non-cooperative mode of the application; otherwise the output of the Response Estimator is applied by the Mitigator in place of the output of the Decision Computation Module.

5   Prediction Models

The central component of REDEM is the construction of the machine learning models to be used in the predictor (and response estimator). These components are implemented and trained on a trusted cloud platform, and are refined with training data from subscribed vehicles through on-board data collector component. Obviously, the quality of the models, in addition to the training data, depends crucially on the model parameters. The communication pattern among vehicles or between vehicles and infrastructure depends on a variety of parameters, including terrain (*e.g.*, hilly, rural highway, city), time of day or night, ambient weather, etc. Furthermore, there is trade-off between the quality of prediction induced by the model and the complexity of computation and storage requirements induced by a high-precision model.

There is no reason to believe there is a unique, uniform deep learning model that will be suitable across all cooperative connected car applications. Nevertheless, some models can be easily ruled out, *e.g.*, simplistic prediction models that depend on linearity assumptions are clearly unsuitable, and so are highly complex computation-intensive or storage-intensive models which might be difficult to implement within the limited resources of automotive ECUs. For our initial CACC work, we have found a multilayer perceptron (MLP) model sufficient for both the Predictor and the Response Estimator. We suspect that such a model provides the sweet spot between accuracy needs and computation cost for most major applications.

Another key question to address is whether (for a specific application) one unified model NBM is sufficient or whether a different model is necessary for each driving scenario (*e.g.*, terrain, weather, time of day, etc.). If effective prediction requires a custom model for each specific driving scenario, then there must be facility to download/switch models as the vehicle drives from one scenario to another (*e.g.*, moving from highway to city or sunny to cloudy weather).

It would appear that such custom models might have higher accuracy than a single model that has to predict normal behavior under all potential driving scenarios. Consequently, the question of one unified model vis-a-vis custom models for different scenarios might appear to be a trade-off between prediction accuracy and cost of switching. On the other hand, our very recent experiments suggest that this trade-off might actually be spurious. In a recent experiment we found that in fact a single unified model may turn out to be *more accurate* than custom models, at least for some specific applications. The reason for this apparent paradox is that a single global model that predicts normal behavior for all scenarios usually has more in-field data for training, causing it to be a better source of prediction than custom models for different scenarios trained with less data.

6   REDEM Evaluation

The success of research targeted at connected car applications critically depends on effective evaluation framework that enables clear comprehension of the effects of different architectural trade-offs on the resiliency and efficiency of the applications. Roughly, there are two critical requirements in addressing the evaluation needs as described below, *e.g.*, effective adversary models and realistic datasets on vehicle behavior.

– *Adversary Modeling.* As discussed in Sect. 3.1, a key requirement for an automotive resiliency solution is that it must provide protection against the spectrum of (known and unknown) potential adversaries. On the other hand, evaluating this requirement requires developing a set of adversary models that can be justified as comprehensive, and demonstrating the robustness of a proposed solution against this set. Unfortunately, no such comprehensive set of adversaries exist for communication attacks. Indeed, determining adversaries is typically a reactive process: given a specific resiliency solution, one comes up with an adversary to subvert the specific solution. The result of this process is typically a collection of specific "point adversaries". For communication attacks, specific adversaries include masquerade, man-in-the-middle, Sybil, wormhole, etc. However, simply evaluating the solution against a collection of specific, known adversaries does not provide any confidence on its resiliency against unknown, zero-day attacks.
– *Evaluation Platform.* Since autonomous vehicles are complex, safety-critical systems, it is essential to evaluate the performance, safety, and effectiveness of any resiliency solution before deployment. Since REDEM is a machine learning solution, this additionally implies training and evaluation of the proposed prediction models. Unfortunately, this is challenging because of the lack of available datasets. Existing benchmark driving datasets do not comprehensively represent different driving environments, nor do they provide sufficient data corresponding to rare driving scenarios that are particularly important for evaluation of security attacks.

We address the challenges above in REDEM as follows. To address the problem of adversary models, we are developing an adversary taxonomy to enable comprehensive evaluation of the resiliency architecture. The key idea is to eschew specific adversary types (*e.g.*, Sybil, MITM, wormhole, etc.) but focus on adversary capabilities given the threat model of Sect. 3.3. In particular, we classify adversaries along three vectors, *e.g.*, (1) *stealth* or frequency of malicious communication, ranging from independent discrete attacks at very infrequent time instants to a continuous sequence of attacks at each instant over a time interval; (2) the effect of the attack on V2X, *e.g.*, message mutation, injection of fabricated message, delivery prevention; and (3) potential effect on the target vehicle, *e.g.*, accident, string instability, inefficient use of infrastructure, etc. The attack taxonomy incorporates a diverse spectrum of attacks considered in wireless and networking communities, including wormhole, masquerade, misdirection, Sybil, and man-in-the-middle attacks. On the other hand, since the focus of the taxonomy is on *effects* rather than on specific point adversaries, we can be confident that a system demonstrated to be resilient to adversaries across the taxonomy is also resilient against other zero-day adversaries.

In addition to the above classifications, the possibility of adversarial machine learning attacks can be addressed by considering a special class of attacks, which we refer to as *Predictor Subversion Attacks*. These attacks involve an adversary with complete knowledge of the REDEM architecture (including the anomaly detection threshold) and the trained predictor configurations. Predictor subversion attacks can bypass the REDEM's anomaly detection system and go undetected. The application will be considered robust against adversarial machine learning if the Predictor Subversions cannot create a perceptible impact (*e.g.*, compromising safety or loss of efficiency of the cooperative application) on the target vehicle.

We address the problem of evaluation platform by using a physical research simulator. The specific simulator we use in REDEM is RDS1000® (https:// www.faac.com/realtime-technologies), but other physical simulators that provide similar functionalities will also be sufficient. The simulator gives us the flexibility to define and simulate driving environments at a fine detail, and capture realistic driving data pertaining to normal behavior models. Note that we generally need more sophisticated platforms than desktop simulators used in previous research, *e.g.*, VENTOS [5] or Carla (http://carla.org). In particular, RDS1000 enables flexible programming and simulation of virtually any environmental, terrain, or traffic conditions, and any (autonomous) maneuver of the vehicle. Data pertaining to each of these environments can be used for training and testing machine learning components of REDEM. It also enables gathering data that reflects the real-time behavior of a vehicle. Data pertaining to each of these environments can be used for training and testing machine learning components of REDEM. Driving environments are classified based on various major parameters that impact the driving patterns: (i) Road terrain (Highway, Suburban and Urban); (ii) Weather (Clear, Windy, Snowy, Rainy); and (iii) Time of

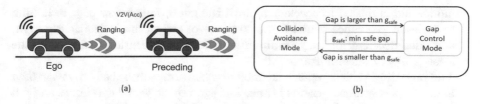

Fig. 2. (a) Represents two vehicles engaged in CACC; (b) represents the modes of operation of a conventional CACC decision computation module.

day (Day, Night). Different combinations are considered with these factors and the environments are simulated accordingly.

7   Case Study: Secure CACC

To determine viability of the REDEM vision, we are realizing it on a specific connected car application, *viz.*, Cooperative Adaptive Cruise Control. CACC forms the basis for several connected car applications such as platooning, cooperative on-ramp merging etc. In CACC, the ego vehicle autonomously adapts its velocity in accordance to the acceleration of the vehicle in front (received through V2V communication), as well as the relative velocity and gap between the two vehicles (obtained from the ranging sensor readings). CACC enables improved road safety and efficiency (*e.g.*, a much smaller headway) compared to its non-cooperative counterpart, Adaptive Cruise Control (ACC) which does not utilize V2V communication.

7.1   CACC Functional Overview

Figure 2(a) depicts vehicles engaged in CACC. Figure 2(b) is used to demonstrate the high-level functionality of a CACC decision computation module implementing a constant time headway policy. The specific CACC implementation considered here [18] targets a constant time headway of 0.55 s from the preceding vehicle. The safety goal of CACC is to maintain a space gap that is greater than a safety threshold g_{safe} computed as a function of relative velocity between the vehicles. CACC operates in two modes: collision avoidance and gap control, based on the instantaneous space gap between the vehicles. The vehicle normally operates in gap control mode where it follows the leading car as closely as possible while maintaining a space gap greater than g_{safe}; if space gap is less than g_{safe}, it switches to collision avoidance mode and the vehicle is decelerated at its maximum value.

Obviously, CACC is susceptible to attacks targeting the V2V communication. Consider the following attack scenarios.

1. The preceding vehicle reports falsified acceleration values that are *higher than actual* for a continued period of time. The ego vehicle operates in gap control

mode, and is misled to accelerate, until the gap g falls below g_{safe} switching to collision avoidance mode. If the speed v_f of the victim is sufficiently high, a sudden deceleration may result in a collision, a precarious skid, or at the least, a highly uncomfortable jolt.

2. The preceding vehicle reports falsified acceleration values that are *lower than actual* for a continued period of time. The ego vehicle would decelerate and fall behind, resulting in degraded fuel efficiency and travel time. In extreme cases, the vehicle might switch to collision avoidance mode, resulting in sudden deceleration, jolt, or even a collision with the vehicles behind.

3. The leading vehicle stops reporting acceleration values completely, or communicates a random sequence of values, with the intent to mislead or confuse the high-level CACC controller of the follower vehicle. One effect could be for the V2V messages to become uncorrelated with the sensor data,e.g., positive acceleration of the leading car accompanied with reduced distance. Depending on the CACC controller implementation, this can result in vehicle stall, sudden deceleration, downgrading of CACC to ACC, etc.

7.2   REDEM for CACC

We developed a realization of REDEM for CACC. Here we discuss some of the initial experimental results from that effort, primarily as a demonstration of viability of REDEM as a means to introduce resiliency in cooperative connected car applications. As shown below, our results are promising. Nevertheless, they should be taken with the caveat that the work is still early at the time of this writing and much more experimentation is necessary to thoroughly vet the REDEM architecture even for this specific application.

Simulation Setup and Training Data Generation

As discussed in Sect. 6, we used a physical automotive simulator for creating the various driving environments and traffic conditions, and recording the necessary data parameters required for training the machine learning based global predictor component. For this analysis, we considered three road parameters (*e.g.*, highway, suburban, and city), four weather parameters (*e.g.*, rain, snow, clear, and windy), and two diurnal parameters (*e.g.*, day and night). A unique model is created and trained for each combination of parameters, resulting in 24 unique models. Each dataset corresponding to about 15 min of driving time and constitutes approximately 90, 000 samples collected at a frequency of 100 Hz. 80% of the data is used to train the machine learning models to learn normal behavior (in each driving environment) while the rest is used for testing and evaluation purposes.

Attack Orchestration

As initial demonstration, we orchestrated a class of simple, independent discrete attacks on the REDEM augmented CACC system. Under these attacks, the ego vehicle receives mutated V2X messages reporting false or anomalous vehicle acceleration values of the preceding vehicle. Discrete samples constituting 30% of

Table 1. Global predictor model accuracy evaluation: testset mean absolute error values

Road infrastructure	Day				Night			
	Rain	Snow	Clear	Windy	Rain	Snow	Clear	Windy
Highway	0.24	0.26	0.27	0.25	0.28	0.19	0.18	0.27
Suburban	0.12	0.29	0.16	0.21	0.18	0.08	0.11	0.23
City	0.08	0.33	0.06	0.02	0.11	0.05	0.16	0.04

Table 2. Anomaly detector accuracy evaluation: % false positives and false negatives

Road infrastructure	Day								Night							
	Rain		Snow		Clear		Windy		Rain		Snow		Clear		Windy	
	%FP	%FN	%FP	%FN	%FP	%FN	%FP	%FN	%FP	%FN	%FP	%FN	%FP	%FN	%FP	%FN
Highway	6.2	0.09	2.11	4.42	4.23	0.92	1.07	5.2	6.4	2.8	0.4	5.9	7.2	5.5	7.4	8.8
Suburban	0.56	0.07	1.1	7.72	2.6	0.65	0.88	2.29	0.62	3.97	2.24	0.95	0.52	3.22	2.23	0.95
City	0.23	0.10	9.59	0.12	0.21	0.22	0	0.15	8.41	0.12	0.11	5.87	0.28	0.17	0.04	1.30

Table 3. Anomaly detector accuracy evaluation: % true positives and true negatives

Road infrastructure	Day								Night							
	Rain		Snow		Clear		Windy		Rain		Snow		Clear		Windy	
	%TP	%TN	%TP	%TN	%TP	%TN	%TP	%TN	%TP	%TN	%TP	%TN	%TP	%TN	%TP	%TN
Highway	93.78	99	97.88	95.57	95.77	99.07	98	94.8	93.6	97.2	99.6	94.1	92.8	94.5	92.6	91.2
Suburban	99.43	99.92	98.89	92.27	97.39	99.35	99.11	97.7	99.38	96.02	97.76	99.05	99.48	96.77	97.76	99.05
City	99.77	99.90	90.41	99.87	99.79	99.77	100	99.85	91.59	99.87	99.88	94.12	99.71	99.82	99.96	98.7

the evaluation data are selected at random and a bias is added to the acceleration values such that the resultant headway between the two vehicles becomes smaller than the safe limit or large enough to cause inefficiency and string instability in the traffic.

Results

We evaluate the predictor models trained on data collected from each driving environment. The resiliency of REDEM depends both on the accuracy of the Predictor and the choice detection threshold of the Comparator. Table 1 shows the predictor accuracy indicated by the deviation from the expected acceleration prediction under normal operating conditions in the absence of malicious activity. The low mean absolute error indicates that the predictor models closely estimate the acceleration output of a conventional CACC Decision Computation Module. The Predictor accuracy under anomalous conditions are shown in Tables 2 and 3. False positive and false negative percentages indicate the percentage of normal samples falsely captured as anomalies and vice versa. Note that REDEM even with this initial realization still achieves a prediction accuracy of about 95%.

8   Conclusion and Future Work

With the trend towards increasing autonomy of automotive systems, cooperative connected applications will become increasingly crucial, together with the need to introduce resiliency in such applications against potential subversions targeting V2X communications. Clearly, a reactive approach to security, *i.e.*, point solutions/patches incrementally fixing the system as newer and newer attacks are discovered, is not viable in this space. In this paper we have introduced a novel vision for introducing resiliency in connected car applications, by providing an architecture to augment the application design with generic components. The architecture is reusable over different connected car applications, can be implemented within the computational/storage constraints induced by automotive systems, and can support real-time detection and mitigation. We have also introduced evaluation mechanisms to evaluate the viability of such resiliency architecture over a wide class of adversaries and driving scenarios. We provided initial evidence of viability of the approach in introducing resiliency in CACC.

Nevertheless, we have only scratched the surface of this vast research area. Even in the realization of REDEM in CACC, much evaluation is left to be done, *e.g.*, viability over the spectrum of attacks in our adversary taxonomy, efficiency of the models defined, effectiveness of the approach against a variety of adversarial machine learning attacks, quality of the dataset generated through our driving simulator, etc. Furthermore, we will work on realizing REDEM for other cooperative applications and consider extending it for scenarios where the sensor system (in addition to V2X) is compromised.

References

1. Cybersecurity for Autonomous Vehicle Platooning. https://digitalcommons.usu.edu/cgi/viewcontent.cgi?article=1559&context=researchweek
2. Abdollahi Biron, Z., Dey, S., Pisu, P.: Real-time detection and estimation of denial of service attack in connected vehicle systems. IEEE Trans. Intell. Transp. Syst. **19**(12), 3893–3902 (2018)
3. Akhtar, N., Mian, A.: Threat of adversarial attacks on deep learning in computer vision: a survey. IEEE Access **6**, 1441–14430 (2018)
4. Alheeti, K.M.A., Al-Ani, M.S., McDonald-Maier, K.: A hierarchical detection method in external communication for self-driving vehicles based on TDMA. PLoS ONE **13**(1), e0188760 (2018)
5. Amoozadeh, M., Deng, H., Chuah, C.-N., Zhang, H.M., Ghosal, D.: Platoon management with cooperative adaptive cruise control enabled by VANET. Veh. Commun. **2**(2), 110–123 (2015)
6. Aygun, B., Lin, C.-W., Shiraishi, S., Wyglinski, A.: Selective message relaying for multi-hopping vehicular networks. In: IEEE Vehicular Networking Conference, pp. 1–8 (2016)

7. Aygun, B., Lin, C.-W., Shiraishi, S., Wyglinski, A.M.: Selective message relaying for multi-hopping vehicular networks. In: 2016 IEEE Vehicular Networking Conference (VNC), pp. 1–8. IEEE (2016)

8. Bergenhem, C., Pettersson, H., Coelingh, E., Englund, C., Shladover, S., Tsugawa, S.: Overview of platooning systems. In: 19th ITS World Congress (2012)

9. Bergenhem, C., Shladover, S., Coelingh, E., Englund, C., Tsugawa, S.: Overview of platooning systems. In: Proceedings of the 19th ITS World Congress, Vienna, Austria, 22–26 October 2012 (2012)

10. Berger, I., Rieke, R., Kolomeets, M., Chechulin, A., Kotenko, I.: Comparative study of machine learning methods for in-vehicle intrusion detection. In: Katsikas, S.K., et al. (eds.) SECPRE/CyberICPS -2018. LNCS, vol. 11387, pp. 85–101. Springer, Cham (2019). https://doi.org/10.1007/978-3-030-12786-2_6

11. Checkoway, S., et al.: Comprehensive experimental analyses of automotive attack surfaces. In: USENIX Security Symposium, San Francisco, vol. 4 (2011)

12. Du, L., Chen, S., Han, L.: Coordinated online in-vehicle navigation guidance based on routing game theory. Transp. Res. Rec.: J. Transp. Res. Board **2497**, 106–116 (2015)

13. Du, L., Chen, S., Han, L.: Coordinated online in-vehicle navigation guidance based on routing game theory. Transp. Res. Rec. **2497**(1), 106–116 (2015)

14. Du, L., Han, L., Li, X.: Distributed coordinated in-vehicle online routing under mixed strategy congestion game. Transp. Res. Part B: Methodol. **67**, 235–252 (2014)

15. Dutta, R.G., Yu, F., Zhang, T., Hu, Y., Jin, Y.: Security for safety: a path toward building trusted autonomous vehicles. In: 2018 IEEE/ACM International Conference on Computer-Aided Design (ICCAD), pp. 1–6, November 2018

16. Dutta, R.G., Yu, F., Zhang, T., Hu, Y., Jin, Y.: Security for safety: a path toward building trusted autonomous vehicles. In: Proceedings of the International Conference on Computer-Aided Design, p. 92. ACM (2018)

17. Hempfield, C.: Why a Cybersecurity Solution for Driverless Cars May be Found Under the Hood (2017). https://techcrunch.com/2017/02/18/why-a-cybersecurity-solution-for-driverless-cars-may-be-found-under-the-hood

18. Jagielski, M., Jones, N., Lin, C., Nita-Rotaru, C., Shiraishi, S.: Threat detection in collaborative adaptive cruise control in connected cars. In: WISEC, pp. 184–189 (2018)

19. Jagielski, M., Jones, N., Lin, C.-W., Nita-Rotaru, C., Shiraishi, S.: Threat detection for collaborative adaptive cruise control in connected cars. In: Proceedings of the 11th ACM Conference on Security & Privacy in Wireless and Mobile Networks, pp. 184–189. ACM (2018)

20. Kang, M.-J., Kang, J.-W.: Intrusion detection system using deep neural network for in-vehicle network security. PLoS ONE **11**(6), e0155781 (2016)

21. Koscher, K., et al.: Experimental security analysis of a modern automobile. In: 2010 IEEE Symposium on Security and Privacy, pp. 447–462. IEEE (2010)

22. Levi, M., Allouche, Y., Kontorovich, A.: Advanced analytics for connected car cybersecurity. In: 2018 IEEE 87th Vehicular Technology Conference (VTC Spring), pp. 1–7 (2018)

23. Lin, Y.-T., Hsu, H., Lin, S.-C., Lin, C.-W., Jiang, I.H.-R., Liu, C.: Graph-based modeling, scheduling, and verification for intersection management of intelligent vehicles. ACM Trans. Embed. Comput. Syst. (TECS) **18**(5s), 95 (2019)

24. Madry, A., Makelov, A., Schmidt, L., Tsipras, D., Vladu, A.: Towards deep learning models resistant to adversarial attacks. arXiv, abs/1706.06083 (2018)

25. Miller, C., Valasek, C.: A survey of remote automotive attack surfaces. Black Hat USA 2014, p. 94 (2014)
26. Miller, C., Valasek, C.: Remote exploitation of an unaltered passenger vehicle. Black Hat USA 2015, p. 91 (2015)
27. National Highway Traffic Safety Association. Road Accidents in USA. https://www.recalls.gov/nhtsa.html
28. Papernot, N., McDaniel, P., Jha, S., Fredrikson, M., Celik, Z.B., Swami, A.: The limitations of deep learning in adversarial settings. In: IEEE European Symposium on Security and Privacy (2016)
29. Sayin, M.O., Lin, C.-W., Shiraishi, S., Shen, J., Basar, T.: Information-driven autonomous intersection control via incentive compatible mechanisms. IEEE Trans. Intell. Transp. Syst. **20**(3), 912–924 (2019)
30. Tian, Y., Pei, K., Jana, S., Ray, B.: Deeptest: automated testing of deep-neural-network-driven autonomous cars. In: Proceedings of the 40th International Conference on Software Engineering, ICSE 2018, pp. 303–314 (2018)
31. Tiwari, A., et al.: Safety envelope for security. In: Proceedings of the 3rd International Conference on High Confidence Networked Systems, HiCoNS 2014, pp. 85–94 (2014)
32. Uricár, M., Krízek, P., Hurych, D., Sobh, I., Yogamani, S., Denny, P.: Yes, we GAN: applying adversarial techniques for autonomous driving. CoRR, abs/1902.03442 (2019)
33. Zhang, H., Chen, H., Song, Z., Boning, D., Dhillon, I., Hsieh, C.-J.: The limitations of adversarial training and the blind-spot attack. In: International Conference on Learning Representations (2019)

Trust in IoT Devices: A Logic Encryption Perspective

Yasaswy Kasarabada$^{(\boxtimes)}$, David Luria, and Ranga Vemuri

Digital Design Environments Laboratory, University of Cincinnati,
Cincinnati, OH, USA
{kasarayv,luriadm}@mail.uc.edu, vemurir@ucmail.uc.edu

Abstract. Tremendous technological advancement has led to the development of an ecosystem of highly connected ubiquitous computing devices called the Internet of Things (IoT). Considering the sensitive nature of the data collected by the IoT devices, it is essential to ensure the security of these devices. Logic encryption is a popular design-for-trust technique used for protection against hardware IP piracy, design counterfeiting, and hardware Trojan insertion. The introduction of various attack methods that leverage vulnerabilities in known logic encryption techniques has prompted the development of new techniques able to thwart the proposed attacks. Major research effort in the field of logic encryption focuses on increasing resilience to known and potential attacks while often ignoring considerations of cost overhead, especially die area and power consumed. Since area and power optimization are key aspects in the design and development of most IoT devices, it is important to evaluate the cost incurred by logic encryption schemes, especially in the context of these two metrics. In this paper, we survey some of the most popular logic encryption and decryption techniques proposed in the past decade. An analysis of the area and power overhead of these logic encryption techniques using several standard benchmark circuits is presented to assess their suitability for resource constrained systems.

Keywords: Logic encryption · Internet of Things · Trust · Security

1 Introduction

The proliferation of ubiquitous computing devices has led to the creation of a densely connected global network - IoT. Many of these devices (like wearable technology) continuously measure and transmit sensitive and critical data. Therefore, it becomes essential to incorporate a security mechanism into the device to protect against prospective attack scenarios. Implementation of traditional cryptographic algorithms that are effective against cyber attacks is typically not light-weight, an important requirement for the resource-constrained IoT devices. Hardware-based security measures like logic encryption are suitable

© IFIP International Federation for Information Processing 2020
Published by Springer Nature Switzerland AG 2020
A. Casaca et al. (Eds.): IFIPIoT 2019, IFIP AICT 574, pp. 123–141, 2020.
https://doi.org/10.1007/978-3-030-43605-6_8

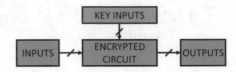

Fig. 1. Overview of logic encryption

alternatives for protecting IoT devices against foundry based attacks like reverse engineering, counterfeiting, and piracy.

Logic encryption is a hardware protection technique that locks the design functionality using a set of newly introduced inputs called *key inputs*. An overview of logic encryption is shown in Fig. 1. If the correct logic value (chosen by the designer) is applied on the key inputs, the design behaves as expected. An incorrect key value causes corruption of the input-output relationship of the circuit. Figure 2 shows a simple encryption scheme. Initial logic encryption schemes [14] proposed to insert these key-controlled gates (*key gates*) randomly into the circuit. This technique was shown to be susceptible to an attack method [12] that was able to sensitize wrong key values to primary outputs. Subsequently, encryption techniques [6,9,32] that focused on increasing the dependency between the key gates were proposed to thwart the sensitization attack. An oracle-guided Boolean Satisfiability (SAT) based attack [20], that uses a SAT-solver to iteratively eliminate multiple incorrect key values to obtain the correct key assignment, was able to defeat many previously proposed logic encryption methods.

The advent of the SAT-based attack led to the proposal of various SAT-resilient techniques [10,24,29,30,33,34]. By inserting SAT-hard blocks, these techniques ensured that the attack was unable to eliminate more than a limited number of incorrect keys per iteration, leading to extremely long, unfeasible attack times. Other SAT-resilient techniques [13,17] focused on preventing the SAT attack from modelling the circuit by introducing key controlled feedback cycles into the design. Although the proposed SAT-resilient schemes were able to defeat the original SAT attack, they were found to be susceptible to other attack methods like approximate-SAT [16], cyclic-SAT [35], removal [31], and bypass [27].

The original SAT attack [20] could directly be applied to sequential circuits if the flip-flops were accessible using scan-chains. It has been asserted in recent works [18] that disabling the scan-chains after the testing procedure is relatively inexpensive. Without a scan-accessible oracle circuit, the traditional SAT attack cannot be applied directly to sequential circuits. Therefore, new unrolling-based SAT attack methods [4,7,18] to decrypt sequential circuits have been proposed. These techniques have been successful in defeating popular sequential logic encryption techniques [3,5,7].

Research in the field of logic encryption primarily focuses on finding new attack methods that are able to defeat known encryption schemes and new defense techniques to thwart proposed attacks. Evaluation of cost metrics such

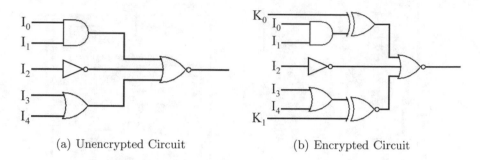

(a) Unencrypted Circuit   (b) Encrypted Circuit

Fig. 2. Logic encryption with key gates

as penalties on IC performance (timing, area, and power) and impact on testing (test coverage and testability) are often overlooked and rarely mentioned in the literature. Application of popular encryption techniques to resource-starved IoT devices must be undertaken after an assessment of (1) the level of security offered by these techniques, and (2) the cost incurred by their implementation. This paper aims to assist in this assessment by performing an analysis of the impact of many popular logic encryption techniques on two important cost parameters - area and power. Selected, well-known combinational and sequential logic encryption techniques are implemented on benchmark circuits from the ISCAS '85 and ITC '99 suites respectively to obtain an estimate of the area and power overhead of these schemes.

The rest of the paper is organized as follows. Section 2 discusses some of the salient features of many popular logic encryption techniques. Major attack methods are summarized in Sect. 3. Resiliency of encryption techniques described in Sect. 2 against these attacks is presented in Sect. 4. Section 5 discusses our analysis of the cost (area and power) incurred by the implementation of these proposed techniques using standard benchmark circuits. Section 6 presents the conclusions derived from this work.

2   Logic Encryption Techniques

In this section, we describe several logic encryption methods proposed over the past decade. We begin by discussing traditional encryption schemes, that are vulnerable to the SAT attack, followed by the SAT-resilient techniques. Finally, we detail the sequential encryption methods and some of their important features.

1. **EPIC** [14] proposed to lock the design by inserting key controlled XOR/ XNOR gates coupled with inverters into the circuit. These gates are placed on randomly chosen nets in the circuit while avoiding critical paths. If the wrong key value is applied on any key gate, its output is inverted. Since the attacker does not know if the inverter is a part of the original design or a part of the added locking mechanism, using a direct reverse engineering attack to infer the key values may be unsuccessful.

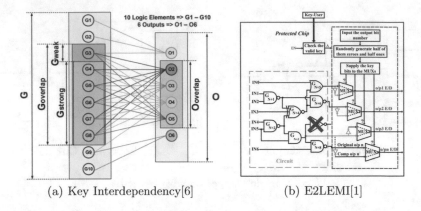

(a) Key Interdependency[6]   (b) E2LEMI[1]

Fig. 3. Traditional logic encryption techniques

2. The **Logic Cone Size based scheme** [11] was proposed as a technique to design a well-obfuscated hardware Trojan. Inserting key gates on nets with large fan-in and fan-out cones is advocated to avoid graph isomorphism-based equivalency attacks. Using a weighted normalized metric [2] for all gates in the design, suitable locations for key gate insertion can be chosen.

3. **Strong Logic Locking** [32] focuses on intelligent insertion of key controlled gates by evaluating two important metrics - *pairwise security* and *dominance*. Two key gates are considered to be pairwise secure if the key value on any one of these key gates cannot be sensitized to a primary output without knowing the correct key value on the other key gate. Meanwhile, a key gate lying on any path from another key gate to any primary output is said to dominate the other key gate. The key gates are inserted such that each key gate is pairwise secure with at least one other key gate. Additionally, a one-way random function like AES is used with a subset of the in-memory key acting as its input while its output is fed to some of the key gates.

4. The **Key Interdependency based technique** [6] uses a three-step pruning process to obtain a set of gates that are considered ideal locations for key gate insertion. The first step involves finding a set of gates (G_{strong}) with the largest number of primary outputs ($O_{overlap}$) in the combined output cone of dependency of G_{strong}, as shown in Fig. 3(a). Following this, the fault impact metric $FI(g) = NoP_0 \cdot NoO_0 + NoP_1 \cdot NoO_1$ for each gate g ($\in G_{strong}$) is calculated using 10000 random input patterns, where NoP_i ($i \in \{0, 1\}$) is the number of input patterns that are able to sensitize a stuck-at-i fault at g to a primary output and NoO_i ($i \in \{0, 1\}$) is the total number of outputs that are affected by the sensitization of the stuck-a-i fault at g. A dependency graph, constructed with $O_{overlap}$ and the set of gates (G_{oc}) with highest FI values, is used to calculate the *dependency* metric for each gate in G_{oc}. The gates with the highest dependency values are chosen and key gates are inserted at the inputs of these gates. The motivation behind

this techniques is to increase the overlap in output cones of dependency of the added key gates while ensuring maximum interference between them.

5. A light-weight logic encryption method called **Hardware Enlightening** [15] was proposed to thwart the insertion of hardware Trojans [23] into the design. To avoid detection during the testing procedure, nets with low controllability/observability values are chosen as trigger signals for the Trojan. The encryption algorithm begins by finding nets with low probability values. For each of these signals, a key controlled XOR/XNOR gate is added on the fan-in signal with the lowest probability value and adequate slack time. After the addition of a key gate, the probability values of all nets in the circuit are re-calculated and the process is repeated for the next low probability signal. To avoid direct reverse engineering attacks, an inverter is inserted at the output of the key gate based on a hidden signature (generated by the designer).

6. To reduce power consumption, the **Energy-Efficient Logic Encryption using Multiplexer Insertion (E2LEMI)** [1] proposed to insert multiplexers on all primary outputs of the circuit with the output nets serving as the 'correct' inputs to the multiplexer while the inverted output nets are fed as the 'incorrect' inputs, as shown in Fig. 3(b). The select input of each multiplexer is connected to the output of a linear feedback shift register (LFSR) designed to produce an output pattern with equal number of 0s and 1s. A hardware Trojan based circuit is inserted into the design to check if the correct key value is applied. On the application of an incorrect key, the payload activates the LFSR which feeds half the multiplexer select inputs with 0s and the rest with 1s. Therefore, half the multiplexer's select the correct output values while the rest select inverted output values, thus achieving 50% Hamming distance from the correct output. If the correct key is provided, the Trojan deactivates the LFSR and the correct select pattern is provided to the multiplexers such that the outputs of the design hold the correct value.

7. A part of the first wave of SAT-resilient techniques, **SARLock** [29] focuses on thwarting the SAT attack by making the attack time exponentially large. A comparator block is inserted into the circuit to compare the applied key value with the value on the inputs of a chosen logic cone. The comparator output is connected to an XOR gate placed on the output of the chosen logic cone to ensure that the output of the logic cone is corrupted when the key value is the same as the value on the input of the logic cone. Since this is undesirable for the correct key, a masking block is used to invert the output of the comparator when the correct key is applied and the comparator output is high. Since the output of the comparator becomes high for only one input vector per key value, the error rate of the encrypted circuit is very low. This could lead to the attacker using the encrypted netlist with a wrong key assignment for $2^k - 1$ input patterns, where k is the number of key inputs. To avoid this scenario, the authors propose to use this technique in conjunction with traditional (potentially SAT vulnerable) encryption schemes. Such a compound scheme ensures high error rates due to the traditional scheme

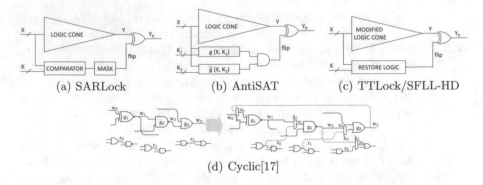

(a) SARLock   (b) AntiSAT   (c) TTLock/SFLL-HD

(d) Cyclic[17]

Fig. 4. SAT-resilient logic encryption techniques

and boasts SAT-resilience due to the SARLock instance. An overview of SARLock is shown in Fig. 4(a).

8. Similar to SARLock, **Anti-SAT** [24] also uses a point function to make the SAT attack infeasible. The construction of the point function in Anti-SAT is achieved using two logic blocks operating on the same set of inputs (of the chosen logic cone) and locked with two different key inputs. The function implemented by each logic block is a complement of the function of the other logic block. When the output of both logic blocks is 1, the output of the Anti-SAT block turns high and flips the output of the chosen logic cone, thus enforcing corruption. The functions of the complementary logic blocks are chosen such that when the correct key value is applied, the output of the Anti-SAT block does not go high for any input value. If an incorrect key is applied, the output of the Anti-SAT block goes high for at most one input pattern. To increase the error rate of the encrypted circuit, Anti-SAT can be used in a compound scheme with a traditional encryption technique. Figure 4(b) shows a high-level representation of Anti-SAT.

9. In **TTLock** [34], a secret input value, called *Protected Input Pattern* (PIP), is removed from the chosen logic cone such that when the PIP is applied to the cone, the output is inverted. A restoration block is added to the circuit as shown in Fig. 4(c). When the input pattern is equal to the applied key value, the output of the restoration block goes high. For all incorrect key values $\vec{K_i}$ ($\neq PIP$), the output of the modified logic cone is incorrect for two input patterns - the PIP and $\vec{X_i}$, where $\vec{X_i} = \vec{K_i}$. For the correct key value $\vec{K_C}$ ($=PIP$), the output of the modified logic cone is inverted when the PIP occurs, thus obtaining the correct output value. Although the error rate for TTLock is higher than that of SARLock/Anti-SAT, it is still very low. Therefore, it is still advisable to use TTLock as a part of a compound scheme.

10. In **Stripped-Functionality Logic Locking (SFLL-HD)** [33], similar to TTLock, the logic cone is modified and a restore logic is used to restore the output of the modified cone when the correct key value is applied. However,

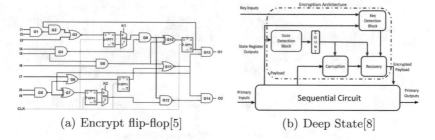

(a) Encrypt flip-flop[5]   (b) Deep State[8]

Fig. 5. Sequential logic encryption techniques

unlike TTLock, SFLL-HD^h inverts the output of the logic cone for multiple
PIPs, where the Hamming distance between each PIP and the k-bit secret
key is h. The restore block checks if the Hamming distance between the
value on the input of the logic cone and the applied key is equal to h and
inverts the output of the modified logic cone if this condition is satisfied.
This technique can protect as many as $\binom{k}{h}$ input patterns.

11. Unlike all SAT-resilient schemes discussed so far, **Cyclic obfuscation** [17]
    focuses on thwarting the SAT attack by impairing the ability of the SAT
    solver in finding a suitable assignment for the input vector. To achieve this,
    combinational feedback cycles are introduced into the design that are acti-
    vated on the application of an incorrect key value. 'Hard' irreducible loops
    with at least two removable edges are used to increase the effort of an attacker
    trying to remove the added cycles. As illustrated in Fig. 4(d), a key controlled
    MUX is added on each edge (net) of these hard loops. Additionally, each
    reducible loop is made irreducible to make the identification and removal of
    the loop using depth first traversal (DFT) non-trivial.

12. **SRCLock** [13] aims at increasing the attack time by densely connecting
    all feedback cycles introduced by Cyclic obfuscation. Several techniques are
    proposed to significantly increase the number of cycles in the netlist. One of
    these techniques focuses on creating *super cycles* out of smaller *micro cycles*,
    such as the ones generated in cyclic obfuscation. The algorithm focuses on
    generating super cycles by strongly connecting all micro cycles with two-way
    signals between micro cycle nets. Additionally, signals in micro cycles that
    are not used to connect a super cycle are used in two-way connections with
    other unused micro cycle signals or random signals in their fan-in cone. This
    method results in a set of strongly connected micro cycles and an exponential
    increase in the number of overall cycles with a linear increase in the number
    of inserted feedback edges.

13. A gate-level sequential logic encryption technique, **Encrypt Flip-Flop** [5]
    proposes to add key-controlled MUXes on the outputs of scan-chain acces-
    sible flip-flops, as shown in Fig. 5(a). The non-select inputs of each MUX
    are connected to the Q and $\overline{Q}$ outputs of the preceding flip-flop. If an incor-
    rect key value is applied to the MUX, the incorrect output of the flip-flop is
    passed on to the next level on the following clock-edge. A placement strategy

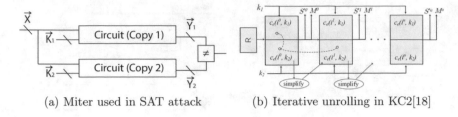

(a) Miter used in SAT attack   (b) Iterative unrolling in KC2[18]

Fig. 6. Logic decryption techniques

similar to the one used in the Key Interdependency technique is followed to increase the overlap in the output cone of dependency of the key gates.

14. Similar to Encrypt Flip-Flop, the **Chain Based Encryption** [7], dictates the placement strategy of key gates, based on the relative position of the flip-flops in the design. Following an analysis of the unrolling-based Sequential SAT attack, the authors argue that encrypting long flip-flop chains ensures that the attacker needs to unroll the design for more number of clock cycles, thus increasing the complexity of the attack process. The depreciation in protection offered by the scheme when encrypting chains with large fan-out (*sneak paths*) leading outside the chain is discussed. The ensuing algorithm recommends the placement of key gates at the inputs of flip-flops with maximum distance from the nearest primary output.

15. **Deep State Encryption** [8] is a SAT-resilient gate-level scheme that incorporates a technique conceptually similar to a hardware Trojan to induce locking on the design. Two unique Monte Carlo methods are proposed to estimate a *deep state* in the design, where depth is the minimum distance (in clock cycles) from the reset state. On a chosen fixed number of occurrences of the deep state, the payload is corrupted by inverting the logic value on these signals. The corrupted signals are inverted back using a restoration block if the correct key value is applied. If an incorrect key value is applied, the payload stays corrupted and the key checking mechanism is disabled, thus forcing the design into a corrupt state forever. Figure 5(b) gives an overview of the proposed encryption architecture.

3 Logic Decryption Strategies

Over the past decade, many innovative decryption techniques against logic encryption have been proposed. In this section, we discuss notable properties of some of the most widely cited attack methods.

1. One of the first oracle guided attacks, the goal of the **Key Sensitization attack** [12] is to decipher the correct key assignment by sensitizing wrong key bits to primary outputs for observation. This is similar to the ATPG technique of sensitizing a stuck-at-fault on a net to the primary output. After finding a suitable input pattern to sensitize the required key bit, the output

pattern from the encrypted circuit is compared with the output from an oracle circuit (acquired from the market) to eliminate an incorrect value on the key bit. Iteratively all incorrect values are identified to derive the correct key assignment.

2. The **SAT attack** [20] uses a SAT solver to satisfy the Quantified Boolean Formula (QBF) of a model of a miter of two encrypted circuits (as shown in Fig. 6(a)). Each copy of the circuit in the miter is assigned unique keys ($\vec{K}_1$ and $\vec{K}_2$) to obtain the initial QBF, $F = C(\vec{X}, \vec{K}_1, \vec{Y}_1) \wedge C(\vec{X}, \vec{K}_2, \vec{Y}_2)$, where $\vec{X}$ is the input vector and $\vec{Y}_1$, $\vec{Y}_2$ are the output vectors. This QBF is solved by the SAT solver with an additional condition that the two output vectors must be different ($\vec{Y}_1 \neq \vec{Y}_2$) to obtain an assignment on the input vector $\vec{X}_d$, called a *distinguishing input pattern* (DIP). The DIP is applied to the oracle IC to obtain the correct output vector $\vec{Y}_d$. Either one or both the keys can be eliminated by comparing $\vec{Y}_d$ with $\vec{Y}_1$ and $\vec{Y}_2$. Additionally, all keys that result in the incorrect output(s), $\vec{Y}_1$ and/or $\vec{Y}_2$, on the application of $\vec{X}_d$ are also eliminated using this DIP. This process is continued to iteratively eliminate all incorrect key values to obtain the correct key assignment.

3. Proposed as a countermeasure to point-function based SAT-resilient schemes, **AppSAT** [16] aims to find a key assignment for which the output corruption is very low. It uses intermediate error estimation and random query reinforcement to optimize the run time of the SAT attack. After every d DIP queries, error ε is estimated using r random queries and the attack is stopped if ε stays below a chosen threshold. The disagreeing inputs from the error estimation process are added to the QBF as additional constraints. Using this strategy, AppSAT assists in the convergence of the SAT solver when stuck in point-functions.

4. **CycSAT** [35] overcomes the disability of the SAT solver in finding a satisfiable assignment for a QBF when the model of the circuit is not a directed acyclic graph (DAG), such as in the presence of key-controlled feedback cycles. A pre-processing step that identifies key conditions resulting in the creation of these feedback cycles is performed. These conditions, expressed in the Conjunctive Normal Form (CNF), are added to the QBF before the SAT solver is invoked. The added cycle avoidance clauses make the QBF satisfiable, thus enabling the solver in finding a suitable key assignment.

5. **Removal attacks** [31] use structural and functional analysis of the netlist to strip away the SAT-resilience of the circuit. The *Signal Probability Skew* (SPS) attack calculates the probability skew ($P(1) - 0.5$) of each net in the circuit to identify the highly skewed outputs of point-function based SAT-resilient blocks. Once identified, these nets are broken and are set to their respective skew value, thus nullifying the protection offered by the SAT-hard blocks. The *AppSAT Guided Removal* (AGR) attack uses AppSAT to first identify the key bits belonging to the SAT-resilient locking block. Next, a structural analysis starting from these key bits reveals the output of the SAT-resilient block, which is then removed.

Table 1. Logic encryption resiliency matrix

	Sens. [12]	SAT [20]	AppSAT [16]	CycSAT [35]	Removal [31]	SeqSAT [7]	KC2 [18]
Random [14]	✗	✗				✗	✗
LCB [11]	✗	✗					
SLL [32]	✓	✗					
KeyDep [6]	✓	✗					
AntiHT [15]	✓	✗					
E2LEMI [1]	✓	✗					
SARLock* [29]	✓	✓	✗		✗		
AntiSAT* [24]	✓	✓	✗		✗/†		
TTLock* [34]	✓	✓	≈		✓		
SFLL* [33]	✓	✓	✓		✓		
Cyclic [17]	✓	✓		✗	✓		
SRCLock [13]	✓	✓		≈	✓		
EFF [5]	✓				✓	✗	?
CBE [7]	†				✓	✗	?
DSE [8]	✓				≈	✓	?

✓ Denotes resilience, † Denotes potential resilience
✗ Denotes susceptibility, ≈ Denotes potential susceptibility
? Denotes unknown, * Denotes compound scheme with SLL

6. To attack encrypted sequential circuits, an unrolling based **Sequential SAT attack** [7] has been proposed. In this technique, the attacker unrolls the encrypted design S_e and the unencrypted design S_o for an iteratively increasing number of clock cycles (unr) to obtain equivalent combinational circuits C_e^{unr} and C_o^{unr}. These circuits are decrypted using the combinational SAT attack to obtain a key assignment $\vec{K}_C^{unr}$. The correctness of the obtained key is checked by applying a sufficiently large number of input vectors to S_e (mounted on an FPGA) and comparing the outputs with the outputs of S_o. When a correct key assignment is obtained, the algorithm stops and returns $\vec{K}_C^{unr}$ as the correct key. Note that the combinational SAT attack [20] can be applied directly to sequential circuits if the flip-flops in the design are scan-accessible. However, recent works have shown that the scan-access pin can either be disabled (by burning a fuse) or obfuscated (using additional key gates). In such a scenario, the flip-flops in the oracle IC are no longer scan-accessible for the attacker to launch the combinational SAT attack.

7. A more powerful attack on encrypted sequential circuits, **KC2** [18] combines a traditional sequential SAT attack [4] with several dynamic optimization techniques to implement a faster deobfuscation method. This technique uses incremental SAT solving along with BDD/SAT-based key condition sweeping, conversion of key-conditions to BDDs, and negative key-condition crunching while avoiding unnecessary clause inflation to boast a speedup in decryption times of up to two orders of magnitude in comparison to previous methods [4]. Experimental results have demonstrated the success of KC2 against random XOR/XNOR locking techniques.

4   Attack Resiliency of Encryption Schemes

In this section we evaluate the resiliency of the logic encryption schemes discussed in this paper against the attack methods from the previous section. Table 1 summarizes the resiliency analysis presented in this section.

1. **EPIC (Random)** - Due to the random key gate placement, EPIC is susceptible to the key sensitization attack and all SAT-based attacks.

2. **LCB** - Although the insertion of key gates on nets with large fan-in and fan-out cones is able to thwart graph equivalence based attacks, this scheme is susceptible to the sensitization attack since no requirement is placed on the interference between the key gates. Additionally the absence of SAT-hard instances makes it vulnerable to the SAT-based attacks.

3. **SLL** - Since the key gate placement strategy in SLL ensures maximum interference between each pair of key gates, the sensitization attack is unable to propagate an incorrect key value to a primary output without knowing the correct assignment on all interfering key gates. Also it is claimed that due to the presence of the AES block, the SAT-based attacks would not be able to determine the in-memory key (AES input) by determining the value at the inputs of the key gates (AES output). However, it has been asserted that AES blocks are highly recognizable and hence prone to removal.

4. **Key Interdependency** - This technique ensures large overlap between inserted key gates, in terms of affected primary outputs, thus thwarting the logic cone based attack [9]. Also, selecting nets with large fault impact values greatly increases the effort in sensitizing a wrong key value to the primary outputs. However, since this technique only dictates the placement strategy of the key gates, a metric that does not directly affect the complexity of the SAT attack, it is vulnerable to all SAT-based attacks.

5. **Hardware Enlightening** - By improving the probability values of low probability nets, this technique increases the effort in finding suitable locations in the netlist to insert a hardware Trojan. Also, the authors have shown that with sufficiently large key values, a 50% Hamming distance between the correct output value and the incorrect values can be achieved. Absence of SAT-hard instances makes this technique vulnerable to SAT-based attacks.

6. **E2LEMI** - Since each incorrect key activates the LFSR and corrupts the primary outputs, potentially a single DIP can be used to eliminate the entire equivalence class of incorrect keys to obtain the correct key assignment using the SAT attack. Additionally, insertion of MUXes directly on the primary outputs makes this technique prone to a reverse engineering attack that is capable of removing the MUXes and rendering the circuit defenseless.

7. **SARLock** - When used in conjunction with SLL, the resultant compound scheme is able to thwart the sensitization attack as well as the SAT attack. The SAT attack is able to eliminate at most one key per DIP, thus requiring 2^k-1 DIPs to obtain the correct key value, where k is the number of key inputs. Newer attack methods like AppSAT and Removal are able to identify the key bits associated with the point function and can either ensure that

the SAT solver does not get stuck solving the point function or can remove the SAT-resilient block.

8. **AntiSAT** - Similar to SARLock, a compound scheme of Anti-SAT and SLL is able to defeat sensitization and SAT attacks while being susceptible to AppSAT and Removal attacks. Improvement to the Anti-SAT architecture [26] using wire entanglement and design withholding has been successful in thwarting the Removal attack.

9. **TTLock** - In addition to being resilient to the SAT attack, the modification of the logic cone ensures that the Removal attack is unable to obtain the original logic cone after removing the point-function. Since the error rate of the SAT-hard instance is low, TTLock is still susceptible to attacks that derive approximate keys, like AppSAT.

10. **SFLL-HD** - Similar to TTLock, removing input patterns from the logic cone increases the resiliency of SFLL-HD against the removal attack, since a corrupted logic cone is obtained after removal of the restore logic. However, increasing the number of PIPs decreases resiliency against the SAT attack which is now able to eliminate more than one key per DIP. Newer attack methods like FALL [19] and Gaussian elimination [28] have been able to defeat SFLL-HD without the use of an oracle.

11. **Cyclic** - Since the resultant circuit cannot be represented as a directed acyclic graph (DAG), the SAT solver is unable to satisfy the given QBF to find a required DIP. However, the pre-processing step in CycSAT is able to identify the key condition that results in cycles and add this condition to the initial QBF. Experimental results have shown CycSAT to be successful against cyclic obfuscation.

12. **SRCLock** - Authors have shown that adding feedback edges between the cycles generated by cyclic obfuscation can lead to an exponential increase in the number of cycles that need to be handled by the CycSAT pre-processing step. Also, the use of an input-dependency based cycle generation technique causes one of the condition checking steps in CycSAT to return an unsatisfiable model. However, experimental results have shown that even after the cyclification of chosen Boolean functions, other condition checking steps in CycSAT are able to defeat SRCLock.

13. **Encrypt Flip-flop** - By restricting controllability/observability of the scan-chain, this technique can defeat the combinational SAT attack. However, the complexity of the unrolling-based Sequential SAT attack does not depend on scan-access to the flip-flops in the design. Therefore it is able to decipher the correct key values within a reasonable amount of time.

14. **Chain Based Encryption** - Due to the limited ability of finding large flip-flop chains with low number of sneak paths, it has been shown [7] that the Chain Based technique is susceptible to the Sequential SAT attack and offers very little additional protection over a random insertion technique.

15. **Deep State Encryption** - The attack time of the Sequential SAT attack increases exponentially with increase in unroll count. By choosing a state with a sufficiently large depth value, this technique can force the attack to unroll for a large number of clock cycles, thereby greatly increasing the time

Table 2. Benchmark circuits used for evaluation

ISCAS '85 benchmarks				ITC '99 benchmarks				
Circuit	#PI	#PO	#Gates	Circuit	#PI	#PO	#Gates	#DFF
c432	36	7	160	b04	11	8	632	66
c499	41	32	202	b05	1	36	821	34
c880	60	26	383	b07	1	8	380	49
c1355	41	32	546	b11	7	6	622	31
c1908	33	25	880	b12	5	6	963	121
c2670	233	140	1269	b13	10	10	310	53
c3540	50	22	1669	b14	32	54	9767	245
c5315	178	123	2307	b15	36	70	8367	449
c6288	32	32	2416	b21	32	22	20027	490
c7552	207	108	3513	b22	32	22	29162	735

required to find the correct key. However, the proposed structure of the State Detection and Key Detection blocks may make this technique susceptible to the SPS Removal attack. The effectiveness of the KC2 attack on this technique is unknown and needs further investigation.

5   Cost Analysis - Area and Power

Typical IoT devices operate under the restriction of limited resources. Harsh area and power constraints are placed on these devices during the design process to which the added logic encryption blocks must also adhere. Therefore large logic encryption blocks are undesirable. In this section, we evaluate the area and power overhead of the discussed logic encryption techniques.

5.1   Experimental Setup

The combinational logic encryption techniques were implemented on benchmark circuits chosen from the ISCAS '85 suite while the sequential techniques were implemented on ITC '99 benchmarks. The benchmark details are listed in Table 2. These circuits were chosen due to their wide usage in other works on logic encryption. The chosen benchmark circuits were encrypted using the discussed techniques with key sizes of 32, 64, and 128. For larger benchmarks (more than 300 gates), key size 256 was also used. Some of the salient features of the encryption process are listed below.

- **Random, SLL, LCB** - The combinational benchmark circuits for these techniques were obtained from Trust-Hub [2]. Sequential circuits encrypted using the random technique were generated in-house.

Table 3. Encryption scheme rankings - cost and security

Combinational						Sequential		
Technique	Cost	Security	Technique	Cost	Security	Technique	Cost	Security
Random	A	D	Cyclic	B	B	CBE	A	C
LCB	A	D	SRCLock	B	A	Random	B	D
SLL	A	C	SARLock	C	B	EFF	C	B
KeyDep	B	C	AntiSAT	C	B	DSE	D	A
AntiHT	B	C	TTLock	C	A			
E2LEMI	B	C	SFLL	D	A			

- **Key Interdependency** - Algorithm 1 from [6] was used as the key gate placement strategy. If the number of gate locations found was less than the number of key bits, the remaining locations were chosen randomly.
- **Hardware enlightening** - Key gates were inserted using the technique described in Algorithm 1 of [15]. The threshold values for $PROBAMIN$ and $SLACKMIN$ were chosen to be 0.
- **E2LEMI** - Key controlled MUXes were inserted on all primary inputs while the (sequential) LFSR was omitted, since combinational benchmarks were used for E2LEMI. Instead, a static 'incorrect' selection pattern with equal number of 0s and 1s was stored in the design and applied to the MUXes if the correct key value was not provided. A small hardware Trojan was inserted to detect the application of the correct key.
- **Cyclic** - The light-weight implementation algorithm from [17] was used to insert the key gates into the netlist. A loop length of 8 was chosen and $k/8$ key gates were added for each loop, where k is the number of key bits.
- **SRCLock** - Each micro-cycle generated by the cyclic obfuscation technique was connected with another micro-cycle using a key controlled gate to form the required super-cycle.
- **SARLock, AntiSAT, TTLock** - A compound scheme was used for these techniques. SLL with $k = 32$ was chosen as the traditional scheme while internal signals were used as inputs to the SAT resilient block. The number of internal signals (proportional to the number of SAT resilient keys) was chosen such that the total key sizes were equal to 64, 128, and 256.
- **SFLL** - In addition to the strategy followed for TTLock, all input patterns with a hamming distance of $(h=)2$ from the applied key input were chosen as the PIPs. The restore logic was designed to detect these $\binom{k}{2}$ PIPs and restore the modified output when the correct key was applied.
- **Encrypt Flip-flop** - The flip-flop selection technique described in Algorithm 2 of [5] was used to obtain suitable key gate locations. For circuits with number of flip-flops less than the chosen key size, the remaining key gates were placed on randomly chosen combinational gate inputs.
- **Chain Based Encryption** - Using the chain-based selection technique described in [7], key gates were inserted at the inputs of the flip-flops with

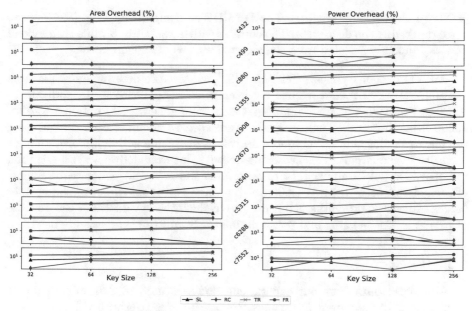

(a) Combinational Logic Encryption

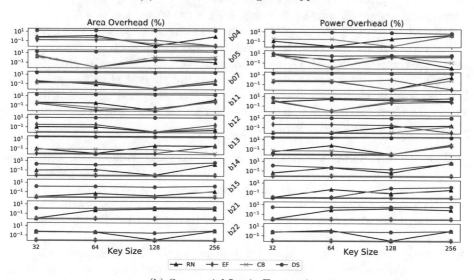

(b) Sequential Logic Encryption

Fig. 7. Cost overhead analysis

maximum distance from the nearest primary output. Again, if the number of flip-flops in the design was less than the key size, randomly chosen combinational gates were encrypted.

- **Deep State Encryption** - The DESIDE-SIM algorithm from [8] was used to determine the deep state. The counter width was set to 5 while the payload was randomly selected from the internal signals in the circuit.

An ATPG tool, Synopsys TetraMax [22], was used to determine test patterns for 100% stuck-at-fault coverage for each unencrypted circuit. In addition to these test patterns, unique random patterns were generated to obtain a total of 10000 input patterns. These patterns were used to simulate each design using the Icarus Verilog simulation tool to derive the switching activity information for each net in the circuit. This switching activity data was fed to a synthesis tool, Synopsys Design Compiler [21], to determine the area and power requirements of each circuit using the SAED90nm_typ library. Note that these area and power values are post logic synthesis but pre phsycial synthesis values. For the purpose of this analysis, the area and power estimates from logic synthesis are used.

5.2   Results

The overhead data from our experimentation was used to determine the cost efficiency of the surveyed techniques. Using the area overhead A_{ib}^k and power overhead P_{ib}^k values, a rank value $R(E_i) = \sum_{\forall b} \sum_{\forall k} A_{ib}^k \cdot P_{ib}^k / |B||K|$ for each encryption scheme E_i applied to benchmark b ($\in B$) for key size k ($\in K$) was calculated, where B is the set of all benchmarks and K is the set of all key sizes. Using these rank values and the resiliency matrix from Sect. 4, the encryption techniques were graded, in terms of cost and security efficiency, as shown in Table 3 (lower letter grade is better). For each unique cost efficiency grade (A-D), the scheme that offers the best security is chosen and the cost overhead values for these schemes are plotted in Fig. 7[1]. Our observations regarding the obtained cost metrics are listed below.

- The area and power overheads for traditional (SAT-vulnerable) techniques are negligible. This follows from the fact that the number of key gates added by these techniques is linear to the number of key bits. This value stays relatively low compared to the size of the circuit. It can be postulated that for large key sizes ($k > 512$), the overhead introduced by the key gates may become significant for small designs.
- In many benchmark circuits, an increase in key size led to a decrease in cost for several encryption schemes. This can be attributed to the optimization techniques used by the synthesis tool to achieve a better fit. This leads to an important conclusion that, unlike attack times, area and power overhead values may not follow a direct correlation with key size.
- Cyclic locking techniques exhibit low cost overhead values because the number of key gates added by these techniques increases linearly with key size, similar to traditional schemes.

---

[1] The raw data used to generate these plots is made available online at https://github.com/kasarayv/costanalysis.

- The combinational point-function based SAT-resilient techniques introduce a large number of gates into the design, thus contributing significantly to the cost overheads. An average 200% cost overhead is observed for smaller benchmarks; this decreases to 50% for larger benchmarks.
- SARLock and AntiSAT have relatively lower overhead values in comparison to TTLock and SFLL. The reason for this is the modification of the original logic cone in the latter two techniques, which in many cases adds additional gates to the circuit. Also, on average the overhead for SFLL is larger than that of TTLock due to SFLL's complex restoration block.
- Similar to corresponding combinational techniques, sequential techniques that are SAT-vulnerable also exhibit low area and power overheads due to the addition of low number of key gates to the design.
- The cost of using the sequential SAT-resilient technique is high due to the introduction of two detection blocks in addition to the corruption and restoration gates.

In summary, SAT-vulnerable techniques exhibit low overhead (high efficiency in cost) whereas SAT-resilient schemes incur higher cost due to the insertion of SAT-hard blocks. Cyclic locking techniques exhibit low cost overhead while offering high level of security. Techniques like delay locking [25] and parametric locking [34] that alter other properties of the design, instead of corrupting signals, have shown success in thwarting SAT-based attacks. However, these methods need to be evaluated for area and power requirements.

6   Conclusion

In this work, we have surveyed several logic encryption and decryption techniques. Benchmark circuits encrypted using these schemes are utilized to derive an estimate of the cost incurred (area occupied and power consumed) by these techniques. Traditional logic encryption methods are light-weight with negligible overhead, but are susceptible to SAT-based attacks. Successful SAT-resilient schemes introduce large overheads and are therefore undesirable for applications where resources are constrained. Although sequential logic encryption techniques exhibit relatively lower cost overheads, they are still attackable by newly proposed decryption methods. Therefore, a new light weight robust logic encryption scheme for application in IoT device security is desired.

References

1. Alasad, Q., Bi, Y., Yuan, J.S.: E2LEMI: energy-efficient logic encryption using multiplexer insertion. Electronics **6**(1), 16 (2017)
2. Amir, S., et al.: Development and evaluation of hardware obfuscation benchmarks. J. Hardw. Syst. Secur. **2**(2), 142–161 (2018)
3. Chakraborty, R.S., Bhunia, S.: HARPOON: an obfuscation-based SoC design methodology for hardware protection. IEEE Trans. Comput. Aided Des. Integr. Circuits Syst. **28**(10), 1493–1502 (2009)

4. El Massad, M., Garg, S., Tripunitara, M.: Reverse engineering camouflaged sequential circuits without scan access. In: 2017 IEEE/ACM International Conference on Computer-Aided Design (ICCAD), pp. 33–40. IEEE (2017)
5. Karmakar, R., Chatopadhyay, S., Kapur, R.: Encrypt flip-flop: a novel logic encryption technique for sequential circuits. arXiv preprint arXiv:1801.04961 (2018)
6. Karmakar, R., Kumar, H., Chattopadhyay, S.: On finding suitable key-gate locations in logic encryption. In: 2018 IEEE International Symposium on Circuits and Systems (ISCAS), pp. 1–5. IEEE (2018)
7. Kasarabada, Y., Chen, S., Vemuri, R.: On SAT-based attacks on encrypted sequential logic circuits. In: 20th International Symposium on Quality Electronic Design (ISQED), pp. 204–211. IEEE (2019)
8. Kasarabada, Y., Thulasi Raman, S.R., Vemuri, R.: Deep state encryption for sequential logic circuits. In: 2019 IEEE Computer Society Annual Symposium on VLSI (ISVLSI), pp. 338–343, July 2019
9. Lee, Y.W., Touba, N.A.: Improving logic obfuscation via logic cone analysis. In: 2015 16th Latin-American Test Symposium (LATS), pp. 1–6. IEEE (2015)
10. Li, M., et al.: Provably secure camouflaging strategy for IC protection. IEEE Trans. Comput.-Aided Des. Integr. Circuits Syst. (2017)
11. Narasimhan, S., Chakraborty, R.S., Chakraborty, S.: Hardware IP protection during evaluation using embedded sequential trojan. IEEE Des. Test Comput. **29**(3), 70–79 (2012)
12. Rajendran, J., Pino, Y., Sinanoglu, O., Karri, R.: Security analysis of logic obfuscation. In: Proceedings of the 49th Annual Design Automation Conference, pp. 83–89. ACM (2012)
13. Roshanisefat, S., Mardani Kamali, H., Sasan, A.: SRClock: SAT-resistant cyclic logic locking for protecting the hardware. In: Proceedings of the 2018 on Great Lakes Symposium on VLSI, pp. 153–158. ACM (2018)
14. Roy, J.A., Koushanfar, F., Markov, I.L.: Ending piracy of integrated circuits. Computer **43**(10), 30–38 (2010)
15. Samimi, M.S., Aerabi, E., Kazemi, Z., Fazeli, M., Patooghy, A.: Hardware enlightening: no where to hide your hardware trojans! In: 2016 IEEE 22nd International Symposium on On-Line Testing and Robust System Design (IOLTS), pp. 251–256. IEEE (2016)
16. Shamsi, K., Li, M., Meade, T., Zhao, Z., Pan, D.Z., Jin, Y.: AppSAT: approximately deobfuscating integrated circuits. In: 2017 IEEE International Symposium on Hardware Oriented Security and Trust (HOST), pp. 95–100. IEEE (2017)
17. Shamsi, K., Li, M., Meade, T., Zhao, Z., Pan, D.Z., Jin, Y.: Cyclic obfuscation for creating SAT-unresolvable circuits. In: Proceedings of the on Great Lakes Symposium on VLSI 2017, pp. 173–178. ACM (2017)
18. Shamsi, K., Li, M., Pan, D.Z., Jin, Y.: KC2: key-condition crunching for fast sequential circuit deobfuscation. In: 2019 Design, Automation & Test in Europe Conference & Exhibition (DATE), pp. 534–539. IEEE (2019)
19. Sirone, D., Subramanyan, P.: Functional analysis attacks on logic locking. In: 2019 Design, Automation & Test in Europe Conference & Exhibition (DATE), pp. 936–939. IEEE (2019)
20. Subramanyan, P., Ray, S., Malik, S.: Evaluating the security of logic encryption algorithms. In: 2015 IEEE International Symposium on Hardware Oriented Security and Trust (HOST), pp. 137–143. IEEE (2015)
21. Synopsys: Design compiler (2018). https://www.synopsys.com/
22. Synopsys: Tetramax (2018). https://www.synopsys.com/

23. Xiao, K., Forte, D., Jin, Y., Karri, R., Bhunia, S., Tehranipoor, M.: Hardware
    trojans: lessons learned after one decade of research. ACM Trans. Des. Autom.
    Electron. Syst. (TODAES) **22**(1), 6 (2016)
24. Xie, Y., Srivastava, A.: Mitigating SAT attack on logic locking. In: Gierlichs, B.,
    Poschmann, A.Y. (eds.) CHES 2016. LNCS, vol. 9813, pp. 127–146. Springer, Hei-
    delberg (2016). https://doi.org/10.1007/978-3-662-53140-2_7
25. Xie, Y., Srivastava, A.: Delay locking: security enhancement of logic locking against
    IC counterfeiting and overproduction. In: Proceedings of the 54th Annual Design
    Automation Conference 2017, p. 9. ACM (2017)
26. Xie, Y., Srivastava, A.: Anti-SAT: mitigating SAT attack on logic locking. IEEE
    Trans. Comput. Aided Des. Integr. Circuits Syst. **38**(2), 199–207 (2018)
27. Xu, X., Shakya, B., Tehranipoor, M.M., Forte, D.: Novel bypass attack and BDD-
    based tradeoff analysis against all known logic locking attacks. In: Fischer, W.,
    Homma, N. (eds.) CHES 2017. LNCS, vol. 10529, pp. 189–210. Springer, Cham
    (2017). https://doi.org/10.1007/978-3-319-66787-4_10
28. Yang, F., Tang, M., Sinanoglu, O.: Stripped functionality logic locking with ham-
    ming distance based restore unit (SFLL-hd)-unlocked. IEEE Trans. Inf. Forensics
    Secur. **14**, 2778–2786 (2019)
29. Yasin, M., Mazumdar, B., Rajendran, J.J., Sinanoglu, O.: SARLock: SAT attack
    resistant logic locking. In: 2016 IEEE International Symposium on Hardware Ori-
    ented Security and Trust (HOST), pp. 236–241. IEEE (2016)
30. Yasin, M., Mazumdar, B., Sinanoglu, O., Rajendran, J.: CamoPerturb: secure IC
    camouflaging for minterm protection. In: 2016 IEEE/ACM International Confer-
    ence on Computer-Aided Design (ICCAD), pp. 1–8. IEEE (2016)
31. Yasin, M., Mazumdar, B., Sinanoglu, O., Rajendran, J.: Removal attacks on logic
    locking and camouflaging techniques. IEEE Trans. Emerg. Top. Comput. 1 (2017)
32. Yasin, M., Rajendran, J.J., Sinanoglu, O., Karri, R.: On improving the security
    of logic locking. IEEE Trans. Comput. Aided Des. Integr. Circuits Syst. **35**(9),
    1411–1424 (2015)
33. Yasin, M., Sengupta, A., Nabeel, M.T., Ashraf, M., Rajendran, J.J., Sinanoglu,
    O.: Provably-secure logic locking: from theory to practice. In: Proceedings of the
    2017 ACM SIGSAC Conference on Computer and Communications Security, pp.
    1601–1618. ACM (2017)
34. Yasin, M., Sengupta, A., Schafer, B.C., Makris, Y., Sinanoglu, O., Rajendran, J.J.:
    What to lock?: functional and parametric locking. In: Proceedings of the on Great
    Lakes Symposium on VLSI 2017, pp. 351–356. ACM (2017)
35. Zhou, H., Jiang, R., Kong, S.: CycSAT: SAT-based attack on cyclic logic encryp-
    tions. In: Proceedings of the 36th International Conference on Computer-Aided
    Design, pp. 49–56. IEEE Press (2017)

Latent Space Modeling for Cloning Encrypted PUF-Based Authentication

Vishalini Laguduva Ramnath[1(✉)], Sathyanarayanan N. Aakur[1,2], and Srinivas Katkoori[1]

[1] Department of Computer Science and Engineering, University of South Florida, Tampa, FL 33620, USA
vishalini@mail.usf.edu
[2] Department of Computer Science, Oklahoma State University, Stillwater, OK 74078, USA

Abstract. Physically Unclonable Functions (PUFs) have emerged as a lightweight, viable security protocol in the Internet of Things (IoT) framework. While there have been recent works on crypt-analysis of PUF-based models, they require physical access to the device and knowledge of the underlying architecture along with unlimited access to the challenge-response pairs in plain text without encryption. In this work, we are the first to tackle the problem of encrypted PUF-based authentication in an IoT framework. We propose a novel, generative framework based on variational autoencoders that is PUF architecture-independent and can handle encryption protocols on the transmitted CRPs. We show that the proposed framework can successfully clone three (3) different PUF architectures encrypted using two (2) different encryption protocols in DES and AES. We also show that the proposed approach outperforms a brute-force machine learning-based attack model by over 20%.

Keywords: Physically Unclonable Function · Cloning · Encryption · Latent space modeling

1 Introduction

Rapid progress in computing technologies, especially space and power-efficient devices, have enabled the advent of the *"age of Internet of Things (IoT)"*. The IoT ecosystem refers to the massive collection of ubiquitous and pervasive devices that have been deployed across a variety of environments to collect and process massive amounts of data. Applications of IoT devices range from wearable computing devices, bio-implantable devices to monitor vital bodily functions for direct human interaction, as well as for "smart" devices that we interact with on a day-to-day basis. Due to the somewhat limited scope of computing resources, the IoT nodes themselves do not process such information. Instead, they are used as data collection agents that transmit the collected data to more powerful edge servers for information processing. This information transmission is

© IFIP International Federation for Information Processing 2020
Published by Springer Nature Switzerland AG 2020
A. Casaca et al. (Eds.): IFIPIoT 2019, IFIP AICT 574, pp. 142–158, 2020.
https://doi.org/10.1007/978-3-030-43605-6_9

often done through wireless networks, which are prone to attacks and hence require robust security protocols for ensuring the integrity of the transmitted data. Security protocols, such as node authentication, have to be sufficiently lightweight, yet highly secure to ensure that these protocols can be performed on power-constrained IoT nodes.

Authentication protocols can vary from being very simple, such as physical storage of a secret key on silicon devices, to complex cryptography-based algorithms that can require significant power and area requirements on the device. It has, however, been shown that the most straightforward authentication that of physically storing the secret key on the node device can be bypassed through physical and side-channel attacks [19]. Recovering the secret key through such physical attacks can compromise the entire IoT network and hence compromise the integrity and anonymity of the transmitted data. With the need for lightweight, yet secure authentication protocols increasing with the rapidly growing use of IoT nodes, physically unclonable functions (PUFs) [15] have emerged as a viable option for IoT node security [3].

Physically unclonable functions, or PUFs for short, are physical random functions that exploit the unique physical variations that can occur during the manufacturing process to create a "digital signature" for the device. This digital signature is dependent on the uniqueness of the device's physical microstructure. Since the physical structure is dependent on random physical aspects introduced in the manufacturing process, it is not feasible to clone or duplicate the exact physical structure of the device. In addition to their unclonable nature, the PUF-based authentication protocol extends the single key-based authentication to using the challenge-response pair (CRP) based authentication. CRPs are characterized by the application of an external stimulus (the challenge) to the PUF and receiving an unpredictable, but a repeatable response. Each challenge-response pair is unique to a PUF and hence can be used to verify the identity of a given device. These characteristics of PUFs have made them highly conducive for their widespread use in cryptography applications such as for identification and authentication [21], digital rights management [14], bit-commitment protocol [21], and secure multi-party communication [23], to name a few.

The use of PUFs as the basis for IoT node authentication has gained momentum in recent times [1,2,6–8]. PUF-based IoT node authentication has two fundamental processes - (1) an enrollment phase and (2) an authentication phase. The enrollment phase involves the building of a database of CRPs between the authenticating edge server and a data node. This is typically done before the data node is *"deployed"* into the wild and involves the collection of a large number of CRPs to ensure that the *"replay"* attack is prevented. The authentication phase is the application of an authentication protocol, typically the use of the challenge to the PUF and verification of the corresponding response. Figure 1 illustrates these processes in a typical IoT framework. While proven to be effective, the enrollment phase allows for a malicious attacker to eavesdrop and construct a complementary database of CRPs that they can then use to emulate, or rather *clone* the PUF and thus compromise the integrity of the data node. There have

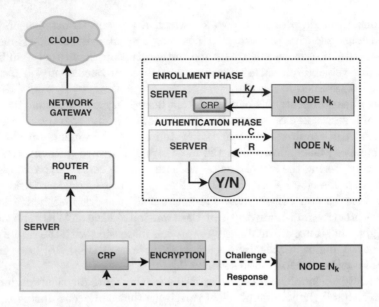

Fig. 1. A typical IoT architecture is illustrated. The inner figure shows the enrollment phase and the authentication phase of a PUF-based IoT node authentication scheme.

been advances that have now been proposed that the extraction of CRPs is then destroyed, i.e., fuse the extraction wires, thereby eradicating the possibility of cloning via this method.

The use of PUFs for IoT node security holds some **security assumptions** as defined in [20]. Many of the proposed IoT networks using PUF authentication in existing literature [1,6,7] make the following underlying assumptions: (1) a malicious agent can have access to the collection of CRPs obtained in the enrollment phase through malicious software attacks, although secret keys are not explicitly known, (2) the challenge-response characteristics of the PUF within the data IoT node is an implicit property and is not accessible to an adversary, (3) the malicious agent has unrestricted to the communication channel and (4) the modeling of PUF characteristics, either physical, mathematical or otherwise is a complex task. Given that current designs of IoT nodes ensure that they are tamper-proof [18,33], physical access to the PUF such as micro-probing is somewhat tricky. Hence, PUF-based authentication has proven to be an effective strategy for securing data nodes in an IoT framework.

While highly sophisticated and secure, PUF models are susceptible to cloning using complex mathematical models and cryptanalysis. Common modes of cryptanalyses include side-channel attacks [19,25], machine-learning (ML) attacks [24] and software attacks, for example, worms and viruses [28]. Machine learning models are particularly adept at cloning PUF models. The pioneering work of Rühmair et al. [24], have shown great success in cloning PUFs, gaining cloning accuracy of up to 99.99%. Most approaches to PUF cloning make two critical assumptions: (1) the underlying architecture must be known *a priori*, either through invasive physical intrusions or explicit architecture knowledge and (2) the challenge and response are sent through the communication channel in plain text i.e., no encryption masks the direct relationship between challenge and response characteristics of the PUF within the data node. Given that most, if not all, communication in the wireless channel is encrypted through some hashing or encryption technique, and most IoT data nodes are tamper-proof, these are very strong assumptions to make, especially in the context of node security in an IoT framework.

In this work, we aim to address these challenges and propose an *architecture independent* modeling approach based on machine learning that does not require any prior knowledge of the underlying PUF architecture. Additionally, we do not assume that the challenge-response authentication is done via clear text transmission, as is the case with existing approaches in the literature. This does, however, come with an additional set of challenges that need to be addressed for successful cloning of the PUF-based authentication. Namely, the challenges are as follows: (1) the encryption protocols mask the relationship between external challenge and the corresponding response, (2) most encryption protocols are not easily broken and hence require us to uncover the secret key, which might not be even possible if the challenges are encrypted using a one-way hash function and (3) lack of physical access to the data node does not give us any auxiliary data such as the PUF architecture type and/or other PUF characteristics.

We aim to overcome these challenges by learning an auto-generative model which helps us to learn a discriminative latent space. This latent space modeling allows us to bypass the need to correlate the input challenge and the corresponding response. This is achieved through the use of a variational autoencoder (VAE). A variational autoencoder (VAE) consists of two parts, an encoder and a decoder. We decrease the dimensionality of the input challenge into a smaller dimensional subspace called the latent space. We then reconstruct the original input using a decoder model from this latent representation. Hence, the latent space forms a bottleneck, forcing the model to effectively compress the input data to a more discriminative representation for easier PUF response modeling. However, in addition to the traditional decoder, which attempts to regenerate the input challenge, we also introduce a decryption decoder head. The decryption head attempts to decrypt the original challenge from the encrypted version without the need for knowing the secret key. This allows us to ensure that the bottleneck layer, or the latent space, to be influenced by both the discriminative nature of the compressed representation as well as the original, plain text challenge.

In short, our paper makes the following novel contributions:

- we propose a machine learning-based cloning model on PUF architectures that do not require any prior knowledge and physical access to the IoT node,
- we show that the proposed approach can successfully clone the PUF model even if the challenge-response pair is encrypted,

- we show that the use of a generative model such as a variational autoencoder can help learn a discriminative latent space that is robust to noise, encryption, and masking which are common traits of many cryptography models used for data encryption, and
- we show that generative modeling can potentially lead to more effective probing of the PUF models to create or *recreate* the PUF's CRP database without explicit access to the server.

To the best of authors' knowledge, this is the first such framework to evaluate the case of PUF-based IoT node authentication with encryption techniques while not requiring any prior knowledge of the PUF architecture. We show that the proposed approach can successfully clone three (3) common PUF architectures encrypted using two (2) common encryption protocols. Combined, they form some of the more common IoT node authentication protocols proposed in the existing literature.

The rest of the paper is laid out as follows. We give a brief introduction to physically unclonable functions (PUFs), their use in IoT node security and the associated encryption protocols in Sect. 2. We introduce the proposed latent space modeling using a variational autoencoder and the training strategy for cloning an encrypted PUF protocol in Sect. 3. We present a baseline approach for cloning an encrypted PUF protocol by brute-force machine learning models in Sect. 4.1 following the experimental evaluation of the proposed approach in Sect. 4.2. Finally, in Sect. 5, we conclude with a discussion on the feasibility of the proposed approach.

2   Background and Related Work

In this section, we introduce the necessary terms and background knowledge that are relevant to the proposed approach. We begin with an introduction to physically unclonable functions and their application in IoT node security. We then review existing work on cloning or attack models on PUF models. We conclude with a short review of commonly used encryption protocols.

2.1   Physically Unclonable Functions

Physically Unclonable Functions [14,15], or physical random functions, are an embodied version of physical functions that maps an external stimulus (the challenge) to a random, but a repeatable response. The physical function is characterized by the inherent randomness introduced during the manufacturing process and is nearly impossible to replicate given a polynomial amount of resources. A PUF model's characteristics are best expressed through the collection of challenge-response pairs (CRPs) and hence form the basis of most, if not all, PUF-based security protocols. PUFs can be categorized into two types based on the number of valid CRPs, namely weak PUFs and strong PUFs [26]. A PUF is said to be a *weak* PUF if it has a fixed, small set of CRPs that are valid and are assumed to be access restricted. *Strong* PUFs, on the other hand, leverage large amounts of the inherent unpredictability and hence possess a large number of CRPs. They are also considered to have an unprotected physical interface and are more commonly used in security applications. We refer the reader to [26] for an extensive review of weak and strong PUF models.

There have been numerous PUF models introduced and evaluated over the years. Broadly, they can be divided into two major groups - the time-delay based models and the memory-based models. *Time delay-based models* include ring oscillator PUFs and Arbiter PUFs or APUF and its variations such as feed-forward arbiter PUFs. Such PUF models can generate real-time, chip-specific signatures without the need for expensive memory for key storage and thus, have been particularly conducive to device authentication, intellectual property, and data privacy preservation to name a few. *Memory-based PUF* models, on the other hand, exploit the variations between matched silicon devices of memory elements to characterize the inherent random function. Some common bistable memory elements that are exploited for the PUF functions are SRAM, latches, and flip-flops. Again, we refer the reader to [16] for a more detailed review of PUF architectures, which is beyond the scope of this paper.

2.2 PUFs for IoT Node Security

The use of PUFs for IoT node security [1,2,6–8,17] has gained momentum in recent days. Such approaches can be classified into two major categories - PUF-based authentication and PUF-based key generation for cryptography-based approaches [30]. In PUF-based device authentication, the nature of strong PUF models to possess a large number of CRPs is exploited to build a robust authentication protocol. A trusted party, the authentication server, randomly applies a set of external stimuli or challenges to create a database of valid CRPs for authentication. This process is called the enrollment phase. Every time there is a need for authenticating the node of data transmission within the IoT framework, the server authenticates the node with a random challenge from the database of CRPs. This process is called the authentication phase. Figure 1 illustrates both these processes in a typical IoT framework. The other approach consists of using the PUF response to generate cryptographic keys. The keys are typically generated by hashing the PUF's response to a given challenge, which is processed through an error-correcting circuit.

2.3 Cloning Attacks on PUF Models

The widespread introduction of PUF models into IoT node authentication has seen an increase in approaches that attempt to test their effectiveness through attacking or *cloning* the PUF model. Cloning a PUF model typically involves the fitting of a complex mathematical function to capture the correlation between the input challenge and the corresponding PUF response. There have been several approaches, including leveraging machine learning models and physical modeling. Perhaps the most influential approach was introduced by Rührmair *et al.*

[24], who proposed a machine learning-based modeling of strong PUF models using a predictive approach. The authors were able to clone the functionality of the underlying PUF given the PUF model by evaluating model parameters using LR with RProp and ES. While highly successful, they make the assumptions outlined in Sect. 1 and as such cannot be widely applied to practical IoT node cloning using PUF models. The other type of approach [4,11] involves physical access to the PUF model beyond just knowledge about PUF architecture and model. They typically involve the use of machine learning approaches to model the PUF response by exploiting the physical characteristics obtained through side-channel approaches. Recently efforts have shifted to a combined ML and side-channel (timing and power) to present an improved hybrid attack surface [19,25]. A mathematical model-free ML attack using PAC (Probably Approximately Correct) learning framework has been proposed in [12]. The authors presented that an influential bit, if present in stable PUF response, can predict the future response corresponding to a challenge with low probability.

2.4   Encryption Protocols for IoT Node Authentication

With the use of CRPs for IoT node authentication, the need for encryption protocols has risen due to the need for added security from eavesdropping protocols. The use of encryption protocols in IoT node communication and authentication has seen staggering rise [5,27,29,31,32]. In summary, the encryption protocols used are the Data Encryption Standard (DES) [9] and the Advanced Encryption Standard (AES) [10]. While there has been successful cryptanalysis of DES, it still takes an extraordinary amount of compute and access to data to achieve it, whereas there has not been a successful attack on the 128-bit AES encryption protocol. While encryption protocols have been used extensively in IoT node communication, it requires some semblance of computation to get working. Hence, there have been other protocols proposed to overcome such computation power such as obfuscated CRPs [13] and substring matching [22], to name a few. In this work, we consider the encryption protocols AES and DES as the encryption mechanisms used for encrypting the CRPs in the IoT framework.

3   Learning a Latent Subspace for Encrypted CRPs

In this section, we introduce the proposed approach for learning a discriminative latent subspace that can be used for machine learning-based cryptanalysis of the security protocols in a typical IoT ecosystem. We begin with a brief introduction to *variational autoencoders*, which form the backbone of the proposed approach. We then introduce the proposed approach with a multi-headed decoder, which helps learn a more robust subspace for better modeling of the encryption protocols. Finally, we expand on the strategy employed in the optimization process for end-to-end training of the proposed network.

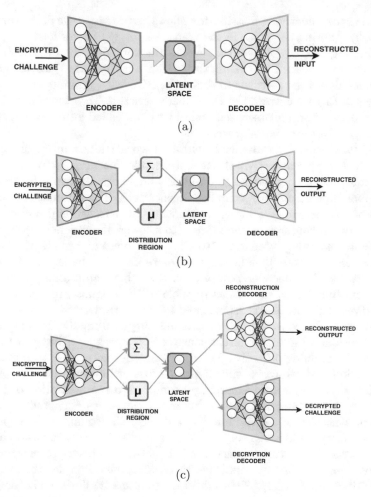

Fig. 2. We illustrate the architecture of (a) typical autoencoder, (b) a typical variational autoencoder and (c) the proposed approach with multi-headed decoders.

3.1 Variational Autoencoders

Encryption techniques such as AES and DES, to name a few, secure the transmitted data by injecting noise into the data through various techniques including, but not limited to hashing and block cipher. By doing so, the actual data within the transmitted information is hidden from prying influences. Hence, any attempt to break the security of the encryption must either (1) know the encryption techniques and the hidden cipher to recover the original data, or (2) model the underlying data distribution effectively to learn a model for manipulating the information stream. While there have been existing work in crypt-analysis for the former approach, the latter has not been explored extensively. Modeling the internal structure of the data distribution offers three significant advantages:

(1) knowing the underlying distribution allows us to reduce the dimensionality of the data by ignoring the noise in the transmission, (2) allows for the possibility of learning a generative model that clones the source of the data distribution, which in our case is the PUF within the IoT data node, and (3) learning a generative model allows the attacker to probe the PUF with genuine, or rather, valid challenges to further extract the PUF characteristics. To achieve the above, we employ the use of an unsupervised neural network called autoencoders, or more specifically, *variational autoencoders.*

An *autoencoder* is an artificial neural network trained in an unsupervised manner. The major objective of the autoencoder network is to compress the input data into an encoded representation and, more importantly, *reconstruct* the original input from the compressed encoding. The autoencoder typically consists of two networks working in tandem - an *encoder* and a *decoder.* The encoder network compresses the input into a lower-dimensional representation, called the *latent space,* by learning to ignore the noise and modeling the underlying data distribution. This latent space is represented by the *bottleneck layer* of the network. The decoder network, on the other hand, aims to reconstruct a representation that is as close as possible to the original input from the bottleneck layer. This process is represented in Fig. 2(a), where it can be seen that the input to the encoder and reconstructed output from the decoder have the same dimensions whereas the latent space or bottleneck layer has a lower dimensionality. The training objective for an autoencoder network is to minimize the reconstruction loss, which is typically an $L2$ loss or binary cross-entropy.

While incredibly useful in learning a compressed representation of a (potentially) noisy input data, there is no way to restrict, or rather, *predict* the latent space representation of a given input in a deterministic manner. This poses two critical concerns. First, while very useful for compression, the latent space learned in a traditional autoencoder is scattered. This leads to better reconstructions of the input image but is not conducive to *generate* new samples that match the valid distribution. Second, a deterministic latent space allows for better probing of the PUF model through generating legitimate challenges. It also allows us to model the PUF characteristics in a model agnostic manner. To overcome these limitations, we employ the use of a *variational autoencoder.* A modification on the traditional autoencoder network paradigm, a variational autoencoder aims to restrict the latent space into a more deterministic manner by introducing an additional optimization constraint. Figure 2(b) illustrates the typical architecture of a variational autoencoder. As can be seen, the bottleneck layer is not passed through to the decoder network directly. Rather, it is used to generate a normal distribution $N(\mu, \sigma)$ (i.e. mean μ and standard deviation σ). The latent space is then sampled from this distribution to ensure that the bottleneck layer follows a given set of distribution and hence is deterministic. The training objective then becomes the reconstruction loss and the KL divergence loss to ensure that the distribution follows the standard normal distribution $N(0, 1)$. This additional loss ensures that the parameters μ and σ do not regress such that the latent space of the encoder network is preserved. The objective function is given by

$$\mathcal{L}(\theta, \phi, X) = E_{z \sim q_\phi(Z|X)}(log P_\theta(X|Z)) - \mathcal{D}_{KL}(q_\phi(Z|X)||p_\theta(Z)) \qquad (1)$$

where X is the input to be modelled (the encrypted challenge in our case), Z is the hidden variables (the latent space) from which to generate new challenges, $p_\theta(X|Z)$ is the generative process done by the decoder and $q_\phi(Z|X)$ represents the encoding process. θ and ϕ represent the parameters of the decoding and encoding processes, respectively.

3.2   Multi-headed Decoding for Robust Latent Subspace Modeling

The use of a variational autoencoder helps in providing a deterministic latent space by forcing the encoder representations to follow a normal distribution. Given that the only task of the encoder is to learn representations that can be reconstructed, there can be a tendency to overfit to the sample distribution due to the single-task learning paradigm. To overcome this inhibition, we propose the use of a multi-headed decoder network to introduce a form of multi-task learning. This provides a form of inductive transfer and allows us to form better representations for modeling the PUF characteristics. In addition to the traditional reconstruction head, we introduce a second decoder which acts as a brute-force decrypting mechanism. We assume that a minimal amount of CRPs is available to the attacker in both plain-text and encrypted forms. Given the multitude of possible eavesdropping mechanisms, this is not an unreasonable assumption. The proposed architecture is shown in Fig. 2(c), where it can be seen that a joint representation, learning by the encoder, is used as the latent space for both reconstructing the original challenge as well as the decrypted challenge. This allows the model to learn a latent space representation that captures the inherent structure of a valid CRP while learning to ignore the noise induced by the encryption protocols. In Sect. 4.2, we can see that the use of the second decoder network as a brute-force decryption method offers better modeling of the underlying PUF architecture.

Formally, the objective of the proposed network differs from the traditional variational autoencoder (Eq. 1). First, there is another generative process to uncover the plain-text challenge represented by $d_\psi(\widetilde{X}|Z)$, where $\widetilde{X}$ represents the plain-text challenge. Second, the generation of the decrypted challenge must also be dependent on the encoded representation Z. This results in the updated objective function given by

$$\mathcal{L}(\theta, \phi, \psi, X, \widetilde{X}) = E_{z \sim q_\phi(Z|X)}(log P_\theta(X|Z) + log P_\theta(\widetilde{X}|Z))$$
$$- \mathcal{D}_{KL}(q_\phi(Z|X)||p_\theta(Z)) \qquad (2)$$

where $\widetilde{X}$ is the clear text challenge, X is the input to be modelled (the encrypted challenge in our case), Z is the hidden variables (the latent space) from which to generate new challenges, $p_\theta(X|Z)$ is the auto-generative process done by the first decoder, $d_\theta(\widetilde{X}|Z)$ is the decrypted generative process done by the second decoder and $q_\phi(Z|X)$ represents the encoding process. θ, ψ and ϕ represent the parameters of the two decoding processes and the lone encoding process, respectively.

The addition of the second decoder network introduces the notion of multi-task learning (MTT). The use of multi-task learning is crucial in many aspects, especially considering that the number of CRPs available are often very low, ranging from the low hundreds to a thousand. Since the encoder network is shared among the two decoders, this reduces the possibility of the network to overfit to the training set of the CRPs and helps generalize to unknown CRPs. In addition to preventing overfitting, the hard parameter sharing paradigm offers other benefits such as attention focusing, implicit data augmentation, reducing representation bias, and regularization, to name a few.

3.3 Implementation Details and Training Strategy

Since the proposed architecture has a complex structure, we detail the implementation details and the training strategy for the approach here. The encoder consists of four (4) densely connected layers, with each layer interspersed with a dropout layer. Each dropout layer has a dropout probability of 50%. We reduce the dimensionality of the input by $0.5\times$ at each fully connected (dense) layer. This follows the standard protocol in autoencoders to induce the bottleneck at the end of the encoding network. Each of the two decoders (reconstruction and decryption) consist of two fully connected layers that increase the dimensionality back to the original dimension and decrypted challenge dimensions, respectively. We also have a series of two (2) fully connected layers that take the latent space as input and produces the PUF response as output. This is the only part of the network that is trained in a supervised manner, i.e., using labels and target dimensions. The encoder and two decoders are trained in an unsupervised manner.

Since the training data is limited, most neural networks tend to overfit to the smaller amounts of data and do not generalize well to the other, unobserved challenge-response pairs. To overcome this, we propose the following training regimen. For ten epochs, we first train the network end-to-end only with the reconstruction decoder as active i.e., it is trained first as a traditional variational autoencoder. For the next ten epochs, we then train the decryption decoder for ten epochs while freezing the weights of the reconstruction decoder. This represents the unsupervised training portion of the proposed training regimen. We then begin the supervised training process. In this part of the training, we freeze the layers of the decoding structures and take the latent space produced by the encoder network and feed it to a series of fully connected layers and model the PUF response to the input challenge. The neural network's target is the PUF response. We train for a total of 100 epochs, with the unsupervised and supervised portions interspersed together.

4   Experimental Evaluation

In this section, we present the experimental evaluation of the proposed approach. We begin with a description of a baseline approach against which we compare the proposed approach. We then continue with the presentation of the quantitative metrics from the experimental evaluation. We then conclude with a discussion on the qualitative aspects of the proposed approach.

4.1   Baseline Approach: A Brute Force Attack on Encrypted PUFs

Given the one-to-one nature of the challenge-response mappings, it could be argued that a simple mathematical model, such as any of those used in various machine learning approaches, could be a viable alternative for cloning an encrypted PUF architecture. To this end, we train and evaluate two (2) machine learning-based models and one (1) neural network-based model. The two machine learning-based models that we trained were logistic regression (LR) and random forest (RF). We chose logistic regression as a baseline approach due to the fact the pioneering work of Rührmair *et al.* [24] successfully used the method to clone various PUF architectures. While successful for cloning plain-text challenge-response characteristics of PUF architectures, we evaluate the ability of logistic regression-based approaches on the encrypted CRP setting. We chose the random forest algorithm as another baseline approach due to its tendency to reduce the overfitting nature of decision trees. Given the limited training data and the inherent non-linear nature of the data distribution, the ensemble of decision trees generated by the random forest algorithm provides a strong baseline. As a final baseline, we use a neural network that is similar to the proposed approach.

Table 1. ML Model cloning accuracy and the time required for cloning a 64-Stage Arbiter PUF encrypted with 128-bit DES and AES algorithms.

PUF model	Encryption	Approach	Accuracy (%)	Cloning time
64-Stage Aribter	DES	LR *(Brute)*	46.9	1.2 s
		RF *(Brute)*	51.6	0.001 s
		MLP *(Brute)*	56.1	35.8 s
		Ours *(no decrypt)*	69.4	84.7 s
		Ours *(no reconstr.)*	67.8	45.3 s
		Ours *(full)*	**75.6**	98.6 s
	AES	LR *(Brute)*	48.7	1.9 s
		RF *(Brute)*	54.7	0.005 s
		MLP *(Brute)*	53.6	33.1 s
		Ours *(no decrypt)*	68.2	83.3 s
		Ours *(no reconstr.)*	65.2	48.6 s
		Ours *(full)*	**73.9**	93.2 s

Instead of pretraining the feature extraction using the proposed approach of variational autoencoders with multiple decoders, we use a standard multilayer perceptron (MLP) network. It consists of an input layer, followed by two (2) hidden layers (analogous to the encoder) that reduce the dimensionality of the input and two hidden layers that increase the dimensionality (comparable to the decoder) followed by the output layer that models the PUF's characteristic response. We choose this MLP architecture to emphasize the importance of the proposed approach, which enhances the ability of the neural network to learn discriminative features.

Table 2. ML Model cloning accuracy and the time required for cloning a 3 XOR PUF encrypted with 128-bit DES and AES algorithms.

PUF model	Encryption	Approach	Accuracy (%)	Cloning time (s)
3-XOR PUF	DES	LR *(Brute)*	60.9	26.2 s
		RF *(Brute)*	59.4	0.31 s
		MLP *(Brute)*	51.1	70.8 s
		Ours *(no decrypt)*	61.5	87.0 s
		Ours *(no reconstr.)*	62.4	51.9 s
		Ours *(full)*	**64.8**	83.6 s
	AES	LR *(Brute)*	53.8	30.2 s
		RF *(Brute)*	54.7	0.29 s
		MLP *(Brute)*	52.3	46.7 s
		Ours *(no decrypt)*	65.4	76.9 s
		Ours *(no reconstr.)*	62.1	42.6 s
		Ours *(full)*	**68.9**	73.6 s

4.2   Quantitative Evaluation

Following experimental setup by [24], we report the upper bound of the attacker's ability to successfully clone a given PUF architecture as its accuracy in a supervised setting. To evaluate the ability of the proposed approach to cloning a given PUF successfully, we consider two strong PUF architectures in a 64-stage Arbiter PUF and XOR PUFs. We consider two (2) variations of the XOR PUF - 3-XOR and 4-XOR PUFs to evaluate the ability of the proposed approach to generalize to more complex architectures. We also consider two (2) conventional encryption techniques - the Data Encryption Standard (DES) and the Advanced Encryption Standard (AES). We use the 128-bit versions of both encryption methods. This gives us a total of six (6) different strong PUF architectures for validating the efficacy of the proposed method. We present the average results of the experiments conducted over ten (10) trials and on a limited CRP regime of less

than 250 CRP pairs for both training and testing. Although DES is susceptible to crypt-analysis, it is a non-trivial task. 128-bit AES is resistant to brute
force attacks, given that there can exist as much as 3.4×10^{38} key combinations.
Such characteristics make the task of cloning an encrypted PUF a challenging
problem.

Arbiter PUFs are often considered by many to be strongly predictable and
hence more susceptible to machine learning-based attacks. However, with the
added security of an encryption protocol, the predictability of an arbiter PUF
model can be considered to lower significantly. We can corroborate this in our
experiments with a 64-stage arbiter PUF. We present these results in Table 1.
It can be seen that the brute force attacks do not perform well on this task,
although some, such as logistic regression, have shown up to 99.9% accuracy in
cases when the challenge is not encrypted. Additionally, the addition of even a
relatively weak encryption scheme such as 128-bit DES significantly degrades
the performance of machine learning models. On the other hand, our proposed
approach can clone the Arbiter PUF model with significantly higher accuracy.
There is a significant difference in performance between the proposed approach
and the brute force models, even considering the similarly structured MLP approach, which differs from the proposed approach only in that the unsupervised
training regime is not conducted on it during the training phase.

XOR PUFs offer a significantly higher challenge to the cloning problem compare to the arbiter PUFs. As the number of stages grows, the predictability
of the PUF architecture reduces. This makes the XOR PUF more suitable for
nodes requiring additional security. The addition of encryption protocols such
as DES and AES makes it even more challenging to clone a given PUF architecture. We summarize the results of our experiments with 3 XOR and 4 XOR
PUFs in Tables 1 and 2 respectively. We can see that as the number of stages
increases, the ability of the machine learning models to clone the PUF device
reduces drastically. It is important to note that in the literature [23,24], the
maximum number of XORs used is 6. We experiment up to 4 XOR PUFs in
this paper. We also find that in XOR PUFs, the role of the decryption head
is significantly higher than in arbiter PUFs. This could arguably be attributed
to the fact that each of the XOR nodes in the PUF architecture adds to the
non-linearity of the PUF characteristics, thereby reducing its predictability and
hence providing added security against machine learning attacks.

We also perform **ablation studies** to evaluate the impact of each of the components that are part of the proposed framework: (1) decryption decoder head,
(2) the reconstruction decoder head and (3) the use of variational autoencoders
for unsupervised pretraining of the encoder network. It can be seen from each of
Tables 1, 2 and 3 that each decoder head adds significant improvements over the
base model. The performance improvement due to the addition of the decryption
decoder can be as high as 5.7% (Table 1). Additionally, the mere use of neural
networks is not sufficient to guarantee successful cloning of a PUF architecture,
especially with the employment of encryption schemes. We can see that the use
of the objective functions described in Eqs. 1 and 2 and the unsupervised pre-

training regimen described in Sect. 3.3 add significant performance gains over the vanilla neural networks (MLP). We observe as much as 20.6% improvement in cloning accuracy for arbiter PUFs.

Table 3. ML Model cloning accuracy and the time required for cloning a 4 XOR Arbiter PUF encrypted with 128-bit DES and AES algorithms.

PUF model	Encryption	Approach	Accuracy (%)	Cloning time (s)
4-XOR PUF	DES	LR *(Brute)*	43.75	53.9 s
		RF *(Brute)*	42.2	1.8 s
		MLP *(Brute)*	50.1	98.7 s
		Ours *(no decrypt)*	55.5	86.7 s
		Ours *(no reconstr.)*	57.9	65.7 s
		Ours *(full)*	**60.3**	82.6 s
	AES	LR *(Brute)*	40.62	49.9 s
		RF *(Brute)*	48.43	1.3 s
		MLP *(Brute)*	50.23	112.9 s
		Ours *(no decrypt)*	57.6	93.1 s
		Ours *(no reconstr.)*	59.7	81.4 s
		Ours *(full)*	**63.9**	97.6 s

5 Conclusion and Future Work

In this work, we introduce and evaluate a novel, generative framework using based on a variational autoencoder to clone PUF models over an encrypted communication channel, which is a realistic scenario. We are, to the best of our knowledge, the first to address the problem of encrypted CRPs. We show that the use of the unsupervised pretraining using the proposed framework and training regimen allows us to successfully clone a given PUF model without the need for knowing the secret key used in the encryption protocol. Extensive experiments show that the proposed approach can generalize even with a limited number of CRPs and can show significantly higher cloning accuracy compared to brute force machine learning models. In the future, we aim to show that the proposed approach can generate or recover CRPs that are transmitted with obfuscation and noisy channels.

References

1. Aman, M.N., Chua, K.C., Sikdar, B.: Hardware primitives-based security protocols for the internet of things. In: Cryptographic Security Solutions for the Internet of Things, pp. 117–141. IGI Global (2019)

2. Aman, M.N., Taneja, S., Sikdar, B., Chua, K.C., Alioto, M.: Token-based security for the internet of things with dynamic energy-quality tradeoff. IEEE Internet Things J. **6**(2), 2843–2859 (2018)
3. Aman, M.N., Chua, K.C., Sikdar, B.: Position paper: physical unclonable functions for IoT security. In: Proceedings of the 2nd ACM International Workshop on IoT Privacy, Trust, and Security, pp. 10–13. ACM (2016)
4. Becker, G.T., Kumar, R., et al.: Active and passive side-channel attacks on delay based PUF designs. IACR Cryptology ePrint Archive 2014, 287 (2014)
5. Bokefode, J.D., Bhise, A.S., Satarkar, P.A., Modani, D.G.: Developing a secure cloud storage system for storing IoT data by applying role based encryption. Procedia Comput. Sci. **89**, 43–50 (2016)
6. Braeken, A.: PUF based authentication protocol for IoT. Symmetry **10**(8), 352 (2018)
7. Chatterjee, U., Chakraborty, R.S., Mukhopadhyay, D.: A PUF-based secure communication protocol for IoT. ACM Trans. Embed. Comput. Syst. (TECS) **16**(3), 67 (2017)
8. Chatterjee, U., et al.: Building PUF based authentication and key exchange protocol for IoT without explicit CRPs in verifier database. IEEE Trans. Dependable Secure Comput. **16**(3), 424–437 (2018)
9. Coppersmith, D.: The data encryption standard (DES) and its strength against attacks. IBM J. Res. Dev. **38**(3), 243–250 (1994)
10. Daemen, J., Rijmen, V.: The Design of Rijndael: AES-the Advanced Encryption Standard. Springer, Heidelberg (2013). https://doi.org/10.1007/978-3-662-04722-4
11. Delvaux, J., Verbauwhede, I.: Side channel modeling attacks on 65nm arbiter PUFs exploiting CMOS device noise. In: 2013 IEEE International Symposium on Hardware-Oriented Security and Trust (HOST), pp. 137–142. IEEE (2013)
12. Ganji, F., Tajik, S., Fäßler, F., Seifert, J.P.: Strong machine learning attack against PUFs with no mathematical model. Cryptology ePrint Archive, Report 2016/606 (2016). https://eprint.iacr.org/2016/606
13. Gao, Y., et al.: Obfuscated challenge-response: a secure lightweight authentication mechanism for PUF-based pervasive devices. In: 2016 IEEE International Conference on Pervasive Computing and Communication Workshops (PerCom Workshops), pp. 1–6. IEEE (2016)
14. Gassend, B., Clarke, D., van Dijk, M., Devadas, S.: Controlled physical random functions. In: Proceedings of the 18th Annual Computer Security Applications Conference, ACSAC 2002, pp. 149–160. IEEE Computer Society, Washington (2002). http://dl.acm.org/citation.cfm?id=784592.784802
15. Gassend, B., Clarke, D., Van Dijk, M., Devadas, S.: Silicon physical random functions. In: Proceedings of the 9th ACM Conference on Computer and Communications Security, pp. 148–160. ACM (2002)
16. Herder, C., Yu, M.D., Koushanfar, F., Devadas, S.: Physical unclonable functions and applications: a tutorial. Proc. IEEE **102**(8), 1126–1141 (2014). https://doi. org/10.1109/JPROC.2014.2320516
17. Idriss, T., Idriss, H., Bayoumi, M.: A PUF-based paradigm for IoT security. In: 2016 IEEE 3rd World Forum on Internet of Things (WF-IoT), pp. 700–705. IEEE (2016)
18. Ishai, Y., Prabhakaran, M., Sahai, A., Wagner, D.: Private circuits II: keeping secrets in tamperable circuits. In: Vaudenay, S. (ed.) EUROCRYPT 2006. LNCS, vol. 4004, pp. 308–327. Springer, Heidelberg (2006). https://doi.org/10. 1007/11761679_19

19. Mahmoud, A., Rührmair, U., Majzoobi, M., Koushanfar, F.: Combined Modeling and Side Channel Attacks on Strong PUFs. Cryptology ePrint Archive, Report 2013/632 (2013). https://eprint.iacr.org/2013/632
20. Ostrovsky, R., Scafuro, A., Visconti, I., Wadia, A.: Universally composable secure computation with (malicious) physically uncloneable functions. In: Johansson, T., Nguyen, P.Q. (eds.) EUROCRYPT 2013. LNCS, vol. 7881, pp. 702–718. Springer, Heidelberg (2013). https://doi.org/10.1007/978-3-642-38348-9_41
21. Pappu, R., Recht, B., Taylor, J., Gershenfeld, N.: Physical one-way functions. Science **297**(5589), 2026–2030 (2002). https://doi.org/10.1126/science.1074376. http://science.sciencemag.org/content/297/5589/2026
22. Rostami, M., Majzoobi, M., Koushanfar, F., Wallach, D.S., Devadas, S.: Robust and reverse-engineering resilient PUF authentication and key-exchange by substring matching. IEEE Trans. Emerg. Top. Comput. **2**(1), 37–49 (2014)
23. Rührmair, U.: Oblivious transfer based on physical unclonable functions. In: Acquisti, A., Smith, S.W., Sadeghi, A.-R. (eds.) Trust 2010. LNCS, vol. 6101, pp. 430–440. Springer, Heidelberg (2010). https://doi.org/10.1007/978-3-642-13869-0_31
24. Rührmair, U., Sehnke, F., Sölter, J., Dror, G., Devadas, S., Schmidhuber, J.: Modeling attacks on physical unclonable functions. In: Proceedings of the 17th ACM Conference on Computer and Communications Security, CCS 2010, pp. 237–249. ACM, New York (2010). https://doi.org/10.1145/1866307.1866335. http://doi.acm.org/10.1145/1866307.1866335
25. Rührmair, U., Xu, X., Sölter, J., Mahmoud, A., Koushanfar, F., Burleson, W.: Power and Timing Side Channels for PUFs and their Efficient Exploitation. Cryptology ePrint Archive, Report 2013/851 (2013). https://eprint.iacr.org/2013/851
26. Rührmair, U., Holcomb, D.E.: PUFs at a glance. In: Proceedings of the Conference on Design, Automation & Test in Europe, p. 347. European Design and Automation Association (2014)
27. Sehgal, A., Perelman, V., Kuryla, S., Schonwalder, J.: Management of resource constrained devices in the internet of things. IEEE Commun. Mag. **50**(12), 144–149 (2012)
28. Stallings, W., Brown, L., Bauer, M.D., Bhattacharjee, A.K.: Computer Security: Principles and Practice. Pearson Education, London (2012)
29. Stergiou, C., Psannis, K.E., Kim, B.G., Gupta, B.: Secure integration of IoT and cloud computing. Future Gener. Comput. Syst. **78**, 964–975 (2018)
30. Suh, G.E., Devadas, S.: Physical unclonable functions for device authentication and secret key generation. In: 2007 44th ACM/IEEE Design Automation Conference, pp. 9–14, June 2007
31. Suo, H., Wan, J., Zou, C., Liu, J.: Security in the internet of things: a review. In: 2012 International Conference on Computer Science and Electronics Engineering, vol. 3, pp. 648–651. IEEE (2012)
32. Wang, X., Zhang, J., Schooler, E.M., Ion, M.: Performance evaluation of attribute-based encryption: toward data privacy in the IoT. In: 2014 IEEE International Conference on Communications (ICC), pp. 725–730. IEEE (2014)
33. Yang, K., Forte, D., Tehranipoor, M.: Protecting endpoint devices in IoT supply chain. In: Proceedings of the IEEE/ACM International Conference on Computer-Aided Design, pp. 351–356. IEEE Press (2015)

Lightweight Countermeasure to Differential-Plaintext Attacks on Permutation Ciphers

Matthew Lewandowski$^{(\boxtimes)}$ and Srinivas Katkoori

University of South Florida, Tampa, FL 33620, USA
{mlewando,katkoori}@mail.usf.edu

Abstract. Many lightweight permutation based block ciphers have emerged for the use of encryption and security in the Internet of Things (IoT). However, recent work has shown a critical vulnerability in these ciphers due to the employment of static permutation networks in their architectures; Side-Channel Analysis and Differntial-Plaintext Attack (SCADPA) can be effectively performed on any cipher utilizing permutation networks. In this work, we present a lightweight solution for combating SCADPA. We demonstrate how this countermeasure can be employed on existing ciphers using the lightweight IoT PRESENT-80 cipher, providing multiple architectural implementations, and comparing the performance of these modified architectures against the unaltered PRESENT-80 cipher. Additionally, we analyze how this countermeasure impacts the resilience for all permutation ciphers when considering this attack scheme and provide alternative implementations and possible enhancements.

Keywords: Ciphers · Countermeasures · Differential-Plaintext Attack · Encryption · Permutation networks · Side-Channel Analysis · SCADPA

1 Introduction

As Integrated Circuit (IC) technologies continuously advance we have seen many computing devices (μcomputer, μcontroller, etc. . .) being made affordably and widely available to the public; driving curiosity & innovation for many through rapid prototyping, deployment, or even exploitation, of hardware systems. Similarly, the technology and capabilities of consumer goods has also largely grown over the decades; for instance, toys, cars, garage doors, washers & dryers, are all some of the commonplace devices that are now being equipped with embedded systems and wireless communication capabilities for enhancing the end-user experience. However, as technology continued to advance and grow so too did the vastness of information that was becoming readily available and accessible by nearly everyone around the world, and at the touch of their fingertips. As a

© IFIP International Federation for Information Processing 2020
Published by Springer Nature Switzerland AG 2020
A. Casaca et al. (Eds.): IFIPIoT 2019, IFIP AICT 574, pp. 159–176, 2020.
https://doi.org/10.1007/978-3-030-43605-6_10

result, it has become possible for many without prior knowledge or experience to adequately obtain the skills necessary for designing and implementing hardware systems that can enhance or exploit everyday technology.

Even though the devices that contribute to this Internet of Things (IoT) were intended for improving quality-of-life and furthering the smart home revolution, they have since become a common targets among many hardware hackers; with home devices being targeted for vulnerability, enhancement, or simply repurposing. While it may be understandable that many of these home devices (toys, washer, etc.) don't necessarily require proper access & control mechanisms, it would be expected that devices otherwise designed for the purpose of access control (garage door) would implement some form of secure communication protocol. However, websites such as YouTube have become commonplace for hardware hackers to demonstrate exploitation of these IoT devices that we otherwise naïvely expect to keep our homes secure from others; videos for cloning Radio Frequency Identification (RFID) security badges, hacking: electronic home locks, magnetic door locks, wireless doorbells, garage doors, and even cars, can all be found. While this can be seen simply as an innocent dissemination of knowledge and educational content, its darker side exposes the general lack of concern for security by device manufacturers and existing susceptibilities of systems with respect to the ever evolving technology; allowing for those with ill-intent to easily and affordably construct malicious systems that can be used for personal gain.

In this work we present a practical and lightweight design method for incorporating key-dependent substitution and permutation networks within cryptographic algorithms and hardware through Interconnection Network (ICN) primitives. This design method is demonstrated via modification to the PRESENT-80 cipher with several architectural variations to demonstrate flexibility. Additionally, we show that, for this cipher, incorporation of this key-dependent design methodology has little-to-no impact on resulting performance or power results obtained during synthesis and only serve to increase the resilience while acting as a countermeasure to the critical susceptibility exhibited by permutation based ciphers.

While ICNs have been shown to be applicable to cryptosystems, the novelty of this work stems from the previously unexplored applications of ICNs at the scope of a single switch rather than just providing methods of permutation via routings (omega, baseline, etc.); exploring how resilience of cryptosystems can be enhanced via switching networks and do not require the use of additional complex mathematical operations in-order to provide security. Further, we provide viable countermeasures and discuss how this design methodology can be applied to alternative key methods or even constructing ciphers solely from this methodology.

The rest of this work is organized as follows: Sect. 2 provides necessary background on cryptographic fundamentals, ICNs, and the attack model considered. Section 2.5 details related works relevant to the approach presented in Sect. 3, where Sect. 4 provides experimental results compared against an unaltered implementation of the PRESENT-80 cipher. Section 5 performs an in-depth analysis of the presented approach with respect to existing attacks on the cipher and implications of this design methodology against these attacks. Finally in Sect. 6 we draw conclusions.

2   Background and Related Work

In this section we cover the necessary background information and related works relevant to the proposed approach; beginning by covering the basics of information security and follow with the attack model considered throughout this work. We then provide information relevant to the proposed approach and review existing works that present countermeasures to differential-plaintext attacks.

2.1   Cryptography and Information Security

The National Institute of Standards and Technology (NIST) defines what may now be commonly referred to as the *CIA Triad* [14], and is composed of the three fundamental services required for information security: (1) Confidentiality, (2) Integrity, (3) Availability [7]; simply requiring: (1) privacy and protection of data from unauthorized parties, (2) the data may not be altered by unauthorized parties, and (3) the the confidential data to be readily accessible and in a timely manner. However, it is commonly believed that information security is incompletely represented by this triad alone, requiring additional services: (4) Authenticity and (5) Non-repudiation [14]; simply requiring: (4) that data be verifiable as genuine, and (5) that data/actions can be adequately linked to the appropriate originating entity.

While this set of services are basic principles & requirements for information security they are also applicable to cryptography and must be upheld. However, behind any and all cryptographic algorithms are Shannon's [13] properties of (1) confusion and (2) diffusion; more simply, (1) the resulting ciphertext should be dependent on more than one part of the key and (2) changing a single bit in the plaintext should produce a larger change in the resulting ciphertext. This small alteration to the plaintext that results in a larger change in the ciphertext is known as the *avalance effect*. *Confusion*, commonly performed using the Substitution-Box (S-Box), replaces blocks of bits in the plaintext with some other block, e.g., the character *c* is replaced by *a*. *Diffusion*, potentially using the Permutation-Box (P-Box), permutes the plaintext, e.g., *cat* becomes *tca*. These two concepts ultimately relate to the integration of substitution and transposition for the plaintext to ciphertext transformation through some involved process.

2.2   PRESENT-80 Cipher

In order to provide a better relational understanding of the attack model to permutation based ciphers, here we will first detail the PRESENT-80 cipher, as first presented [3]. The 80-bit implementation of the cipher utilizes an 80-bit secret key, wherein only 64-bits of the key are used each round and in conjunction with an additive value from the round counter; as 32 rounds are performed on the plaintext data. This key-schedule is illustrated by Fig. 1 and depicts the round subkey (64 of 80-bits) and the update operation for constructing the next round subkey; additionally, the 5-bit Exclusive OR (XOR) operation depicts the additive round counter data. The round architecture is shown by Fig. 2, wherein the series of boxes labeled with S denote the SBox operations, detailed by Table 1, with the subsequent routing depicting the PBox operation.

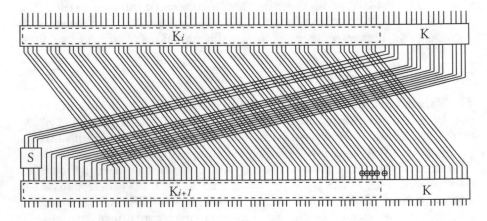

Fig. 1. PRESENT-80 key schedule

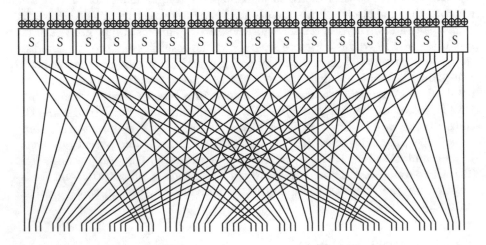

Fig. 2. PRESENT-80 round architecture

Table 1. PRESENT-80 substitution box

x	0	1	2	3	4	5	6	7	8	9	A	B	C	D	E	F
S(x)	C	5	6	B	9	0	A	D	3	E	F	8	4	7	1	2

2.3 Attack Model

The attack model we consider here is that first presented [4], which constructs an attack method on the permutation network of the PRESENT-80 cipher which is ultimately shown applicable to all permutation based ciphers.

The SCADPA methodology utilizes a differential-plaintext attack and is initially performed by capturing power/Electromagnetic (EM) leakage in order to obtain SBox differential at the round output. To better illustrate this consider the following example, exemplified by Fig. 3, wherein if we consider any single bit change to the leftmost nibble then the resulting bits/locations that are potentially always impacted by this change are shown in red.

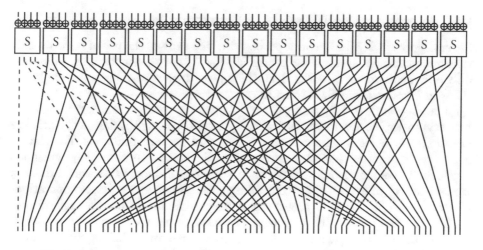

Fig. 3. Bits affected from changing a single bit input (Color figure online)

The SCADPA method serves to exploit this architectural design limitation/convention, and as to the best of our knowledge, all SPN based ciphers utilize such an exploitable design methodology; thus, the bits that are potentially affected by changing a single nibble will always be in the same position.

2.4 Interconnection Networks

ICNs can be used for a variety of routing applications: network switching, high-performance/parallel computing, and even sorting. Non-blocking IDNs are networks wherein the endpoints are outside (indirect) and that any permutation of

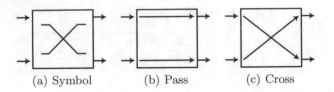

(a) Symbol   (b) Pass   (c) Cross

Fig. 4. Contention free Banyan switch

source-destination is possible via switching (non-blocking). The most basic non-blocking indirect switching element, shown by Fig. 4, is known as the *Banyan Switch* and is the foundation for intermediate flow-control of data for a variety of network topologies. For clarity, we note that *Contention Free* in Fig. 4 denotes that no two starting endpoints will attempt to utilize the same route. Additionally, the focus of the focus of this work will not be on the routing topologies between these Banyan structures, rather, it will focus on the use of solely these Banyan structures within cryptographic architectures.

2.5   Interconnection Networks in Crpytography

Several works [5,9,15] have been proposed which explore the use of ICNs outside telecommunication systems for producing low latency permutations. Similarly, only a limited number of works [8,11,16] appear to have been proposed exploring ICNs in cryptographic algorithms.

The first work [11] that appears to present the concept of integrating ICNs into cryptographic architectures does so by demonstrating the design of a one-key cryptosystem using a combination of ICNs and boolean functions. For clarity, a one-key system is that of a turn dial padlock, i.e., only one key will open the lock. To combat contention issues in switching elements this work utilizes a *control-setting function* (h) for controlling passthrough and crossover operations of Banyans. This function h, generated from some set of boolean operations, controls all Banyans in the topology; further showing that h can be enhanced through the use of a pseudo-random function generator. Ultimately this work shows that the use of ICNs in cryptography is a viable method for performing permutations while fulfilling the *avalanche* property.

Another work [8] shows that integration of ICNs for performing permutations in cryptographic software can successfully reduce the number of instructions and cycles needed in n-bit permutations. This is achieved through the development of four different permutation methods, wherein they show that each of these methods reduce cycle & instructions when compared to using Lookup-table (LUT) primitives; thus further showing that the application of network primitives can be advantageous in cryptosystems. A significant difference between this work [8] and [11] is how controlling bits for switching elements are generated, unlike that of [11] a variety of methods generate control sequences and switching element functionality is extended to handle *don't care* control values. Additionally, this method doesn't implement at rue switching network per say, it utilizes a series of registers with routing topologies (benes, butterfly, etc.) and connects register locations with 2-to-1 multiplexers; the output selected by the control value is passed to a temporary register.

More recently, [16] presents an On-Chip-Network (OCN) specifically targeting hardware based cryptographic cores. This work utilizes what is known as a *wormhole* ICN which is based on a *Flit* control method, rather than function generators. Flits are essentially data contained within a packet of information; with the format of a packet as: $\{Head, Flit, Flit, ..., Tail\}$. The wormhole ICN is simply a large mesh based ICN where communication of packets is done through single pieces of a packet and in a manner where the tail follows flits which follow the head that is initially sent through the wormhole. Conversely, as previous methods [8, 11] utilize non-blocking networks, a wormhole is inherently blocking and does not have contention free routing. In the event that two packets attempt to utilize the same route then one will be blocked and all subsequent pieces following the head will also stop. Additionally, this method explores the use of both randomized and pipelined scheduling for burst encryption of data. Results provided from the randomized scheduling method further enforce the fact that collision/contention is not handled in this system as [16] states that this method incurs longer transmission times due to increased collisions and disordering of packets; with the pipelined method presented to alleviate this drawback.

2.6   Key-Dependency in Cryptography

Several works exist in literature presenting the concept of key-dependent structures in cryptographic [2, 10]. However, they currently only pertain to, and demonstrate, enhanced security and avalanche properties for dynamic key-dependent Substitution Box (SBox) networks. While enhancing SBox resilience via key-dependent mechanisms provides enhanced security in one aspect it still does not aim to address other susceptibilities of many algorithms based on the previously detailed attack model.

3   Key-Dependent Interconnection Network Structures

As mentioned, existing key-dependent implementations do not aim to address the most recent susceptibilities in cryptographic algorithms, for this reason we aimed to provide a lightweight mechanism that can produce both key-dependent SBox and PBox networks. Thus, in this section we introduce the proposed approach for combating such differential-plaintext attacks applicable to not only IoT based, but all permutation based ciphers.

The proposed approach utilizes a controlled version of the Banyan switch for inducing key-dependent permutations of round data in PRESENT-80; however, this approach is still applicable to any cipher using permutation networks, not just PRESENT-80. To better illustrate this we depict how the operations of a controlled Banyan switch via Fig. 5.

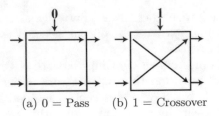

Fig. 5. Controlled Banyan switch

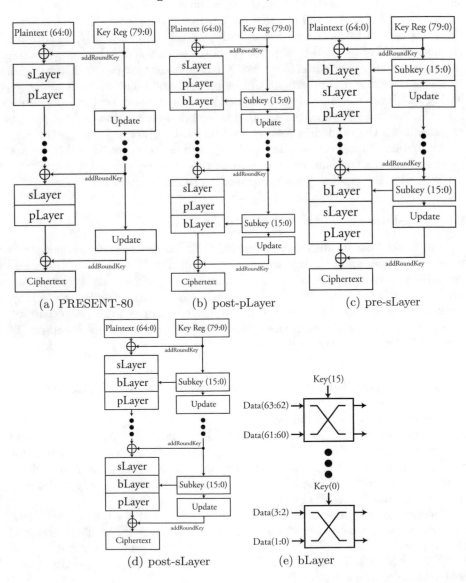

Fig. 6. PRESENT-80 architectures examined & bLayer implementation

Following, the architecture shown by Fig. 6(a) was constructed based on the original presentation and detailing of the PRESENT-80 cipher [3], and subsequent architectures Fig. 6(b)–(d) are those modified to incorporate a layer of controlled Banyan structures (*bLayer*), implemented as shown by Fig. 6(e), at various points in the round architecture. For simplicity, the bLayer was constructed around the PRESENT-80 cipher, such that, the input/output bus widths of the Banyan switches was based on the number of Banyans that were easily integrated: 16, as 16-bits of the 80-bit key went unused per round.

4 Experimental Evaluation

The architectures, shown by Fig. 6, were constructed and verified using Xilinx ISE 14.6, VHDL-93, and the Nexys 3 development board from Digilent (XC6SLX16-3CSG324). The remainder of this section, we provide results in terms of performance, area, and power data gathered during the synthesis process for each of the architectural implementations, while comparing it against the unaltered PRESENT-80 cipher.

We first present the synthesis results for each of these architectures in Table 2, where Lookup-Tables (LUTs) and Registers are reported in terms of Slice Logic Utilization as reported by Xilinx ISE when utilizing the default synthesis design goal & strategy: Balanced, Xilinx Default (unlocked). Additionally, for clarity, the parenthetically enclosed percentages reported in Table 2 denote the overall percentage of slice logic usage for the Nexys 3 development board used; the total number of slices for both LUTs and registers for this package are 9112 and 18224, respectively.

Table 2. Summary of synthesis results

Architecture	MHz	LUTs	Registers	$\%\Delta$ M	$\%\Delta$ L	$\%\Delta$ R
PRESENT-80 (Fig. 6(a))	223.821	589 (6%)	741 (4%)	–	–	–
Figure 6(b)	223.821	497 (5%)	757 (4%)	0	−15.62	2.16
Figure 6(c)	223.821	589 (6%)	741 (4%)	0	0	0
Figure 6(d)	223.821	482 (5%)	745 (4%)	0	−18.17	0.54

Following this, the architectures were mapped to the Nexys 3 board and power reports generated. Each of the designs was run with default signal activity for simplicity. Table 3 details the Total, Dynamic, and Static power for each of the PRESENT-80 architectures as reported by the Xilinx Power Estimator tool.

Table 3. Summary of I/O power results

Architecture	Total	Dynamic	Static	%Δ T	%Δ D	%Δ S
PRESENT-80 (Fig. 6(a))	91.5 mW	69.3 mW	22.2 mW	–	–	–
Figure 6(b)	69.6 mW	47.58 mW	22.0 mW	−23.93	−31.34	−0.9
Figure 6(c)	91.5 mW	69.3 mW	22.2 mW	0	0	0
Figure 6(d)	75.0 mW	52.95 mW	22.1 mW	−18.03	−23.59	−0.45

For clarity, values less than zero reported in the %Δ columns of Tables 2 and 3 denote improvements/reductions while those greater than zero indicate deterioration/increase of the corresponding metric.

4.1 Analysis of Results

Here we provide possible explanations for the results reported for both synthesis and power; as it can be seen that in nearly all cases modification of the original architecture to include the bLayer has shown to reduce power and slice usage. As this is otherwise counter-intuitive when considering hardware systems: more is generally not less. Thus, in the remainder of this section we will explore potential reasons for which the addition of logic produced both lower overall slice logic and power consumption.

When examining the Spartan-6 Configurable Logic Block (CLB) documentation, provided via [1], more insight is given; specifically, the XC6SLX16 architecture has 9,112 LUTs. More importantly, these LUTs are specifically 6-input LUTs which is completely less obvious from the Xilinx ISE post synthesis report,

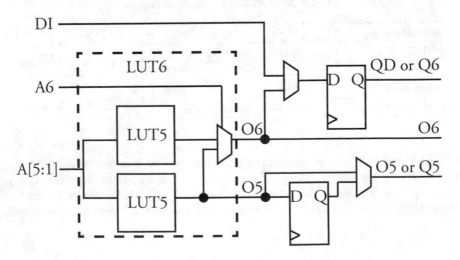

Fig. 7. Xilinx Spartan-6 slice LUT logic

as they are only reported as Slice LUTs. Now, consider Table 2, while a maximum difference of 1% in overall slice LUT usage appears minimal, or even negligible, when considering the %Δ difference we can see that the overall change is relatively large in comparison. Thus, we hypothesize that additional bLayer logic allowed for the synthesis process to greater utilize the 6-input LUTs via logic reduction and optimization efforts provided by the strategy. This becomes more clear given Fig. 7, the simplified implementation of an [1], and consider how given outputs of a bLayer can be condensed into the logic of an LUT6 better than solely that of the logic for a static permutation network.

Additionally, we secondarily hypothesize that through the reduction of 6-input LUTs and optimization of switching logic we also saw a reduction in total/dynamic/static power. We do note that further experiments utilizing other cryptographic algorithms and this method will need to be performed in order to confirm/deny this hypothesis. In addition to this we believe that because slice logic differs between development boards and logic cores, that it must also be explored across multiple development boards and packages. Such that, this benefit is not exclusive to both the PRESENT-80 and Nexys 3/Spartan-6 FPGA/development boards.

5 Analysis

Here we examine concepts applicable to this work that aim to increase cipher resilience, how it can be applied to other ciphers, and existing works which further support the proposed approach.

5.1 Differential-Plaintext Attacks

Here we examine the implications of these additions and architectural modifications with respect to existing susceptibilities exhibited by the PRESENT-80 algorithm. We first examine one of the most recent works that not only attacks the PRESENT-80 cipher but is applicable to all bit permutation based ciphers, and is presented [4].

This methodology, called SCADPA, utilizes a differential-plaintext attack and is initially performed by capturing power/Electromagnetic (EM) leakage in order to obtain SBox differential at the round output. However, while SCADPA captures leakage to capture entropy and determine SBox differential at the round output given that the permutation of bits is known, or static, consider this scenarios when examining the architecture presented by Fig. 6(b).

If these permutations and observable round outputs were not static but rather a key-dependent outcome then the observable differential represents two possible values. For example, when using the bLayer, an output of '0001' for bits (63:60) of a given round has the potential to be either '0001' or '0100' based on key-dependency and controlled permutations. When considering the PRESENT-80 cipher this is significant, as the SBox is predetermined for 4-bit nibbles of round data, and is provided by Table 1. This means that based on such a key-dependent

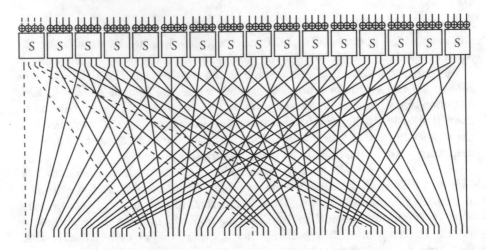

Fig. 8. Bits affected by changing first plaintext nibble

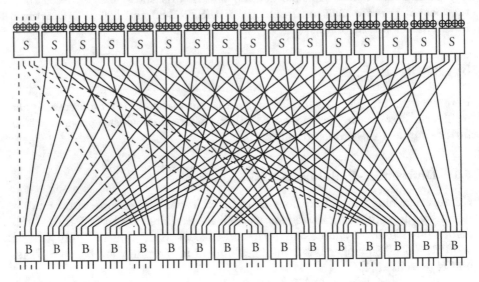

Fig. 9. Bits affected by changing first plaintext nibble when using bLayer for Fig. 6(b); twice as many

permutation the data substituted could have either originally been an 'E' or '3' and, thus, disrupts the ability to clearly ascertain an exact value of substitution from an otherwise static permutation network. Conversely, without use of the bLayer, a value of '0001' statically represented a substitution of '5' and allowed for a nibble of plaintext to be determined from the resulting permuted round data.

To best illustrate this, Fig. 8 shows the potential bits that can be affected by changing the first nibble of plaintext in the cipher, conversely, by employing a key-dependent Banyan layer Fig. 9 now illustrates the bits potentially affected, this increasing the number of possibilities and reducing the amount of static differential. For clarity, boxes labeled B in Fig. 9 and subsequent figures denotes a controlled Banyan.

Potential Improvements. Due to the ordering of Banyan structures only roughly twice the number of bits are potentially affected; however, it is possible to implement an architecture which yields a larger number of bits being affected when changing the first nibble, which is illustrated by Fig. 10. Similarly, through the use of bitwise Banyan operations the number of bits affected are five times as many, Fig. 11, and round dependency can be integrated through utilization of Banyans and bits from the round counter Fig. 12. For clarity the five Banyan structures at the bottom in Fig. 12 would be controlled by round counter bits (Fig. 13).

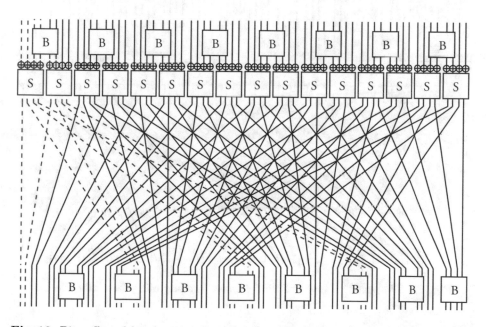

Fig. 10. Bits affected by changing first plaintext nibble; 3 times as many bits potentially affected

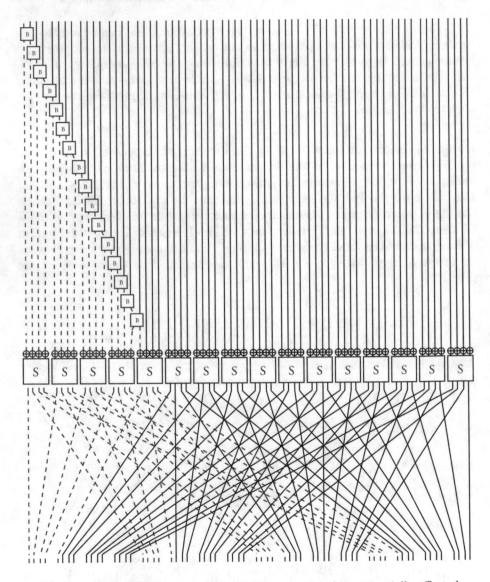

Fig. 11. "Waterfall" Banyan of Bits; 4 times as many bits potentially affected

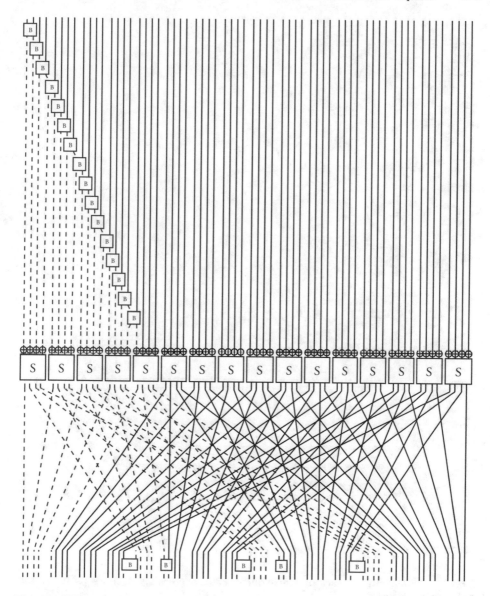

Fig. 12. "Waterfall" Banyan of Bits and Round Dependency; 6 times as many bits potentially affected

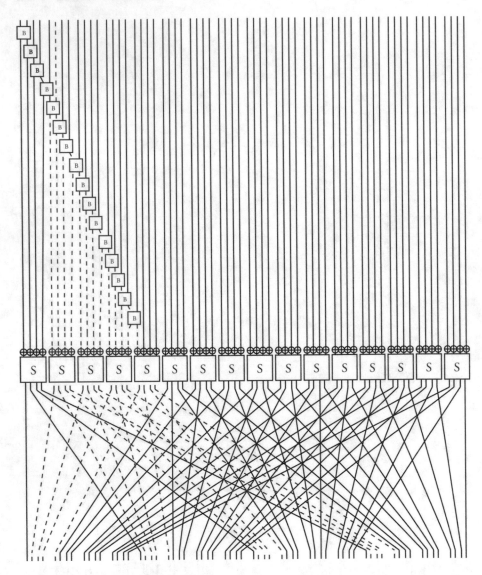

Fig. 13. "Waterfall" impact on Subsequent Bits, decreasing; 4 times as many bits potentially affected

5.2   Application to SBox

While the demonstration of this methodology was only applied to the PBox (pLayer) of the PRESENT-80 cipher it can easily be extended to enabling the use of key-dependent SBox permutations. If one were to apply controlled Banyan switches to some unique patterning of SBox data, where no collisions would occur for all combinations, then the incorporation of key-dependent SBox data is easily computed. For example, consider the two least significant bits in a binary representation of hexadecimal 0-F, if a controlled Banyan is applied to these 16 numbers then a unique key-dependent ordering of substitution values can be produced and requires no complex ordering.

5.3 Application to Other Ciphers

While we demonstrated this methodology using the PRESENT-80 cipher, due to 16-bits of unused round keys during a given round, it is easily applicable to other ciphers and can require minimal effort for incorporation. Doing so would be simply dictated by cipher owner and extension of key length for incorporation of key-dependent permutation based networks is a simple and feasible solution, as demonstrated for existing ciphers, while an additional key-schedule for such key-dependent permutation and substitution based networks can easily be developed and implemented as well, further expanding the key-space, complexities, and securities involved in attacking such systems.

5.4 Use with Other Methods

While this method shows to increase the differential of affected bits via key-dependent structures, the PRESENT-80 cipher is also known to be susceptible to both fault-injection and side-channel analysis, with a proven countermeasure to both of these attacks presented [6]. The application of this countermeasure is via SBox decomposition into shared registers using the system proposed [12] and implementation of masking circuitry. As alterations we present to the PRESET-80 cipher round structure are minimal impact and only serve to further reduce leakage, in applicable cases, altering the round structure for use with existing methods can trivially be implemented.

6 Conclusion

As shown, the use of controlled key-dependent ICN primitives enhances resilience against differential-plaintext attacks while demonstrating, via PRESENT-80, that no impacts to performance were incurred and in the most optimal scenario system power was reduced. Additionally, the use of this design methodology is highly flexible, applicable to SPN based networks while easily integrated into existing cipher architectures and still able to be seamlessly used with other methods and countermeasures to further enhance overall cipher security.

References

1. Spartan-6 fpga configurable logic block user guide. https://www.xilinx.com/support/documentation/user_guides/ug384.pdf

2. Ara, T., Shah, P.G., Prabhakar, M.: Dynamic key dependent S-Box for symmetric encryption for IoT devices. In: 2018 Second International Conference on Advances in Electronics, Computers and Communications (ICAECC), pp. 1–5 (2018). https://doi.org/10.1109/ICAECC.2018.8479442

3. Bogdanov, A., et al.: PRESENT: an ultra-lightweight block cipher. In: Paillier, P., Verbauwhede, I. (eds.) CHES 2007. LNCS, vol. 4727, pp. 450–466. Springer, Heidelberg (2007). https://doi.org/10.1007/978-3-540-74735-2_31

4. Breier, J., Jap, D., Bhasin, S.: SCADPA: side-channel assisted differential-plaintext attack on bit permutation based ciphers. In: 2018 Design, Automation Test in Europe Conference Exhibition (DATE), pp. 1129–1134 (2018). https://doi.org/10.23919/DATE.2018.8342180

5. Bin Dai, Z., Xiang, N.: Fast bit permutation instruction based on omega+omega network. In: 2007 7th International Conference on ASIC, pp. 153–156 (2007). https://doi.org/10.1109/ICASIC.2007.4415590

6. De Cnudde, T., Nikova, S.: Securing the present block cipher against combined side-channel analysis and fault attacks. IEEE Trans. Very Large Scale Integr. (VLSI) Syst. 25(12), 3291–3301 (2017). https://doi.org/10.1109/TVLSI.2017.2713483

7. Guttman, B., Roback, E.A.: SP 800–12. An Introduction to Computer Security: The NIST Handbook (1995)

8. Lee, R.B., Shi, Z., Yang, X.: Efficient permutation instructions for fast software cryptography. IEEE Micro 21(6), 56–69 (2001). https://doi.org/10.1109/40.977759

9. Li, H., Gao, F.: Design and implementation of reconfigurable bit permutation system based on Waksman network. In: 2010 Third International Conference on Information and Computing, vol. 2, pp. 113–116 (2010). https://doi.org/10.1109/ICIC.2010.122

10. Nejad, F.H., Sabah, S., Jam, A.J.: Analysis of Avalanche effect on advance encryption standard by using dynamic S-Box depends on rounds keys. In: 2014 International Conference on Computational Science and Technology (ICCST), pp. 1–5 (2014). https://doi.org/10.1109/ICCST.2014.7045184

11. Portz, M.: On the use of interconnection networks in cryptography. In: Davies, D.W. (ed.) EUROCRYPT 1991. LNCS, vol. 547, pp. 302–315. Springer, Heidelberg (1991). https://doi.org/10.1007/3-540-46416-6_26

12. Poschmann, A., Moradi, A., Khoo, K., Lim, C., Wang, H., Ling, S.: Side-channel resistant crypto for less than 2300 GE. J. Cryptol. 24(2), 332–345 (2011)

13. Shannon, C.E.: Communication theory of secrecy systems

14. Stallings, W., Brown, L.: Computer Security: Principles and Practice, 1st edn. Prentice Hall Press, Upper Saddle River (2008)

15. Yang, X., Lee, R.B.: Fast subword permutation instructions using omega and flip network stages. In: Proceedings 2000 International Conference on Computer Design, pp. 15–22 (2000). https://doi.org/10.1109/ICCD.2000.878264

16. Young, C.P., Chia, C.C., Chen, L.B., Huang, I.J.: On-chip-network cryptosystem: a high throughput and high security architecture. In: APCCAS 2008–2008 IEEE Asia Pacific Conference on Circuits and Systems, pp. 1276–1279 (2008). https://doi.org/10.1109/APCCAS.2008.4746260

Smart and Low Power IoT

Challenges in the Design of Integrated Systems for IoT

Ricardo Reis[✉]

Instituto de Informática, Universidade Federal do Rio Grande do Sul (UFRGS), Caixa Postal 15.064, Porto Alegre, RS 91501-970, Brazil
reis@inf.ufrgs.br

Abstract. The Internet of Things is moving fast to be the Internet of Everything. This brings several challenges in several areas of Computing Systems, as in Embedded Systems, Computer Architectures, Fault Tolerance and Integrated Circuits and Systems. One common point is the power optimisation, as the demanding energy is increasing year by year. Optimisation must be done in all levels of design abstraction, system, computer architecture till the physical design. Another issue is reliability and fault tolerance as systems at ground level can be affected by radiations reaching the ground. Also, as several devices in IoT are related to sensitive applications, security is also an important issue in different design levels, including the physical one. The talk will present an overview of all these issues, proposing also some solutions.

Keywords: Internet-of-Things · Optimization · Physical design · Fault Tolerance · Radiation effects · Embedded systems · Computer Architectures · VLSI · Nanoelectronics

1 Introduction

In Reis (2018) was shown that the Internet of Things (IoT) demands new challenges in the design of computing and electronics components. One of the major challenges is the power reduction of this expanding network of connected devices, where the majority is permanently connected. In a large set of applications, another significant issue is reliability, especially on critical areas as health and transport. It was presented an overview of design strategies that we have developed to reduce power consumption and to increase reliability in circuits that are components of the IoT, as the reduction of the number of transistors in IoT devices by using optimisation techniques and the physical design of circuits tolerant to radiation effects.

In this paper the goal is to discuss challenges in several areas of Computing Systems, as in Embedded Systems, Computer Architectures, Fault Tolerance and Integrated Circuits and Systems. Power optimization is a major issue, as the demanding energy to run all electronics devices is increasing year by year. In Reis (2018) was shown a figure with the number of transistors fabricated each year till 2014. Figure 1 shows a new version, including data about the number of transistors produced in 2017. It is possible to see that in 3 years, the production of transistors in the world increased

A. Casaca et al. (Eds.): IFIPIoT 2019, IFIP AICT 574, pp. 179–196, 2020.
https://doi.org/10.1007/978-3-030-43605-6_11

by 4 times, reaching the amount of 1 sextillions of transistors. How many power plants we will need to cope with increasing level of production of transistors?

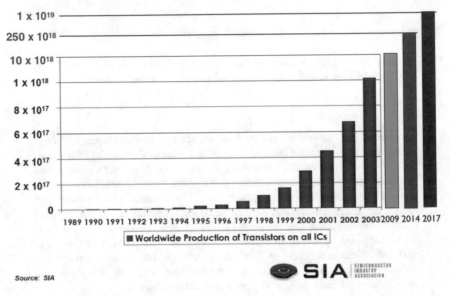

Fig. 1. Number of transistors produced annually in the world (adapted from (SIA 2005))

An essential keyword on the Internet of Things is **optimisation**, especially the optimisation of power consumption, which must be addressed at all levels of abstraction in the design flow of a computer or electronic system. The total power optimisation is a summation of the optimisation done at each level of design abstraction. So, sustainable computing requires optimisation at all design levels of a computer or electronic system design.

So, it is needed, more and more, to reduce the transistor count in each application specific design, which means the design of dedicated chips for embedded systems and new computer architectures (that nowadays means the design of new systems on chip). In other words, the use of Application Specific Integrated Circuits (ASICS). Also, due to reduction in voltages, the circuits are becoming more sensitive to radiation effects, even at ground level. Then, dedicated circuits to be used in critical applications, like in medicine and transport, must use fault tolerant techniques.

2 Internet of Things

Devices connected to the Internet of Things (or the Internet of Everything), can have many different complexities. If the complexity is considered by the number of components, the IoT includes small devices (with few transistors) and large devices (with billions of transistors). Large devices will consume much more power, but it should be considered that most devices on the Internet of Things are small ones with a low number of transistors. But, because they are found in large quantities, they can represent a total consumption more important than the consumption of the so-called large devices that, in general, are in a lower number. Therefore, consumption optimisation must be performed on both large and small devices that are present in large quantities. Another aspect to consider is that some devices require the application of reliability techniques (such as those related to transport or health systems), which can increase the number of components. Other devices are not critical, such as a camera or video, where an error in viewing a pixel of an image does not cause significant problems. Also, there is several cases where there is the need to consider security, as the protection of intellectual property.

It can be expected that many systems connected to the Internet of Everything (IoE) will be Cyber Physical Systems (CPS), that are systems composed by different classes of components like electronic elements, mechanical elements, optical elements, physical sensors, chemical sensors, organic components, and many others. So, it is needed to develop Electronic Design Automation (EDA) tools to cope with the design of CPS composed of all these classes of devices.

Figure 2 The Connectivist (2014) shows an estimate of the number of devices connected to the Internet since 1992 when they were about 1 million devices. By 2020 it is estimated that there will be more than 50 billion devices connected in the network, and just two years ago it was around 35 billion devices connected to the IoT. That means a 50% increase in just two years. This significant growth in the number of connected devices to the Internet has naturally led to a considerable increase in the energy need to run the IoT.

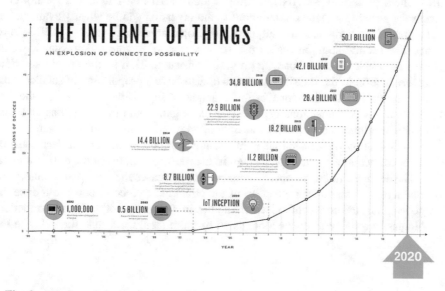

Fig. 2. Number of devices connected in the IoT (adapted from (The Connectivist 2014))

In critical areas such as the design of implanted devices (chips) in humans and chips to be used in transportation, the reliability of the implanted systems in humans and embedded systems in automobiles is obviously a critical issue. Some of the used techniques are based on the triplication of circuits and the temporal analysis of the propagation of a signal. Previously, the design of fault-tolerant circuits, to cope with radiation effects, was mainly in circuits that were sent to space. With the reduction of the value of the supply voltage of integrated circuits, nowadays the integrated circuits for use at ground level are also sensitive to errors caused by the radiation incident on the earth. Therefore, in critical applications it is necessary to implement radiation effects tolerance techniques (Velazco et al. 2007). Any critical systems used in the Internet of Health should be tolerant to any kind of noise (internal or external to the human body). They also must have a larger lifetime as possible, for obvious reasons and also should cope with environmental variability.

3   Power Consumption

The reduction of the power consumption of a System on a Chip (SoC) is a function of a sum of techniques and design strategies applied in different levels of abstraction in the design flow of an integrated system (Reis 2011a, b). The summation of the gains is that will define the total gain in power reduction. When we deal with the physical synthesis of a system on a chip, one technique is the optimisation of the number of components, that is, the transistor count. In Fig. 3, it can be observed two solutions for the implementation of the same equation. The first solution makes use of 4 basic logic gates (2 NOR 2-input ports and 2 NANDs), using a total of 16 transistors. We are not considering the possible inverters in the input as the inversion can be already available (as for example, if the variable is the output of a flipflop that has both values available in its output). The second solution makes use of only one logic gate (a supergate), which performs the same function but with only 10 transistors. That is, the second solution, having a reduction in the transistor count, will also have a proportionally smaller static power consumption. Furthermore, in the example of Fig. 3, we can see that the first solution also has 3 connections between the basic gates (and therefore vias and contacts) that are eliminated in the second option, with only one larger logic gate.

This elimination of connections is increasingly important because it decreases the number of connections to be implemented in the routing step, using the different metal layers. The decrease in the number of connections decreases the density of connections and, therefore, increases the routability of the circuit. It also contributes to reduce the average length of the connections, which implies in a reduction of the delay. In modern technologies, the delay in connections is so or more significant than the delay in the switching of logic gates. A greater spacing between the connections also contributes to an increase of reliability, due, for example, to the reduction of the possibility of electromigration (Posser et al. 2017).

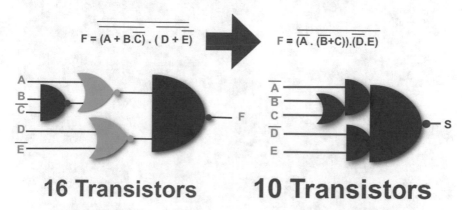

Fig. 3. Two options for the implementation of the same function (Reis 2011a)

The reduction of the transistor count depends on the use of efficient EDA tools that transform the logical equations of a system so that in addition to mapping equations in CMOS gates, make optimal use of complex logic gates. In Conceição and Reis (2019) we present a tool to reduce the number of transistors in a circuit through the fusion of networks of transistors that present fanout equal to 1. Also, it is fundamental the use of an automatic synthesis tool that can perform the automatic layout of any logical function. There is no way to achieve a logical optimisation when it should be used a technology mapping step to transform the equations according to the logic gates available in a traditional cell library (which have few functions, in general, no more than 100 functions), as is done when using a traditional EDA system for standard cell-based designs. The technology mapping represents a step of deoptimization. With this aim, we have developed automatic layout synthesis tools such as ASTRAN (Ziesemer and Reis 2015) (Fig. 4), which allows the automatic layout generation of any network of transistors (Reis 2011a).

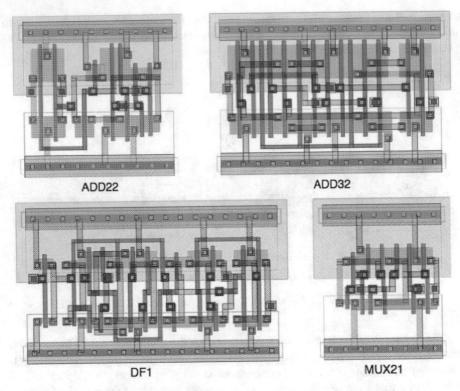

ADD22

ADD32

DF1

MUX21

Fig. 4. Transistor network layouts generated automatically (Ziesemer and Reis 2015)

Another technique to reduce consumption is through the sizing of the transistors. Modern integrated circuit manufacturing technologies show a significant increase in static power consumption that is often greater than dynamic power consumption. One way to mitigate power consumption, especially the static one, is to carry out a sizing of transistors to optimise power consumption. In Reimann et al. (2016) significant decreases in consumption are obtained through the use of automatic transistor sizing tools. This method is also called cell selection, when the cells are selected from a cell library. In this case, cell selection means the selection of cells with a specific size and Vth (threshold voltage). In traditional cell libraries, one function has in general 3 sizings (one for smaller area, one for less power, and one for smaller delay) and 3 Vth (threshold voltage).

It is possible to investigate different strategies to do the automatic layout generation, one is ASTRAN that was referred above, another one is presented in Fig. 5, where transistors are placed and routed using some metal bricks and contacts/vias, to construct the layout of a transistor network.

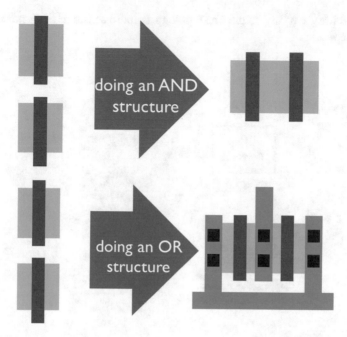

Fig. 5. Placement and routing of transistors to obtain the layout a transistor network

4 Reliability

The design of critical systems demands the use of techniques to increase reliability at different levels of design abstraction. At the architectural level, a traditional method is the redundancy of modules, especially triple module redundancy (TMR) (Kastensmidt et al. 2006). Another is the temporal redundancy (Nicolaidis 1999) where a signal traverses two paths, one with higher delay and another one with less delay. The difference of delay must be longer than the duration of a transient. Comparing the signal after traversing the two paths indicates if there was a transient propagation or not. At the physical level, we can apply different techniques to reduce or avoid problems such as electromigration (Posser et al. 2017). In Velazco et al. (2007) it is presented a series of works aimed at mitigating the effects of radiation on integrated circuits. In Kastensmidt et al. (2006), Neuberger et al. (2014), Gennaro et al. (2017), Aguiar et al. (2016), Lazzari et al. (2011), Brendler et al. (2018), Brendler et al. (2019) it is presented some of the results that our research group has obtained in the development of techniques aiming the design tolerant to faults due to transients, as the ones due to radiation effects.

It was observed that there is an influence of the transistor arrangement in the sensitivity of gates to radiation effects (Brendler et al. 2018; Zimpeck et al. 2018). In Fig. 6 it is presented an AOI21 gate designed using (a) close and (b) far topologies for a 7 nm predictive Finfet technology. It was observed that for short pulse width the Far topology was less sensitive to radiation effects and more sensitive when the pulse width is above 1200 ps for a LET of 10 MeV.cm^2.mg^{-1}. But for Linear Energy Transfer

(LET) of 58 MeV.cm^2.mg^{-1}, the Far topology is more sensitive from pulse width of 350 ps or more.

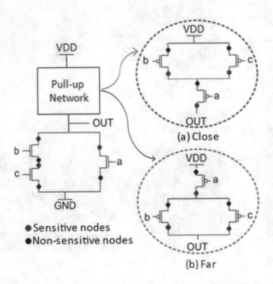

Fig. 6. Influence of transistor arrangement in the sensitivity of gates to radiation effects (Brendler et al. 2018)

5 Security

Security is a critical issue in the design of many circuits and systems for IoT. Chip content security has increasingly become one of the significant issues for the Semiconductor (IC) Industry, and the reasons range from counterfeiting to the theft of core technologies and trade secrets. This concern is even more significant in the IoT context, that uses more and more embedded systems and embedded devices on a large scale. An extensive set of IoT circuits are small ones and typically using mature process technology, which implies in a circuit more accessible to suffer reverse engineering by delayering the set of layers. These characteristics make these embedded systems susceptible to intellectual property infringement using reverse engineering attacks (El Massad et al. 2015). However, there are also more and more IoT devices using modern technologies using several layers and making the reverse engineering more complicated, but still possible.

Let's consider the design security in IoT from the perspective of the physical design. One action is to make reverse engineering more laborious by using camouflage techniques. Another way to make reverse engineering difficult is to use different transistor arrangements for the same function, or yet to use complex logic functions beyond the available ones in a standard cell library. Also, it can be considered the generation of different layout approaches for a same function. This task is more comfortable with the help of an EDA tool to generate several different layouts for a same function. Chip-level reverse engineering is an analysis of electronic circuits that focus on getting back the circuit functionality description from the layout view, by first identifying the transistors and how they are connected. Chip-level reverse engineering is a more and more complex task that demands advanced equipment like high-resolution optical and electronic microscopes, probe stations and logic analysers. It comprises several main steps, as illustrated in Fig. 7.

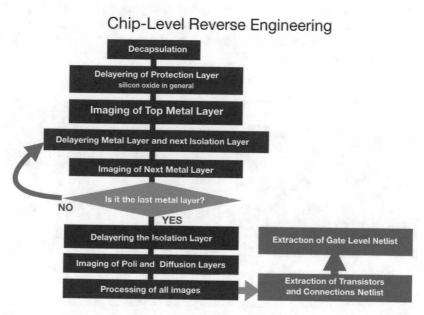

Fig. 7. Influence of transistor arrangement in the sensitivity of gates to radiation effects (Brendler et al. 2018)

The decapsulation step exposes the IC internal components like the die and pad interconnections. Delayering consists in taking out the material of layer by layer. It is a destructive process done by using acids and allowing to see each metal layer, polysilicon, active areas and substrate. In each imaging step, an image is taken of each layer using an ultra-high-resolution optical microscope. Each image related to each metal layers, via layers, polysilicon layer and diffusion layers are saved in a database. Then, it is done a post-processing to analyse the obtained images of each layer to build up first a transistors and connections netlist. Then, from this netlist it is obtained a gate level one. From a gate level netlist it is possible to go to higher abstraction levels and to discover the functionality of the chip. Let's present some alternative physical design approaches to prevent this kind of attack by making harder the reverse engineering steps.

Post-processing steps in chip-level reverse engineering cover the activities of annotation, gate-level schematic extraction, and schematic analysis and organization. These steps are partially automated by extraction tools and pattern recognition tools that are used to annotate wire names, identify connections, and recognize logic cells. Anti-reverse engineering strategies rely on reducing the power of such tools, making the activities more time consuming, complicated, and expensive willing to discourage most forms of attack.

The camouflage technique is a way to provide security for the circuit in the cell level. Instead of only using cells from a typical standard cell library, it works by selecting some gates from the original netlist to be camouflaged (Rajendran et al. 2013). It uses a look-alike technique where camouflaged gates share the same layout and include dummy lines, as well as dummy and true pins, as shown in Fig. 8. The choice of which pins will be true or dummy defines the gate functionality. Therefore, some cells in the circuit layout will differ just by the contact layers, thus making a pattern recognition more difficult.

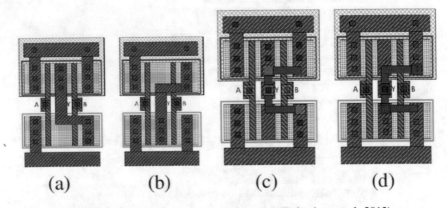

Fig. 8. Influence of transistor arrangement (Rajendran et al. 2013)

The work of Gomez et al. (2019) proposes to use many different layouts for the same cell as an alternative to a look-alike method. Besides NOR and NAND gates, they propose to automate the layout of inverters, latches, and flip-flop cells to generate different layouts as a way to improve security. They argue that an imaging tool is trained with a database of regular optimal cells. So, it will not be able to identify other gates that have a non-optimal geometry shape, and therefore they cannot extract a full netlist.

The use of more complex AOIs (And Or Inverters) is also a way to complicate a reverse engineering, mainly if a same AOI can have different layouts. Transistor reordering is a simple technique based on rearranged transistor networks keeping the same logic function. In the design of AOI gates, it is possible to consider different orderings of the transistors for the same function as shown in Fig. 9. Different transistor combinations change the electrical and physical characteristics of logic cells, and consequently, it also alters the susceptibility to process variations and radiation-induced soft errors. However, it can also be used to complicate reverse engineering.

Figure 9 shows the layout of an AOI21 logic cell implemented using two different transistor ordering. The layouts are related to a FinFet technology using three fins per transistor. It is possible to see that the metal layer is different in both solutions. So, the use of different transistor ordering for the same function also helps to difficult reverse engineering. However, it is also known that a different transistor ordering means different sensitivity to radiation effects (Zimpeck et al. 2019).

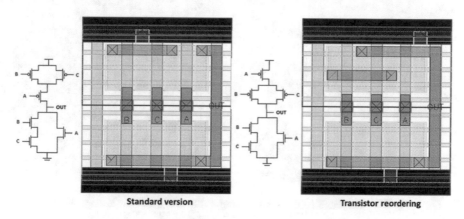

Fig. 9. An AOI using two different transistor reordering

As mentioned, instead of making similar layouts for different logic functions to make reverse engineering difficult, we can also use an opposite option, that is to have many different layouts for a same logic function. It is possible by generating transistor networks on the fly using a layout generator tool as ASTRAN (Ziesemer and Reis 2015). Even better if the logic function is not a conventionally one found in a traditional cell library.

The use of complex cells composed by several transistors provides a more extensive set of layout options as well as a big design exploration with transistor reordering. As an example, Fig. 10 shows four layout options for the same logic function, also using transistor reordering, that enables four different metal layer artworks. Other layout artworks are still possible for the same netlist varying the parameters of the cell layout generator.

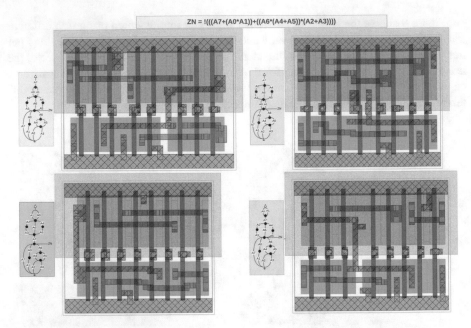

Fig. 10. The same AOI function using 4 different transistor arrangements

This approach does not show the limitations that we have when using a standard cell library, that contains a limited set of logic functions and a limited set of sizing. By using a layout generator tool, we overcome this limitation and extend the number of logic functions that a circuit can use, as well to generate cells with a large set of sizing options. This push reverse engineers to analyse circuit from a transistor level instead of a gate level, thus considerably increasing the complexity of a reverse engineering approach.

The tool we developed can be set to generate new complex cells (supercells) with up to a limiting number of transistors defined by the designer, as well as the limit of allowed serial transistors.

6   3D Circuits

There are two main types of 3D circuits. The basic 3D circuits are composed of several tiers (layers) of silicon fabricated separately and mounted one over the other and connected by using TSV (through-silicon vias) (see Fig. 11). They are called TSV 3D Circuits or Stacked 3D Circuits.

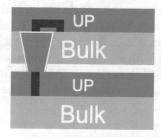

Fig. 11. Scheme of a TSV 3D circuit (Hentschke 2007)

Another type of 3D Circuits, shown in Fig. 12, is the Monolithic ones (M3D), where the tiers of transistors are placed one over the others by deposition. The connections between tiers in a monolithic 3D Circuits (MIVs) are much smaller than the TSVs used in stacked 3D Circuits. Also, the layers of transistors in a monolithic 3D are separated by an isolation layer much thinner than in stacked 3D circuits. In one main type of monolithic circuits, one tier is used to do the NMOS transistors (the top one), and a next tier is used to do the PMOS transistors. The implementation of connections is divided into two set of connections, the interlayer one, that mainly does the connections inside a network of transistors (logic cell) and are located between P and N tiers. The longer connections use a back-end level of connections in the top of the NMOS layer (see Fig. 12).

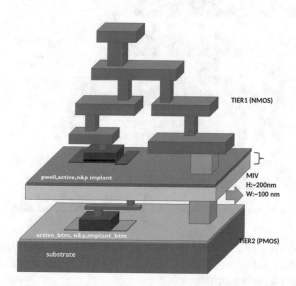

Fig. 12. Scheme of a Monolithic 3D circuit (source: Carolina Metzler)

It is also possible to conclude that 3D circuits are more protected to reverse engineering, mainly the monolithic ones, as they are more difficult and more laborious to do delayering. The use of different tiers to do PMOS and NMOS transistors also help to improve security. It can also be concluded that 3D circuits are more tolerant to radiation effects as lower tiers will be less sensitive to radiation.

In Monolithic 3D, a gate is folded and implemented using two tiers (Fig. 13). The use of more regular layout of transistor networks is important to allow an easier way to implement MIVs as a vertical one, connecting top and bottom layer elements.

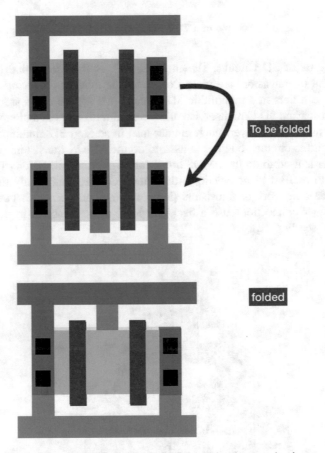

To be folded

folded

Fig. 13. In Monolithic 3D, a gate is folded and implemented using two tiers

The different tiers of a 3D circuit can correspond to different types of circuits as well to different technologies. The only concern is to well adjust the placement of TSVs or MIVs. Figure 14 shows an example.

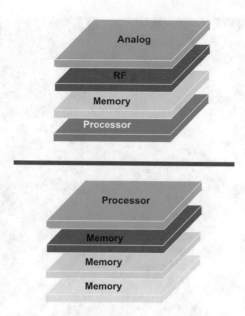

Fig. 14. The different tiers of a 3D circuit can correspond to different types of circuits

7 Hardware Accelerators

The evolution of computer architectures, which today means, the evolution of micro-processor architectures has been very significant. Nowadays, there are chips with multiple CPUs and several GPUs, as can be seen in Fig. 15 (Techinsights 2018) showing the floorplan of the A12 microprocessor (from Apple). In this same figure, it can be observed that about half of the area is occupied with hardware accelerators, which are modules dedicated to the execution of a specific function. For example, an encryption module placed next to the output/input pins and which will encode the output data and decode the received data. The execution of this function will be faster, because it is done by a dedicated module (that means a smaller one) and with only the needed number of transistors to perform that function. It also will consume less power.

A more important fact is that the use of hardware accelerators leads to greater energy efficiency (allowing more sustainable computing), mainly due to the reduction in the number of components used to perform a function. At any given time, only the hardware accelerators in use at that time are being powered. So, the hardware accelerators that are not in use are disconnected from the power supply (shut down). This strategy is also known as "Dark Silicon". We can even predict architectures consisting essentially of hardware accelerators, with only one or two small CPUs to manage these hardware accelerators.

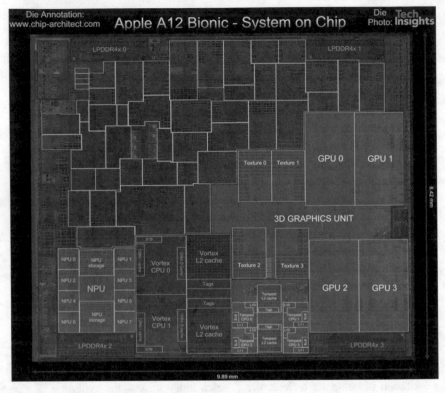

Fig. 15. Apple 12 Floorplan with an NPU (Techinsights 2018)

The introduction of an Neural Processing Unit (NPU) in A11 is another element characterising the heterogeneity of the SoC. And we can expect increasingly heterogeneous architectures, with dedicated modules for different operations to be performed by a SoC. In Fig. 15 (Techinsights 2018) the floorplan of the Apple A12 microprocessor is presented, where one of the modules is an NPU. NPU is mostly dedicated to facial recognition (Techinsights 2018), processing machine learning tasks more efficiently, consuming less energy than CPUs do. The 2 high performance CPUs plus the 4 lower power CPUs, occupy about 15% of the area of the chip and 4 GPUs occupy about 20% of the area. Most of the area is filled with the hardware accelerators. That is, it is increasing the use of hardware accelerators in the architecture of Apple microprocessors/systems on chip.

8   Conclusions

The main challenges in several areas of Computing Systems, as in Embedded Systems, Computer Architectures, Fault Tolerance and Integrated Circuits and Systems, are mainly power consumption, reliability and security. To have sustainable computing, it is fundamental that the design of the devices connected to the IoE, includes optimization in all abstraction levels of a design, mainly with the goal of reducing power consumption. At architectural level, the use of hardware accelerators is a great strategy, not only to reduce power consumption but also to speed up the execution of functions.

At physical level, it can be observed that most of the chips being designed nowadays use many more transistors than necessary to perform a function. There is a significant space for the optimisation of the transistor count at logical level. In devices related to critical applications, like medical and transport ones, it is needed the application of techniques for fault tolerance, as nowadays circuits at ground level can have faults due to radiation effects. The keyword in the IoT/IoE is **optimisation**.

Acknowledgements. We thank CNPq, FINEP, Fapergs, and CAPES for financial support for the development of our team's work, as well as the master's and doctoral students of PGMICRO and PPGC and students of Scientific Initiation who have contributed to the research works that served as the basis for this paper.

References

Reis, R.: Strategies for reducing power consumption and increasing reliability in IoT. In: Strous, L., Cerf, V.G. (eds.) IFIPIoT 2018. IAICT, vol. 548, pp. 76–88. Springer, Cham (2019). https://doi.org/10.1007/978-3-030-15651-0_8

Semiconductor Industry Association: Rebooting the IT revolution. http://www.semiconductors. org/clientuploads/Resources/RITR%20WEB%20version%20FINAL.pdf

The Connectivist (2014). http://ow.ly/i/5vph6/original

Velazco, R., Fouillat, P., Reis, R.: Radiation Effects on Embedded Systems. Springer, Dordrecht (2007). https://doi.org/10.1007/978-1-4020-5646-8. ISBN 978-1-4020-5645-1

Reis, R.: Design automation of transistor networks, a new challenge. In: IEEE International Symposium on Circuits and Systems, ISCAS 2011, Rio de Janeiro, Brasil, 15–19 May 2011, pp. 2485–2488. IEEE Press (2011a). https://doi.org/10.1109/iscas.2011.5938108

Reis, R.: Power consumption & reliability in NanoCMOS. In: IEEE NANO, 11th International Conference on Nanotechnology, Portland, USA, 15–19 August 2011, pp. 711–714 (2011b). (invited talk). https://doi.org/10.1109/nano.2011.6144656

Posser, G., Sapatnekar, S., Reis, R.: Electromigration Inside Logic Cells, 118 p. Springer, Cham (2017). https://doi.org/10.1007/978-3-319-48899-8

Conceição, C., Reis, R.: Transistor count reduction by gate merging. IEEE Trans. Circuits Syst. I **66**(6) (2019). https://doi.org/10.1109/tcsi.2019.2907722

Reimann, T., Sze, C., Reis, R.: Challenges of cell selection algorithms in industrial high performance microprocessor designs. Integration **52**, 347–354 (2016). https://doi.org/10. 1016/j.vlsi.2015.09.001. ISSN 0167-9260

Ziesemer, A., Reis, R.: Physical design automation of transistors network. Microelectron. Eng. **148**, 122–128 (2015). https://doi.org/10.1016/j.mee.2015.10.018. ISSN 0167-9317

Kastensmidt, F., Carro, L., Reis, R.: Fault-Tolerance Techniques for SRAM-Based FPGA, 183 p. Springer, New York (2006). https://doi.org/10.1007/978-0-387-31069-5. ISBN 0-387-31068-1

Nicolaidis, M.: Time redundancy based soft-error tolerance to rescue nanometer technologies. In: 1999 Proceedings of the IEEE VLSI Test Symposium, vol. 17, pp. 86–94. IEEE Computer Society (1999)

Neuberger, G., Wirth, G., Reis, R.: Protecting Chips Against Hold Time Violations Due to Variability, 107 p. Springer, Dordrecht (2014). https://doi.org/10.1007/978-94-007-2427-3. ISBN 978-94-007-2426-6

Gennaro, R., Rosa, F., Oliveira, A., Kastensmidt, F., Ost, L., Reis, R.: Analyzing the impact of fault tolerance methods in ARM processors under soft errors running Linux and parallelization APIs. IEEE Trans. Nucl. Sci. **64**(8) (2017). https://doi.org/10.1109/tns.2017. 2706519. ISSN 1558-1578

Aguiar, Y., Zimpeck, A., Meinhardt, C., Reis, R.: Permanent and single event transient faults reliability evaluation EDA tool. Microelectron. Reliab. **64**, 63–67 (2016). ISSN 0026-2714

Lazzari, C., Wirth, G., Kastensmidt, F., Anghel, L., Reis, R.: Asymmetric transistor sizing targeting radiation-hardened circuits. J. Electr. Eng. (2011). https://doi.org/10.1007/s00202-011-0212-8

Brendler, L.H., Zimpeck, A.L., Meinhardt, C., Reis, R.: Evaluating the impact of process variability and radiation effects on different transistor arrangement. In: 2018 VLSI-SOC - International Conference on Very Large Scale Integration (VLSI), Verona, vol. 1, pp. 1–6 (2018)

Brendler, L., Zimpeck, A., Meinhardt, C., Reis, R.: Multi-level design influences on robustness evaluation of 7 nm FinFET technology. IEEE Trans. Circuits Syst. I (2019). https://doi.org/10.1109/tcsi.2019.2927374

Zimpeck, A., Meinhardt, C., Artola, L., Hubert, G., Kastensmidt, F., Reis, R.: Impact of different transistor arrangements on gate variability. Microelectron. Reliab. **88–90**, 111–115 (2018). https://doi.org/10.1016/j.microrel.2018.06.090. ISSN 0026-2714

El Massad, M., Garg, S., Tripunitara, M.: Integrated circuit (IC) decamouflaging: Reverse engineering camouflaged ICs within minutes. In: Network and Distributed System Security Symposium (NDSS), January 2015. https://doi.org/10.14722/ndss.2015.23218

Rajendran, J., Sam, M., Sinanoglu, O., Karri, R.: Security analysis of integrated circuit camouflaging. In: CCS 2013, Berlin, Germany, 4–8 November 2013 (2013)

Gomez, H., Duran, C., Roa, E.: Defeating silicon reverse engineering using a layout level standard cell camouflage. IEEE Trans. Consum. Electron. **65**(1), 109–118 (2019). https://doi.org/10.1109/TCE.2018.2890616

Hentschke, R.: Algorithms for wire length improvement of VLSI circuits with concern to critical paths. Ph.D. thesis, PPGC/UFRGS (2007)

Zimpeck, A., Meinhardt, C., Kastensmidt, F., Hubert, G., Reis, R., Artola, L.: Mitigation of process variability effects using decoupling cells. Microelectron. Reliab. **100-101**, 6 p., paper 113446 (2019). https://doi.org/10.1016/j.microrel.2019.113446. ISSN 0026-2714

Techinsights (2018). http://techinsights.com/

Mixed Precision Quantization Scheme for Re-configurable ReRAM Crossbars Targeting Different Energy Harvesting Scenarios

Md Fahim Faysal Khan[1], Nicholas Anton Jao[1], Changchi Shuai[2],
Keni Qiu[2(✉)], Mehrdad Mahdavi[3], and Vijaykrishnan Narayanan[3(✉)]

[1] Department of Electrical Engineering,
Pennsylvania State University, University Park, PA, USA
[2] Capital Normal University, Beijing, China
qiukn@cnu.edu.cn
[3] Department of Computer Science and Engineering,
Pennsylvania State University, University Park, PA, USA
vxn9@psu.edu

Abstract. Crossbar arrays with non-volatile memory have recently become very popular for DNN acceleration due to their In-Memory-Computing property and low power requirements which makes them suitable for deployment on edge. Quantized Neural Networks (QNNs) enable us to run inference with limited hardware resource and power availability and can easily be ported on smaller devices. On the other hand, to make edge devices self sustainable a great deal of promise has been shown by energy harvesting scenarios. However, the power supplied by the energy harvesting sources is not constant which becomes problematic as a fixed trained neural network requires a constant amount of power to run inference. This work addresses this issue by tuning network precision at layer granularity for variable power availability predicted for different energy harvesting scenarios.

Keywords: Quantization · Deep learning · ReRAM · Crossbar · Energy harvesting · Power predictor

1 Introduction

Deep Neural Networks (DNNs) have gained enormous popularity by solving tasks such as object recognition and detection at human level accuracy over the past few years [10]. One of the key factors responsible for the rapid progress, is the availability of compute power such as GPUs. Although these hardware facilitate the training and running of the DNNs at high precision, they consume a huge amount of power. Excessive power consumption is a major bottleneck while running inference using DNNs on edge devices such as smartphones, smartwatches or training them in a distributed fashion using edge nodes. Quantization of these

Published by Springer Nature Switzerland AG 2020
A. Casaca et al. (Eds.): IFIPIoT 2019, IFIP AICT 574, pp. 197–216, 2020.
https://doi.org/10.1007/978-3-030-43605-6_12

networks offer lower state representation, transforming expensive floating point computations into integer arithmetic. Hence, quantization makes the networks more amenable for execution on systems with low compute capability and limited power. Consequently, research in Quantized Neural Networks (QNNs) is promising and is the focus of this work.

Non-volatile memories such as Resistive Random Access Memory (ReRAM) arranged in a crossbar structure permit intrinsic and efficient computation of multiply-accumulate (MAC) operations which dominate the run-time of convolutional neural networks (CNNs). This is due to the notion of leveraging Kirchoff's current law using the ReRAM cells as the weight modulators to perform analog current summation and exploit the crossbar's intrinsic parallelism to compute MAC [3,17]. However, this analog method of computation is impractical on full-precision floating point data representations and therefore more suitable to run low-precision fixed point computations. This work leverages ReRAM based crossbars as the underlying hardware platform for the proposed low-precision neural networks.

The scenarios of deploying energy harvesting processors and accelerators have drawn researchers' interest in the area of Internet of Things (IoTs). Various techniques have been proposed to reconfigure tasks or execution patterns to match the widely fluctuating harvested energy and thus achieve the optimal energy efficiency [7,12,23]. For an energy harvesting system, it is important to have the ability of power prediction to be aware of the future power in advance. In this work, with the ability of power prediction, we can proactively configure the last incomplete inference's network structure to fit the next coming power cycle, but not discarding the obtained partial results.

Inference using a given deep network requires a fixed amount of power. As a result, when the amount of harvested power varies due to inherent fluctuations in an energy-harvesting environment, there exists a mismatch between the power producer and the deep network consumer. It can happen that a high precision fixed network cannot be executed in many power cycles due to its high power demand. It can also happen that a low precision fixed network may achieve high throughput but very low accuracy. In order to adapt to this variable power scenario, dynamic precision quantization could be a solution. That is, we accommodate different mix-precision network structures to different power supply levels to achieve a balance among accuracy, performance and power.

This work makes the following contributions:

- We propose a mixed precision quantization scheme to find different network configurations to support operation at different levels of harvested power. Our approach builds upon an existing multi-precision framework and modifies it to incorporate power-aware tuning.
- A high-accuracy power predictor is designed to be able to predict multiple power levels. Specifically, a SMOTE algorithm is embedded into the predictor to pre-process the data set so as to achieve balanced data group density for the training phase.

- Both QNN learning results and the system-level results (*throughput, energy efficiency, energy utilization* etc.) show that the proposed mixed precision quantization scheme can manage a good trade-off among throughput, energy efficiency and accuracy.

The remainder of the paper is organized as follows. Section 2 describes background information and related work to QNN, ReRAM crossbar and energy harvesting systems. Section 3 presents the quantization schemes for different power levels. Section 4 shows the ReRAM circuit parameters and different network configurations. In Sect. 5, we present a power predictor which can predict multilevel future power with a high accuracy. Section 6 shows the experimental results. Finally, we conclude the paper in Sect. 7.

2   Background and Related Work

2.1   Quantized Neural Networks

Quantized Neural Networks (QNNs) enable us to run inference using low compute capability and power availability. One approach towards QNN investigates post training quantization, where the training is done in full precision and then the trained model is quantized [1,13]; Another approach deals with quantization during training [4,5,14,16,24,25]. Both approaches result in a compressed version of the model with reduced bit precision to have a lighter inference requirement. However, all of the above mentioned works offer a uniform precision quantized network i.e. bit precision of each layer is fixed.

Recently, there have been a few studies on training mixed precision networks as well where each layer inside the network can have different bit representation. It has recently been showed by [22] that different layers inside a neural network serves different purposes and should not be treated as same. The mixed precision approaches support the statement [6,19–21] by showing that the accuracy can be preserved even though a good number of layers are quantized to lower precision while keeping a few at higher precision. HAQ [20] and ReLeQ [21] are reinforcement learning based approaches where the agent learns the bit precision for each of the layers after a large number of training episodes. HAWQ [6] finds mixed precision configurations by using second order information like calculating hessian. C2Q [19] takes a full precision or quantized network at higher state and quantizes it to a lower bit representation gradually layer by layer based on a competitive-collaborative approach.

2.2   ReRAM Crossbar-Based Accelerator

ReRAM crossbar is a promising device to perform MAC operations in a In-Memory Computing style. PRIME [3] presents the architecture-level design of ReRAM crossbar-based accelerator where the ReRAMs function as dual modes of both computing module and storage module. Custom peripheral circuits are designed to achieve the reusability of the ReRAM crossbars. The ISAAC [17]

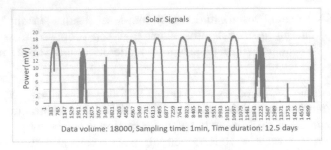

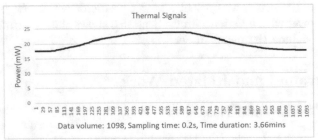

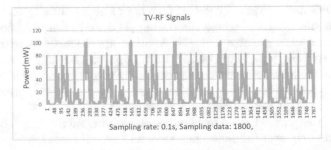

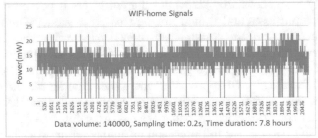

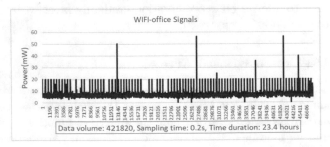

Fig. 1. Five energy harvesting sources.

architecture supports a pipeline execution to boost the MAC throughput based on the ReRAM tiles. The hybrid ReRAM structure [15] is proposed to combine sequential and parallel execution fashions to meet some power budget.

2.3 Energy Harvesting System

Energy harvesters accumulate energy from the surrounding environment, such as solar energy, piezo electricity, thermal gradients, radio frequency (RF) radiation, as shown in Fig. 1. The harvested energy can be first charged to energy stores or directly fed to devices. In this work, we consider the "Harvest-Direct Use" architecture to use the harvested energy. Because the environmental energy is not stable, the system may suffer frequently power-down and has to restart. Even with power on, the system has to operate under a fluctuating powering condition.

It is known that power consumption requirements of different system architectures vary. Ma et al. proposed three hardware structures to fit the changing power of energy harvesters [11]. This work targets the ReRAM crossbar-based CNN deployment. The goal is to accommodate different quantization solutions to the changing harvested power. Since we need to reconfigure the ReRAMs given a power level and a corresponding quantization solution, it is highly demanded to know the power level of future power cycles.

3 Quantization for Different Power Levels

In this section, we briefly describe our methodology for training mixed precision networks. We choose a layer by layer gradual quantization strategy to find networks with different bit precision granularity following C2Q [19]. The quantization framework can incorporate any of the existing quantization strategies and deliver a quantized model within a targeted size, power or accuracy threshold. Figure 2 gives an overview of this framework.

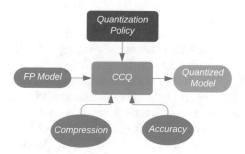

Fig. 2. Competitive-Collaborative Quantization (CCQ or C2Q) framework. It takes a full precision model and gives a quantized model under different size, power and accuracy constraints.

In this particular problem, the power supplied by the energy harvesting sources is not constant. A constant fixed network requires a specific amount of power to execute. When the energy harvesting sources can deliver that amount of power, the network can operate. However, when the available power is less than the required, it cannot operate. Interestingly, if the energy harvesting sources deliver more power, the network cannot make use of that either without an energy storage device. This work tries to find out a way to make use of that extra available power to boost the accuracy. In general, quantization makes the network run using integer arithmetic enabling it to be deployed on edge devices. Existing policies are capable of quantizing the network to lower precision levels such as 8 bits, 4 bits, 2 bits or even 1 bit. The lower the bit precision, the smaller the required compute, requiring less power for execution. However, using lower precision causes degradation in accuracy. Hence, there is a clear trade-off between precision and accuracy. As higher precision networks requires comparatively higher power to operate, we can easily draw a connection among power→precision→accuracy providing us a very interesting knob to tune. This work proposes a scheme where we can boost the accuracy upon availability of sufficient power by increasing the precision of the network.

While quantizing, most of the prior works used uniform bit precision i.e. used same precision such as 2 bits, 4 bits etc. for all the layers. There are however a couple of issues of using the whole network operating at constant precision such as 4 bits or 8 bits. First of all, the separation among these levels in terms of power is quadratic and we cannot scale the precision linearly. On the other hand, mixed precision networks where different layers operate using different precision levels can offer better linearity. Moreover, C2Q argued that the uniform bit-precision may not be optimal representation for a network. According to them, some layers might need higher precision to preserve the accuracy while others can operate at much lower precision levels. In order to find out these mixed precision networks they use a quantization framework which can deliver a mixed precision network under different constraints such as size, power, accuracy etc. Consequently, this framework becomes a perfect choice for our desired goal. We use it to find different mixed precision networks working at different power levels providing accuracy numbers accordingly. In brief the quantization framework works as follows,

- Starts from a uniform precision network working at higher accuracy, and then quantizes each layer gradually one by one
- During quantization, the layers compete with each other in order to get quantized. In competition, each layer gets quantized and a score is calculated for that layer based on the network's performance on a small portion of the validation set. Once the scores for all the layers are obtained, a probability for each of the layers gets calculated. For each layer, the corresponding probability is calculated using the following equation:

$$p^{(t)} = \frac{\alpha_m^{(t)}}{\sum_{i=1}^{m} \alpha_i^{(t)}}, \tag{1}$$

where, $p^{(t)}$ is the probability at tth quantization step, α is the score for each layer and m is the number of layers. Finally, a layer gets selected based on the probability vector $p^{(t)}$. This is called the *competition* stage.

- The selected layer is quantized to the next level (usually, the steps are 8 bits $\rightarrow$ 6 bits $\rightarrow$ 4 bits $\rightarrow$ 2 bits). Due to quantization, the accuracy gets degraded which is then recovered by retraining of the network where all the layers participate. This is called *collaboration* stage.
- The whole procedure is repeated until a desired compression level (in terms of size or power) is achieved.

We follow a similar strategy to find out different configurations of a network for different power levels. In order to take the compute power into account, we modify the probabilities calculated using Eq. 1 by introducing a parameter λ. The final probability becomes:

$$p_{new}^{(t)} = (1 - \lambda)p^{(t)} + \lambda \frac{|U_m^{(t)}|}{\sum_{i=1}^{m} |U_i^{(t)}|} \qquad (2)$$

where, $p_{new}^{(t)}$ is the new probability at t_{th} quantization step and $U_m^{(t)}$ is the compute power for m_{th} layer at that quantization step. The parameter λ determines how aggressively the layers requiring higher power will get quantized. A higher value will try to quantize the expensive layers first. Typical values for λ is around 0.6 to 0.7. Following this, we find out different mixed precision configurations for different power levels. One of these networks gets employed into the ReRAM crossbar depending on the power availability predicted by the power predictor. This makes the accuracy boosting based on power availability possible.

4   Precision Configurable ReRAM Crossbar

We evaluate the network on a ReRAM crossbar to perform the MAC operation at variable precision. We perform HSPICE circuit simulation to evaluate the latency and energy consumed by the components of a ReRAM crossbar. Each crossbar comprises of a row driver, ReRAM cells, analog-digital converters (ADC) and shift-add output accumulators illustrated in Fig. 3.

The row driver logic is designed to switch between one-hot and MAC modes. During one-hot mode, the row driver acts as a row decoder for the ReRAM arrays to behave as a basic read/write memory. To enable the MAC operation, the drivers select 16 rows of the array simultaneously as a bit-serial input. By bit-slicing the data in to processing one bit at a time, the driver circuits avoid costly digital-to-analog converters proposed in prior works [3].

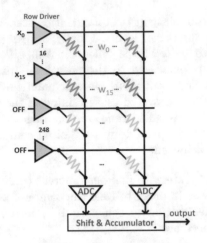

Fig. 3. Circuits of ReRAM-based Neural Network Accelerator.

For the crossbar array, ReRAM memory devices are employed to store the weights of the quantized neural networks. To reduce the variation challenges associated with the technology, each ReRAM cell only supports two resistance states, high resistance and low resistance. The SET operation sets the device into low resistance and the RESET operation switches it back to high resistance state. Therefore, multiple ReRAM cells are used to represent the weights in binary format.

The ADC unit is composed of a current sense amplifier (CSA) used to quantize the output current from the ReRAM crossbar coupled with a feedback circuit made of reference ReRAM devices and registers. The CSA is a comparator circuit which compares the two current inputs and outputs which input is greater than the other. The feedback control logic is employed for the reference input to perform a binary search on the ReRAM current like a successive-approximation register ADC (SAR-ADC).

Finally, the shift-add output accumulator is required to add the partial product results generated from the ADC units to generate the final product of the MAC operation [8,17]. When the weights are represented by multiple ReRAMs, multiple ADC units are employed to digitize the current summation from least significant to most significant bits. Consequently, the shift and add units are the key logic components to ensure mathematical correctness of the analog computation of both bit-sliced weights and activations.

Table 1 shows the measured power breakdown of each component of a crossbar for different weight configurations. The crossbar's peripheral components employ power gating circuit techniques on ADC units to support lower precision weights as the weight quantization varies the number of columns that are active during convolution. Consequently, the inputs of the shift-add units for inactive columns are shut-off, reducing the dynamic power of the partial product compression. Lastly, the power consumed by the row driver and output registers do

Table 1. Power breakdown of each component of a crossbar for different weight configurations.

Config.	Crossbar power breakdown (per convolution)						
	Row driver (nW)	ReRAM (μW)	CSA (μW)	ADC logic (μW)	Shift-add (μW)	Output reg. (μW)	**Total** (μW)
1-bit	414	20.2	110.7	148.6	28.2	124	432
2-bit	414	40.5	221.3	269.5	51.8	124	718
3-bit	414	60.7	332	410.4	74.1	124	1000
4-bit	414	80.9	442.7	541.3	94.5	124	1280
5-bit	414	101.2	553.3	672.2	113	124	1560
6-bit	414	121.4	664	803.1	131	124	1840
7-bit	414	141.6	774.7	934	148	124	2100
8-bit	414	161.8	885.3	1060	163.7	124	2400

not change with weight precision and are measured to be constant as long as the crossbar is active.

Understanding the QNN quantization principles and the ReRAM circuit design paradigm, we study five different quantization configurations of *Network-1*, *Network-2*, *Network-3*, *Network-4* and *Network-5*. Each of these network

Table 2. Five precision-fixed quantization schemes

	Network-1	Network-2	Network-3	Network-4	Network-5
Feature.0 (bit)	8	8	6	4	2
Feature.3 (bit)	8	2	2	2	2
Feature.7 (bit)	8	6	2	2	2
Feature.10 (bit)	8	4	2	2	2
Feature.14 (bit)	8	2	2	2	2
Feature.17 (bit)	8	6	4	2	2
Feature.20 (bit)	8	8	6	4	2
Feature.24 (bit)	8	4	2	2	2
Feature.27 (bit)	8	4	2	2	2
Feature.30 (bit)	8	8	6	4	2
Feature.34 (bit)	8	6	6	4	2
Feature.37 (bit)	8	6	4	4	2
Feature.40 (bit)	8	8	4	2	2
Classifier (bit)	8	6	4	2	2
Accuracy	90.92%	89.58%	89.16%	89.11%	87.54%
Power (mW)	21.4	14.1	10.6	8.5	7.0
Latency (s)	0.0049	0.00313	0.00202	0.00158	0.00125

structures consumes different amounts of power and incurs different latency and achieves different output accuracy as shown in Table 2. The *Network-1* configuration with the highest data precision can achieve the best accuracy, while consuming the highest power and longest latency, and vice versa. Motivated by this reconfigurable design possibility, this paper proposes to apply different quantization designs to accommodate to the unstable harvested power while achieving as high as possible output accuracy. In other words, when a minimum amount of power is available from the energy harvesting sources, the smallest configuration can be used and upon availability of more power, other configurations can be used to boost the accuracy.

5   Power Prediction

In energy harvesting systems, a key issue is to give the system the ability of predicting the future harvested power in advance. In this work, if we can understand the power level in the next power cycle in advance, we may be able to transfer the incomplete computations to the next power cycle, instead of discarding them. For high sample rate power sources, it is of great value, because only a few inferences can be completed in one power cycle and it is worthwhile to save one more inference through an early action.

Power prediction is not easy for multi-level situations. Prior efforts have presented that the existing neural network algorithms can predict three harvesting power levels with an accuracy of 80%. However, those techniques are not able to predict greater power levels while maintaining a high accuracy. This work augments an existing machine learning-based approach to predict 5-/6-level power with a very high accuracy in order to accommodate 4/5 quantization configurations. This can be realized through a proposed SMOTE algorithm to re-sample and provide more friendly training data set. Our augmented power predictor can achieve an accuracy of up to 90% for several power sources.

5.1   NN-Based Power Prediction

In this work, we use a lightweight fully-connected neural network (NN) algorithm to do power prediction.

Feature Extraction. To train the NN algorithm of the power predictor, the following parameters are used for training inputs and output.

(1) *Power level classification*: Recalling that the ambient energy keeps changing as shown in Fig. 1, so we need to partition power levels to indicate different favorable quantization schemes. In this work, we address a six-level classification scenario.
(2) *Energy intensity*: The energy intensity indicates the strength of the power signal. It is calculated by the product of power and sample rate.

(3) *Average energy intensity*: Corresponding to each energy intensity of a power cycle, this parameter gives the average value of its former five energy intensity. It can smooth the instantaneous changes on the power trace.

(4) *Energy standard deviation*: For each power cycle, this parameter denotes the standard deviation of the energy intensity of the former five samples, showing the stability of energy changes.

Before data are fed to the neural network, normalization is done as shown in Eq. 3 to improve the convergence.

$$F_{nor} = (F_{org} - Min(F_{org}))/(Max(F_{org}) - Min(F_{org})) \tag{3}$$

Here F_{nor} and F_{org} denote the normalized feature vector and the original feature vector, respectively.

NN Structure. The NN structure used for our power predictor is shown in Fig. 4. The deep neural networks used in our power predictor can be illustrated by the layers of input layer, hidden layer, and output layer.

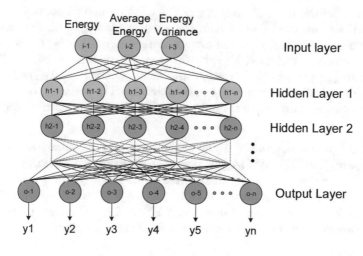

Fig. 4. NN structure of the power predictor.

The input layer receives the feature vectors of the energy intensity, average energy intensity and energy standard deviation.

The hidden layer is the key part of the deep neural network as shown in Eq. 4. The term $x_{l,n}$ denotes the output of the n-th neuron in the l-th layer, $w_{l,n,s}$ denotes the s-th weight value of the n-th neuron in the l-th layer, and $b_{l,n}$ denotes the offset of the nth neuron in the l layer. The hidden layer contains the activation function, s_l denotes the number of weights of the l-th layer, and f_{act} is the activation function. This work uses *Sigmoid* as the activation function as shown in Eq. 5. In this work, we set 30 neurons for the first hidden layer, and 10 neurons for the remaining hidden layers.

$$x_{l,n} = f_{act}(\sum_{s=0}^{S_t} x_{l-1,s} \times w_{l,n,s} + b_{l,n}) \tag{4}$$

$$sig(x) = \frac{1}{1 + e^{-x}} \tag{5}$$

When dealing with multi-classification problems, *one-hot* is used as the output of the neural network. In other words, only one of the N-bit status registers outputs 1, while the others all output 0. The output is processed by the *Softmax* algorithm as shown in Eq. 6. The value of S_i denotes the normalized probabilities of the *i-th* class. The maximal S_i represents the inferred class.

$$S_i = \frac{e^i}{\sum_j e^j} \tag{6}$$

5.2   Augmented Power Prediction

As discussed before, if we directly apply the existing neural network algorithm to predict the multi-level (>3) power, the accuracy is not ideal. For multi-level power prediction, we find that the uneven data distribution is the cause of the accuracy problem. Motivated by this, this paper proposes to use the SMOTE algorithm to pre-process the data set and then obtain friendly training data. Finally, a high prediction accuracy can be obtained. The training, validation and accuracy assessment are implemented in the *Keras* machine learning framework.

SMOTE Algorithm. As Fig. 1 depicts, most power distributions are significantly uneven. Take the *WiFi-office* power as an example as shown in Table 3, the data sets are very unevenly distributed in different power levels. The harvested power numbers are pretty large in the 1st level while very small in the last level, showing a variance of more than 100×. The imbalance property may cause the model to over-fit and induce low prediction accuracy.

Table 3. Power level range and sample number of *WiFi-office* source

Power level	Upper bound (μW)	Lower bound (μW)	Sample number
1	920	400	385914
2	1440	921	30954
3	1960	1441	3299
4	2480	1961	1623
5	3000	2481	36

This paper exploits the SMOTE algorithm to upsample the data and increment the small data set [2]. The SMOTE algorithm can well solve the problem of imbalanced data sets. The underlying principle is to create new data from the original data so as to increase the distribution density of low-density group.

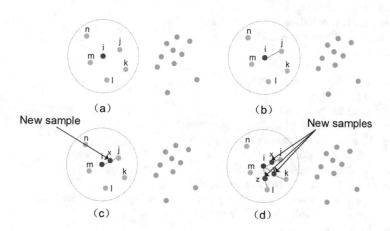

Fig. 5. New sample data generation in the SMOTE algorithm.

Algorithm 1 gives the pseudo code of the SMOTE algorithm. First, we count the sample number of each group (Line 1–3). For each low-density group, we calculate the Euclidean distances between a randomly selected sample and any other samples, and then collect the five nearest samples (Line 4–8). For each sample pair, we generate a new sample between them following the Eq. 7 (Line 11–17). And so forth, we can obtain a density-balanced data samples for retraining (as showed in Fig. 5).

$$X_{new} = x + rand(0, 1) \times (\hat{x} - x) \tag{7}$$

Cross Validation. *Ten-Fold* cross validation is used to evaluate the fitting of the to-be-inferred data sets. Specifically, the power traces are divided into ten parts. Each time nine parts are selected as the training set while the remaining one part is for test. Meanwhile, the SMOTE algorithm is applied on the training set to increase the data density of minority groups. Finally, we use the test set to evaluate the model accuracy.

Figure 6 shows the final accuracy of the *Softmax* output layer. It can be seen that more than 90% accuracy can be achieved for 5-/6-/7-level classification with the proposed augmented power predictor, even though that the accuracy is only ~85% for 3-level prediction. The proposed scheme guarantees high prediction accuracy of power traces in this work.

Algorithm 1. New sample data generation with the SMOTE algorithm.

Input:
 samples(e, e_eva, e_var, label);
 label = [0, m];
 e : energy;
 e_ave : average energy;
 e_var : energy variation;
 k : number of nearest neighbors;
 K : increment rat;

Output:
 smote_samples(e, e_eva, e_var, label);
 find the minority;
1: count samples group by label;
2: majo = the amount of majority of samples;
3: save the rest samples as mino_samples[m-1];
4: **for** i = 0 to m-1 **do**
5: randomize the mino_samples[i];
6: **for** each ITEM in mino_samples[i] **do**
7:   compute k nearest neighbors for ITEM, and save as neighbor_arr;
8:   populate(ITEM, i, neighbor_arr);
9: **end for**
10: **end for**
11: Define populate{ITEM, i, neighbor_arr}
12: **while** count(mino_samples[i]) ¡= R*majo **do**
13: Choose a random number between 1 and k, set it as x;
14: dist = neighbor_arr[x] - ITEM;
15: gap = random(0, 1);//random from 0 to 1
16: synthetic = ITEM + gap * dist;
17: mino_samples[i].add(synthetic)//add the synthetic node to mino_samples
18: **end while**

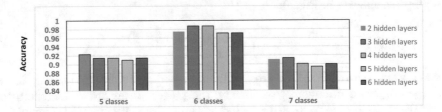

Fig. 6. Prediction accuracy of different power levels with 2–6 hidden layers.

6   Experiments

In this section, we first describe our experimental settings and then move onto discussing our results & findings to demonstrate the plausibility of our idea.

6.1 Experimental Settings

For our experiments, we use CIFAR10 [9] dataset with VGG16 [18] architecture. CIFAR10 is an image classification dataset of 10 classes with 50000 training and 10000 validation images of size $3*32*32$. VGG16 is a popular DNN architecture consisting of 16 layers (15 convolutional and 1 fully connected). However, to adjust the network for CIFAR10 dataset, two convolution layers are dropped and the size of final classifier is changed.

6.2 Results

Learning Curve. The layer-wise quantization scheme is best illustrated by Fig. 7. Starting with a fully converged network, the quantization scheme selects one layer at a time, then quantizes it followed by a recovery step. This behavior is very well reflected in the figure. The valleys indicate the accuracy loss after each quantization step and the peaks indicates the recovery following that step. In this experiment we start with uniform 8-bit precision network and then gradually quantize it to 2-bit. In between uniform 8-bit to uniform 2-bit networks, we take few snapshots each of which is basically a mixed precision network. The compute power requirements of these networks decreases gradually as the average precision decreases. Accuracy of these networks follows the same trend which is why we have been able to do power aware inference where the accuracy depends on the available power.

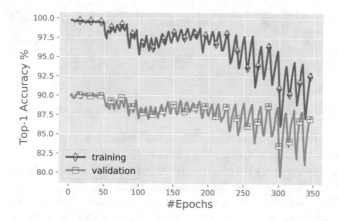

Fig. 7. Learning curve for mixed precision models. The zigzag pattern represents the quantization and subsequent recovery steps.

System-Level Results. In the system-level simulation, we built an in-house coarse-grain simulator to evaluate the throughput, energy efficiency and average accuracy on top of different power sources as shown in Fig. 1. The parameters in

Table 2 are fed into the simulator. In order to support the VGG computation, we assume there are multiple harvesters together to power the ReRAMs. The harvester number for the sources of *Solar, Thermal, TV-RF, WiFi-home* and *WiFi-office* are 18, 8, 4, 25 and 20, respectively. Seven quantization versions are evaluated in total: *Network-1, Network-2, Network-3, Network-4, Network-5, Network-adaptive* and *Network-predictive*. For the first five versions, we use fixed quantization solution as shown in Table 2. The *Network-adaptive* version employs dynamic quantization solutions in different power cycles. That is, we always select the quantization network structure with as high as possible accuracy as long as the harvested power in the power cycle can meet the requirement. The *Network-prediction* perform the same dynamic quantization policy as the *Network-adaptive* based on the predicted power traces.

Figure 8 shows the normalized results of throughput, energy efficiency and energy utilization and output accuracy in (a), (b), (c) and (d) respectively. The normalized results are referred to the *Network-adaptive* version. Further, Table 4 gives the absolute values of the *Network-adaptive* version.

Table 4. Throughput, energy efficiency, energy utilization and average accuracy of *Network-adaptive*.

Power source	Throughput (#inference/s)	Energy efficiency (#inference/J)	Energy utilization	Average accuracy
Solar	12.49	2810.6	1.4%	89.35%
Thermal	25.6	1241.6	42.0%	90.17%
TV-RF	17.6	842.3	44.3%	90.09%
WiFi-home	6.09	1911.4	42.7%	89.18%
WiFi-office	44.4	7122.4	30.8%	87.98%

We can make the following observations and analyses from the results:

- It is not surprising that the *Network-5* version always achieves the best throughput because it incurs the shortest latency to complete an inference. However, this version also has the lowest accuracy due to the lowest data precision. It can be seen that the *Network-adaptive* version can achieve the best balance between the throughput and the accuracy. The reason is that the *Network-adaptive* version can well trade throughput of accuracy by adopting dynamic quantization configurations. Consistent with the throughput observation, the proposed *Network-adaptive* can achieve a balanced trade off between energy efficiency and accuracy.
- For each power source, the *Network-adaptive* version always achieves the highest energy utilization. This is because we apply the policy of adopting the quantization degree of the VGG network structure to best meet the available power level. As a result, the proposed policy can make the best effort to convert the harvested energy to the classification accuracy.

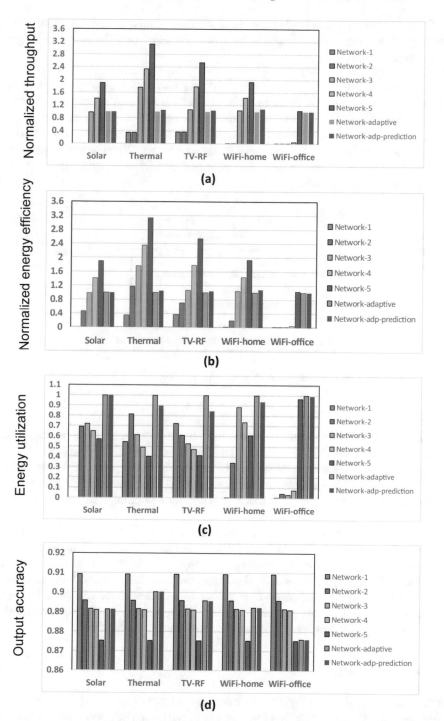

Fig. 8. (a) Throughput, (b) Energy efficiency, (c) Energy utilization and (d) Average accuracy across the power sources.

- Overall, the *Network-adaptive* version can manage the tradeoff among throughput, energy efficiency and output accuracy by efficiently utilizing the harvested energy.

As discussed in Sect. 5, the power predictor can direct us to proactively configure the last incomplete inference's computation with an appropriate network structure, so that the incomplete computation results can be transferred to the next power cycle under a *High-to-Low* power level transition situation. Further, Fig. 9 shows the increase in number of inferences when using the power predictor. It is interesting to have the following observations by comparing to the results without power prediction.

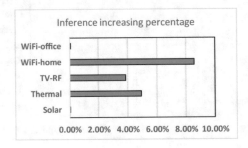

Fig. 9. The percentage of inference increasing with power prediction.

- The increased number of inferences for the power sources of *Solar* and *WiFi-office* is much smaller than that of the power sources of *Thermal, TV-RF* and *WiFi-home*. This can be explained by the fact that the power level transitions, especially the *High-to-Low* power level transitions, occur much less with the former two power sources. Therefore, there is less chance to benefit from the incomplete computation saving.
- The energy utilization with the *Network-adaptive* version is always higher than that with the *Network-prediction* version. However, it does not imply that the performance of the *Network-adaption* is better as shown in Fig. 8. The real underlying reason is that the computations of the last incomplete inference under the *High-to-Low* power level transitions will be terminated early, directing by the power predictor. This is why we can see paradoxical results from the angles of throughput and energy utilization.

7   Conclusion

With the increasing deployment of deep neural networks in edge devices, their operation in energy-harvesting environments with varying power-levels becomes a necessity. Further, in applications without an energy storage device, the ability to dynamically adapt the complexity of the deep neural network becomes essential to best utilize the incoming harvested power. This work deploys a quantized deep network with varying degrees of quantization to meet varying degrees of available power. At execution time, we vary the instantiated network configuration to match the available power. Additionally, we have proposed an approach that predictively ensures that partial results from the network are best retained when power levels change. The results from this work show that the proposed adaptive quantization scheme can exploit the energy to achieve as much as possible high accuracy and maintain good throughput.

Acknowledgements. This work was supported in part by Semiconductor Research Corporation (SRC), Center for Brain-inspired Computing (C-BRIC), Center for Research in Intelligent Storage and Processing in Memory (CRISP), NSF Expeditions in Computing CCF-1317560, National Natural Science Foundation of China [NSFC Project No. 61872251] and Beijing Advanced Innovation Center for Imaging Technology.

References

1. Banner, R., Nahshan, Y., Hoffer, E., Soudry, D.: ACIQ: analytical clipping for integer quantization of neural networks. arXiv preprint arXiv:1810.05723 (2018)
2. Chawla, N.V., Bowyer, K.W., Hall, L.O., Kegelmeyer, W.P.: SMOTE: synthetic minority over-sampling technique. J. Artif. Intell. Res. **16**, 321–357 (2002)
3. Chi, P., et al.: PRIME: a novel processing-in-memory architecture for neural network computation in reram-based main memory, June 2016
4. Choi, J., Wang, Z., Venkataramani, S., Chuang, P.I.-J., Srinivasan, V., Gopalakrishnan, K.: PACT: parameterized clipping activation for quantized neural networks. arXiv preprint arXiv:1805.06085 (2018)
5. Courbariaux, M., Hubara, I., Soudry, D., El-Yaniv, R., Bengio, Y.: Binarized neural networks: training deep neural networks with weights and activations constrained to +1 or −1. arXiv preprint arXiv:1602.02830 (2016)
6. Dong, Z., Yao, Z., Gholami, A., Mahoney, M., Keutzer, K.: HAWQ: Hessian aware quantization of neural networks with mixed-precision. arXiv preprint arXiv:1905.03696 (2019)
7. Gong, Z., et al.: Retention state-enabled and progress-driven energy management for self-powered nonvolatile processors. In: 2017 IEEE 23rd International Conference on Embedded and Real-Time Computing Systems and Applications (RTCSA), pp. 1–8 (2017)
8. Jao, N., Ramanathan, A.K., Sengupta, A., Sampson, J., Narayanan, V.: Programmable non-volatile memory design featuring reconfigurable in-memory operations. In: 2019 IEEE International Symposium on Circuits and Systems (ISCAS), pp. 1–5, May 2019
9. Krizhevsky, A., Hinton, G.: Learning multiple layers of features from tiny images. Technical report, Citeseer (2009)
10. LeCun, Y., Bengio, Y., Hinton, G.: Deep learning. Nature **521**(7553), 436–444 (2015)
11. Ma, K., Li, X., Liu, Y., Sampson, J., Xie, Y., Narayanan, V.: Dynamic machine learning based matching of nonvolatile processor microarchitecture to harvested

energy profile. In: Proceedings of the IEEE/ACM International Conference on Computer-Aided Design, pp. 670–675 (2015)

12. Ma, K., et al.: Architecture exploration for ambient energy harvesting nonvolatile processors. In: 2015 IEEE 21st International Symposium on High Performance Computer Architecture (HPCA), pp. 526–537 (2015)

13. Migacz, S.: 8-bit inference with tensorrt. In: GPU Technology Conference, vol. 2, p. 7 (2017)

14. Mishra, A., Nurvitadhi, E., Cook, J.J., Marr, D.: WRPN: wide reduced-precision networks. arXiv preprint arXiv:1709.01134 (2017)

15. Qiu, K., Chen, W., Xu, Y., Xia, L., Wang, Y., Shao, Z.: A peripheral circuit reuse structure integrated with a retimed data flow for low power RRAM crossbar-based CNN. In: 2018 Design, Automation Test in Europe Conference Exhibition (DATE), pp. 1057–1062 (2018)

16. Rastegari, M., Ordonez, V., Redmon, J., Farhadi, A.: XNOR-Net: imagenet classification using binary convolutional neural networks. In: Leibe, B., Matas, J., Sebe, N., Welling, M. (eds.) ECCV 2016. LNCS, vol. 9908, pp. 525–542. Springer, Cham (2016). https://doi.org/10.1007/978-3-319-46493-0_32

17. Shafiee, A., et al.: ISAAC: a convolutional neural network accelerator with in-situ analog arithmetic in crossbars. In: 2016 ACM/IEEE 43rd Annual International Symposium on Computer Architecture (ISCA), pp. 14–26, June 2016

18. Simonyan, K., Zisserman, A.: Very deep convolutional networks for large-scale image recognition. arXiv preprint arXiv:1409.1556 (2014)

19. Khan, Md.F.F., Kamani, M.M., Mahdavi, M., Narayanan, V.: Learning to quantize deep neural networks: a competitive-collaborative approach. In: Proceedings of the 57th Annual Design Automation Conference (2020)

20. Wang, K., Liu, Z., Lin, Y., Lin, J., Han, S.: HAQ: hardware-aware automated quantization with mixed precision. In: Proceedings of the IEEE Conference on Computer Vision and Pattern Recognition, pp. 8612–8620 (2019)

21. Yazdanbakhsh, A., Elthakeb, A.T., Pilligundla, P., Mireshghallah, F., Esmaeilzadeh, H.: ReLeQ: an automatic reinforcement learning approach for deep quantization of neural networks. arXiv preprint arXiv:1811.01704 (2018)

22. Zhang, C., Bengio, S., Singer, Y.: Are all layers created equal? arXiv preprint arXiv:1902.01996 (2019)

23. Zhao, M., Qiu, K., Xie, Y., Hu, J., Xue, C.J.: Redesigning software and systems for non-volatile processors on self-powered devices. In: 2016 IFIP/IEEE International Conference on Very Large Scale Integration (VLSI-SoC), pp. 1–6 (2016)

24. Zhou, S.-C., Wang, Y.-Z., Wen, H., He, Q.-Y., Zou, Y.-H.: Balanced quantization: an effective and efficient approach to quantized neural networks. J. Comput. Sci. Technol. **32**(4), 667–682 (2017)

25. Zhou, S., Wu, Y., Ni, Z., Zhou, X., Wen, H., Zou, Y.: DoReFa-Net: training low bitwidth convolutional neural networks with low bitwidth gradients. arXiv preprint arXiv:1606.06160 (016)

Smart Network Architectures

Toward Holistic Integration of Computing and Wireless Networking

Kwang-Cheng Chen[1]([✉]), Yingze Wang[1,2], Zixiang Nie[1], and Qimei Cui[2]

[1] University of South Florida, Tampa, FL 33620, USA
kwangcheng@usf.edu
[2] Beijing University of Posts and Telecommunications, Beijing 100876, China

Abstract. To systematically cop complex systems engineering in Internet of Things, this paper looks into a technological challenge to effectively and efficiently integrate computing and wireless networking. One aspect is how machine learning and artificial intelligence to influence wireless networking, and another aspect is how wireless networking to enhance artificial intelligence computing. Finally, a holistic computing and networking architecture is introduced to examine implementation of holistic computing and wireless networking.

Keywords: Artificial intelligence · Machine learning · Wireless networks · Internet of Things · Edge computing

1 Introduction

Internet of Things (IoT) is well known to involve technology of computing, control, and wireless networking, under wide-range of application scenarios. Complex systems engineering of IoT complicates efficient realization of IoT systems. While control of intelligent systems such as robots is widely implemented by artificial intelligence (AI) computing, holistic integration of computing and networking emerges a critical technology for future IoT. This article presents a unique aspect to look into this new technological paradigm, we first review the applications of machine learning (ML) in the wireless networking of IoT systems (in Sect. 2), then turn to a particular scenario of applying AI and ML into smart factory of networking (in Sect. 3). By investigating the facilitation of ML in wireless networks and the requirements of wireless networking into multi-agent AI systems, the possible picture of holistic integration of AI computing and wireless networking in IoT, particularly involving mobile agents such as autonomous vehicles, mobile robots, smart factory, has been initially investigated in this paper.

K.-C. Chen and Z. Nie appreciate the grant from the Cyber Florida to conduct this research.

A. Casaca et al. (Eds.): IFIPIoT 2019, IFIP AICT 574, pp. 219–234, 2020.
https://doi.org/10.1007/978-3-030-43605-6_13

2   Applications of ML in IoT Wireless Networking

Currently, a vary of remarkable developments of the network, notably wireless networks, are breaking the boundaries between virtual and reality and evolve narrow cyber towards the Internet of Things (IoT). The terminals of the internet are no longer limited to PCs, mobile phones. TVs, lamps, mirrors, water heaters, air conditioners, taxis, elevators, workstations and so on are all surprisingly connected to the Internet. The interconnection of all things dramatically facilitates people's work and life. And wireless sensor networks (WSN), the main part of IoT, extend human physiological perception limits. These vast changes also pose profound challenges to theoretical research.

Unlike a series of "excellent" features of traditional wireless communication systems, IoT has been a significant impact on wireless communication technologies. For example, the number of network nodes has increased dramatically, the network topology has become more dynamic, links and interference have become denser, and network transmission has demand fluctuates sharply, etc. Recently, Machine Learning, particularly Reinforcement Learning, has been used as an emerging tool to effectively address the above problems and challenges. Different from classic convex optimization or optimization methods, ML shows exciting performance in solving complicated mathematical structures and instability decisions.

According to our investigation of published articles, the current research directions of applying ML in IoT can roughly divide into three categories: MAC protocol design, cache and offload in MEC scenarios, and network security. Besides, there are some explorations for unique scenarios and particular problems that not included in this list. (The framework is shown in Fig. 1).

2.1   MAC Protocol: Wireless Access, Routing and Others

Modern networks, particularly IoT, become more decentralized and ad-hoc and more dynamic in topology and routing. In IoT, entities such as sensors and mobile users need to make independent decisions, e.g., multi-routing selections, channel selections, to achieve their own goals, e.g., throughput maximization. However, this is challenging due to the dynamic and the uncertainty of network status. The reinforcement learning represented by Q-learning and Deep Q-learning Network (DQN) can intuitively adapt to the design requirements of such mac protocols. Therefore, extensive research has been carried out in this direction, such as dynamic wireless access schemes, dynamic routing, multi-point cooperative communication, etc.

Focus on multiple Access for Heterogeneous Wireless Networks, [54] proposed and investigated a MAC protocol based on deep reinforcement learning for heterogeneous wireless networking, referred to as Deep-reinforcement Learning Multiple Access (DLMA). A salient feature of DLMA is that it can learn to achieve an overall objective (e.g., α-fairness objective) by a series of state-action-reward observations while operating in the heterogeneous environment. In particular, it can achieve near-optimal performance with respect to the objective without

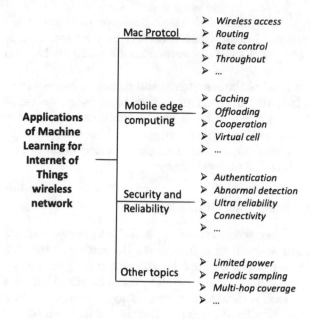

Fig. 1. The appli of Machine Learning for IoT wireless network

knowing the detailed operating mechanisms of the coexisting MAC. For dynamic routing implementation issues, [49] devises the off-policy Q_{ssp} algorithm and the on-policy $SARSA_{ssp}$ algorithm to solve the routing problem in Wireless Sensor Networks. Specifically, the authores tackle the stochastic shortest path problem using reinforcement learning schemes by modeling the path searching procedure as an appropriate discounted Markov decision process. [41] considers the multi-hop routing algorithm plays an important role in the exploration and monitoring of deep-sea environments. For this A proposed a routing algorithm based on the Q-learning for 3D under water WSN. Combined with defined distance and energy paths, the researchers derived the iterative formula of the Q-table. The proposed QL-EDR algorithm can extend the network lifetime and improve the efficiency of the data collection, compared to the conventional protocol. In addition, the authors defined a regulatory factor to adjust the network performance. According to the realistic demands, choose appropriate values of factor to improve the network throughput, to reduce the average end-to-end delay or to prolong the network lifetime.

[62] works on improving the packet transmission efficiency using Cognitive networks. A Q-learning-based transmission scheduling mechanism using deep learning for the cognitive radio-based IoT is proposed to solve the problem of how to achieve the appropriate strategy to transmit packets of different buffers through multiple channels to maximize the system throughput. [23,43] have also tried machine learning applications in the field of IoT congestion control, and has gained some valuable experience. [57] proposed a cooperative spectrum sensing algorithm for cognitive radio networks. By implementing DQN based

on upper confidence bounds with Hoeffding-style to improve the exploration efficiency, the proposed algorithm can achieve better reward performance with faster convergence speed than the conventional algorithms based on Q-learning with ε-greedy.

We note that most of the research in this direction models the network state of IoT as MDP. In addition, the DQN method receives more attention than other algorithms. The future network will involve multiple network slides, and these network slides have multiple conflicting goals, which brings many challenges to the traditional resource management mechanism and network standard formulation that are worthy of in-depth study.

2.2   MEC: Caching and Offloading

MEC is one of the key scenarios of IoT, and the intra-network cache can effectively reduce duplicate content transmission. Research on wireless caching shows that by caching content in wireless devices, you can significantly reduce access latency, energy consumption, and overall traffic. This direction has also attracted many studies. As each node's storage, computing, and energy consumption capabilities are limited, how to coordinate collaboration between nodes, such as decision cache content, has become a focus of attention.

Most recent studies focus on "attention" tagging of content and tasks and caching and calculation offload allocation based on importance. But there are still many attempts to provide new ideas for research. [25] cares about that rare wireless network resources are difficult to meet the influx of a huge number of terminal devices. Specifically, the authors use two potential recurrent neural network approaches, the echo state network (ESN) and the long short-term memory (LSTM) network, to make predictions about user mobility and content popularity. Finally, use DQN algorithm to make cached decisions for prediction results. [61] formulated the cache replacement problem as a MDP problem and proposed a DRL-based caching policy. In the model S, A and $reward$ are definded as values of information about cached/arrived data items, the caching action selected by the edge node and the sum utility of all data items which are requested, respectively. [44] tries to simultaneously tackle the issues of content caching strategy, computation offloading policy, and radio resource allocation, in fog computing. Authors use the actor-critic reinforcement learning framework to solve the joint decision-making problem with the objective of minimizing the average end-to-end delay, due to wireless signals and service requests have stochastic properties. The deep neural network (DNN) is employed as the function approximator to estimate the value functions in the critical part due to the extremely large state and action space in the problem. The actor part uses another DNN to represent a parameterized stochastic policy and improves the policy with the help of the critic.

At the same time, some scholars have also noticed the connectivity of the MEC devices in this scenario. [29] focus on the connectivity solutions especially for those covering the wide remote areas in the scale of kilometer squares.

Although many low-power wide-area network technologies are supposed to support long-range low-power wireless communication, underneath star topology limits the scalability of the networks due to the need for a central hub. To provide connectivity to a wider area, the authors propose to build the mesh topology upon these LPWAN technologies and propose a distributed as well as energy-efficient reinforcement learning based routing algorithm for the wide-area wireless mesh IoT networks. [16]'s goal is to acquire an online algorithm that optimally adapts task offloading decisions and wireless resource allocations to the time-varying wireless channel conditions. This requires quickly solving hard combinatorial optimization problems within the channel coherence time, which is hardly achievable with conventional numerical optimization methods. The authors propose a Deep Reinforcement learning-based Online Offloading (DROO) framework that implements a deep neural network as a scalable solution that learns the binary offloading decisions from the experience. It eliminates the need for solving combinatorial optimization problems, and thus greatly reduces the computational complexity especially in large-size networks.

MEC scenarios involve very complicated system analysis, which is due a unified study on caching, offloading, networking, and transmission control. Strong couplings among mobile users with heterogeneities in application demand, QoS provisioning, mobility pattern, radio access interface, and wireless resources also cause for above. A model-free reinforcement learning approach becomes a promising candidate to manage huge state space and optimization variables.

2.3   IoT Security and Reliability

In IoT, physical devices, sensors, appliances, and other different objects can communicate with each other without the need for human intervention in IoT. And IoT has many critical and non-critical applications. The security of IoT became a crucial problem. Future networks become more decentralized and ad-hoc in nature which is vulnerable to various attacks such as Denial-of-Service (DoS) and cyber-physical attacks. Recently, the DQL has been used as an effective solution to avoid and prevent the attacks [31].

In [52], the Markov game framework is employed to model and analyze the anti-jamming defense problem. Based on Q-learning, the authors development a collaborative multi-agent anti-jamming algorithm. As machine learning and artificial intelligence can be used for the protection of devices by analyzing traffic or devices behavior, the [48] development a model of increasing security of wireless environment for IoT appliance through creating a fingerprint by Machine Learning algorithm. The experimental result shows that the model is able to detect anomaly flooding traffic in Wi-Fi networks based on characteristic patterns that separate normal traffic from malicious activity.

A wide variety of low-cost radio technologies, that being used to enable wireless communication in IoT, brings a security problem due to the fact that it is very easy for a malicious user to perform passive wireless signal scanning on these networks and use this information to launch identity-based attacks. In [34], the authors propose a learning-based strategy to detect spoofing attacks in wireless sensor networks. Based on detailed analytical models for the mobile radio channel, the proposed algorithm combines two classifiers to process and analyze the instant samples of received signal strength to detect attacks. In [11], a watermarking algorithm is proposed for dynamic authentication of IoT signals to detect cyber-attacks. The proposed watermarking algorithm, based on a deep learning long short- term memory structure, enables the IoT devices to extract a set of stochastic features from their generated signal and dynamically watermark these features into the signal. This method enables the IoT gateway, which collects signals from the IoT, to effectively authenticate the reliability of the signals.

The sharp increase in interference caused by the dense network is also an aspect that needs to be explored in depth. [14] considers the optimization of the cache-enabled opportunistic interference alignment network as a so complex problem. The results in the literature were demonstrated that the performance of cache-enabled opportunistic IA networks can be significantly improved by using the proposed deep reinforcement learning approach.

We found that the research on reinforcement learning applied to network security is mainly focused on anomaly detection and identity authentication, and research on interference in network transmission needs to be further promoted.

2.4   Low-Power Operation and Sensor Networks

In addition to the above directions in which the studies are concentrated, scholars have also conducted extensive explorations on the application of machine learning in wireless networks. Such as power supply problems in low power networks, network structure update problems, etc.

Sensing devices operating in the upcoming IoT are likely to rely on the radio frequency (RF) transmissions of a hybrid access point (HAP) for energy [51]. The HAP is also responsible for setting the sampling or monitoring time of these devices according to their harvested energy. A challenging issue is that setting the HAP's charging time and also the sampling time of each device with imperfect channel gains information. [51] also propose a scheme, through the improvement of Actor-Critic algorithm, to minimize the sampling time of the device. Wireless sensor network has the characteristics of scattered network requirements and uneven information. [46] study the WSN-based field sensing and reconstruction problem. The authors establish a two-layer learning framework based on reinforcement learning, and present the detailed design for an adaptive sampling policy which can actively determine the most informative sensing location and thus significantly reduce the communication cost.

3   Machine Learning in Smart Factory

A smart factory is an IoT system of particular interest. Factories, especially manufacturing factories are embracing the notion of integrating cyber resources such as computation, networking and physical processes together to drive the development of smart factory, which is Cyber-Physical Systems (CPS) [38,42]. Several technologies are believed to bring evolutionary changes to the traditional factories in industry, they are: Internet of Things (IoT), Wireless Sensor Networks (WSN), Cloud Services and Artificial Intelligence [38,42,47]. The main goal is to accommodate product variants and production number variance to fulfill the demands from major customers down to individual customers. That requires the real-time collection of relevant information, a fast reintegration of resources within the factory and an optimized re-setup or reconfiguration solution of physical entities within the factory [40]. In addition to that, the call for sustainability requirement smart factory to improve the utility of raw materials and energy [40], even a higher efficiency of supply chain, product packing and logistics among factories.

The integration of cyber resources and physical entities happens on top of automated manufacturing equipped factories. By regarding each physical entity after integration a system, the whole CPS is actually a system of systems. The integration of cyber resources and physical entities is considered in two ways: vertical integration that emphasis on the real-time information collection and control, and horizontal integration that emphasis on cooperation among physical entities [40,59].

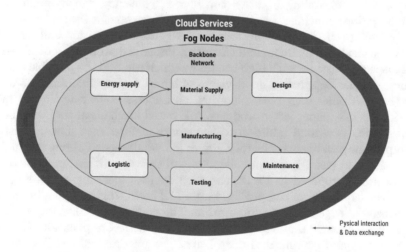

Fig. 2. A horizontal integration towards smart factory.

3.1   Computing and Networking Systems in Smart Factories

By regarding each physical entity after integrating a system, the whole CPS is actually a system of systems. As shown in Fig. 2, illustrative systems including product design, materials supply (raw materials), energy use to drive the manufacturing, entities in manufacturing process, product test (inspection), maintenance of the factory, logistic (local logistic within the factory dealing with semi-products, packing and shipping of the finished products), local fog nodes(including storage, computing and etc.), cloud service (including cloud storage, cloud computing and etc.) and backbone network (with internet access) are considered to be the import systems in smart factories [38]. Paper [4,38] expounded data powered "smart design" in future industry. The sensing devices integrated to the traditional factory brings tremendous amount of data from every stage of manufacturing. After proper data processing and visualization, the designers could refine the manufacturing processes, part design and etc towards more flexible and energy saving manufacturing. Paper [4,17,38] discussed the supply chain in smart factory. Since the fact that the production requirement is dynamic in the smart factory age, the short-term supply system paves a solid foundation of smart manufacturing. Paper [17] proposed a multi-objective, multi-stage flexible flow-shop scheduling model for fast response supply chain and manufacture agent collaboration. Resource and energy efficiency is another important indicators toward next generation industry in that it's directly related to the profit and environment. Smart energy supply gives energy consumption data as a feedback to the designer and management to improve the plant organization and production design [19,42,59]. A lot of paper in literature focus on Multi-agent System (MAS) in manufacturing system. Paper [17,39] proposed algorithms for scheduling in MAS considering efficiency and dynamic. Paper [10,27,36] adopt Machine Learning (ML), Reinforcement Learning (RL) and Deep Learning (DL) to give solutions to MAS task allow cation and scheduling considering the load balancing and efficiency. Paper [24] proposed a deep learning based inspection system with high accuracy, which can find the possible defective products. Paper [35] gives a good vision of smart factory maintenance considering the task offloading, path planning, and access point selection in mobile scenario. Besides, paper [45] introduced ML based mechanical tool wearing prediction, which is a good addition to the smart maintenance. Local logistics is also important part of smart factory. Paper [38,40] discussed about raw material distribution and (semi-)product collection and delivery within smart factory. In the framework proposed in Fig. 2, the edge devices, local fog nodes and cloud all have the capability of computing. Paper [24] and [27] give a possible solution that utilize the edge and fog computation. The good side is edge/fog computing delivers lower latency than cloud computing in practical application. Of course, data intensive and complicated deep learning algorithms may still good to be executed on the cloud, but edge computing and fog computing are more in line with the needs of smart factories for real-time environment and requirement changes.

3.2   Vertical Integration

As shown in Fig. 3, seven important elements in traditional factory could all get integrated with WSN, actuators, computing and AI to become a system. Each one of four technology is a layer put on top of traditional element, so it's called vertical integration. After equipped with WSN, the traditional element in

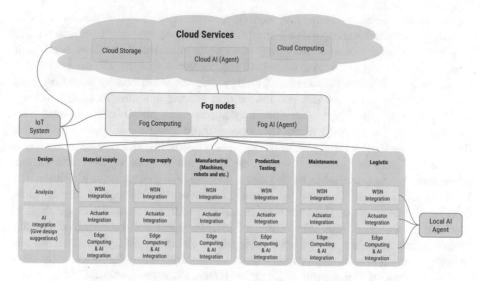

Fig. 3. A vertical integration towards smart factory.

addition to the backbone network and fog or cloud becomes a IoT system. After equipped with actuator (either software or physical part that could control the entity), the traditional element becomes a cloud controlled IoT system. After the integration of computing capability and AI algorithms (software), the traditional element becomes a complete local AI agent. For example, the energy meter in the energy supply system will keep monitoring the energy consumption data and then upload to cloud storage. The related designer could utilize those data for further refining the design of the product in purpose of green manufacturing. Another example is, after collecting maintenance data from the cloud service, the AI on the cloud send an instruction that one of the robots in manufacturing need to get maintenance. Therefore, the other robots will get more tasks to make up that change for the overall goal. In this example, the actuator is the software running on manufacturing robots. Like just mentioned, the IoT integration brings data that hard to access in traditional factory. This makes machine learning, deep learning and reinforcement learning based AI integration possible to facilitate the smart manufacturing.

3.3 Horizontal Integration

As shown in Fig. 2, after the vertical integration, seven systems are connected to the backbone network of the smart factory. Also, they play a part of the smart factory network. The connections indicate the physical interaction that could happen in the smart factory, of course, along with data exchange. For example, the AI agent within the manufacturing system find the materials are running out. It could send material requirement to the material supply system. The material supply system then prepares the materials and send requirement to the local logistic system. The logistic system then initiates a material distribution. Another example is all the machine related systems (manufacturing, product test, logistics and etc.) may need daily maintenance. They send their daily running statistics and AI agent in maintenance system will analysis those data and gives a cost-optimized and energy efficient maintenance schedule. This kind of integration emphasis the interaction among systems in smart factory, making a better quality, higher efficiency automation possible. Horizontal integration is vital especially when there are human involved in the overall work flow or the vertical integration is incomplete considering the cost. The reason is that, when there are human involved or incompleteness of vertical integration, some data are not available to the cloud service. For example, in a factory, the local logistics has to be done by human. However, the output of human part, that is, the delivery of the raw material is dynamic because of the variance of working efficiency. At the same time, no measurement will be acquired directly from human in terms of, for example, the working efficiency considering the privacy. Thus, those measurement could be acquired from the next, fully integrated process of the manufacturing by interaction: the manufacturing robot received the raw materials, as a variable in the whole manufacturing. Therefore, the horizontal integration requires sensing and data exchange among systems in the smart factory, which will need extra sensors or related parts. Other reasons such as latency of a centralized cloud based control, failure of the data collection system and etc. brings the necessarily of the horizontal integration. Paper [3] introduces a Parallel Reinforcement Learning (PRL) based IoT system to reduce the learning time of Reinforcement Learning (RL) considering the communication overhead. The simulation based on the multi-agent system in smart factory gives a good vision of horizontal integration.

4   Future Networking and Computing Architecture

The holistic networking and computing architecture can be facilitated from two aspects: (1) machine learning for communications and networks (2) networking for AI agents to form a networked multi-agent system, which will be detailed in the following two sub-sections.

4.1   State-of-the-Art Applications of Machine Learning to Future Wireless Network Architecture

Future wireless network architecture accommodating machine learning (ML) emerges as an important technology for next decades, while ITU-T forming a focus group (FG) to study from 2018 to 2020. When incorporating ML functionalities into network architecture, there are two mechanisms to execute ML algorithms: online ML and offline ML. The online ML computing means the ML functionality is embedded into networking algorithms or protocols, and thus must be implemented into the corresponding network entities. On the other hand, if the ML functionality is executed then used to assist network functionalities, it is known as offline ML computing that can be executed in a co-locating computing facility connected to the corresponding network entities. The offline ML can be also computed in another far-away computing facility and then transfer the model of learning to the target network entity. As shown in Fig. 4, the ML computing can be executed and co-located with the user equipment (UE) or agents, radio access network (RAN), or core network (CN), in addition to the cloud. The emerging edge computing or edge artificial intelligence (AI) [33] can be considered co-locating with RAN.

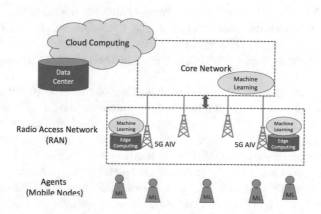

Fig. 4. Alternatives, agent computing with UE, edge computing co-locating with RAN, and cloud computing through CN to implement machine learning or AI in the wireless network architecture

Generally speaking, ML can be applied in a few possible networking and communication scenarios:

- Channel State Information (CSI): CSI is critical to air-interface technology for networking algorithms and physical layer communication, which has been considered to be inferred or estimated with the aid of deep learning [18,53], or calibration the channel models for preferred CSI [1].
- User Behavior: User behavior such as human/vehicular mobility patterns can be useful to network management and mobility management functionalities [7], and autonomous system operation [8], through big data analysis by ML or reinforcement learning [28].
- Traffic Prediction: Deep packet inspection, network intelligence, and user mobility patterns, can be used to predict wireless network traffic for more efficient network/radio resource allocation [20,55].
- Cybersecurity: ML might be one of the most attractive tools to enhance network security, detect attacks and intrusions to networks [13,56].
- Anticipatory Networking Mechanism: Except using reinforcement learning or multi-armed bandit mechanisms for radio resource or network resource allocation [32,58], existing applications of ML to wireless networking is generally offline learning to assist or enhance existing solutions. However, another

advantage of ML is to develop predictive networking mechanism via online learning such that ML can enable networking functionalities that are nor possible before. One of such rare examples is the anticipatory mobility management using Naive Bayesian and recursive belief update [6, 26] as online learning to enable proactive communication and virtual cell for ultra-low latency wireless networking, where anticipatory is widely adopted in AI.

4.2   Networked Multi-agent Systems

In addition to apply ML to wireless networks, another question of AI computing and wireless networking arises: what is the desirable wireless networking for agents using ML? More precisely, how to design a wireless network for agents of machine intelligence, say a multi-robot system (MRS) or a multi-agent system (MAS).

Legg and Hutter gave an informal definition of machine intelligence in [22]: *Intelligence measures an agent's ability to achieve goals in a wide range of environments.* Distributed artificial intelligence (DAI) has been brought into attention in AI research well over 3 decades [2], which has two common sub-disciplines: distributed problem solving (DPS) and multi-agent system (MAS). DPS typically decomposes task into several not completely independent sub-problems that can be executed on different processors and then synthesizes a solution. On the other hand, MAS considers an agent is an intelligent entity, which can be a robot or an AV, with goals and actions in an operating environment. In state-of-the-art CPS/IoT that are highly parallel in computing, a MAS typically represents a complex system of multiple agents and the mechanism for coordination of agents' behaviors. Please recall that Demazeau inspiringly defined MAS consisting of four major aspects: agents, environments, interactions, and organization [9]. When RL deals with agent's action and environment, communication for decisions was brought into MAS of agents using RL by modeling as partially observed MDP [37,50]. Though communication or exchange of actions by agents has been studied in MAS and DAI for a long time, the features of wireless networks have been hardly considered in literature. In [37], finite number of communication channels with so-called fast communication was considered for information sharing among a team of cooperative agents. [12,30,60] indirectly considered the communication in MAS. However, realistic wireless communications and networking has not well taken into consideration, nor impacts on ML mechanisms.

An interesting study looks into collective behavior of autonomous vehicles moving across a region of Manhattan streets, by treating the behavior of each autonomous vehicle as an agent using reinforcement learning. It is shown that wireless networking reduces average delay [21]. In such wireless networking, different from human-to-human personal communication, the reward map and policy of another autonomous vehicle in the interaction range would be useful information to exchange. The age of such information is critical and thus ultra low-latency wireless networking is highly preferred, in which the real-time ALOHA has been considered as multiple access. For collaborative robots that each has own machine learning algorithms (such as moving actions and planning) to execute toward a common goal, wireless networking would be extremely beneficial to collective efficiency [5]. A lot of issues remain open in such networked MAS, such as network topology [15] and innovative machine learning for networked MAS.

5   Conclusions

Holistic integration and interaction of AI computing and wireless networking for IoT systems still has a long way to develop. This paper initially brings up the literature survey and in-depth discussions toward this ultimate goal. Many open issues still require remarkable technological innovations in the future.

References

1. Adeogun, R.: Calibration of stochastic radio propagation models using machine learning. IEEE Antennas Wirel. Propag. Lett. **18**(12), 2538–2542 (2019)
2. Bond, A.H., Gasser, L.: Readings in Distributed Artificial Intelligence. Morgan Kaufmann, San Mateo (2014)
3. Camelo, M., Claeys, M., Latré, S.: Parallel reinforcement learning with minimal communication overhead for IoT environments. IEEE Internet Things J. **7**, 1387–1400 (2019)
4. Chen, B., Wan, J., Shu, L., Li, P., Mukherjee, M., Yin, B.: Smart factory of Industry 4.0: key technologies, application case, and challenges. IEEE Access **6**, 6505–6519 (2017)
5. Chen, K.C., Hung, H.M.: Wireless robotic communication for collaborative multi-agent systems. In: ICC 2019-2019 IEEE International Conference on Communications (ICC), pp. 1–7. IEEE (2019)
6. Chen, K.C., Zhang, T., Gitlin, R.D., Fettweis, G.: Ultra-low latency mobile networking. IEEE Netw. **33**(2), 181–187 (2018)
7. Chih-Lin, I., Sun, Q., Liu, Z., Zhang, S., Han, S.: The big-data-driven intelligent wireless network: architecture, use cases, solutions, and future trends. IEEE Veh. Technol. Mag. **12**(4), 20–29 (2017)
8. Cui, Q., et al.: Big data analytics and network calculus enabling intelligent management of autonomous vehicles in a smart city. IEEE Internet Things J. **6**(2), 2021–2034 (2018)
9. Demazeau, Y.: From interactions to collective behaviour in agent-based systems. In: Proceedings of the 1st European Conference on Cognitive Science, Saint-Malo. Citeseer (1995)
10. Elango, M., Nachiappan, S., Tiwari, M.K.: Balancing task allocation in multi-robot systems using K-means clustering and auction based mechanisms. Expert Syst. Appl. **38**(6), 6486–6491 (2011)
11. Ferdowsi, A., Saad, W.: Deep learning for signal authentication and security in massive Internet-of-Things systems. IEEE Trans. Commun. **67**(2), 1371–1387 (2019)
12. Ge, X., Han, Q.L.: Distributed formation control of networked multi-agent systems using a dynamic event-triggered communication mechanism. IEEE Trans. Ind. Electron. **64**(10), 8118–8127 (2017)

13. He, D., Liu, C., Quek, T.Q., Wang, H.: Transmit antenna selection in MIMO wiretap channels: a machine learning approach. IEEE Wirel. Commun. Lett. **7**(4), 634–637 (2018)
14. He, Y., et al.: Deep-reinforcement-learning-based optimization for cache-enabled opportunistic interference alignment wireless networks. IEEE Trans. Veh. Technol. **66**(11), 10433–10445 (2017)
15. Hsiao, J.H., Chen, K.C.: Communication methodology to control a distributed multi-agent system. In: ICC 2019–2019 IEEE International Conference on Communications (ICC), pp. 1–6. IEEE (2019)
16. Huang, L., Bi, S., Zhang, Y.J.: Deep reinforcement learning for online computation offloading in wireless powered mobile-edge computing networks. IEEE Trans. Mob. Comput., 1 (2019)
17. Ivanov, D., Dolgui, A., Sokolov, B., Werner, F., Ivanova, M.: A dynamic model and an algorithm for short-term supply chain scheduling in the smart factory Industry 4.0. Int. J. Prod. Res. **54**(2), 386–402 (2016)
18. Jiang, Z., He, Z., Chen, S., Molisch, A.F., Zhou, S., Niu, Z.: Inferring remote channel state information: Cramér-Rae lower bound and deep learning implementation. In: 2018 IEEE Global Communications Conference (GLOBECOM), pp. 1–7. IEEE (2018)
19. Kang, H.S., et al.: Smart manufacturing: past research, present findings, and future directions. Int. J. Precis. Eng. Manuf.-Green Technol. **3**(1), 111–128 (2016). https://doi.org/10.1007/s40684-016-0015-5
20. Kim, J., Hwang, G.: Adaptive bandwidth allocation based on sample path prediction with gaussian process regression. IEEE Trans. Wirel. Commun. **18**(10), 4983–4996 (2019)
21. Ko, E., Chen, K.C.: Wireless communications meets artificial intelligence: an illustration by autonomous vehicles on Manhattan streets. In: 2018 IEEE Global Communications Conference (GLOBECOM), pp. 1–7. IEEE (2018)
22. Legg, S., Hutter, M.: Universal intelligence: a definition of machine intelligence. Mind. Mach. **17**(4), 391–444 (2007). https://doi.org/10.1007/s11023-007-9079-x
23. Lei, L., Xu, H., Xiong, X., Zheng, K., Xiang, W., Wang, X.: Multiuser resource control with deep reinforcement learning in IoT edge computing. IEEE Internet Things J. **6**(6), 10119–10133 (2019)
24. Li, L., Ota, K., Dong, M.: Deep learning for smart industry: efficient manufacture inspection system with fog computing. IEEE Trans. Ind. Inf. **14**(10), 4665–4673 (2018)
25. Li, L., Xu, Y., Yin, J., Liang, W., Li, X., Chen, W., Han, Z.: Deep reinforcement learning approaches for content caching in cache-enabled D2D networks. IEEE Internet Things J. **7**(1), 544–557 (2020)
26. Lin, C.Y., Chen, K.C., Wickramasuriya, D., Lien, S.Y., Gitlin, R.D.: Anticipatory mobility management by big data analytics for ultra-low latency mobile networking. In: 2018 IEEE International Conference on Communications (ICC), pp. 1–7. IEEE (2018)
27. Lin, C.C., Deng, D.J., Chih, Y.L., Chiu, H.T.: Smart manufacturing scheduling with edge computing using multi-class deep Q network. IEEE Trans. Ind. Inform. **15**, 4276–4284 (2019)
28. Liu, X., Liu, Y., Chen, Y., Hanzo, L.: Trajectory design and power control for multi-UAV assisted wireless networks: a machine learning approach. IEEE Trans. Veh. Technol. **68**, 7957–7969 (2019)
29. Liu, Y., Tong, K.F., Wong, K.K.: Reinforcement learning based routing for energy sensitive wireless mesh IoT networks. Electron. Lett. **55**(17), 966–968 (2019)

30. Liu, Z., Dai, J., Wu, B., Lin, H.: Communication-aware motion planning for multi-agent systems from signal temporal logic specifications. In: 2017 American Control Conference (ACC), pp. 2516–2521. IEEE (2017)

31. Mamdouh, M., Elrukhsi, M.A.I., Khattab, A.: Securing the Internet of Things and wireless sensor networks via machine learning: a survey. In: 2018 International Conference on Computer and Applications (ICCA), pp. 215–218. IEEE, Beirut, August 2018

32. Nguyen, D.D., Nguyen, H.X., White, L.B.: Reinforcement learning with network-assisted feedback for heterogeneous RAT selection. IEEE Trans. Wirel. Commun. **16**(9), 6062–6076 (2017)

33. Park, J., Samarakoon, S., Bennis, M., Debbah, M.: Wireless network intelligence at the edge. Proc. IEEE **107**(11), 2204–2239 (2019)

34. Pinto, E.M.d.L., Lachowski, R., Pellenz, M.E., Penna, M.C., Souza, R.D.: A machine learning approach for detecting spoofing attacks in wireless sensor networks. In: 2018 IEEE 32nd International Conference on Advanced Information Networking and Applications (AINA), pp. 752–758. IEEE, Krakow, May 2018

35. Rahman, A., Jin, J., Cricenti, A.L., Rahman, A., Kulkarni, A.: Communication-aware cloud robotic task offloading with on-demand mobility for smart factory maintenance. IEEE Trans. Ind. Inf. **15**(5), 2500–2511 (2018)

36. Shiue, Y.R., Lee, K.C., Su, C.T.: Real-time scheduling for a smart factory using a reinforcement learning approach. Comput. Ind. Eng. **125**, 604–614 (2018)

37. Stein, S., Williamson, S.A., Jennings, N.R.: Decentralised channel allocation and information sharing for teams of cooperative agents. In: Proceedings of the 11th International Conference on Autonomous Agents and Multiagent Systems, vol. 1, pp. 231–238. International Foundation for Autonomous Agents and Multiagent Systems (2012)

38. Tao, F., Qi, Q., Liu, A., Kusiak, A.: Data-driven smart manufacturing. J. Manuf. Syst. **48**, 157–169 (2018)

39. Tereshchuk, V., Stewart, J., Bykov, N., Pedigo, S., Devasia, S., Banerjee, A.G.: An efficient scheduling algorithm for multi-robot task allocation in assembling aircraft structures. arXiv preprint arXiv:1902.08905 (2019)

40. Thoben, K.D., Wiesner, S., Wuest, T.: "Industrie 4.0" and smart manufacturing-a review of research issues and application examples. Int. J. Autom. Technol. **11**(1), 4–16 (2017)

41. Wang, S., Shin, Y.: Efficient routing protocol based on reinforcement learning for magnetic induction underwater sensor networks. IEEE Access **7**, 82027–82037 (2019)

42. Wang, S., Wan, J., Li, D., Zhang, C.: Implementing smart factory of Industrie 4.0: an outlook. Int. J. Distrib. Sens. Netw. **12**(1), 3159805 (2016)

43. Wang, Z., Zhang, J., Zhang, X., Wang, W.: Reinforcement learning based congestion control in satellite Internet of Things. In: 2019 11th International Conference on Wireless Communications and Signal Processing (WCSP), pp. 1–6. IEEE, Xi'an, October 2019

44. Wei, Y., Yu, F.R., Song, M., Han, Z.: Joint optimization of caching, computing, and radio resources for fog-enabled IoT using natural actor-critic deep reinforcement learning. IEEE Internet Things J. **6**(2), 2061–2073 (2019)

45. Wu, D., Jennings, C., Terpenny, J., Gao, R.X., Kumara, S.: A comparative study on machine learning algorithms for smart manufacturing: tool wear prediction using random forests. J. Manuf. Sci. Eng. **139**(7), 071018 (2017)

46. Wu, H., Zhang, Z., Jiao, C., Li, C., Quek, T.Q.S.: Learn to sense: a meta-learning-based sensing and fusion framework for wireless sensor networks. IEEE Internet Things J. **6**(5), 8215–8227 (2019)
47. Wuest, T., Weimer, D., Irgens, C., Thoben, K.D.: Machine learning in manufacturing: advantages, challenges, and applications. Prod. Manuf. Res. **4**(1), 23–45 (2016)
48. Xia, F., Song, H., Xu, C.: Securing the wireless environment of IoT. In: 2018 IEEE International Conference of Safety Produce Informatization (IICSPI), pp. 315–318. IEEE, Chongqing, December 2018
49. Xia, W., Di, C., Guo, H., Li, S.: Reinforcement learning based stochastic shortest path finding in wireless sensor networks. IEEE Access **7**, 157807–157817 (2019)
50. Xuan, P., Lesser, V., Zilberstein, S.: Communication decisions in multi-agent cooperation: model and experiments. In: Proceedings of the Fifth International Conference on Autonomous Agents, pp. 616–623. ACM (2001)
51. Yang, C., Chin, K.W., He, T., Liu, Y.: On sampling time maximization in wireless powered Internet of Things. IEEE Trans. Green Commun. Netw. **3**(3), 641–650 (2019)
52. Yao, F., Jia, L.: A collaborative multi-agent reinforcement learning anti-jamming algorithm in wireless networks. IEEE Wirel. Commun. Lett. **8**(4), 1024–1027 (2019)
53. Ye, H., Li, G.Y., Juang, B.H.: Power of deep learning for channel estimation and signal detection in OFDM systems. IEEE Wirel. Commun. Lett. **7**(1), 114–117 (2017)
54. Yu, Y., Wang, T., Liew, S.C.: Deep-reinforcement learning multiple access for heterogeneous wireless networks. IEEE J. Sel. Areas Commun. **37**(6), 1277–1290 (2019)
55. Zhang, C., Zhang, H., Qiao, J., Yuan, D., Zhang, M.: Deep transfer learning for intelligent cellular traffic prediction based on cross-domain big data. IEEE J. Sel. Areas Commun. **37**(6), 1389–1401 (2019)
56. Zhang, L., Restuccia, F., Melodia, T., Pudlewski, S.M.: Taming cross-layer attacks in wireless networks: a Bayesian learning approach. IEEE Trans. Mob. Comput. **18**(7), 1688–1702 (2018)
57. Zhang, Y., Cai, P., Pan, C., Zhang, S.: Multi-agent deep reinforcement learning-based cooperative spectrum sensing with upper confidence bound exploration. IEEE Access **7**, 118898–118906 (2019)
58. Zhao, P., Tian, H., Cheny, K.C., Fan, S., Nie, G.: Context-aware TDD configuration and resource allocation for mobile edge computing. IEEE Trans. Commun. **68**, 1118–1131 (2019)
59. Zheng, P., et al.: Smart manufacturing systems for Industry 4.0: conceptual framework, scenarios, and future perspectives. Front. Mech. Eng. **13**(2), 137–150 (2018). https://doi.org/10.1007/s11465-018-0499-5
60. Zhou, L., Yang, P., Chen, C., Gao, Y.: Multiagent reinforcement learning with sparse interactions by negotiation and knowledge transfer. IEEE Trans. Cybern. **47**(5), 1238–1250 (2016)
61. Zhu, H., Cao, Y., Wei, X., Wang, W., Jiang, T., Jin, S.: Caching transient data for Internet of Things: a deep reinforcement learning approach. IEEE Internet Things J. **6**(2), 2074–2083 (2019)
62. Zhu, J., Song, Y., Jiang, D., Song, H.: A new deep-Q-learning-based transmission scheduling mechanism for the cognitive Internet of Things. IEEE Internet Things J. **5**(4), 2375–2385 (2018)

The Thing About the Internet of Things: Scoping the Social Science Discourse in IoT Research

Viktor Mähler[(⊠)] [iD]

Department of Informatics, Umeå University, 90187 Umeå, Sweden
viktor.mahler@umu.se

Abstract. Internet of Things (IoT) is predicted to change not only industry, businesses and commerce, but also our everyday lives. Social science research surrounding IoT is important and necessary because of this predicted change. In this 'scoping study' keyword-clusters are being used to identify key-concepts within the social science subject area, giving an overview of the scopes within said concepts, and where social science stands to benefit from further research. The result is the thematization of 25 keywords, spread within 5 clusters; *Organization, Logistics, Infrastructure, Technology* and *Protection*. This paper argues that more research is needed in human-centric aspects, and that in doing this - a potential sixth theme regarding *ethics* can emerge where the subject field of social science can stand to generate a larger impact on IoT research.

Keywords: Internet of Things · Scoping study · Themes · Social science · Ethics

1 Introduction

Internet of Things is a buzzword. Not in the negative sense, but rather in the everybody-is-talking-about-it sense, as evident by the conferences, special editions and symposiums that are springing up all around the globe in regards to this phenomenon.

The interest in IoT show no indication of stopping in the foreseeable future and estimations predict that in 2020 there will be 30 billion connected devices worldwide and that the value surrounding IoT will reach up to 1.3 trillion dollars (Statista 2019; Ericsson 2016). If these estimations prove correct then IoT will truly change the modern landscape as we know it, and IoT research have already rapidly transcended the scope or concept of a single field of research. Today IoT is influencing both governmental and private sectors, transport, e-health, customer behavior, manufacturing, privacy and the very cities that we live in (Porter and Heppelmann 2014).

These areas are all aspects within the social sciences, each with their own research traditions and methodologies, which will need to be able to work together and conduct research alongside one another in order to contribute to the body of knowledge. This knowledge then serves to inform researchers, decision-makers as well as social science undergraduates and graduates that will eventually play a role in *e.g.* policymaking and politics – affecting the lives of many, for good or bad (Tarschys and Lachapelle 2010).

© IFIP International Federation for Information Processing 2020
Published by Springer Nature Switzerland AG 2020
A. Casaca et al. (Eds.): IFIPIoT 2019, IFIP AICT 574, pp. 235–251, 2020.
https://doi.org/10.1007/978-3-030-43605-6_14

Most of the IoT research that is being performed today concerns technological advancements and incremental improvements on sensors and hardware. Examining publications indexed by the research database Scopus, the subject-fields of Engineering and Computer Science are currently over-represented within the database when searching for "IoT" or "Internet of Things" (as shown in the literature selection).

The field of information systems research has already studied and showcased the need for co-operation and involvement of employees to facilitate adoption of IT within organizations (Gallivan et al. 2005; Botta-Genoulaz and Millet 2006). And while individuals previously have had the ability to opt-out of connectivity and technology outside of work, the massive implications of IoT can shift that ability on a societal level. Technological adoption on such a massive scale, as for instance a city, is a new phenomenon - one where the focus now risks being on the technology of the smart city, rather than the inhabitants within. Because of this the social science subject-area was selected for this scoping study, in order to understand key concepts within, provide an overview for researchers and practitioners, and to make suggestions for future research.

The research question that this scoping study aims to answer is; *"What areas are being addressed within the social science subject-field of IoT-literature in research journals and where can further social science research stand to contribute?"*

Through the analysis of 8290 keywords, and a selective reading of peer-reviewed journal articles, the scopes for different key concepts within IoT research is presented and thematized. The primary aim for this study is to explore how IoT is addressed within Social Science literature, to examine key concepts that are discussed and also to present an argument for strengthening inter-disciplinary co-operation within Social Sciences. Based on the analysis and results from the scoping study, an additional argument is made for the need of further research in social science concerning human-centric aspects and ethics. This study concludes that five themes can be observed in terms of IoT in social science, and that a sixth theme (*ethics*) has a potential to emerge. The study identified a lack in human-centric and ethics research, and argue that such research could prove beneficial to the field. The implications, should the Social Sciences fail to establish themselves within the human-centric aspects of IoT discourse, is that adaptions and implementations of IoT risks being left to the devices of individuals or organizations with the intent of monetizing personal data generated by users, selling user information and infringing on the privacy of millions.

2 Research Methodology

A scoping study, as described by Arksey and O'Malley (2005) focuses towards quickly mapping key concepts within a research area, mapping the main sources as well as providing a comprehensive study – where the depth of the study can vary depending on the review. This type of study can also function in terms of deciding whether or not the undertaking of a full systematic literature review would be valuable, summarizing research findings and identifying gaps in the literature (ibid.).

This research methodology was selected because of its aim to give an overarching view of research within a field – which fit well with the research question at hand.

The subject field of Social Science was the main interest, and in order to get as wide of a selection among research journals, no exclusions were made on journals within the selected subject field. This scoping study focuses on breadth in terms of literature selection in order to showcase key concepts and adhere to the aspect of 'relevance' rather than the 'rigor' of a full systematic literature review in terms of in-depth analysis (Senn 1998).

Scopus was selected as the research database for this study. Scopus is a part of the Elsevier publishing company, and the largest abstract and citation database of peer-reviewed literature (Elsevier 2019) being the reason for its selection.

In order to assist with the analysis and charting of the data, the software "VOS-viewer" was used. VOSviewer is a tool used to construct as well as visualize bibliometric networks (Centre for Science and Technology Studies 2018).

Using the VOSviewer-software a keyword map was created by examining the bibliographic data collected from 1489 articles – directing the study towards the co-occurrence of keywords relating to the chosen subject-fields within every published journal paper in the Scopus database. 8290 keywords were identified, where 25 were refined into five clusters detailing key concepts, and through analysis of these key concepts five themes emerged that were expanded upon and examined.

2.1 Literature Selection

Scopus was selected as the reference database, and only journal articles were selected for the analysis. Delimitation of the scope to 'journals only' was made in order to assure reputable outlets, and to condense keywords grown out of rigorous research, compared to the lesser rigor associated with conference proceedings in some subject fields. In order to capture as many facets as possible, articles were selected from the subject-areas of; Social Science, Business, Management and Accounting, Psychology as well as Arts and Humanities – within Scopus own preassigned subject-area search options.

The reason for including Psychology and Arts and Humanities into the subject-area was to capture eventual cross-disciplinary publications, such as Human-Computer Interaction or otherwise related areas. Engineering and computer science journals were not excluded from the search, provided that the article itself was in relation to the subject area of Social Sciences. This was done in order to expand the scope of the search and to get an idea of where the social scientific discourse is being held.

In order to look at the most recent research, it was decided that publications should be no older than 2014, to capture the trend of the last five years. In order to see the current trend being discussed, as well as the areas of focus within the body of knowledge, the following search string was generated:

(TITLE-ABS-KEY (iot) OR TITLE-ABS-KEY ("Internet of Things")) AND PUBYEAR > **2013** AND PUBYEAR < **2020** AND (LIMIT-TO (SUBJAREA , "**SOCI**") OR LIMIT-TO (SUBJAREA , "**BUSI**") OR LIMIT-TO (SUBJAREA , "**ARTS**") OR LIMIT-TO (SUBJAREA , "**PSYC**")) AND (LIMIT-TO (DOCTYPE , "ar")) AND (LIMIT-TO (LANGUAGE , "**English**"))

The final search was performed 20/6 -2019 and the criteria yielded 1489 articles, where 786 were from Social Sciences, 730 from Business, Management and Accounting, 85 from psychology and 84 from Arts and Humanities. The discrepancy when looking at the number of articles (1489) and the number of articles when adding up the aforementioned subject areas (1685) could be explained by some articles being in multiple differing categories. The selection for this scoping study is described in the flowchart below, with the decision of which items to keep and remove, respectively.

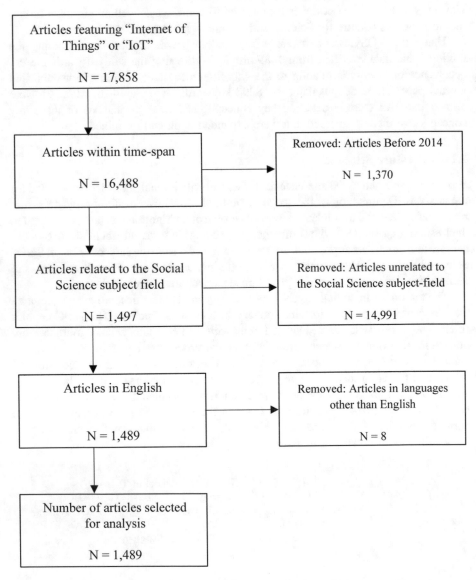

Fig. 1. Flowchart of literature selection process.

2.2   Literature Analysis

The total number of available keywords was 8290. Keywords that appeared in at least 29 different articles were selected to be part of the study, leaving 34 keywords in total. Keyword duplicates were removed (e.g. "Smart City" and "Smart Cities") where the word with the lowest scoring link strength was the one that were removed. Keywords such as "Internet of Things", "IoT" and variations thereof were also removed, leaving a total of 25 keywords remaining, split into five different clusters that can be observed as differentiated by colors. In regards to "Privacy", "Data Privacy", "Security" and "Network Security", they were chosen to remain separated; due to each keyword having different implications in the literature. The strength of the connection between the keywords is visualized in differing boldness of the lines connecting each of the keywords (Fig. 2).

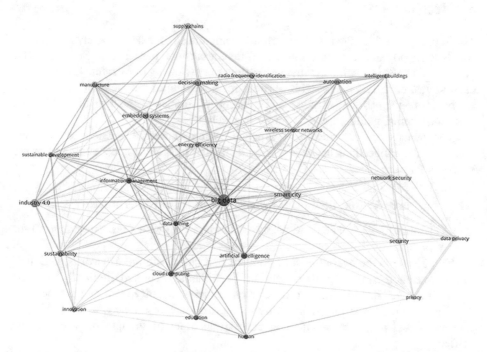

Fig. 2. The 25 most common keywords out of 8290 available, divided into 5 clusters.

Based on the keywords produced by the literature analysis, each cluster was examined and a select reading of the most cited articles for each keyword was performed.

In order to summarize the keyword-clusters into *Themes* the related articles were analyzed in terms of what topic they covered and their connection to each other. What Arksey and O'Malley (2005) describes as 'key concepts' was identified within each cluster, and the theme emerged from the identified concept. Heavily cited articles were generally premiered over lesser cited – unless the article could be considered to be related to a specific scope within the theme.

When articles were selected for the inclusion to describe the scope of a particular theme, the search included the same keyword duplicates that previously had been separated from the analysis. This was made in order to increase the breadth of the search without straying from the examination of associated scopes. An example of this would be that the search string included "Smart City OR Smart Cities" or "RFID OR Radio Frequency Identification".

3 Results

The scoping study resulted in 1489 articles being chosen for deeper analysis. 25 keywords emerged, and were split into five different clusters, presented in Sect. 3.1. The clusters were used to formulate themes through the reviewing of literature connected to each keyword, and its theme. This allowed for a scoping of the literature within each theme leading up to the selection and addition of articles deemed to fit within that particular theme, guiding towards future research.

The themes are described and expanded upon in Sect. 3.2 where an analysis regarding the connections between keywords is presented alongside a summary of the scope of for each theme.

3.1   Keywords Within the Social Science Subject-Field Literature

The *Keywords* for each theme are displayed firstly, along with a corresponding *ID* for each Keyword.

The *Theme* is the overall area of concern that deals with the *Keywords*, and their link to one another, making them a cluster. Each theme is colored differently from the other which was done in order to make them easier to identify from one another.

The *Occurrence* is how many times *Keywords* are mentioned in the published journals – and they are presented in descending order of strength for each *Theme* (Table 1).

Table 1. Keywords, their ID, Theme of Cluster and Keyword Occurrence.

Keyword	ID	Theme	Occurrence
Industry 4.0	A-1	Organization	65
Sustainability	A-2	Organization	43
Innovation	A-3	Organization	40
Sustainable Development	A-4	Organization	34
Decision Making	B-1	Logistics	54
Embedded Systems	B-2	Logistics	50
Manufacture	B-3	Logistics	41
Radio Frequency Identification	B-4	Logistics	39
Supply Chains	B-5	Logistics	36
Smart City	C-1	Infrastructure	77
Automation	C-2	Infrastructure	49
Energy Efficiency	C-3	Infrastructure	36
Wireless Sensor Networks	C-4	Infrastructure	36
Intelligent Buildings	C-5	Infrastructure	29
Big Data	D-1	Technology	121
Artificial Intelligence	D-2	Technology	43
Cloud Computing	D-3	Technology	40
Information Management	D-4	Technology	39
Data Mining	D-5	Technology	34
Education	D-6	Technology	30
Human	D-7	Technology	29
Network Security	E-1	Protection	48
Security	E-2	Protection	44
Data Privacy	E-3	Protection	39
Privacy	E-4	Protection	37

3.2   Themes Based on Keywords from the Social Science Subject-Field Litterature Analysis

The articles related to each theme has been chosen in order to provide an understanding of different aspects within the scope of the theme, in which journals they are being addressed and the number of citations, according to the Scopus database for each article (Which has been abbreviated as #C in the tables below).

Each theme will be presented, with their respective table color-coded to correspond with the themes in the keyword Sect. (3.1). The scope of the theme itself will also be laid out, based on selected reading. It should be noted that while the themes have been isolated based on the clustered keywords, it does not mean that the themes are isolated from each other – where *e.g.* the keyword *big data* plays a part in every theme.

Certain themes have stronger links towards each other than others, and will therefore overlap one another. Noteworthy keyword connections (or lack-there-of) identified in VOSviewer will be also be presented, and later discussed.

The table of articles for each theme will feature articles presented in order of descending citations, however they should be considered of equal importance, functioning as scope overview for further reading and referencing. Some articles within one theme may touch upon aspects within other themes, where it serves to highlight that the themes are not in isolation.

Organization – The keywords for the organization theme was identified as; *Industry 4.0, Sustainability, Innovation* and *Sustainable Management*. The theme revolves around IoTs role on industrial aspects and future improvement within an organizational or production-oriented setting. The following articles have been chosen to highlight the different scopes of the Organization theme (Table 2):

Table 2. List of keyword ID, connected article, author(s), journal, year and number of citations for the "Organization" theme.

Article	Author(S)	Journal, Year	#C
The Internet of Things (IoT): Applications, investments, and challenges for enterprises	Lee, I., Lee, K.	Business Horizons, 2015	349
Business models for the Internet of Things	Dijkman, R.M., Sprenkels, B., Peeters, T., Janssen, A.	International Journal of Information Management, 2015	109
A Complex View of Industry 4.0	Roblek, V., Meško, M., Krapež, A.	SAGE Open, 2016	86
Industry 4.0: State of the art and future trends	Xu, L.D., Xu, E.L., Li, L.	International Journal of Production Research, 2018	76
Sustainable industrial value creation: Benefits and challenges of industry 4.0	Kiel, D., Müller, J. M., Arnold, C., Voigt, K.-I.	International Journal of Innovation Management, 2017	33

The keyword **analysis** from showcases that the most commonly occurring keyword *industry 4.0* connects towards both the logistics, infrastructural and technical themes. Notably in the Protection theme; *industry 4.0* connected to *network security* but not to any of the keywords relating to *privacy* or *data privacy*. This does not mean that privacy was a non-issue, but in terms of the Protection theme, the *network security* was of greater interest within the Organization theme. Unsurprisingly there was also strong connection between *industry 4.0* and the keywords *manufacture* and *embedded systems* within the Logistics theme. The keyword *innovation* was one of the few keywords that connected to both *human* and *education*, albeit weakly.

The **scope** of the Organization theme primarily focuses on the business aspect of IoT, where it is examined the extent to which production can be improved upon (Roblek et al. 2016), which way IoT will change the way that businesses operate (Dijkman et al. 2015; Kiel et al. 2017), and wherein monetary value will present itself and how to utilize sensor-based technology (Lee and Lee 2015; Xu et al. 2018). The surveyed articles reveals a generally positive outlook on what IoT will come to entail – and many articles theorize about a considerable growth of revenue, but of course challenges are also presented, but these mainly relate towards technology and sustainability. Less reflections in terms of Organizations are related to the change IoT will mean for workers within the industry – and changing aspects of their work, whereas change for customers is covered in a wider sense.

Discussed challenges within the Organization theme-literature relate to data storage, disruptive changes to business models and emergence of new business eco-systems and how these can be utilized. Opportunities that are being discussed within the literature revolve around monetary gains, optimizing production and maintenance as well as the benefits towards customers.

Logistics – Keywords related to the Logistics theme were; *Decision Making, Embedded Systems, Manufacture, Radio Frequency Identification* and *Supply Chains*. The logistics theme focuses on IoTs impact on transportation, production and overview of goods or machinery. The following articles have been chosen to highlight the different scopes of the Logistics theme (Table 3):

Table 3. List of keyword ID, connected article, author(s), journal, year and number of citations for the "Logistics" theme.

Article	Author(S)	Journal, Year	#C
Smart manufacturing: Past research, present findings, and future directions	Kang, H.S., Lee, J.Y., Choi, S., Kim, H., Park, J. H., Son, J.Y., Kim, B.H., Noh, S.D	International Journal of Precision Engineering and Manufacturing - Green Technology, 2016	203
The Future of Retailing	Grewal, D., Roggeveen, A. L., Nordfält, J.	Journal of Retailing, 2017	91
Smart manufacturing	Kusiak, A.	International Journal of Production Research, 2018	76
ICT in multimodal transport and technological trends: Unleashing potential for the future	Harris, I., Wang, Y., Wang, H.	International Journal of Production Economics, 2015	61
Bottom-up approach based on Internet of Things for order fulfillment in a collaborative warehousing environment	Reaidy, P.J., Gunasekaran, A., Spalanzani, A.	International Journal of Production Economics, 2015	49

The keyword **analysis** show that *decision making* is the most commonly occurring keyword for this theme, where it connects to many of the other themes except for *innovation* in the Organization theme, and *education* in the Technology theme.

The keyword *supply chains,* despite having a low occurrence were connected towards all themes, but *radio frequency identification* had no connections towards the Organizational theme, showing that it was less frequently occurring, even in relation to *industry 4.0* – where the connection instead were towards *embedded systems*. In this theme *decision making* has a strong connection towards every other keyword within the theme and the other major keyword within the other themes as well.

The **scope** of the logistics theme deals with IoT within transportation, production, factories and the equipment within them. RFID is an important aspect of this theme, and research explores the introduction and implementation of embedded systems (Reaidy et al. 2015) and freighting/shipping (Harris et al. 2015). The keyword *decision making* and its facilitation (Grewal et al. 2017; Harris et al. 2015) remains a central aspect throughout this theme, as well as effects on retail in relation to transportation, delivering and storing. Another aspect that is prevalent in the Logistics theme is that of Smart Manufacturing and Smart Factories (Kang et al. 2016; Kusiak 2018) – and how IoT will come to affect the modes of production and machines.

Discussed challenges within the Logistics theme literature includes utilization of Big Data in terms of simplifying supply-chains, the technological transition towards smart manufacturing and expected consumer effect. Opportunities that were discussed within the Logistics literature were productivity increases, easier cargo tracking, increased revenue streams in retail and manufacturing.

Infrastructure – The keywords identified for the infrastructure theme was; *Smart City, Automation, Energy Efficiency, Wireless Sensor Networks* and *Intelligent Buildings*. The Infrastructure theme deals with the improvements IoT can have in terms of public services, tourism, energy, cities and networks. The following articles have been chosen to highlight the different scopes of the Infrastructure theme (Table 4):

Table 4. List of keyword ID, connected article, author(s), journal, year and number of citations for the "Infrastructure" theme.

Article	Author(S)	Journal, Year	#C
Smart tourism: foundations and developments	Gretzel, U., Sigala, M., Xiang, Z., Koo, C.	Electronic Markets, 2015	217
The role of big data in smart city	Hashem, I.A.T., Chang, V., Anuar, N.B., Adewole, K., Yaqoob, I., Gani, A., Ahmed, E., Chiroma, H.c	International Journal of Information Management, 2016	170
Urban computing in the wild: A survey on large scale participation and citizen engagement […]	Salim, F., Haque, U.	International Journal of Human Computer Studies, 2015	40
A Unified Smart City Model (USCM) for smart city conceptualization and benchmarking	Anthopoulos, L., Janssen, M., Weerakkody, V.	International Journal of Electronic Government Research, 2016	30
Towards the next generation of intelligent building: An assessment study of current automation and future IoT based systems […]	Lilis, G., Conus, G., Asadi, N., Kayal, M.	Sustainable Cities and Society, 2017	25

The keyword **analysis** show *smart city* as the most prominent keyword, where it connecting to every other keyword in every other theme with the notable exception of *education* and *human*. In this theme *automation* was also connected to every other theme with a strong connection towards *embedded systems, smart city, intelligent buildings* and *big data*. The Infrastructure theme also has a closer link towards the Protection theme than the other themes. The keyword *energy efficiency* connected to every other theme, however it did not connect to the keywords *industry 4.0* or *supply chains*. The keyword of *wireless sensor networks* were most connected towards the Logistics theme, and the Technology theme, where it only had one connection to the Organization and Protection theme, being; *industry 4.0* and *network security*.

The **Scope** of the Infrastructure theme deals in IoT within a cityscape, e-health, the energy management required and networks. Benefits towards tourism with the help of IoT implementations (Gretzel 2015) were discussed and explored. Like the Logistics theme, transports and optimization of these were also of interest – however these transports relate to infrastructure such as waste management and tracking of service vehicles (Hashem et al. 2016) rather than cargo transportation. Models on how to design the smart city concept is explored (Anthopoulos et al. 2016), along with the design of intelligent buildings (Lilis 2017). Another, smaller, scope was towards exploring the design of the smart city in terms of interaction (Salim and Haque 2015).

Discussed challenges within the Infrastructure theme were related towards the generation of big data, increased energy demands and digitalization of older buildings. Opportunities that are frequently discussed are; automation of services, increased city monitoring capabilities and the creation of eco-systems.

Technology – Within the Technology theme the keywords that were found was; *Big Data, Artificial Intelligence, Cloud Computing, Information Management, Data Mining, Education* and *Human*. The technology theme deals with the IoT in relation to hardware, management of data, and technological advancements. This theme features a heavy focus towards "Big Data". The following articles have been chosen to highlight the different scopes of the Technology theme (Table 5):

Table 5. List of keyword ID, connected article, author(s), journal, year and number of citations for the "Technology" theme.

Article	Author(S)	Journal, Year	#C
Significance and Challenges of Big Data Research	Jin, X., Wah, B.W., Cheng, X., Wang, Y.	Big Data Research, 2015	205
The role of big data in smart city	Hashem, I.A.T., Chang, V., Anuar, N.B., Adewole, K., Yaqoob, I., Gani, A., Ahmed, E., Chiroma, H.c	International Journal of Information Management, 2016	170
The Internet-of-Things: Review and research directions	Ng, I.C.L., Wakenshaw, S.Y.L.	International Journal of Research in Marketing, 2017	56
Conceptualizing and measuring quality of experience of the internet of things [...]	Shin, D.-H..	Information and Management, 2017	39
Putting things to work: Social and policy challenges for the Internet of things	Dutton, W.H.	Info, 2014	33

The keyword **analysis** showed *big data* to be the most prominent keyword, where it had a connection towards every other keyword. The keyword *human* surprisingly had the shared lowest occurrence out of all keywords – with only 29 occurrences (tied with *intelligent buildings*), and the weakest link strength to the other themes. The *human* keyword was mostly featured within the technology theme, only having one connection to the Organizational theme (*innovation*) and the Infrastructural theme (*automation*). In the Protection theme *human* was linked to *network security* and *privacy* and in the Logistics theme *human* was connected to *decision making* and *radio frequency identification*.

The **scope** of the theme proved difficult to portray, even if the theme itself became clear after analyzing the keywords. As described in the introduction of Sect. 3.2, many areas have some overlap, and this especially noticeable in the Technology theme – where it becomes more of a reference category, as the 'hard sciences' of engineering and computer science were left out. The literature in terms of the technological aspect revolved heavily around *big data*, its implications (Ng and Wakenshaw 2017), the opportunities and challenges (Jin et al. 2015) and implementations towards other themes (Hashem et al. 2016). The *human* keyword was included in this theme, and where humans were discussed as a scope in the Technology theme, it was mostly in terms of usability (Shin 2017), with less of a focus on policy challenges (Dutton 2014).

Discussed challenges within the Technology theme were related to data storage, interconnectivity and the complexity of the data. Opportunities that were discussed were; improvements in industry, predictions, addition of artificial intelligence.

Protection – The protection theme features the keywords *Network Security, Security, Data-Privacy* and *Privacy*. It revolves around the security of IoT protocols, threat detection and the aspects of intrusions both in hardware and private data. The following articles have been chosen to highlight the different scopes of the Protection theme (Table 6):

Table 6. List of keyword ID, connected article, author(s), journal, year and number of citations for the "Protection" theme.

Article	Author(S)	Journal, Year	#C
Regulating the internet of things: First steps toward managing discrimination, Privacy, Security, And consent	Peppet, S.R.	Texas Law Review, 2014	75
Low-energy security: Limits and opportunities in the internet of things	Trappe, W., Howard, R., Moore, R.S.	IEEE Security and Privacy, 2015	65
The Internet of Things: a security point of view	Li, S., Tryfonas, T., Li, H.	Internet Research, 2016	56
Internet of Things: Convenience vs. privacy and secrecy	Weinberg, B.D., Milne, G. R., Andonova, Y.G., Hajjat, F.M.	Business Horizons, 2015	55
SecKit: A Model-based Security Toolkit for the Internet of Things	Neisse, R., Steri, G., Fovino, I.N., Baldini, G.	Computers and Security, 2015	50

Analysis of the clusters in VOSviewer showed that in general the *Protection* theme was relatively disconnected from the other themes, they linked towards other themes, however the strongest connection within the *Protection* theme was within itself. The keyword *privacy* was the only word within the cluster connecting to *human*, with other the strongest connections being within its own cluster. Other connections were towards the *Technology*, *Infrastructure* and *Logistics* themes. The only keyword connecting towards the *Organization* theme was *network security*. The strongest link in this theme were between *data privacy* as well as *big data*, which is indicative of the literature.

In terms of **scope**, the Protection theme were less consistent than the other themes. Where most other themes would have a fairly clear delimitation, the protection theme had a wider area of interest, and the scoping was fairly spotty – ranging between the technical and the personal. One of the prominent scopes within this theme dealt with data security – connected to keywords *Network Security* and *Security* in terms of networks, hardware and security in an organizational setting (Neisse et al. 2015; Trappe et al. 2015; Li et al. 2016).

The second scope related to personal security in regards to informing, lawmaking, individual privacy and data privacy issues (Peppet 2014; Weinberg 2015) – worth noting is that this scope appeared to be somewhat smaller than litterature dealing with technical security issues.

Discussed challenges within the Protection theme were related to encryption, data transfer, the human factor and hacking. Opportunities identified within the Protection theme entails novel security solutions, advances in cryptography.

4 Discussion

4.1 Suggestions for a New Thematic Scope

Looking at the themes and the scopes within them, it can be argued that they show consistency with each other in terms of the key concepts, and the areas of interest within each one. While this is to be expected, it also highlights the exceptions to these expectations, making eventual outliers stand out in comparison. In this case, three notable exceptions were identified as part of the analysis, the first two being the keywords *education* and *human* within the Technology theme, and *privacy* from the Protection theme.

Within the Technology theme the keywords *human* and *education* stood out in comparison to the more consistent tech-oriented keywords - these two keywords were weak in their connection towards the other themes, and one speculation as to why could be that they do not fit particularly well within the Technology theme itself. However, they do not fit particularly well in any of the other themes either.

The same could be said about the keyword *privacy* within the Protection theme. It was the only keyword from the Protection theme that had a connection towards *human*, and examined papers with this keyword tended to have a scope closer to human-centric aspects rather than techno-centric aspects. In lacking a clear thematic connection, these three keywords form the weakest connections to the other themes and keywords, where one could expect *human* to play a larger role within the social science literature.

However low, the occurrence of the keywords still made them relevant, showing that an interest still exists and it could be argued that if the keywords *privacy, education* and *privacy* were instead used together more often in connection to other themes, a sixth theme could emerge filling a research gap in terms of the human-centric aspect, which does appear to be lacking. Such keywords as *human, education* and *privacy,* could make up the beginning of an Ethics theme – a concept with a scope that this study deems to be understudied within the IoT literature in the social science subject field.

4.2   Why Should the Social Sciences Care

As described in the introduction of this study, the value of IoT by 2020 is estimated to reach 1.3 trillion dollars, with 30 billion connected devices, and having the potential to change the technological world (Statista 2019; Ericsson 2016; Porter and Heppelmann 2014). These estimations should get the attention for more than just business opportunities and IoT-driven economic gains.

Social scientists should arguably be at the forefront of this phenomenon, examining the effect of this paradigm shift on the individuals and groups that are exposed to it. In the paper by Lee and Lee (2015) a study is referenced where only 22% of the participants felt that the benefits provided by a smart device made up for any privacy issues, and in the paper by Weinberg (2015) privacy was highlighted as an important factor among consumers, and it was expressed as something that managers needed to adhere to in terms of *privacy* and *education.*

The literature selection highlighted an over-representation of IoT-articles outside the subject field of social science – where 14,991 articles were removed, because of the subject fields differing from the ones chosen *(See* Fig. 1*).* It can be assumed that ethical concerns will most likely not be a primary issue among the engineers and computer scientists working on technical aspects, which is why this paper argue that the social sciences can stand to add value and enrich research through cross-disciplinary co-operation (Wittrock 2010). Because of the social sciences ongoing involvement in IoT-research, a cross-disciplinary co-operation should not pose any major difficulties and allow for either field to learn from one another and in turn produce higher quality research.

Addressing the concerns surrounding ethical and human-centric aspects can further examine issues and opportunities raised within the five identified themes, for example the engagement of small businesses (Kusiak 2018), identifying incentives for participation (Salim and Haque 2015) or formulating customer relationships (Dijkman et al. 2015). Shifting research, and exploring IoT from a human-centric perspective can contribute towards research, and help facilitate participation, and education towards research and practice, and – if indicative of research from other areas – help with acceptance amongst the users (Gallivan et al. 2005; Botta-Genoulaz and Millet 2006).

5   Conclusions and Suggestions for Future Research

This scoping study has aimed at identifying topics of discussions surrounding IoT in social science journals.

The research question asked was: *"What areas are being addressed within the social science subject-field of IoT-literature in research journals - and where can further social science research stand to contribute?"*

This study have identified 25 commonly occurring keywords, in regards to IoT literature within the social sciences, and divided them into 5 clusters. Keyword clusters were used to formulate five key IoT-themes; *Organization, Logistics, Infrastructure, Technology* and *Protection*. Based on the keyword analysis a sixth theme of *Ethics* was suggested in order to increase focus on human-centric aspects around IoT research.

This study have presented 24 articles from 20 different journals and given an overview in order to guide and inform where the discussions are happening in terms of IoT within the social sciences. In doing this, the study is providing a contribution in terms of thematizing common keyword-clusters allowing for to the identification of key concepts connected to each keyword as well as highlighting where further research can stand to gain. In doing so this study allows for both practitioners and researchers to get an overview of IoT-themes that are prevalent in literature related to the social science subject field and the scopes within them - assisting with future research.

This study also makes the argument that additional value can be created through increased research towards the human-centric side of IoT, and that the subject-field of social science can contribute by offering a deeper discussion into both ethics and policy making surrounding IoT. In doing this, the social sciences has the potential to influence the public, inform law- and policy makers, and ensure that the privacy and integrity of individuals are not being breached as we move towards an even more connected future.

Suggestions for future research is to further deepen the analysis through a structured literature review into either some or all of the themes – in order to test the validity of this scoping study and the themes within it. Further, wile this study is focusing on research journals, it should be compared towards a similar analysis of conference proceedings; in order to contrast them against each other and examine whether they differ from one another, and if so, in what aspect.

References

Anthopoulos, L., Janssen, M., Weerakkody, V.: A Unified Smart City Model (USCM) for smart city conceptualization and benchmarking. In: Smart Cities and Smart Spaces: Concepts, Methodologies, Tools, and Applications, pp. 247–264. IGI Global (2019)

Arksey, H., O'Malley, L.: Scoping studies: towards a methodological framework. Int. J. Soc. Res. Methodol. **8**(1), 19–32 (2005)

Botta-Genoulaz, V., Millet, P.A.: An investigation into the use of ERP systems in the service sector. Int. J. Prod. Econ. **99**(1–2), 202–221 (2006)

Centre for Science and Technology Studies, Leiden University: "VOSviewer - Visualizing scientific landscapes". VOSviewer (2018). http://www.vosviewer.com/. Accessed 10 June 2019

Dijkman, R.M., Sprenkels, B., Peeters, T., Janssen, A.: Business models for the Internet of Things. Int. J. Inf. Manag. **35**(6), 672–678 (2015)

Elsevier: The largest database of peer-reviewed literature – Scopus—Elsevier Solutions (2019). https://www.elsevier.com/solutions/scopus. Accessed 20 June 2019

Ericsson: Cellular Networks for Massive IoT, Enabling Low Power Wide Area Applications. Ericsson White Paper (Uen 284 23-3278), January 2016. https://www.ericsson.com/assets/local/publications/white-papers/wp_iot.pdf. Accessed 25 June 2019

Gallivan, M.J., Spitler, V.K., Koufaris, M.: Does information technology training really matter? A social information processing analysis of coworkers' influence on IT usage in the workplace. J. Manag. Inf. Syst. **22**(1), 153–192 (2005)

Gretzel, U., Sigala, M., Xiang, Z., Koo, C.: Smart tourism: foundations and developments. Electron. Mark. **25**(3), 179–188 (2015)

Grewal, D., Roggeveen, A.L., Nordfält, J.: The future of retailing. J. Retail. **93**(1), 1–6 (2017)

Harris, I., Wang, Y., Wang, H.: ICT in multimodal transport and technological trends: unleashing potential for the future. Int. J. Prod. Econ. **159**, 88–103 (2015)

Hashem, I.A.T., et al.: The role of big data in smart city. Int. J. Inf. Manag. **36**(5), 748–758 (2016)

Dutton, W.H.: Putting things to work: social and policy challenges for the Internet of Things. Info **16**(3), 1–21 (2014)

Jin, X., Wah, B.W., Cheng, X., Wang, Y.: Significance and challenges of big data research. Big Data Res. **2**(2), 59–64 (2015)

Kang, H.S., et al.: Smart manufacturing: past research, present findings, and future directions. Int. J. Precis. Eng. Manuf.-Green Technol. **3**(1), 111–128 (2016). https://doi.org/10.1007/s40684-016-0015-5

Kiel, D., Müller, J.M., Arnold, C., Voigt, K.I.: Sustainable industrial value creation: benefits and challenges of Industry 4.0. Int. J. Innov. Manag. **21**(08), 1740015 (2017)

Kusiak, A.: Smart manufacturing. Int. J. Prod. Res. **56**(1–2), 508–517 (2018)

Li, S., Tryfonas, T., Li, H.: The Internet of Things: a security point of view. Internet Res. **26**(2), 337–359 (2016). https://doi.org/10.1108/IntR-07-2014-0173

Lee, I., Lee, K.: The Internet of Things (IoT): applications, investments, and challenges for enterprises. Bus. Horiz. **58**(4), 431–440 (2015)

Lilis, G., Conus, G., Asadi, N., Kayal, M.: Towards the next generation of intelligent building: an assessment study of current automation and future IoT based systems with a proposal for transitional design. Sustain. Cities Soc. **28**, 473–481 (2017)

Neisse, R., Steri, G., Fovino, I.N., Baldini, G.: SecKit: a model-based security toolkit for the Internet of Things. Comput. Secur. **54**, 60–76 (2015)

Ng, I.C., Wakenshaw, S.Y.: The Internet-of-Things: review and research directions. Int. J. Res. Mark. **34**(1), 3–21 (2017)

Peppet, S.R.: Regulating the Internet of Things: first steps toward managing discrimination, privacy, security and consent. Tex. L. Rev. **93**, 85 (2014)

Porter, M.E., Heppelmann, J.E.: How smart, connected products are transforming competition. Harv. Bus. Rev. **92**(11), 64–88 (2014)

Reaidy, P.J., Gunasekaran, A., Spalanzani, A.: Bottom-up approach based on Internet of Things for order fulfillment in a collaborative warehousing environment. Int. J. Prod. Econ. **159**, 29–40 (2015)

Roblek, V., Meško, M., Krapež, A.: A complex view of Industry 4.0. Sage Open **6**(2), 2158244016653987 (2016)

Salim, F., Haque, U.: Urban computing in the wild: a survey on large scale participation and citizen engagement with ubiquitous computing, cyber physical systems, and Internet of Things. Int. J. Hum.-Comput. Stud. **81**, 31–48 (2015)

Senn, J.: The challenge of relating IS research to practice. Inf. Resour. Manag. J. (IRMJ) **11**(1), 23–28 (1998)

Shin, D.H.: Conceptualizing and measuring quality of experience of the Internet of Things: exploring how quality is perceived by users. Inf. Manag. **54**(8), 998–1011 (2017)

Internet of Things Statista: Number of connected devices worldwide 2012–2025 (2019). https://www.statista.com/statistics/471264/iot-number-of-connected-devices-worldwide/. Accessed 30 June 2019

Tarschys, D., Lachapelle, G.: 2010 Social scientists in the corridors of power. In: ISSC, IDS and UNESCO, World Social Science Report 2010, Knowledge Divides, chap. 8. UNESCO Publishing, Paris (2010)

Trappe, W., Howard, R., Moore, R.S.: Low-energy security: Limits and opportunities in the Internet of Things. IEEE Secur. Priv. **13**(1), 14–21 (2015)

Weinberg, B.D., Milne, G.R., Andonova, Y.G., Hajjat, F.M.: Internet of Things: convenience vs. privacy and secrecy. Bus. Horiz. **58**(6), 615–624 (2015)

Wittrock, B.: Shifting involvements: rethinking the social, the human and the natural. In: ISSC, IDS and UNESCO, World Social Science Report 2010, Knowledge Divides, chap. 6. UNESCO Publishing, Paris (2010)

Xu, L.D., Xu, E.L., Li, L.: Industry 4.0: state of the art and future trends. Int. J. Prod. Res. **56**(8), 294 (2018)

Evaluating Edge Processing Requirements in Next Generation IoT Network Architectures

Brooks Olney[✉], Shakil Mahmud[✉], and Robert Karam[✉]

University of South Florida, Tampa, FL 33620, USA
{brooksolney,shakilmahmud}@mail.usf.edu, rkaram@usf.edu

Abstract. The Internet of Things (IoT) is a massively growing field with billions of devices in the field serving a multitude of purposes. Traditionally, IoT architectures consist of "edge" sensor nodes which are used purely for data collection, actuators for intermediary connectivity, gateways for transmitting data, and cloud servers for processing. However, as application requirements change, IoT architectures must evolve. In the next generation of IoT, traditional architectures may not hold due to power limitations, privacy concerns, or network reliability in certain environments. In particular, Artificial Intelligence (AI) and Machine Learning (ML) applications – especially image/video processing – have become increasingly widespread, and are famously data and compute intensive applications. In this paper, we give an overview and describe the shortcomings of traditional IoT architectures, and outline key scenarios where local processing may be preferred over transferring data to the cloud. We then describe and evaluate metrics which designers can use to assess the needs of their IoT platform. This framework will be beneficial to IoT device manufacturers and network architects for improving usability and reliability, while protecting privacy in the next generation of IoT.

Keywords: Internet of Things (IoT) · Artificial Intelligence · Machine Learning · Image processing · Low power

1 Introduction

The Internet of Things (IoT) has become a pillar of the integrated circuit (IC) market in recent years, with an estimated 212 billion devices predicted to be deployed globally by the end of 2020 [11]. Today, more devices are connected to the internet than ever before. Traditional IoT architectures consist of sensor nodes which are used for data collection, and/or provide some basic means of remote control [33]. For example, smart home components such as smart thermostats, smart fridges, and smart TVs allow consumers to control them using

© IFIP International Federation for Information Processing 2020
Published by Springer Nature Switzerland AG 2020
A. Casaca et al. (Eds.): IFIPIoT 2019, IFIP AICT 574, pp. 252–269, 2020.
https://doi.org/10.1007/978-3-030-43605-6_15

apps on their mobile devices, or perform self regulation based on a list of settings configured by the user. One reason that the market for IoT devices has experienced tremendous growth is because of the ability to provide convenience to consumers in their own home. Another application space seeing a surge in IoT usage is in health care, where devices may provide monitoring services to patients in hospitals, as well as assisted living services at home [4]. In this architecture, devices typically send data through gateways to the cloud for processing. However, as the nature of these workloads changes, e.g. becoming increasingly data intensive, the cost of data transfer may eventually exceed that of processing the data locally. Power constraints, concerns for data privacy in cloud services, or network reliability issues may ultimately lead to more reliance on *edge computing*, where edge nodes are responsible not only for data collection, but some data preprocessing as well. For example, many individuals use their smart phones to capture pictures and video which they then share to social media platforms. In this case, the image or video is rather large due to the improvement of camera quality in smart phones, incurring large overhead in network bandwidth requirements. Such devices typically have the ability to adjust and compress the image or video data before transferring to the cloud, reducing bandwidth overhead at the cost of requiring additional local processing power. However, this is just one example of a need for sophisticated edge computing. Other examples include self-driving automobiles, which may generate almost one Gigabyte of data every second [22]. In the case for self-driving automobiles, suitable compute platforms are implemented within the vehicles as cloud processing cannot be relied on due to latency. Local processing in real-time is required because the on-board computer must make decisions as quickly as possible to avoid collision with other vehicles or pedestrians. So, Artificial Intelligence (AI) and Machine Learning (ML) applications like visual processing in autonomous vehicles make up a large percentage of current compute and data requirements in the cloud.

There are many different sub-fields within AI and ML, with one of the most popular being deep learning or Deep Neural Networks (DNNs) and Convolutional Neural Networks (CNNs) [15, 23]. The concept of deep learning involves the use of a backpropagation algorithm that fine tunes the machine's model based on the error between the values computed by the model and the true target value in the training dataset. With repeated backpropagation during training, the model is able to update the weights in each layer to be more accurate to predict or classify items in real-time. Because of this, DNNs have had tremendous breakthroughs in processing and classifying images, video, speech and audio [3, 34]. Recurrent Neural Networks (RNNs) have also gained popularity in problem spaces with sequential data inputs [7]. In general, the fields of AI and ML have hinted at promising, robust solutions for diverse problem spaces; however, they are also famously demanding on compute and memory resources, both in training of the model and in prediction and classification during feedforward operation [21].

General purpose processors (GPPs) such as central processing units (CPUs) are not preferred for processing of ML workloads as they are more optimized for solving sequential problems, whereas neural networks are highly parallel in nature. The fundamental building block in such networks is the multiply-and-accumulate operation (MAC). Each MAC consists of three memory reads - to read the filter weight, filter map activation, and partial sum. Because of this, memory access becomes the largest bottleneck for processing these networks. For example, feedforward in the AlexNet architecture consists of 724 million MACs, which requires nearly 3 billion DRAM accesses [29]. Thus, cloud processing of these workloads typically leverages the parallel architecture and abundance of on-chip dynamic random-access memory (DRAM) in graphics processing units (GPUs). However, GPUs are very power hungry, and often consume extra power through static power requirements of the given GPU. Because of this, GPUs are only seen in edge devices like self-driving automobiles. An example of this is Nvidia's DRIVE PX Pegasus program which is capable of level 5 (i.e. no human intervention required at all) autonomous driving [18]. For autonomous vehicles, the extra power overhead *may* be acceptable considering the design requirements. However, the same may not be said for edge devices which are required to operate with low power, and/or in environments with minimal internet connectivity. In recent years, Field Programmable Gate Arrays (FPGAs) have been explored as an alternative to conventional ML workload accelerators due their power efficiency, which is measured as the number of Giga-operations per second per Watt, GOP/s/W [14, 25]. The in-field reconfigurability of FPGAs makes them an attractive option for designers implementing deep learning models, as the models themselves have variance in terms of layers, filter size, optimizers, activation functions, etc. Because FPGAs have the advantage in terms of maximizing performance per Watt of power consumption, and can be configured for customized acceleration of ML workloads, they may be especially suited to assess the needs of edge computing in IoT.

Because IoT devices generate data in such large quantities, and deep learning is highly efficient in analyzing complex data, deep learning is becoming an attractive technology for IoT applications [16]. However, ML workloads (including deep learning) are very compute and data intensive tasks. Thus, the typical architecture where data processing is offloaded to the cloud may not be amenable to ML applications. There are several reasons why a designer may wish to perform such computation at the edge. One such reason is that there may be limited or unreliable network connectivity. Many IoT applications require redundancy and minimal latency. So, offloading tasks to the cloud may not be able to meet those design requirements. Besides the fact that transmitting images in real-time may not be efficient in terms of power and bandwidth, transmitting images over the network for cloud processing presents some security and privacy risks as well. Additionally, privacy may be a critical design requirement for the device, and *no* data should be shared with the cloud. Finally, the power consumed to transmit the images to the cloud may exceed the processing power to perform analysis locally. In environments where there is limited or unreliable network connectivity - and potentially in an untrusted environment - local processing may be a *requirement*. In cases where the power consumption of data transmission exceeds local processing power, it may be beneficial to trade off local processing with cloud processing. For example, high level or partial processing of images to determine "important" events may be done prior to transmission in order to minimize power consumption. To the best of our knowledge, there is no comprehensive framework for designers to determine whether local or cloud processing (or some combination of the two) is more appropriate for the application they are targeting.

The main contributions of this paper are as follows:

1. We summarize the current state of the art for IoT architectures and common use cases, as well as relevant image preprocessing in edge computing workloads
2. We describe a framework for balancing design requirements with capabilities of edge nodes for compute and data intensive applications using different optimization metrics
3. We evaluate the framework in real-world situations using current standards for IoT processing and transmission hardware in typical network environments

In summary, this paper establishes a comprehensive framework for IoT device and network design as application requirements evolve towards more data and compute intensive workloads, in the context of ever-increasing privacy concerns.

The rest of the paper is structured as follows: Sect. 2 discusses common IoT architectures present today, and describes some image processing techniques that may be employed by edge nodes. Section 3 presents our framework for determining when it may be more appropriate for designers to opt for local processing over cloud processing, and provides metrics for each individual case. Example case studies are provided to illustrate how the framework can be used to support using a particular edge compute fabric over alternatives. Finally, we conclude in Sect. 5.

2 Background

In this section, we provide a background on common trends in IoT architectures and give context for shifting processing power to the edge. We also elaborate on various image processing techniques used to minimize processing or network transmission overhead with AI and ML applications.

2.1 IoT Architectures

Generic Architecture: There is currently no general agreement on a "standard" IoT architecture. In recent years, researches have proposed various types of architectures. Conventional IoT architecture usually consists of the 3 layers: Perception Layer, Network Layer, and Application Layer. Besides these, the Middleware layer and Business layer were introduced in [13]. Figure 1 shows all of the five layers which are briefly described below:

Perception layer refers to the "layer of sensing", consisting of sensors which are used to identify relevant subjects and gather pertinent information, and actuators, which respond to electrical inputs and perform some physical action. This physical layer may contain various types of sensors and/or actuators which are chosen based on the application's requirement. The data collected in this layer could be information about the environment, physical objects, or programmable parameters. A few of the technologies in this layers include Radio Frequency Identification (RFID) tags, wearable sensing devices, barcodes, and smart sensors.

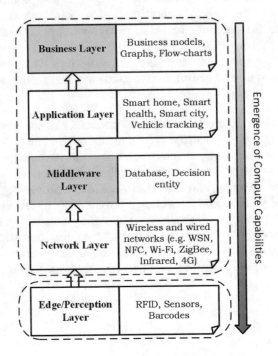

Fig. 1. The five-layered IoT architecture showing the different technologies or applications belonging to each layer, as well as move towards the edge for integrated compute capabilities.

Network layer connects the Perception layer and the Application layer. It also connects network devices, smart devices, and any service in the network. This layer is responsible for transmitting information gathered by the sensors from the perception layer to the internet, using, for example, Wireless sensor networks (WSN), Near Field Communication (NFC), and Bluetooth.

Middleware layer is also known as a processing layer which receives the information sent from the Network layer. In this layer, the received data gets processed, analyzed, and stored in the database. Based on the information processing and computational results, this layer can make decisions automatically.

Additionally, it manages various type of services and has a connection to the database [13].

Application layer receives the processed information from the Middleware layer and based on the user demand, it manages service delivery globally. Smart home, smart city, smart health, vehicle tracking and smart farming are some applications which are implemented by IoT defined in this layer [13].

Business layer gets the data from the application layer and based on the information it generates charts, diagrams, business models, and profit models. This layer serves as a controller managing the application-specific services of the entire IoT system and is also responsible for the end user's privacy.

Cloud Computing, Edge Computing and Gateway Architecture According to National Institute of Standards and Technology (NIST), "Cloud computing is a model for enabling ubiquitous, convenient, on-demand network access to a shared pool of configurable computing resources (e.g., networks, servers, storage, applications, and services) that can be rapidly provisioned and released with minimal management effort or service provider interaction" [17]. Resources in distributed environments are well managed by cloud computing, realizing greater performance. Instead of having a large storage and computing devices, cloud computing offers global access to the data. Highly manageable, schedulable and scalable virtual servers, networks, computational power, and storage are provided by the cloud computing [1]. A few essential characteristics of cloud computing are extensive, multiple service providers, dynamic resource sharing, high reliability, network access from all over the place, flexibility in service management, adaptability, and cost-effective [35, 36].

Based on the type of the provided service, there can be three principal models of cloud computing which are briefly described below:

1. **Infrastructure as a Service (IaaS):**
   IaaS provider provides infrastructural resources such as Virtual Machines (VMs), data center space, network equipment or servers as a service on-demand. With IaaS clients are benefited with great flexibility of managing their resources.
2. **Software as a Service (SaaS):**
   User applications are commonly mentioned as Software as a Service. In SaaS, a finished product is provided to the end-users which are managed by the service provider. Human resource management system and enterprise resource planning generally use SaaS [36].
3. **Platform as a Service (PaaS):**
   PaaS is another type of SaaS, where service is provided as a platform to develop and manage applications. PaaS provides a relaxed environment to the developers by not to think about software maintenance, patching, resource management, or any additional factors. The developers only need to concentrate on developing their programs and provide that to the end-users.

In recent years, vast amounts of data have been produced at the edge of the network, initiating another type of system architecture, *edge computing*. The basic idea behind edge computing is when the data is produced by the devices, it is processed closer to its origin rather than being offloaded to the cloud. Edge computing has been evolving and growing rapidly to lower latency and to improve the efficiency when data is processed locally. As the cloud possesses significant computing power compared to the edge devices, this has been effective for compute, but not data-intensive, workloads. However, with a rapid increase of data at the edge devices introduce the delay of data transportation to the cloud as the *bandwidth bottlenecks* [26]. Autonomous vehicles exemplify this local computing requirement.

IoT Gateway is the point of connection between multiple smart devices and the cloud. It serves as the entry or exit point of the data to or from the cloud. A smart home is a good example of IoT gateway functionality. Inside the home, it creates a local network of all the smart devices connected which can communicate internally. Generally, a gateway will support one or more wireless communication standards in addition to WiFi, enabling it to transfer data to and from edge devices from different manufacturers.

In general, all smart devices are connected to the internet and synchronize with each other by exchanging information seamlessly. However, there may arise a state when - for a very short time - there is no requirement of data transportation to the cloud as that data is not required at the given moment. In certain situations, either the IoT Gateway needs to be intelligent enough to interpret the environment and stop sending the data to the cloud. Or, the smart devices must stop producing data to have efficient usage of the network resources. Such a scenario introduces the "Smart Gateway" which performs some additional data processing and decides when and what type of data must be uploaded to the cloud [1, 2]. In the context of AI/ML, certain preprocessing techniques performed locally to compress or filter the data and minimize transmission overhead may serve similar purposes to a Smart Gateway.

2.2   Image Processing

In AI and ML applications, image processing techniques are used prior to inference or training of a neural network. Some goals of such techniques are to preprocess the images in order to prepare them for analysis through a DNN or other network, compress them for storage or network transmission, and filtering out certain images which do not contain pertinent information. Multiple techniques in image processing are typically used together to achieve these goals. In particular, they are necessary for optimizing ML workloads on IoT edge devices which operate under power and connectivity constraints.

Preprocessing consists of operations that are performed on images at the lowest level of abstraction - that is, input data to preprocessing algorithms is the original, unfiltered image. The main goals of preprocessing techniques differ between the application. For images which are to be fed through a DNN, the main goals are to improve the quality of the image data, remove distortions that may skew the model, and enhance latent features which are important for further processing by a DNN. preprocessing of images when training a model have similar goals in mind, but may also apply certain transformations to each image.

With image compression - especially prior to inference in a DNN - it is important to compress the images in such a way that minimizes the loss in quality and feature distinction, while maximizing the amount of storage space saved. Compressing the image too much can cause the model to miss features and misclassify certain events because of it. Thus, image and video compression algorithms have been an important contribution in image processing research [6,8,37]. Some widely used image/video compression algorithms are:

1. **JPEG** (Joint Photographic Experts Group) [30] is used for single-frame image compression, and is the most widely known and used standards for such tasks. It is typically performed with up to a 16:1 compression ratio without a visible degradation in quality or detail.
2. **PNG** (Portable Network Graphics) is a lossless, portable compression algorithm that was designed to work very well for web-applications.
3. **H.264/MPEG-4** (Motion Picture Experts Group) is used for video compression for very low bitrates with aims for applications that target "conversational" and "non-conversational" applications [32]. Basically an approach that can be applied to streaming/broadcast and storage applications.

Filtering in the context of edge computing devices can be viewed as the process of filtering out images based on their content. For example, consider an edge sensor serving as a security camera which uses facial detection processed in the cloud to identify subjects of the camera feed. The device should not continually stream the video footage to the cloud for processing, as this is a clear waste of power to transmit over the network. Thus, the device should filter out images using some method of motion detection to tell whenever a person has entered the field-of-view (FOV) of the lens. This way, the device will only transmit when absolutely necessary, and minimize the power consumed to transmit, as well as the impact on bandwidth and the cloud.

Visual surveillance (including motion detection) has been a highly influential research topic in computer vision. Intelligent surveillance systems are much more practical than traditional passive surveillance which requires a human operator to constantly view security tapes [31]. Motion detection is incredibly important for edge devices which capture video feeds. Relating back to the security camera; in addition to filtering out images (video feed) that do not contain a person of interest, filtering can further minimize the amount of data transmission required by determining the frames with the *highest quality* capture of the subject of interest. For instance, assume that a suspect remains within the FOV of a security camera for 2 min. But, for most of the time the suspect has their back turned, and only reveals their face for a few seconds of that time. An advanced filtering technique could analyze this segment of data for facial features, and isolate the frames at which the subject is the most identifiable, and then transmit those frames to the cloud for processing. Assuming a camera which captures at 1080 p (1920 × 1080 pixel array) with 30 frames per second (FPS), and 8-bit color depth, the total size of the 2 min segment would be

$1920 \times 1080 \times 8 \times 30 \times 120 = 179,159,040,000$ bits. If we consider the codec for compression being H.264, and a bitrate for video quality of 8 Mbit/sec, then the size of the video would be around 120 MB. However, most of the data in the video is unsuitable for facial detection. In this case, the only suitable frames may be within a few seconds of the entire footage. This means that the amount of data required to transmit could be reduced by up to 94% (considering 1 s of usable data). Thus, filtering can be a powerful tool to minimize overhead in edge devices, but requires significant computing resources to achieve such a reduction in data complexity.

Analysis of images is done using some form of DNN or CNN, depending on the application. The process of inputting an image into a neural network is referred to as an *inference* or feedforward operation. This may be done either locally, or in the cloud. Analysis will be done after preprocessing and filtering, or in real-time when filtering is not used. preprocessing is important to ensure that the images have the correct structure for the input layer to the network, and filtering is important to minimize the dynamic power consumption when running inference on a neural network locally, or for transmitting to the cloud for processing. In some cases, it may be beneficial to do local inference to conserve power and limit network bandwidth overhead. We quantify this in more detail in the next section.

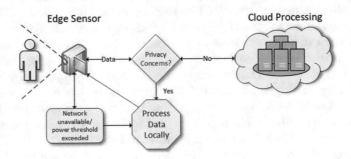

Fig. 2. Flow diagram of proposed framework. The device can do some basic checks to determine if latency and power thresholds are met, and if there are security/privacy concerns before choosing between local or cloud processing.

In general, the image processing techniques we have described are very useful for edge devices. Whether certain methods like compression and filtering are done locally before transmitting to the cloud, or as part of the local processing paradigm, they can alleviate the overhead of storage and transfer from large amounts of data generation. Such techniques are important design considerations and can be integrated within our proposed framework for trading off between local and cloud processing.

3   Edge Node Design and Analysis Framework

In this section, we describe the design and analysis framework for edge nodes handling data and compute intensive tasks. We outline three specific scenarios where more robust edge computing capabilities will be beneficial, providing an in-depth description for each particular case where designers may opt for local processing, or some combination of local and cloud processing for their IoT platform. Finally, we offer sample case studies which quantify the requirements in each scenario using state-of-the-art wireless network hardware for data transfer to the cloud, as well as efficient FPGA implementations of common neural network models from literature. Figure 2 provides a basic flow diagram of the proposed framework.

3.1   Limited Network Connectivity

In Sect. 2, we have described the generic architecture of IoT consisting of 5 layers. Of the 5-layers, the perception/edge layer is the lowest physical layer and consists of different types of sensors, which are the key elements of that layer. To quantify when designers may opt for edge computing over cloud computing in limited or poor network connectivity, we first need to understand the flow from the sensor to the actuator. Sensors sense the data, gather information, and transmit to the gateway. The gateway then sends the data to the cloud and receives a response after the data has been processed. After that, the actuator functions according to the response received from the cloud. Efficiency of this entire process depends on bandwidth, latency, and throughput.

Bandwidth is defined as the maximum amount of data that can be sent through a wired or wireless transmission link from one node to another in a given amount of time. It is the data transfer rate across a network and expressed in bits per second (bps). *Latency* is the time required for a data packet transmitting from its source node to the destination node. One of the common ways of measuring latency is calculating the *Round Trip Time (RTT)*, which is the duration a single packet requires to travel from the source node, reach the destination node and back to the source node. Latency is an accumulation of all the delays involved in the transmission. Specifically, the type of transmission medium, and the time required for propagation, routing, switching, or storage are several factors which affect network latency. We will use the term latency and round-trip-time interchangeably. Another important term in measuring network performance is *throughput*, which is the maximum amount of data that successfully travels through the transmission link, and is expressed in bits per second (bps). The maximum throughput of a system can be calculated by Eq. 1. The Transmission Control Protocol (TCP) is a connection-oriented protocol where both the sender and the receiver keep track of the transmitted data so that any non-received data can be re-transmitted to maintain stable data transportation. TCP window size, expressed in bytes, is the maximum possible data sent before receiving an acknowledgment (ACK) message which can be computed by Eq. 2. When the network is unstable, it is better to maintain a small TCP window to refrain from re-transmitting the data, but with a reliable network, the TCP window size can be considerably large. Another feature of TCP is the sliding window protocol, where the devices can dynamically scale the TCP window based on the available connectivity.

$$\text{Max. Throughput} = \frac{\text{TCP Window Size}}{\text{RTT}} \tag{1}$$

$$\text{TCP Window Size} = \text{Bandwidth (BW)} \times \text{RTT} \tag{2}$$

$$\text{RTT or Latency} = \frac{\text{TCP Window Size}}{\text{Bandwidth (BW)}} \tag{3}$$

Edge nodes with compute capability have the opportunity to maintain system functionality even if the network connection is lost. If the network is good, processing can be done in the cloud as before, and the additional compute resources may be turned off to minimize static power dissipation [12]. We propose a dynamic model where the edge nodes automatically decide between performing local computation or cloud-based computation depending on the latency and available bandwidth. We are considering the TCP window size as constant, because dynamic scaling of TCP window is an expensive operation which will not be cost effective for edge devices. We suggest the designers should take into account the packet loss during transmission when determining the TCP window size. The edge nodes can calculate the total RTT or latency using Eq. 3. After that, it compares the calculated latency with the acceptable latency that has been defined earlier by the system designer and makes the decision of either local processing or cloud-based processing.

For example, consider an edge node with an available bandwidth of 100 Mbps, a constant TCP window size of 64 KB, and the acceptable round-trip-time or latency is 50 ms. Using Eq. 3, the edge node calculates the latency as, (64000×8) bits/100000000 bps = 5.12 ms. Comparing the calculated latency with the acceptable latency, the edge node decides to process the data at the cloud as the computed latency is less than the acceptable latency.

Now, we consider the same edge node operating at limited network connectivity. For example, with a bandwidth of 1 Mbps, but with the same TCP window size of 64 KB and acceptable latency of 50 ms. Similar to the earlier calculation, the edge node computes the latency as 512 ms which is much higher than the acceptable latency of 50 ms. Under certain circumstances, processing the data at the cloud is not feasible as it will incur a very high delay. Our approach may suggest that the edge node should process the data locally rather than in the cloud.

3.2   Privacy and Security Concerns

Privacy and security are significant concerns in cloud computing. Designers and end users alike should be wary about the many privacy and security risks associated with IoT devices, such as having credentials compromised, breaches of private data, violation of data sharing agreements, phishing, and other trust issues. A numerical value quantifying the risk associated with sharing different data to the cloud could enable a data gathering edge node to opt for local processing. Specifics of such a metric would necessarily be determined at design time, considering the environment, data, use cases, and other variables. Here, we describe some of the privacy and security concerns relating to edge-gathered data, which may motivate designers to integrate additional compute capabilities into edge nodes.

General Security Threats: Cloud computing suffers from a number of security threats. Multiple scenarios are briefly described below:

- *Botnets and other malware* represent one of the major threats against the security and reliability of cloud computing. It contains many connected devices, storage, and memory. Botnet can be used to execute a distributed denial-of-service (DDoS) attack and steal the organization's data. The attackers execute the attack by controlling a huge number of automated bots which are malware operated [28].
- *Multitenancy in Cloud Servers* When the same physical machine shares resources like a virtual machine (VM), data, or hard disk drive, this may enable unanticipated side-channels between different running processes, especially if there is no separation between data and processes on a virtual level [9]. This may result in data leakage between different applications.

Integrity and Confidentiality of Personal and Private Information: Integrity means the assets can only be modified after an approved agreement from the owner, while confidentiality refers to ensuring private information is only accessible to the appropriate and trusted parties. Examples of Personal Identifiable Information (PII) include name, address or location data, biometric data, and images, among others [19]. Moreover, information related to religion, health, race, sexual orientation, or finance are considered highly sensitive. Preventing unauthorized access and tampering of private and sensitive data is one of the largest challenges for cloud service providers, and one of the greatest concerns for enterprise customers and consumers alike. Providing an option for local data processing obviates the need for trusting third parties with sensitive data.

Military and Government Applications: Military applications may generate a large amount of sensitive data, from creating a cohesive fighting force, to locating an enemy, or observing a soldier's current state, especially from health sensor networks. These data must be secured from any sort of leakage as the contents are highly confidential. Edge computing is preferred for the Internet of Military/Battlefield Things (IoMT and IoBT) because of the sensitive nature of the data produced by IoMT and IoBT devices [5]. More generally, government regulations in non-military contexts still have strict regulations regarding the storage and sharing of certain data. For example, types of PII, how long those data can be saved, or to whom those data an be shared. Either due to dishonest cloud providers or vulnerabilities in the cloud, it can result in transferring the data to an outside country, which is completely against the privacy law. Hence, military and government contexts for IoT applications would greatly benefit from additional edge processing capabilities.

Whether due to an end-user feeling uncomfortable sharing edge-gathered data with cloud services, or strict rules exist regulating the types of data that can be shared, the option to process at the edge rather than in the cloud for the sake of privacy and security is becoming increasingly important. If the edge nodes do not possess the capability of processing data locally, then the end-users have no choice, and little control on how data are used in the cloud.

3.3   Transmission Power Exceeds Local Processing Power

Given the application of the edge device, it may be possible that the power consumed to transmit data to the cloud for processing exceeds that of local processing on the device itself. In this case, a designer may decide to implement some protocol to trade off processing between local and cloud platforms, or do all processing locally. We propose a dynamic model which can be used by the device to assess it's own requirements and circumstances in real-time, and autonomously make the decision to transmit to the cloud, or process its data locally. To quantify the metrics to decide based on the power consumption, we must consider state-of-the-art WiFi components, as well as an example neural network implementation in FPGA to compare the overhead of local processing to offloading to the cloud. There are three factors that play into assessing the power requirements of cloud processing; namely, the size of the payload, the maximum transmission bitrate, and the power consumed by the transmission circuitry during operation.

To determine payload size, there are three main considerations; the size of the image, the number of frames required to transmit for the target application, and the compression and filtering algorithms used. The size of the image will vary based on the quality of the camera in the device, as well as the compression ratio. The number of frames is dependent on the application, and if any form of filtering is done prior to transmission. In our example with the security camera; with proper filtering techniques, the number of frames is dependent on the duration which the subject's face is distinguishable in the FOV. On the other hand, the application could only require a single frame, or a constant feed. So, we denote the size of the image S as $width \times height \times bit\text{-}depth = S$, the number of required frames as F, the energy consumed by compressing the video as C, and energy from filtering as M. For network transmission in edge devices, the relevant attributes of the transmission circuitry are the power consumed during operation P, and the maximum throughput T. The total power consumption of each is then calculated by multiplying S and F together to get the total amount of data to transmit, then dividing by the throughput of the wireless standard, and finally multiplying by the rated power consumption of the same standard. However, this does not complete the picture. As we mentioned, security and privacy are also concerns. So, we have to consider that the data is encrypted before transmission. For data encryption, we denote E as the power consumed by encrypting a byte of data. The total energy expended to transmit a payload of size $S \times F$ is computed by adding the power consumed by encrypting the data, and the power consumed by transmitting. This is represented by Eq. 4 in terms of Joules (J).

$$P_{transmit} = (C \times F) + (M \times F) + (E \times S \times F) + \frac{S \times F \times P}{T} \qquad (4)$$

The power consumed to transmit to the cloud is shown to be directly proportional to the image size and the amount of frames to transmit (total payload size), as the power and throughput of the transmitting circuitry will remain static. These values will changed based on the native quality of the camera used, whether or not there is any preprocessing or compression prior to transmission, any filtering using motion detection, etc. We compare these values to an example state-of-the-art implementation on FPGA. For this purpose, we refer to the work in [10], a low-power CNN accelerator implemented on a Zynq XC7Z045 platform. The authors experimented with CNN-based optimization methods to improve the performance and power efficiency of the VGG16 network [27] in comparison to other FPGA implementations on the same platform. They reported two separate configurations; one with 16-bit fixed precision, and one with 8-bit. We base our estimations on the 8-bit precision implementation. For this implementation, they reported the performance at 84.3 GOP/s, and power consumption at 3.5 W - yielding an energy efficiency of 24.1 GOP/s/W. Additionally, their implementation of VGG16 requires 30.76 GOP per image. Using these values, we can estimate the average power consumption during operation per image as $(30.76/84.3) \times 3.5 = 1.28$ J/img. For image compression, we consider two different types, 4L H.264 and 4L HEVC, with energy consumption values of 461 and 606 mJ/frame, and average compression ratio of 10.49:1 and 12.5:1, respectively [16]. For image filtering, we consider the power consumed by a Texas Instruments TIDA-01398 PIR motion sensor as 1.57 mW. We also consider two of the most widely used wireless standards in IoT. Namely, Bluetooth Low Energy (BLE) and ZigBee. Each are typically used in some combination as they operate fairly complimentary to each other. Each is around the same transmission speed with 270 kbps in BLE and 250 kbps in Zigbee. BLE is effective at shorter ranges with 10 mW transmit power, whereas Zigbee is effective at a much greater distance but with a higher transmit power of 100 mW [20]. For E, we use the value of power consumption in AES at around 4.2 µJ/byte as measured by [24]. Figure 3 shows graphs of the energy consumed to transmit or process a certain number frames (segment of a video). Estimations are made for native resolution at 1080 p (a)(c), and 720 p (b)(d). For comparison, (a–b) use 4L H.264 compression with 8-bit color depth, and (c–d) use 4L HEVC with 12-bit color depth.

For the higher quality resolutions with 1080 p (Fig. 3(a, c)), the larger file size contributes to a larger power consumption to transmit to the cloud. So, in these situations it may be more energy efficient to do processing locally. With lower resolutions (Fig. 3(b, d)), the energy to transmit is lower, so offloading to the cloud may be the best option. While 4L HEVC has a very large compression ratio of 12.5:1, it is much more computationally complex than other compression standards, contributing to a much higher energy consumption. An important characteristic to note is the power consumed by using advanced filtering techniques. In

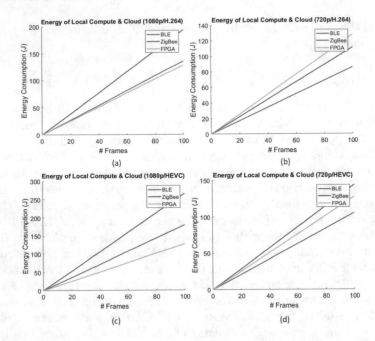

Fig. 3. Comparison of power consumed from local and cloud processing.

these examples, we considered a static power draw from a motion detector that may be used during the duration of the transfer. However, a more sophisticated filtering system would require a frame-by-frame analysis where some frames are excluded due to their content. The energy consumed during such a task is hard to estimate, so we elect to use a static value in this example. To arrive at the optimal solution, one must factor in the energy cost of the frame filtering techniques used, as well as the number of actual frames subject for processing. For example, considering the 2 min security camera example from earlier, we assume that processing such a video locally would be more energy efficient than transmitting to the cloud. However, it could be possible that a filtering technique reduces the amount of frames with pertinent data to 1 s of video, resulting in a much smaller data payload. In that case, transmitting to the cloud may be more efficient, considering the energy consumed to filter and encrypt the video data. Thus, there is a wide range of design space exploration for sophisticated filtering techniques in image processing.

4   Preliminary Results

To provide a comparison between local processing and cloud processing, we conducted a simple image processing experiment using a Raspberry Pi Zero – a cheap off-the-shelf device suitable for IoT applications. In this experiment, we utilized OpenCV to perform simple face detection algorithm that can detect

Fig. 4. Experimental setup of image processing application on Raspberry Pi Zero board.

multiple faces simultaneously. We also set up a Lambda server on Amazon Web Services (AWS) which accepts the video feed from the Raspberry Pi, runs the same face detection code, and sends the resulting images back to the device. We ran these scripts separately and measured the power consumption during operation in both scenarios. The experimental setup is shown in Fig. 4.

Preliminary results are shown in Table 1. In this experiment, processing the data in the cloud was shown to consume less power than processing the data locally. So, if our proposed framework were used in this scenario, the device would elect to process the data in the cloud. However, there are many factors to consider, such as the application used (face detection, face recognition, object detection, etc.), and the underlying hardware and the implementation of the algorithm(s).

Table 1. Preliminary results for local processing and cloud processing.

Experimental procedure	Resolution	Framerate	Throughput	Power
Face detection (without faces)	320 × 240	20 FPS	4.61 MBps	1.4524 W
Face detection (with faces)	320 × 240	20 FPS	4.61 MBps	1.5118 W
Cloud processing	320 × 240	15 FPS	3.46 MBps	1.3714 W

5   Conclusion

In this paper, we have provided a background on different IoT architectures, AI and ML workloads, and staple image processing techniques useful for reducing IoT edge network bandwidth requirements. Edge computing is rapidly becoming a critical design requirement as deep learning workloads consume a disproportionate amount of compute, memory, and network resources. To assess this demand, we have created a framework that considers network capabilities, privacy requirements, and power constraints, enabling designers to more accurately assess whether or not – and the extent to which – local processing capabilities should be considered in edge device design. We envision the integration of this framework within edge nodes, enabling them to independently determine the optimal utilization of computing, memory, and network resources when necessary. This represents a shift from traditional architectures towards a smarter and more scalable IoT.

References

1. Aazam, M., Huh, E.N.: Fog computing and smart gateway based communication for cloud of things. In: 2014 International Conference on Future Internet of Things and Cloud, pp. 464–470. IEEE (2014)
2. Aazam, M., Khan, I., Alsaffar, A.A., Huh, E.N.: Cloud of things: integrating internet of things and cloud computing and the issues involved. In: Proceedings of 2014 11th International Bhurban Conference on Applied Sciences and Technology (IBCAST) Islamabad, Pakistan, 14th-18th January 2014, pp. 414–419. IEEE (2014)
3. Abdel-Hamid, O., Mohamed, A., Jiang, H., Deng, L., Penn, G., Yu, D.: Convolutional neural networks for speech recognition. IEEE/ACM Trans. Audio Speech Lang. Process. 22(10), 1533–1545 (2014)
4. Al-Fuqaha, A., Guizani, M., Mohammadi, M., Aledhari, M., Ayyash, M.: Internet of Things: a survey on enabling technologies, protocols, and applications. IEEE Commun. Surv. Tutor. 17(4), 2347–2376 (2015). Fourthquarter
5. Castiglione, A., Choo, K.K.R., Nappi, M., Ricciardi, S.: Context aware ubiquitous biometrics in edge of military things. IEEE Cloud Comput. 4(6), 16–20 (2017)
6. Christopoulos, C., Skodras, A., Ebrahimi, T.: The JPEG2000 still image coding system: an overview. IEEE Trans. Consum. Electron. 46(4), 1103–1127 (2000)
7. Connor, J.T., Martin, R.D., Atlas, L.E.: Recurrent neural networks and robust time series prediction. IEEE Trans. Neural Netw. 5(2), 240–254 (1994)
8. Delp, E., Mitchell, O.: Image compression using block truncation coding. IEEE Trans. Commun. 27(9), 1335–1342 (1979)
9. Dillon, T., Wu, C., Chang, E.: Cloud computing: issues and challenges. In: 24th IEEE International Conference on Advanced Information Networking and Applications, pp. 27–33. IEEE (2010)
10. Guo, K., et al.: Angel-eye: a complete design flow for mapping CNN onto embedded FPGA. Trans. Comput. Aided Des. Integr. Circ. Syst. 37(1), 35–47 (2018)
11. Gantz, D.R.: The digital universe in 2020: big data bigger digital shadows and biggest growth in the far east. In: IDC iView: IDC Anal Future (2007), pp. 1–16, December 2012
12. Kao, J.T., Chandrakasan, A.P.: Dual-threshold voltage techniques for low-power digital circuits. IEEE J. Solid-State Circuits 35(7), 1009–1018 (2000)
13. Khan, R., Khan, S.U., Zaheer, R., Khan, S.: Future internet: the internet of things architecture, possible applications and key challenges. In: 10th International Conference on Frontiers of Information Technology, pp. 257–260. IEEE (2012)
14. Lacey, G., Taylor, G.W., Areibi, S.: Deep learning on FPGAs: Past, present, and future, February 2016

15. LeCun, Y., Bengio, Y., Hinton, G.: Deep learning. Nature **521**, 436 (2015)
16. Li, H., Ota, K., Dong, M.: Learning IoT in edge: deep learning for the internet of things with edge computing. IEEE Netw. **32**(1), 96–101 (2018)
17. Mell, P., Grance, T., et al.: The NIST definition of cloud computing (2011)
18. NVIDIA: Artificial intelligence computer designed to drive autonomous cars (2017)
19. Pearson, S.: Taking account of privacy when designing cloud computing services. In: ICSE Workshop on Software Engineering Challenges of Cloud Computing, pp. 44–52. IEEE (2009)
20. Ray, B.: A bluetooth & ZigBee comparison for IoT applications, October 2015. https://www.link-labs.com/blog/bluetooth-zigbee-comparison
21. Ray, T.: AI is changing the entire nature of compute—ZDNet. https://www.zdnet.com/article/ai-is-changing-the-entire-nature-of-computer/
22. Rijmenam, M.: Self-driving cars will create 2 petabytes of data, what are the big data opportunities for the car industry? December 2016
23. Rumelhart, D.E., Hinton, G.E., Williams, R.J.: Learning representations by back-propagating errors. Nature **323**(6088), 533–536 (1986)
24. Elminaam, D.S.A., Kader, H.M.A., Hadhoud, M.M.: Performance evaluation of symmetric encryption algorithms on power consumption for wireless devices. Int. J. Comput. Theory Eng. **1**, 343–351 (2009)
25. Shawahna, A., Sait, S.M., El-Maleh, A.: FPGA-based accelerators of deep learning networks for learning and classification: a review. IEEE Access **7**, 7823–7859 (2019)
26. Shi, W., Cao, J., Zhang, Q., Li, Y., Xu, L.: Edge computing: vision and challenges. IEEE Internet Things J. **3**(5), 637–646 (2016)
27. Simonyan, K., Zisserman, A.: Very deep convolutional networks for large-scale image recognition (2014)
28. Somani, G., Gaur, M.S., Sanghi, D., Conti, M., Buyya, R.: Ddos attacks in cloud computing: issues, taxonomy, and future directions. Comput. Commun. **107**, 30–48 (2017)
29. Sze, V., Chen, Y., Yang, T., Emer, J.S.: Efficient processing of deep neural networks: a tutorial and survey. Proc. IEEE **105**(12), 2295–2329 (2017)
30. Wallace, G.K.: The JPEG still picture compression standard. IEEE Trans. Consum. Electron. **38**(1), xviii–xxxiv (1992)
31. Hu, W., Tan, T., Wang, L., Maybank, S.: A survey on visual surveillance of object motion and behaviors. IEEE Trans. Syst. Man Cybern. **34**(3), 334–352 (2004)
32. Wiegand, T., Sullivan, G.J., Bjontegaard, G., Luthra, A.: Overview of the H. 264/AVC video coding standard. IEEE Trans. Circuits Syst. Video Technol. **13**(7), 560–576 (2003)
33. Xu, L.D., He, W., Li, S.: Internet of things in industries: a survey. IEEE Trans. Indust. Inf. **10**(4), 2233–2243 (2014)
34. Yi, D., Lei, Z., Liao, S., Li, S.Z.: Deep metric learning for person re-identification. In: 2014 22nd International Conference on Pattern Recognition, pp. 34–39, August 2014
35. Zhang, Q., Cheng, L., Boutaba, R.: Cloud computing: state-of-the-art and research challenges. J. internet Serv. Appl. **1**(1), 7–18 (2010)
36. Zhang, S., Zhang, S., Chen, X., Huo, X.: Cloud computing research and development trend. In: Second International Conference on Future Networks, pp. 93–97. IEEE (2010)
37. Wang, Z., Bovik, A.C., Sheikh, H.R., Simoncelli, E.P.: Image quality assessment: from error visibility to structural similarity. IEEE Trans. Image Process. **13**(4), 600–612 (2004)

Smart System Design and IoT Education

Good-Eye: A Combined Computer-Vision and Physiological-Sensor Based Device for Full-Proof Prediction and Detection of Fall of Adults

Laavanya Rachakonda[1], Akshay Sharma[2], Saraju P. Mohanty[1(✉)]🆔,
and Elias Kougianos[3]🆔

[1] Department of Computer Science and Engineering,
University of North Texas, Denton, USA
rachakondalaavanya@my.unt.edu, saraju.mohanty@unt.edu
[2] Texas Academy of Mathematics and Science,
University of North Texas, Denton, USA
AkshaySharma@my.unt.edu
[3] Department of Electrical Engineering,
University of North Texas, Denton, USA
elias.kougianos@unt.edu

Abstract. It is imperative to find the most accurate way to detect falls in elders to help mitigate the disastrous effects of such unfortunate injuries. In order to mitigate fall related accidents, we propose the Good-Eye System, an Internet of Things (IoT) enabled Edge Level Device which works when there is an orientation change detected by a camera, and monitors physiological signal parameters. If the observed change is greater than the set threshold, the user is notified with information regarding a prediction of fall or a detection of fall, using LED lights. The Good-Eye System has a remote wall-attached camera to monitor continuously the subject as long as the person is in a room, along with a camera attached to a wearable to increase the accuracy of the model. The observed accuracy of the Good-Eye System as a whole is approximately 95%.

Keywords: Internet of Things (IoT) · Smart healthcare · Healthcare cyber-physical system (H-CPS) · Fall detection · Elderly falls · Edge computing

1 Introduction

Falls are a leading cause of fatal and non-fatal injuries for the aging population. Around a third of elderly people 65 years or older fall each year, and a half of those who do fall tend to fall more than once. As age increases, tendency to fall as well as the injuries one might sustain from falling likewise increases [11].

© IFIP International Federation for Information Processing 2020
Published by Springer Nature Switzerland AG 2020
A. Casaca et al. (Eds.): IFIPIoT 2019, IFIP AICT 574, pp. 273–288, 2020.
https://doi.org/10.1007/978-3-030-43605-6_16

In the United States, fall-related emergency visits are estimated to be around 3 million per year [4].

Seniors' safety, privacy, independence, economic and personal costs are few other factors that are affected since the fall victim requires continuous 24×7 assistance. Over 800,000 hospital admissions, 2.8 million injuries and 27,000 deaths have occurred in the past few years because of falls. Healthcare expenditures were approximately $48 million in Alaska out of which $22 million were due to falls of older people [9]. The risk of hospital admissions has been reduced up to 34% with the constant assistance provided to the elderly as per a study conducted by [27].

With improvements in science and technology in the past decade, the ability to provide more advanced 24×7 protection to elderly people is very important. This can be done by taking advantage of the Internet and its connecting ability to remote devices, which is known as the Internet of Things (IoT). The IoT is defined as the network of devices which can be identified with a unique IP address [17].

In this work we propose Good-Eye, an IoT enabled Edge device that could detect and also predict fall related accidents. The motivation behind Good-Eye is to provide the following:

1. Constant care.
2. Easy to wear accessories convenient to any age.
3. Medical support as per the occurrence of emergencies irrespective of the location.
4. A methodology that promotes that precaution is better than cure.

Fig. 1. Conceptual overview of Good-Eye

The conceptual overview of Good-Eye wherein the sensor data are collected by the wearable along with the camera, and the user is notified about the fall condition through the LED, is represented in Fig. 1.

The paper is organized in the following fashion: Sect. 2 gives an overview of prior related work. Section 3 highlights the novel contributions of the Good-Eye System. Section 4 provides a discussion on the relationships between physiological parameters and falls, along with the possible consideration of signals. Section 5 provides the design and working principles of the Good-Eye System. Section 6 provides the implementation and validation of the system while, Sect. 7 provides the conclusions along with directions for future research.

2   Related Research Overview

Automatic fall detection has been a point of interest for decades. Multiple different implementations of an automatic fall detection sensor have been attempted, but these efforts are either restrictive in nature due to limited range, have low sample sizes, or unsatisfactory success rates [19]. Sole use of accelerometer sensors along with other physiological sensor data is proposed in [2]. The use of accelerometers with an RF signal to capture location is proposed in [5] and the angular velocity of 2D information is used to detect falls in [15]. These however, limit the scope of fall detection accuracy as no other physiological and vision parameters are considered. The scope of fall detection using barometric pressure sensors in floors is proposed in [23]. However, this is not an ideal solution as the location of the user is compromised.

The use of vision by using depth camera images with tangential position changes is used for fall detection in [13]. However, this may not be accurate enough as positions of the fall vary. A Raspberry Pi camera based solution for fall detection is proposed in [30]. However, this will affect the mobility of the user as it is location constrained. None of the solutions that are using sensors or camera, predict the fall before the actual event of fall.

Multiple industries have begun to make commercial products that involve automatic fall detection. However, according to commercial reviewers, these devices fail to accurately predict fall detection and often trigger false alarms [21]. These false alarms are so common that even running may trigger automatic fall detection. Also, none of the products provide prediction of fall before the actual event of fall. The top six marketable products along with their drawbacks are provided in Table 1.

The Good-Eye System not only can ensure that it is detecting a user's fall due to the wearable physiological sensors, but it also has fail-safes in the form of a heart rate sensor and camera in case the accelerometer registers a false positive. Additionally, the novel use of a camera provides unique data in that it can photograph the user's surroundings should they fall, allowing first responders to more accurately find the location of the fallen person.

Table 1. Wearable products and their drawbacks

Wearable	Drawback
Smart Watch [1]	It uses only accelerometers, does not work on low thresholds like double carpet, bathroom, hardwood floors. The user must manually select the option SOS and as a result it fails if the person is unconscious. Users may remain on the floor with no help for long hours
Lifeline [20]	Uses only accelerometers and barometric sensors for pressure changes. After the fall, the system waits for 30 sec and directly connects to help
Lively Mobile [7] and Angel4 [25]	Monitors fluctuations using only accelerometers
Bay Alarm [16] and Medical Guardian [8]	Uses only accelerometers. It has huge base stations limiting the usage and location access

3   Novel Contributions

With a motivation to provide 24×7 care to elders with minimal human interaction, we propose the Good-Eye System. This is a combination of both physiological and computer vision systems which ensures warning the user before the event of fall. The Good-Eye System could be used not only to accurately detect falls but also to capture the environment in which a person has fallen, and their internal physiology for analyzing the reason behind the fall. This information could then be used to treat a patient that has fallen more quickly and effectively.

The flow of the Good-Eye System is represented schematically in Fig. 2. Here, the physiological data, along with the camera input data are taken from the user and the remote wall respectively, and are analyzed at the edge level processing unit. This processed data are sent to the family and doctor for help depending on the emergency.

The significance of the proposed system include the followings:

– To provide a system that not only detects the fall but also predicts the fall.
– To provide an improved method of fall detection that does not involve only accelerometers.
– To provide vision information with a use of camera to the system.
– To provide a system which has both wearable and an off-site devices to obtain much higher accuracy.
– To incorporate the use of other physiological signal data as there is a definite change in the physiology when a person is about to face an accident.

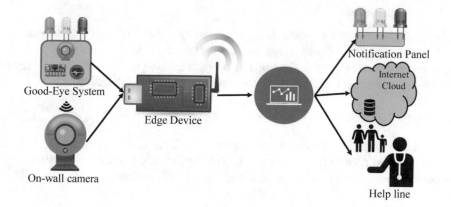

Fig. 2. Broad perspective of Good-Eye

- To capture the environment before and during the fall to accurately analyze the nature of the fall.

4 Are Falls Related to Physiological Parameters?

Emotions and physiology are intimately connected, as explained in [26]. Falls can be considered as one of the stressors in the human body as they elicit a fight-or-flight response. Under stress conditions, active coping strategies and passive coping conditions occur. Hypertension and tachycardia (an increase in the heart rate) as well as hypotension and bradychardia (a decrease in the heart rate) occur under such conditions. A fall would likely trigger an active coping strategy. Thus, we can likely infer that a fall will cause a physiological response. Stress causes the release of epinephrine and has impact on various physiological parameters depending upon the stressors [22]. Some of the frequent physiological parameters that vary with age and that are affected by stress are discussed in the remaining of this Section.

4.1 Sweat

The sweat glands tend to become less effective due to aging skin [24]. This means that older individuals tend to sweat less, which means it might not be a useful factor to consider in fall detection. Sweat gland output per active gland was significantly lower for those aged 58–67 than it was for those aged 22–24 and 33–40 as stated in [12]. Sweat glands typically have decreased sweat output as one ages.

4.2 Heart Rates and Blood Pressures

Cardiac output decreases linearly at a rate of about 1% per year in normal subjects past the third decade [3]. According to [6] the resting supine diastolic blood pressure for younger men was 66 ± 6 and 62 ± 8 for older men.

4.3   Temperature

Significant change in the mean body temperature is not observed in the human body over time [29]. Under stress, temperature fluctuations can sometimes be observed depending on the area of the body. The temperature may not vary at the chest or stomach while it varies at the hands and wrist [22,28].

4.4   Vision

Aging has a significant effect upon vision [18]. This is due to multiple factors, such as spatial contrast sensitivity loss, reduced eyesight in dark situations, and reduced processing potential in terms of visual information.

5   System Level Modeling of Good-Eye

Based on the above factors, the Good-Eye System is proposed in such a way that the behavioral changes in physiological signals are considered not just to detect falls but also to predict falls. The Good-Eye System consists of a wearable that could be placed near the chest portion of the user and an off-site on-wall camera that is connected to the wearable through Internet connectivity. The data collected from the system is processed at the edge device where the parameter analysis and the decision on prediction or detection is made as shown in Fig. 2. While this data is sent to the users as a feedback to notify them about the change, it is also sent to the helpline and cloud for storage.

5.1   Architecture of Good-Eye

The architecture of the Good-Eye System is shown in Fig. 3. Here, the input data are collected from the sensor input unit. These data are processed in the physiological sensor unit and image data unit which process the environmental and orientation change data observed in the on-site and off-site cameras. This data is then compared and analyzed to the set threshold ranges, as explained in Sect. 5.5. The decision is notified to the user by three LED lights.

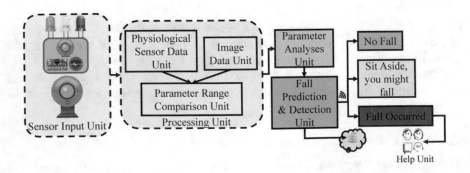

Fig. 3. Architecture of Good-Eye

5.2   The Parameters Considered for Good-Eye System

Modern fall-detection devices have no way to actually detect whether a human is wearing it or if it is being thrown. Additionally, accelerometers can have false alarms due to things like falling into a bed, moving down stairs, etc. So we added new parameters such that we would,

1. be able to detect whether a human is actually using the fall detection device.
2. be able to provide multiple instances of confirmation in order to make the system foolproof.

This would also make it possible to send important data to first responders so humans can verify whether a fall has occurred, such as average heart rate or images of the person's surroundings in the moments before and after they fell. Factors considered in fall predicting and detecting approaches in Good-Eye System are:

– Change in the axes of the accelerometer.
– Sudden change in the heart rate variability of a person compared to the resting heart rate.
– Having an on-site camera in the wearable to measure the change in orientation, to analyze the intensity of fall and provide certain care as per the emergency.
– Having an off-site wall-mounted camera in the surrounding space of a person, enables continuous person detection and tracking to provide proper feedback.

5.3   Design Flow

As the Good-Eye System as a whole comprises of an additional off-site camera, the flow of the system is explained as follows.

On-site Design Flow of Good-Eye System. The physiological sensor data along with the environmental capture are obtained at the on-site portion of the Good-Eye System. The flow of the design is as shown in Fig. 4. Accelerometer sensor changes are considered as a prime source for the system to start running so as to respect the privacy of the user. Whenever an accelerometer reading change is detected, the sudden spike in heart rate variability is checked along with the change in the camera's orientation. The moment there is an observed change in the accelerometer, the camera starts capturing the surroundings of the user.

Even if no change in the camera's orientation is observed, the data obtained from the camera is sent to the parameter analysis unit where the range comparisons are done as explained in brief in Sect. 5.4. This is done in order to maintain a movement log of the user. When there is no sudden spike detected in heart rate variability, the sensor is again taken to an idle state. From the parameter analyses unit, the decision of fall prediction or detection is done as explained in Sect. 5.5. The decisions are sent to family or helpline based on the level of emergency.

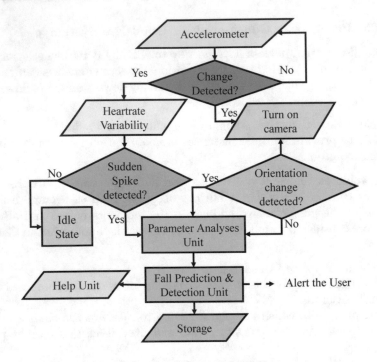

Fig. 4. Design flow of Good-Eye

Off-site Design Flow of Good-Eye System. The off-site or the on-wall camera plays a major role in fall prediction and detection here with a unique design flow as shown in Fig. 5. This is proposed considering facts which include the user forgetting to have an on-site unit. This on-wall camera starts working the moment a motion is detected in the room. This will then continuously start detecting and tracking the person so as to maintain the privacy of other people in the environment. When there is a sudden change in the movement of the user, instead of giving out false positive results, this will connect to the wearable to collect the physiological sensor data. Based on the physiological data and the on-site camera's orientation, the parameter analyses along with the decision of prediction or detection are made.

In the unfortunate case of the user not wearing an on-site wearable or when the on-wall camera isn't able to obtain the physiological sensor data from the wearable, the notification of "No Movement Detected" is sent to the guardian and to the doctors. This will also alert the user as a reminder to wear the wearable. With this notification, not only false positive cases will be reduced but also the incidents of stroke can be quickly addressed instead of waiting for the user to manually ask for help.

5.4   Parameter Analysis Unit

Parameter Data Acquisition. To incorporate the heart rate variability into the overall fall detection program, the Good-Eye System checks if there is a sudden spike in heart rate every few milliseconds, as the human body in such accidents experiences either a higher heart rate or a lower heart rate [26]. It is observed that the maximum heart rate in older men was lower (at around 162 ± 9 beats/min) than the maximum heart rate in younger men (191 ± 11 beats/min) according to [6]. Therefore the heart rate variability to the resting heart rate of every individual is considered as the threshold.

A fall is dependent upon a period of weightlessness followed by a large impact that increases the acceleration of the y-axis of an accelerometer by around 3 g's [10]. The accelerometer would constantly read the x, y, and z values of the g-force exerted upon a human being wearing the device. If the y value of the g-force exceeded ± 3 g's, the accelerometer would pass the threshold required to detect a fall.

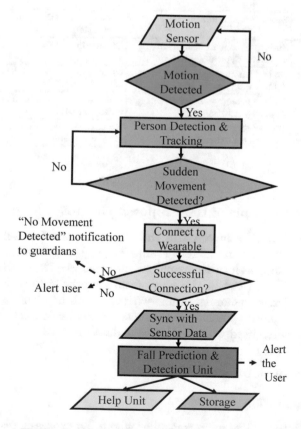

Fig. 5. On-wall camera design flow of Good-Eye.

The camera orientation sensor is implemented using a method that estimates orientation based on sequential Bayesian filtering [14]. The center of the frame is considered, with x and y axes. The respective R, G, and B values are calculated and the distances from each frame are stored for each pixel value. These pixel values are compared to the threshold in order to decide if the event is fall or not. A picture will be snapped when the accelerometer passes the threshold value, and another picture will be snapped when the accelerometer's values return to a new resting position.

5.5   Fall Prediction and Detection Unit

The analysis for the decision if it is a fall or not a fall is based on considering the change in accelerometer data, change in heart rate variability and change in orientation of the camera. It is represented in Table 2.

Table 2. Analyses for fall prediction & detection

Accelerometer sensor data	Heart rate variability	Camera orientation	Decision
Change in y value to ±3 g	Sudden change in heart rate detected; Typically ±10 bpm	Change in 45% of pixels	Fall detected
Change in y value to ±3 g	No sudden change in heart rate detected; Typically ±10 bpm	Change in 45% of pixels	No fall detected
No change in y value to ±3 g	Sudden change in heart rate; Typically ±10 bpm	Change in 45% of pixels	Fall predicted
Change in y value to ±3 g	Sudden change in heart rate; Typically ±10 bpm	No change in 45% of pixels	Fall predicted

5.6   Working Principle of the Proposed Good-Eye Model

The methodology that is involved in the camera of the Good-Eye System is explained as follows for two different Frames through Algorithm 1.

Even if a fall is not seen as occurring but the other two parameters (heart rate and accelerometer) are reached, the camera can send the last few seconds of data to a first responder, who can determine whether a fall has truly occurred. This makes the system more reliable, and prevents waste of resources. The proposed model is again represented with depth image data in Fig. 6.

6   Implementation and Validation

6.1   Implementation

Good-Eye System. The microcontroller where the processing is performed is connected to a tri-axial accelerometer, heartbeat sensor and a camera, as shown in Fig. 7.

Algorithm 1. Algorithm used to build Good-Eye Model

1: Scan a movement of Frame1 at time t_1.
2: Assign X_1 and Y_1 positional values at the center of the scanned frame.
3: Assign garbage values to R_1, G_1, and B_1 variables.
4: Convert the x_1 and Y_1 positional values to R_1, G_1, B_1 values by setting the variable R_1 to $(X_1 + Y_1)/100 * 256$, G_1 to $(1 - (X_1 + Y_1)) * 256$ and B_1 to $(1 - (0.5 - (X_1 + Y_1)/100)^2) * 20$ respectively.
5: Scan a movement of Frame2 at time t_2.
6: Repeat steps 2,3 and 4.
7: Calculate the distance (d_1) between (R_1, G_1, B_1) and (R_2, G_2, B_2) by using the distance formula, $\sqrt{(R_2 - R_1)^2 + (G_2 - G_1)^2 + (B_2 - B_1)^2}$.
8: Store the d_1 value for every pixel, counting whichever pixels are above a set threshold (say, $d_1 = 70$).
9: Checks if this threshold is reached for at least 45% of pixels.
10: If there is a 45% change, a fall has occurred.
11: *Repeat the above steps for all frames.*

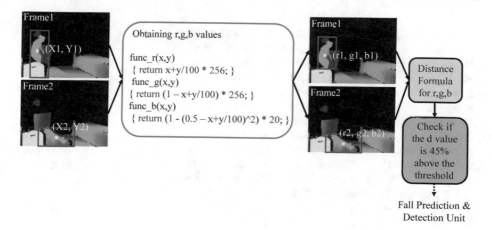

Fig. 6. Proposed model of Good-Eye.

The algorithm involved works by taking both heart rate and accelerometer data simultaneously. It stores the previous data as a means to compare between milliseconds of time. Once the accelerometer's y-axis has a change of more than 2 g's, the heart rates of the user is immediately compared along with the orientation check in camera. If the heart rate of the user has spiked by at least 10 bpm, an alarm triggers. The continued readings from the accelerometer, camera and heart rate are represented in Fig. 8.

Good-Eye Connectivity. The continuous data collected from the Good-Eye system is stored in an open source cloud IoT analytics platform, as shown in Fig. 9. The data stored here can be accessed by the user depending on the requirement.

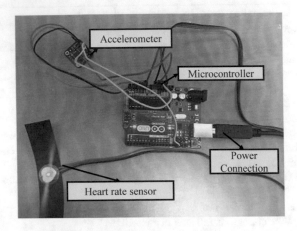

Fig. 7. Implementation of Good-Eye

```
X accel: -0.03    Y accel: 0.04    Z accel: 0.63              BPM: 78
X accel: -0.03    Y accel: 0.04    Z accel: 0.64
X accel: -0.03    Y accel: 0.03    Z accel: 0.62
X accel: -0.03    Y accel: 0.04    Z accel: 0.63              BPM: 78
X accel: -0.03    Y accel: 0.04    Z accel: 0.64
X accel: -0.03    Y accel: 0.04    Z accel: 0.63
X accel: -0.03    Y accel: 0.04    Z accel: 0.63              BPM: 78
X accel: -0.03    Y accel: 0.04    Z accel: 0.63
X accel: -0.03    Y accel: 0.04    Z accel: 0.63
X accel: -0.03    Y accel: 0.04    Z accel: 0.64              BPM: 78
X accel: -0.03    Y accel: 0.04    Z accel: 0.64
X accel: -0.01    Y accel: 0.04    Z accel: 0.64
X accel: -0.03    Y accel: 0.04    Z accel: 0.63              BPM: 79
X accel: -0.03    Y accel: 0.03    Z accel: 0.63
```

(a) Continued readings from the accelerometer, kept on a flat plane, and the heart rate sensor with a live heartbeat.

Center of Rectangle is : (1082, 181)
Output= 'X1082Y181z'
{34 : 322, 626: 914}
X : 626
Y : 34
X+W : 914
Y+H : 322
1083
195

(b) Continued readings from the camera
for every frame.

Fig. 8. Results of Good-Eye.

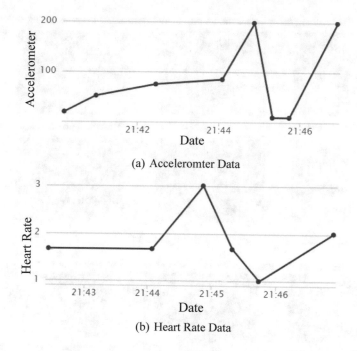

(a) Acceleromter Data

(b) Heart Rate Data

Fig. 9. Signal analysis Good-Eye.

Table 3. Comparison with state of the art research

Research works	Approach used	Automated care?	Fall prediction	Detection accuracy (%)
Bhati et al. [2]	Physiological signal data only	NA	NA	NA
Chen et al. [5]	Physiological signal data only	NA	NA	NA
Liu et al. [15]	Physiological signal data only	NA	NA	NA
Rimminen et al. [23]	Physiological signal data only	NA	NA	NA
Kong et al. [13]	Camera only	NA	NA	97
Waheed et al. [30]	Camera only	NA	NA	NA
Jia Ning [10]	Physiological signal data only	NA	NA	NA
Good-Eye (Current Paper)	Physiological signal data and camera data	Yes, user need not press SOS	Yes	95

6.2   Validation

Event of Fall Vs Event of Sitting. In order to verify the model's algorithm, the validation of the model has been done with the already published Person Falling Dataset [31]. This has 144 instances of data where 6 subjects had performed sitting and falling separately. The process of sitting and falling has been captured by a depth camera in this dataset.

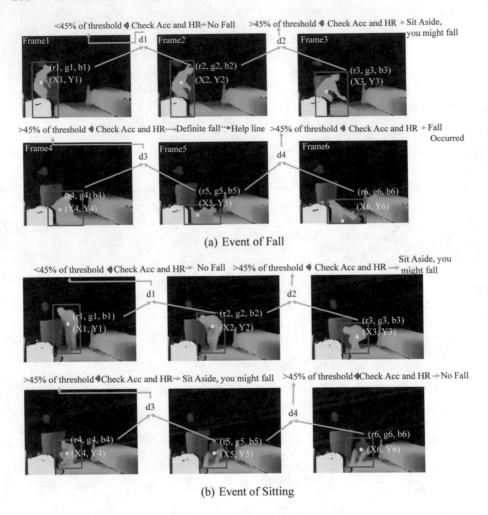

(a) Event of Fall

(b) Event of Sitting

Fig. 10. Validation of Good-Eye.

When these instances were fed to the Good-Eye model, the change in differentiating the sitting to falling has been found with an approximate accuracy of 95%. The differentiation is represented starting from taking the x and y axes, as stated in Algorithm 1 for making decision of fall as stated in Table 2. The event of Falling vs. event of Sitting is represented in Fig. 10.

The methodology implemented in the Good-Eye System is validated with state of the art research and wearables and is provided in Table 3.

7   Conclusions and Future Research

A way to reliably detect falls is of utmost importance for the health of elderly people. The device proposed here not only uses an accelerometer but also other physiological sensor data that enhance the usage of a fall detection device and make it more accurate. The camera inputs and physiological sensor data inputs are independently significant in relaying data and verifying that the device is accurately predicting and detecting the event of fall. This device may greatly increase the importance of fall detection devices as it manages to provide privacy, and convenience to prediction of fall to the user.

The relationship with the physiological data to falls has been explained above and additionally, incorporating all possible sensor data and increasing the model's dataset to further improve the Good-Eye System is our future research.

References

1. Apple: Apple watch. https://support.apple.com/en-us/HT208944
2. Bhati, N.: Health based ubiquitous fall detection for elderly people. In: 8th International Conference on Computing, Communication and Networking Technologies (ICCCNT), pp. 1–7, July 2017. https://doi.org/10.1109/ICCCNT.2017.8204033
3. Boss, G.R., Seegmiller, J.E.: Age-related physiological changes and their clinical significance. W. J. Med. **135**, 434 (1981)
4. Burns, E., Kakara, R.: Deaths from falls among persons aged $\geq$65 years–United States, 2007–2016. MMWR Morb. Mortal. Wkly Rep. **67**(18), 509–514 (2018). https://doi.org/10.15585/mmwr.mm6718a1
5. Chen, J., Kwong, K., Chang, D., Luk, J., Bajcsy, R.: Wearable sensors for reliable fall detection. In: IEEE Engineering in Medicine and Biology 27th Annual Conference, pp. 3551–3554, January 2005
6. Christou, D.D., Seals, D.R.: Decreased maximal heart rate with aging is related to reduced beta-adrenergic responsiveness but is largely explained by a reduction in intrinsic heart rate. J. Appl. Physiol. **105**(1), 24–29 (2008). https://doi.org/10.1152/japplphysiol.90401.2008
7. Greatcall: Lively Mobile (2019). https://www.greatcall.com/devices/lively-mobile-medical-alert-system
8. Medical Guardian: Home Guardian. https://www.medicalguardian.com/products/home-guardian
9. Haddad, Y.K., Bergen, G., Florence, C.S.: Estimating the economic burden related to older adult falls by state. J. Public Health Manag. Pract. (JPHMP) **25**(2), 17–24 (2019)
10. Jia, N.: Detecting human falls with a 3-axis digital accelerometer. Analog Dialogue **43**, 01–07 (2009)
11. Kannus, P., et al.: Fall-induced injuries and deaths among older adults. JAMA **281**(20), 1895–1899 (1999). https://doi.org/10.1001/jama.281.20.1895
12. Kenney, W.L., Fowler, S.R.: Methylcholine-activated eccrine sweat glanddensity and output as a function of age. J. Appl. Physiol. **65**, 1082–1086 (1988)
13. Kong, X., Meng, L., Tomiyama, H.: Fall detection for elderly persons using a depth camera. In: International Conference on Advanced Mechatronic Systems (ICAMechS), pp. 269–273, December 2017. https://doi.org/10.1109/ICAMechS.2017.8316483
14. Lee, J.K., Yoon, K.J.: Real-time joint estimation of camera orientation and vanishing points. In: IEEE Conference on Computer Vision and Pattern Recognition (CVPR). IEEE, June 2015. https://doi.org/10.1109/cvpr.2015.7298796

15. Liu, J., Lockhart, T.E.: Development and evaluation of a prior-to-impact fall event detection algorithm. IEEE Trans. Biomed. Eng. **61**(7), 2135–2140 (2014). https://doi.org/10.1109/TBME.2014.2315784
16. Bay Alarm Medical: Bay Alarm Medical. https://www.bayalarmmedical.com/
17. Mohanty, S.P.: Internet of Things (IoT) - Demystified. In: 16th International Conference on Information Technology (ICIT) (2017)
18. Owsley, C.: Aging and vision. Vis. Res. **51**(13), 1610–1622 (2011). https://doi.org/10.1016/j.visres.2010.10.020
19. Pannurat, N., Thiemjarus, S., Nantajeewarawat, E.: Automatic fall monitoring: a review. Sensors **14**(7), 12900–12936 (2014). https://doi.org/10.3390/s140712900
20. Philips: Philips Lifeline (2019). https://www.lifeline.philips.com/
21. Preece, J.: Best fall detection sensors 2019: send a call for help, April 2019
22. Rachakonda, L., Mohanty, S.P., Kougianos, E., Sundaravadivel, P.: Stress-Lysis: a DNN-integrated edge device for stress level detection in the IoMT. IEEE Trans. Consum. Electron. **65**(4), 474–483 (2019)
23. Rimminen, H., Lindström, J., Linnavuo, M., Sepponen, R.: Detection of falls among the elderly by a floor sensor using the electric near field. IEEE Trans. Inf Technol. Biomed. **14**(6), 1475–1476 (2010). https://doi.org/10.1109/TITB.2010.2051956
24. Rittié, L., Farr, E.A., Orringer, J.S., Voorhees, J.J., Fisher, G.J.: Reduced cell cohesiveness of outgrowths from eccrine sweat glands delays wound closure in elderly skin. Aging Cell **15**, 842–852 (2016)
25. Sense4care: Angel4 Fall Detection. https://www.sense4care.com/tienda/angel4-fall-detection/
26. Steimer, T.: The biology of fear- and anxiety-related behaviors. Dialogues Clin. Neurosci. **4**(3), 231–249 (2002)
27. Stuck, A.E., Egger, M., Hammer, A., Minder, C.E., Beck, J.C.: Home visits to prevent nursing home admission and functional decline in elderly peoplesystematic review and meta-regression analysis. JAMA **287**(8), 1022–1028 (2002)
28. Vinkers, C.H., et al.: The effect of stress on core and peripheral body temperature in humans. Stress **16**(5), 520–530 (2013). https://doi.org/10.3109/10253890.2013.807243
29. Waalen, J., Buxbaum, J.N.: Is older colder or colder older? The association of age with body temperature in 18,630 individuals. J. Gerontol. Ser. A: Biol. Sci. Med. Sci. **66A**(5), 487–492 (2011). https://doi.org/10.1093/gerona/glr001
30. Waheed, S.A., Sheik Abdul Khader, P.: A novel approach for smart and cost effective IoT based elderly fall detection system using Pi Camera. In: IEEE International Conference on Computational Intelligence and Computing Research (ICCIC), pp. 1–4, December 2017. https://doi.org/10.1109/ICCIC.2017.8524486
31. Zhang, Z., Athitsos, V.: Fall Detection Dataset. http://vlm1.uta.edu/~zhangzhong/fall_detection/

Building a Low-Cost and State-of-the-Art IoT Security Hands-On Laboratory

Bryan Pearson[1], Lan Luo[1], Cliff Zou[1(✉)], Jacob Crain[2], Yier Jin[2], and Xinwen Fu[1,3]

[1] University of Central Florida, Orlando, FL 32816, USA
{bpearson,lukachan}@Knights.ucf.edu, czou@cs.ucf.edu
[2] University of Florida, Gainesville, FL 32611, USA
jcrain@ufl.edu, yier.jin@ece.ufl.edu
[3] University of Massachusetts Lowell, Lowell, MA 01854, USA
xinwnefu@cs.uml.edu

Abstract. The popularity of IoT has raised grave security and privacy concerns. The huge IoT botnets Mirai and Reaper were built on compromised IoT devices. In this paper, we propose to develop a low-cost platform with an industrial grade microcontroller (MCU) ESP32 equipped with a crypto co-processor ATECC608A and create teaching materials including labs and case studies for IoT security education. MCUs have broad applications in IoT. Sensor nodes in various smart systems such as smart home, smart health and smart grid can use MCUs to process commands and perform automatic control. We will develop effective, engaging and novel teaching materials on IoT hardware security, operating system/firmware/software security, network security, and data security with the low-cost IoT kit and IDE. The teaching materials will contribute to the Cybersecurity Workforce Development Initiative led by NICE and help respond to a dynamic and rapidly developing array of cyber threats including those resulting from IoT.

Keywords: IoT · Microcontroller · Teaching materials

1 Introduction

Internet of Things (IoT) interconnects everything including physical and virtual objects together through communication protocols. IoT has broad applications in digital healthcare, smart cities, transportation, agriculture, logistics and many other domains. The global IoT market is booming. According to Forbes [13], the IoT Market will reach $520B by 2021.

1.1 Need for Promoting Education in IoT Security

The popularity of IoT has raised grave concerns about security and privacy. When medical devices are connected to the Internet, compromised medical

© IFIP International Federation for Information Processing 2020
Published by Springer Nature Switzerland AG 2020
A. Casaca et al. (Eds.): IFIPIoT 2019, IFIP AICT 574, pp. 289–306, 2020.
https://doi.org/10.1007/978-3-030-43605-6_17

devices may endanger the life of patients. Hacked autonomous cars may crash. Hackers exploited default passwords and user names of webcams and other IoT devices and deployed the Mirai botnet [11]. The huge botnet was then used to conduct the distributed denial-of-service (DDoS) attack against Dyn DNS servers. The IoT reaper botnet was discovered in 2017 and it exploited newly found vulnerable IoT devices [9].

We have also disclosed various vulnerabilities of IoT products on market. We exploited hardware vulnerabilities of the Nest Thermostat, which aims to learn a user's heating and cooling habits to help optimize scheduling and power usage [23]. The hardware architecture of Nest lacked proper protection, allowing attackers to install malicious software into the unit. Through a USB connection, we demonstrated how the firmware verification done by the Nest software stack can be bypassed, providing the means to completely alter the behavior of the unit. Any information stored within the unit was then exposed too. We performed a comprehensive analysis of PurpleAir, a popular low-cost air quality sensor [28]. PurpleAir has one of the largest operational low-cost sensor networks worldwide, being used by individuals and non-profit and governmental agencies for community air quality monitoring. Multiple security vulnerabilities are identified in PurpleAir, including plaintext communication, weak authentication mechanisms, and lack of data integrity measures. By exploiting these vulnerabilities, attackers can impersonate any victim PurpleAir sensor and pollute its data using fabricated data. This is the first security analysis of low-cost and connected air quality monitoring systems. The researchers have been working with PurpleAir to patch their system.

IoT security should be addressed from five aspects [25], including hardware security, operating system (OS)/firmware security, software application security, secure networking protocols and data security. Different IoT systems have different requirements. In this paper, we propose to develop a low-cost platform with the industrial grade microcontroller (MCU) ESP32 [20] and crypto co-processor ATECC608A [30] for IoT security education. While CPUs are more versatile and powerful, MCUs are often used in sensor nodes in various smart systems such as smart home, smart health and smart grid to process commands and provide automatic control.

We will often take an Internet enabled air quality monitoring system as a case study to demonstrate security requirements of an IoT system, and we believe that other IoT systems shall share similar attributes. A secure environmental monitoring system should have hardware security and be able to prevent attackers from reading and changing the data on the device, particularly when the attacker has physical access to the device. Hardware security is a great challenge. For example, advanced attackers may manipulate the flash directly through its I/O interface. The IoT device should have system and firmware security so that it can detect the change of its firmware and protect the overall system. To further protect the firmware and sensitive data stored on the flash, data security through strategies such as flash and file encryption shall be adopted. Secure firmware upgrade of IoT systems is also key to the longevity of an IoT system, since no one can guarantee that a software has no bugs, and security and functionality patches are always expected.

Network security is required to secure network traffic to and from an IoT device, for example, through SSL/TLS (which will be referred to as TLS for simplicity) to establish mutual authentication, communication encryption and integrity between the device and a server. Mutual authentication is critical for any IoT system. Those systems without mutual authentication often have various vulnerabilities [15,24,25,31,32]. Without device authentication, a fake device may obtain security credentials from the server or a smartphone app. Without server/user authentication, a fake server or user can cheat on the device and collect sensitive information. Certificate based mutual authentication based on public key crypto is often the most feasible and simple implementation of mutual authentication. In TLS certificate-based mutual authentication, a client verifies the server's certificate and identity while the server performs similar operations to authenticate the client.

From the discussion above, we can see that there is an urgent need of promoting education in IoT security and privacy given that IoT will be ubiquitous and its security should be systematically addressed from the perspective of the hardware, system/firmware, software, networking and data security.

1.2   Need for Low-Cost and High-Quality Hardware Platforms for IoT Security Education

We propose a low-cost platform with the industrial grade microcontroller ESP32 [20] equipped with a crypto co-processor ATECC608A for IoT security education. A low-cost platform will be easy for dissemination so that schools with low budget can afford it. Pedagogical theories support the use of industry grade hardware platforms for IoT security education. Kaylene Williams and Caroline Williams list various ingredients that can improve student motivation, including student and content [37]. The student ingredient suggests students should be able to connect education results to their future career and even entrepreneurship. The content ingredient requires the content to be accurate, timely, useful, and relevant to students in their life. The hands-on labs and case studies developed in this paper on secure IoT systems are novel, timely and relevant to real life. The platform shall create an environment that students may connect knowledge learned from the school to the industry. With such teaching materials, students will be able to produce practical prototypes such as secure environmental monitoring sensors and generate an impact on the society through innovation. Such an environment will motivate students to learn.

There is also a strong interest among students to learn IoT security and privacy. This is demonstrated by two preliminary surveys performed by us: one tutorial on IoT security at Design Automation Conference (DAC) 2018 and the other from an IoT security and privacy class offered in Fall 2018 at UCF. The survey results from 51 responses in Table 1 reveal that 94.1% of the students do not know how to hack IoT hardware at all or only know somewhat. We cannot expect these students to know how to secure the IoT hardware. 94.1% of the students do not know how to perform traffic analysis of IoT traffic at all or know only somewhat. These students will not be able to perform risk assessment of IoT communication protocols. 89.2% of the students either strongly agree or agree that it is necessary to learn IoT security through hands-on exercises. Overall, the preliminary surveys demonstrated the need and urgency to develop effective education materials to equip the future workforce with adequate knowledge and expertise in IoT security and privacy.

Table 1. Survey on the need for transiting research in IoT security into education

Question	Answer
1. Do you know how to hack hardware of IoT devices through its debugging ports or other hardware interfaces?	68.6% No, 25.5% Somewhat, 5.9% A lot
2. Do you know how to analyze network traffic from IoT devices or the app controlling the devices?	62.7% No, 31.4% Somewhat, 5.9% A lot
3. It is necessary to learn IoT security through hands-on exercises	61.7% Strongly agree, 27.5% Agree

We have following major objectives. Please note: the term "laboratory" in this paper refers to the actual physical laboratory, and the term "lab" refers to a student assignment or project that plays with the IoT kit to learn specific knowledge and skills. While we focus on IoT security, privacy is often mentioned since encrypting data and communication is part of privacy.

Objective 1: Design an affordable low-cost IoT kit with an Integrated Development Environment (IDE) so that schools with low budget can afford such a laboratory on IoT security and privacy education. Given that the kit is small, a physical laboratory may not be necessary. Students can take home the kit in a box and perform the teaching labs and case studies.

Objective 2: Design a suite of teaching labs and case studies using the low-cost IoT kit so that students can learn the state-of-the-art techniques to secure IoT devices. We will design teaching modules covering hardware security, operating system/firmware/software security, network security, and data security. Please note that given the broad areas of IoT security, we focus on those unique and important security features offered by the low-cost IoT kit and do not intend to cover every security topic. For example, in the threat model of an individual defense measure, we will not consider the following physical attacks on hardware platforms: power/electromagnetic side channel attacks [33], laser voltage probing (LVP) based non-destructive reverse engineering [26,27], focused ion beam (FIB) based destructive reverse engineering [36], and other circuit level vulnerabilities. The corresponding solutions to these attacks will lead to the redesign of the microcontrollers and microprocessors. These topics are out of the scope of this paper. The hardware security labs in this paper will address those caused by illegal access to input/output pins. For software security, secure boot can detect the change of the software. We will not cover dynamic security measures such as intrusion detection. However, the covered secure measures will be able to defeat most serious IoT attacks discovered so far.

Objective 3: Integrate the developed IoT teaching labs and case studes into related courses.

2   A Capable and Low-Cost IoT Laboratory

We now introduce the low-cost IoT development kit, the laboratory setup and the integrated development environment (IDE) to use the kit. Such an IoT development kit can be less than $10. For hardware security teaching labs, students need the JTAG debugger and bus pirate, each of which costs around $30. Other laboratory supplies and materials including multimeters and soldering kits are of low cost too.

2.1   Low-Cost IoT Development Kit and Laboratory

We will design a very low-cost and affordable IoT development kit, as illustrated in Fig. 1. It includes a capable industrial grade microcontroller (MCU) – ESP32 development board ($10.99 at Amazon; $4.27 at AliExpress), a crypto co-processor – ATECC608A ($0.86/unit at DigiKey in pack of 25, $0.55/unit at Microchip in pack of 5000), a temperature and humidity sensor – DHT11 ($2.00 at Amazon; $0.83 at AliExpress), a small breadboard ($1.60 at Amazon; $0.90 at AliExpress), a USB to Micro USB cable ($2.00/unit in pack of 5 at Amazon; less than $1.00 at AliExpress) and a few jump wires (less than $1.00). A computer is required to program the MCU and it is assumed that students have computers such as laptops or the school provided computers. If the right seller is chosen, the low cost IoT development kit costs only $8.55, less than $10.

For the hardware security teaching modules, A JTAG debugger ($29.95 at Amazon) is needed to connect to the JTAG interface of ESP32. A Bus Pirate ($29.95 at Amazon) is needed to play with the UART interface and the flash SPI interface. A pair of JTAG debugger and bus pirate costs $59.90.

Figure 2 shows the laboratory setting. If an institution does not have space, there is no need of a physical laboratory. Since the components are small, a small box can hold all the components. A guided lab can be executed in a classroom and lab work can also be performed at home. The laboratory may need soldering iron kits to solder pin headers onto an ESP32 development board, an ATECC608A onto a breakout board, or pin headers onto breakout boards. Multimeters can be used to assist the hardware labs while they are not necessary. One set of soldering kit and multimeter costs only $15.64 at AliExpress. IoT devices must be connected to the Internet and the data from the IoT devices can be saved on a server. ESP32 supports WPA2 Personal or Enterprise, and can be connected to an isolated private network, a campus WiFi network or the widely

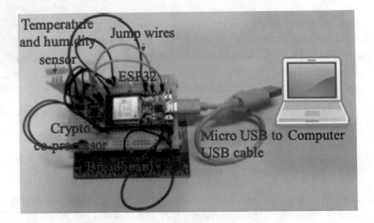

Fig. 1. Single IoT platform

deployed eduroam [29]. Amazon AWS IoT [10] provides a free tier of services including IoT core, database and storage. ESP32 devices can be connected to an open source MQTT (Message Queuing Telemetry Transport) server such as Mosquitto [3], which can use a MySql database to save data. A generic computer can run such a MQTT server and MySql database.

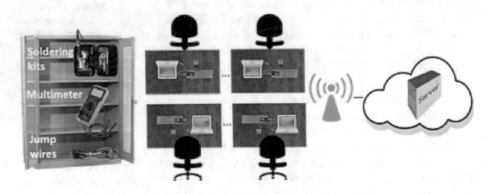

Fig. 2. IoT laboratory

2.2 Creating an Integrated Development Environment (IDE) for IoT Security Education

Hardware is only part of an IoT system. We plan to create a unified IoT IDE (integrated development environment) for the IoT development kit in Fig. 1, which will be used for teaching modules on IoT hardware security, system/firmware/software security, networking security and data security. The native programming environment of ESP32 is Espressif IoT Development Framework (esp-idf) [18], which is a command line based environment. The ESP32 community has migrated the esp-idf into the Arduino core [16] for the ESP32 WiFi and Bluetooth chip so that the Arduino IDE [1] can be used to compile an ESP32 application, flash it into the chip, and monitor debugging messages from ESP32 through a serial port. The Arduino community developers have also developed various libraries such as one for the temperature and humidity sensor DHT11. However, the Arduino IDE has no debug capabilities, and lacks support for multiple files on a project. The alternative is the Eclipse IDE [17], which is integrated with esp-idf and supports JTAG, OpenOCD [6] and GDB debugging [35].

Once the IDE is chosen, we will ensure that the IDE supports the developed teaching modules on configuring ESP32's secure features such as secure boot and programming labs with crypto libraries. (i) Configuring ESP32's secure features. Currently, the configuration is performed at the command line. We plan to develop a GUI for such configuration. (ii) Programming with crypto libraries. We must carefully choose the crypto library, which shall support secure features of both ESP32 and ATECC608A. There are two choices, mbedssl [7] and WolfSSL [8]. ESP32 is shipped with mbedssl and provides an API interface for TLS [19]. WolfSSL is ported to ESP32 and is compatible with Microchip's CryptoAuthLib, a crypto library that supports ATECC608A. Whenever needed, we will extend the crypto library and ensure that the chosen library will support the functionalities of ECC, HMAC and AES of ATECC608A, and can connect to Mosquitto, AWS IoT and other MQTT brokers via TLS.

Since an institution may prefer a private network for all the teaching labs and does not want to use AWS IoT, we plan to extend the open source MQTT project Mosquitto with the database capability and mutual authentication. There are two issues with Mosquitto. The default configuration of Mosquitto does not incorporate MySql. We will extend Mosquitto so that IoT devices can send data to the server, which stores data into a MySql database. The second issue with Mosquitto is its current implementation of SSL/TLS mutual authentication is problematic. In the client authentication, the server verifies the client's certificate and checks if the subject fields of the client certificate include the client's IP. This will tie the client to that IP. This strategy is not flexible and practical. We will adopt the certificate based client authentication used by SSH and AWS IoT for Mosquitto. That is, the client certificate will be stored at the Mosquitto server for the purpose of authentication.

3   Developing Teaching Labs for IoT Security

We now introduce teaching labs and case studies that will be developed for students to master hardware security, secure key storage, secure boot, data security, network security, secure firmware upgrade and crypto co-processor based on the IoT kit in Fig. 1 and the IDE that we will adopt and extend.

3.1   Developing Teaching Modules on Hardware Security

We first introduce hardware security capabilities of ESP32 and then discuss corresponding teaching modules on hardware security based on ESP32.

Hardware Security on ESP32. The first step to accomplishing hardware security is to disable I/O ports that may be present on the device. In the case of ESP32, we must disable the JTAG and UART interfaces, since they provide venues for attackers to read and write on the ESP32.

The Joint Test Action Group (JTAG) formalizes a series of standards for boundary scanning and debugging a chip. With JTAG, the programmer can test each component of the chip separately to verify it is connected and functioning correctly. The Open On-Chip Debugger (OpenOCD) is an open-source project and can interact with the JTAG interface in a GNU Debugger (GDB) environment. OpenOCD was extended to add support for the ESP32 JTAG chain. Programmers can use GDB to communicate with OpenOCD, providing complete flash access of the ESP32. It is possible to read and write to any byte of memory, including registers and instruction flow through the JTAG chain. To disable JTAG, the corresponding eFuse value of ESP32 should be set to 1. The ESP32's eFuse is a 1024-bit partition of one-time programmable memory, separated into four 256-bit blocks. Upon setting a value, hardware "fuses" are burned, rendering these values irreversible.

Universal Asynchronous Receiver/Transmitter (UART) is a circuit which allows two devices to communicate over a serial connection. Both devices in a UART connection can either transmit or receive bytes of data. Using a serial register, UART will convert this data either from serial to parallel or vice versa, depending on whether the data is being transmitted or received. Unlike JTAG, which can debug devices, UART is often used for communication. The primary purpose of UART with respect to the ESP32 is to upload an application or firmware to the flash. Other possibilities with UART include monitoring output from the console, and reading or modifying direct memory addresses. The UART bootloader is implemented through an external interface known as esptool. If flash content is encrypted by the encryption key stored in the eFuse, then the UART bootloader will transparently decrypt this content before reaching the serial monitor. Similarly, the UART bootloader will transparently encrypt data when flashing it via esptool. To disable the insecure properties of the UART bootloader, we must set proper eFuse values. Afterwards, the UART bootloader cannot read or write to the encrypted flash.

Teaching Modules on Hardware Security on ESP32. We will develop JTAG ethical hacking lab, JTAG defense lab, UART ethical hacking lab, UART defense lab, and flash ethical hacking lab.

JTAG hacking lab. Access to a full JTAG chain allows access to all portions of an integrated circuit, some debugging configurations notwithstanding [21]. In this lab, students will learn the different signals that appear on a JTAG port as well as their usage. Students will also be introduced to the standard JTAG state machine, as well as how systems are designed to utilize it. Then students will proceed to identify the JTAG pins of the ESP32 and connect a debug probe to it. We will then provide the students with tools to build the OpenOCD debug bridge and the GNU Debugger (GDB) for the target platform. In doing so, students will get experience on finding and constructing their own debug environment for reverse engineering platforms. With OpenOCD and GDB, students will attempt to reverse engineer a binary provided by the lab instructor. Students will learn to utilize the Python facilities provided by GDB to develop their own plug-ins to facilitate the task at hand. As part of this lab, students will learn to view and modify CPU registers, as well as bypassing the local authentication mechanism provided by the binary. Furthermore, through the JTAG interface, students will modify the contents of memory as the binary runs as to modify its behavior and extract runtime secrets such as ephemeral keys used by the binary to establish secure communications with a remote server. Lastly, students will utilize the JTAG interface to permanently modify the binary within the device introducing a backdoor to allow bypassing local authentication as well as leaking credentials.

JTAG defense lab. The JTAG chain has to be disabled in a final commercial product given that attackers may exploit it to interrupt the microcontroller or access sensitive data on the flash. In this lab, students will learn how to disable the JTAG chain by setting JTAG_DISABLE of the ESP32 to 1. Students will use the debug probe again and test if they can still manipulate the chip after JTAG_DISABLE is set as 1. One thing to note is once JTAG is disabled, it cannot be enabled again since the eFuse is physically burned. Therefore, if the ESP32 will be reused, the JTAG defense lab cannot be truly performed and students should only discuss the principle of disabling the JTAG.

UART hacking lab. For this lab, students will be introduced to communications through UART. The lab will center around using a specially crafted binary provided by the instructor. Students will identify the UART lines of the ESP32 microcontroller and capture data generated by the binary using a cheap signal analyzer such as the Bus Pirate [34]. The students will learn to decode UART frames, as well as to compute the BAUD rate being utilized by the device. With the computed BAUD rate, students will capture all incoming frames and examine the received data for any possible hints on device operation. Students will then interact with the device through a serial terminal emulator, allowing them to dynamically send and receive data from the device. Utilizing Python and the pyserial library, students will then develop a framework to automatically send and retrieve data from the device through UART. The binary will be designed to contain a way to locally authenticate a debug mechanism through its serial port. This is done in a semblance of devices that use the UART as a debug method. Students will utilize this opportunity to brute force the debug authentication credentials, or to perform other styles of attack (such as dictionary attacks) against the authentication prompt. Once authenticated, students will proceed to extract secrets from the device, such as wireless network credentials. Lastly, students will utilize the UART to communicate with the ESP32 Boot ROM code and extract portions of the binary which reside in the on-board flash containing the authentication credentials, modify them, and write them back to the on-board flash utilizing the Boot ROM code.

UART defense lab. The UART has to be either disabled or protected through a strong authentication mechanism in the final commercial product given that attackers may exploit it to access sensitive data on the device. In this lab, students will explore the option to secure the UART. In events where the UART exposes sensitive device information, students will learn ways to securely authenticate with the device to allow access such as timed "knocks", and signed messages. Students will also investigate the option of adding cooldowns after failed authentication attempts and study how it affects the security and usability of the device. The second option is to disable the UART in production devices when it is no longer needed, or to limit its functionality. Students will play with the three eFuse values DISABLE_DL_ENCRYPT, DISABLE_DL_DECRYPT and DISABLE_DL_CACHE, and study the impact. One thing to note is once UART is disabled, it cannot be enabled again since the eFuse is physically burned. Therefore, if the ESP32 will be reused, the UART defense lab cannot be truly performed and students should only discuss the principle of disabling the UART through setting the eFuses.

Flash ethical hacking lab. The ESP32 has multiple SPI channels, with channel 0 dedicated to mapping the external serial flash to memory, and channel 1 for performing writes to this flash. In this lab, students will be provided with a binary by the instructor to be placed in their boards. Students will then probe the SPI lanes and identify read transactions using a cheap signal analyzer such as the Bus Pirate when the device is in operation, identifying the underlying instruction stream being executed by the microcontroller. Students will then interact with the device to allow it to fetch an encrypted secret from the external flash memory. Students will then use the captured instruction stream to decode the secret in order to further their interaction with the device. Students will then use a secret of their own and encrypt it with the binary's algorithm and write it back to flash memory using a cheap programmer such as the aforementioned Bus Pirate. The lab shows the students why flash encryption is needed to protect sensitive data stored in the flash.

3.2 Developing Teaching Modules on Secure Key Storage on ESP32

We first introduce the hardware based secure key storage and then discuss teaching modules on secure key storage on ESP32. Secure key storage is part of ESP32 features securing the system and flash firmware (including the application/software) from unauthorized access. ESP32 uses FreeRTOS to manage the hardware components and run a user task/application [4].

Secure Key Storage on ESP32. Simply encrypting the data will not guarantee that an IoT system is secure. We must also securely store the encryption keys, so that only trusted systems can access it when needed, and even a software malware that has hacked into the system cannot access the keys. That is, secure key storage protects secret keys from being externally revealed or modified. The ESP32's eFuse allows for secure key storage. Recall this eFuse contains four 256-bit blocks. Block 0 is reserved for the MAC address, SPI configurations, and related security settings. Blocks 1 and 2 are actually used for key storage — block 1 stores the flash encryption key, while block 2 stores the secure boot key. Both keys are 256 bits and generated using an internal Random Number Generator (RNG) hardware accelerated algorithm. Block 3 is undefined by default, but a programmer may use it to store application-specific encryption keys.

Teaching Modules on Secure Key Storage. Secure key storage lab. In this lab, students will learn how to utilize the secure key storage and understand the importance of keeping the secret. ESP32 allows pre-generation of a flash encryption key on a host computer, which can be used to burn this key into its eFuse. This approach is recommended for the development phase. Students will be required to use the given flash encryption key to decrypt encrypted data, which may contain sensitive data such as WiFi credentials. However, when the key is kept secret, secure key storage will not leak the key even if a malware gets inside the device. Students will also learn how to enable the secure key storage for the production phase.

3.3   Developing Teaching Modules on System/Firmware Security

We first introduce secure boot, which is part of ESP32 features securing the system and flash firmware from unauthorized access. We then discuss teaching modules on secure boot on ESP32.

Secure Boot on ESP32. ESP32 uses hardware-based secure key storage and secures the booting of the firmware. Secure boot requires all components of the firmware be signed and verified before executing [22]. If either the software bootloader or the application firmware is modified, the device will refuse to boot. Once properly configured, two keys are necessary to enable secure boot. The first key is a 256-bit secure bootloader key and allows the ROM bootloader to validate the software bootloader. The second key is the secure boot signing key, generated with ECDSA with the NIST256p curve. The manufacturer will generate the ECDSA keypair. The signing key is used to generate image signatures, so it must be available to the manufacturer. The software bootloader and the application are validated via a "chain of trust" model.

Teaching Module on Secure Boot. Secure boot lab. The lab has two parts, attack and defense. As introduced above, if secure boot is not enabled, it is possible that an attacker can change the binary code without being detected. In the attack part of this lab, secure boot is not enabled on ESP32. Students will be required to retrieve the binary code from the flash, reverse engineer the binary code, and change the logic of the code. For example, students will be required to change the binary of an air quality monitoring sensor and send fake data to a server. Data integrity is critical for air quality monitoring since air pollution may incur public outcry. In the defense part, students are required to enable secure boot. Students will perform the attack again and observe if secure boot can detect the change of the binary of the device. Secure boot is a critical part of building a trustworthy IoT device.

3.4 Developing Teaching Modules on Data Security

Data Security on ESP32. ESP32 can encrypt the entire flash using a secure AES-256 key. The AES key is stored in block 1 of the eFuse. Once written to the eFuse, the read and write bits for the key are set to prevent anyone from reading or modifying the key. When flash encryption is enabled, application-based flash partitions, i.e., factory and over-the-air (OTA) partitions, are encrypted by default. From there, decryption can only occur at runtime via the flash controller. The flash controller is a hardware component that can perform the following two runtime operations using the AES key: (i) Decryption of memory-mapped read accesses to flash; and (ii) Encryption of memory-mapped write accesses to flash. It is also possible to encrypt other flash partitions by manually setting an "encrypt" flag for a partition. This requires generating a custom partition table rather than using the default table (which only encrypts factory and OTA partitions).

Teaching Modules on Data Security on ESP32. Data security lab. From the flash ethical hacking lab or as instructed by the lecturer, students have learned that attackers can read the content of the flash on a device from the flash's interface (such as SPI). In this lab, students will be guided to enable flash encryption of ESP32 to defeat such flash attacks. Students will understand how a system works with an encrypted flash seamlessly.

3.5 Developing Teaching Modules on Network Security on ESP32

We will first introduce ESP32's security features for network security and then discuss the teaching labs.

Network Security on ESP32. The challenge to implement TLS on an IoT device is often the cost and efficiency of implementing the public key based cryptographic functionalities. As discussed above, the hardware and cost may no longer be the bottleneck. ESP32 has cryptographic hardware acceleration for RSA and Random Number Generator (RNG). Our extensive experiments show that the performance of TLS on ESP32 is satisfactory in various application domains. ESP32 also has cryptographic hardware acceleration for AES and SHA2 so that TLS can be fully implemented. AES encryption can be implemented for communication secrecy and HMAC will achieve communication integrity.

Teaching Modules on Network Security on ESP32. We will develop two teaching labs including network attack lab and network defense lab.

Network attack lab. In this lab, students will use mitmproxy [5] to perform traffic analysis of IoT networking traffic. Mitmproxy is a man-in-the-middle proxy between an http(s) client and a server. It can intercept, modify, replay and save http/s traffic. Students will use mitmproxy to decrypt https traffic between a target IoT device and a server to understand its protocol. Students will set up mitmproxy at a computer. Mitmproxy pretends to be the IoT device for the server because the server normally does not check the identity of the IoT device. Mitmproxy can pretend to be the server for the IoT device too. However, the client normally checks the authenticity of the server by verifying the server's certificate. In this case, the mitmproxy will behave as a fake certificate authority (CA), generate a fake server certificate and send it to the client. Students will have to replace the original CA's certificate on the device with the fake CA's certificate so that the fake server certificate can be authenticated, the binary code can run and the mitmproxy can observe the communicating traffic between the server and client to figure out the communication protocol between them.

Network defense lab. Students are required to program and use SSL/TLS with RSA acceleration to secure network connection to a MQTT server, either Mosquitto or AWS IoT. Mutual authentication between the IoT device and the server will be required. This requires the client have a private key stored locally. Students will learn how to generate the public key pair with openssl or Amazon AWS IoT. Students will understand the issue with the private key hardcoded into the IoT application, given ESP32 does not provide secure key storage for RSA private keys. That is, if a malware gets into the device through means such as buffer overflow vulnerabilities, the malware may steal the private key and then a fake device can be created to impersonate the original device. This shows the necessity of both secure key storage and hardware acceleration of RSA.

3.6   Developing Teaching Modules on Secure Firmware Upgrade

We will first introduce ESP32's security features for secure firmware upgrade, i.e., secure Over-the-Air update (OTA), and then discuss the teaching labs.

3.7   Secure Over-the-Air Updates (OTA) on ESP32

OTA is a process in which the MCU fetches a new image from a remote location, stores this image in the flash, and loads it on successive reboots. OTA updates are seamless and transparent, and many devices can be updated concurrently. The drawbacks are that wireless updates introduce additional attack vectors that must be avoided. The ESP32 offers native library support for https OTA updates. ESP32's partition table includes OTA partitions, which store potential firmware for the ESP32. The otadata partition points to the newer firmware. Upon downloading a new update, the unused partition will be overridden, leaving the current firmware untouched. If the update fails, the device will revert to the previous application. If it succeeds, the system is updated to point to the correct partition, and the system reboots to the new firmware.

Teaching Modules on Secure Over-the-Air Updates (OTA) on ESP32.
We will develop OTA attack lab and OTA defense lab.

OTA attack lab. Students are required to attack a device without secure OTA firmware upgrade and change the firmware. There are two cases students will experiment on. In the first case, the device does not employ secure firmware upgrade and allows arbitrary firmware upgrade. Apparently, this allows the attacker to change the whole system arbitrarily. In the second case, the secure OTA is enabled, but it does not check the version number of the upgrade. Therefore, an old firmware with vulnerabilities can be upgraded into the device.

Secure OTA lab. Students will experiment on two alternatives of upgrading. In the first case, https will be used for secure OTA firmware upgrade. This is convenient since the manufacturers may utilize this strategy to push a new firmware into individual devices. In the second case, WiFi or Bluewooth of ESP32 will be used for secure firmware upgrade. This requires users to perform the upgrade from their smart devices such as smartphone or computers. The users first download the new firmware from the manufacturer and then perform the secure firmware upgrade locally.

3.8   Developing Teaching Modules on Crypto Co-processor

ESP32 does not have ECC hardware acceleration and does not provide secure key storage for its RSA hardware acceleration. It can cause problems when a malware breaks into the system and steals the private key hardcoded in the firmware. We will first introduce the very low-cost crypto coprocessor, Microchip's ATECC608A, which can address these issues, and then discuss the teaching lab.

Microchip's ATECC608A. Microchip's ATECC608A is a cryptographic coprocessor with secure hardware based key storage. It can store 16 keys, and supports ECDSA, ECDH, SHA-256 & HMAC, AES-128 and other features. Communicating with ATECC608A is performed through either a GPIO (general-purpose input/output) pin or a standard Inter-Integrated Circuit (I2C) interface, which is a widely supported serial protocol.

There are two reasons why we want to use a crypto coprocessor with ESP32. First, an old MCU may not have modern support of secure boot, flash/file encryption and hardware crypto acceleration. ATECC608A can be used to secure those MCUs and other processors. ATECC608A can be used with ESP32 to implement those features. Second, ESP32 does not have ECC hardware acceleration while ATECC608A has. Therefore, the use of ATECC608A will boost ESP32 for its SSL/TLS implementation. Software implementation of ECC will hardcode the ECC private key into the software. A malware that gets into the device will be able to read it and use it to impersonate the device. With ATECC608A, the

ECC private key can be burned into ATECC608A's hardware secure storage and will never leave the chip. Even the malware will not be able to get it. It will be also good for students to compare the performance of different implementations of SSL/TLS with RSA and ECC.

Teaching Modules on Microchip ATECC608A. Mutual authentication lab with ATECC608A: One weakness of ESP32 is it does not provide secure key storage for the RSA private key used for SSL/TLS. Even if flash encryption is used, malware that gets into the device will be able to read the private key. In this lab, students are required to generate the ECC key pair and burn the ECC private key into the ATECC608A chip. Since ATECC608A performs the crypto operation inside the chip itself and the private key never leaves the chip, a malware inside the device will not be able to read the private key. Students will be required to connect the ATECC608A enabled device to a MQTT server or AWS IoT through SSL/TLS.

3.9   Developing Case Studies

Case studies show how a theory or concept is applied to real situations. This method requires critical thinking and analysis, allows students to synthesize course contents, encourages active learning, provides an opportunity for development of key skills such as communication, teamwork and problem solving, and increases the students' enjoyment of the topic and hence their desire to learn.

Attack Case: Vulnerabilities of Air Quality Monitoring Networks. We will use the exploit of PurpleAir as a case study [14]. PurpleAir sensors are based on an early version of ESP32 - ESP8266, which does not have security features of ESP32. The measurements of air quality metrics such as PM2.5 are sent to PurpleAir's servers, which show the air quality measurements on Google Map. We explored the system architecture and its communication protocols based on traffic analysis using mitmproxy [14], which is an https proxy tool. We find that the system adopts unencrypted communication and uses MAC addresses to identify sensors in the sensor data sent to the servers. This practice allows us to "pollute" sensor data by conducting a man-in-the-middle (MITM) attack or by sending fabricated data along with a victim sensor's MAC address to the servers. The servers also allow us to check if a specific MAC address exists in the system. This enables us to enumerate all valid MAC addresses of PurpleAir sensors and potentially pollute data from every sensor deployed globally.

We plan to replicate the vulnerabilities of PurpleAir and implement such a vulnerable system on ESP32. Students can play with the system and experiment on man-in-the-middle attack, spoofing attack, device scanning attack, and other ethical hack labs presented in this paper.

Defense Case: Secure Air Quality Monitoring Networks. In this case, students will be required to design a secure air quality sensor and monitoring network and evaluate the pros and cons of various secure measures.

Secure boot should be used to prevent the manipulation of the firmware of the sensor. With secure boot, if the firmware is changed, the sensor will not boot. Such a firmware is trustworthy to some extent. Flash encryption should be used to protect sensitive data on the flash, including the WiFi credentials. Certificate based mutual authentication with TLS should be used to defeat the MITM attacks and protect the communication. The mutual authentication renders the MITM attack invalid and the hash of the sensor's public key can be adopted as the device ID if needed.

Secure storage should be used to store the sensor's private key so that the adversary cannot obtain the private key. Students should realize that a per-device private key is needed. Otherwise, if all devices use the same private key and it is compromised, all these devices will be affected. The location of the sensor can be obtained from either a GPS module on the sensor or WiFi localization. A GPS module can be problematic since a dedicated adversary may replace the GPS module with an artificial one. In addition, the GPS may not work inside buildings. The WiFi localization may be more appropriate since the trusted firmware will retrieve the WiFi information for the purpose of localization. However, students should realize that attackers may deploy rogue access points to mislead the WiFi localization strategy. The server may also validate the reported location from the device via the IP location service [12], which finds the geolocation of a sensor from the IP address of the sensor while the accuracy of the IP location service is limited [2]. Secure firmware upgrade is needed in case that vulnerabilities are found in the system.

4   Conclusion

In this paper, we propose to develop effective, engaging and novel teaching materials on IoT hardware security, operating system/firmware/software security, network security, and data security with the low-cost IoT kit and IDE. Achieving the proposed objectives will lead to an increased capacity in producing cybersecurity professionals. This will be demonstrated by the outcomes in the following two aspects. *Curricula:* (i) New IoT platforms for cybersecurity education, (ii) transferable modules that will be developed and incorporated into curricula at the participating institutions, and (iii) increased IoT security components in interdisciplinary courses. *Students:* (i) Increased student interest in cybersecurity, (ii) improved knowledge and skills in IoT security, (iii) increased exposure of minority students to IoT and cyber security, (iv) increased employment perspective of students in cyber security, (v) increased number of students in IoT security research, (vi) increased student publications, and (vii) increased collaboration among students in the participating institutes.

Acknowledgements. This work was supported in part by NSF grants 1915780, 1931871, 1916175, 1802701 and 1643835. Mr. Jacob Crain is supported through the

REU Supplement of the NSF project (NSF 1802701). Any opinions, findings, conclusions, and recommendations in this paper are those of the authors and do not necessarily reflect the views of the funding agencies.

References

1. Arduino IDE. https://www.arduino.cc/en/Main/Software. Accessed Nov 2018
2. Center for applied Internet data analysis. Internet protocol address (IP) geolocation bibliography. http://www.caida.org/projects/cybersecurity/geolocation/bib/. Accessed Nov 2018
3. Eclipse Mosquitto, an open source MQTT broker. https://mosquitto.org/. Accessed Nov 2018
4. Hello world with ESP32 explained. https://exploreembedded.com/wiki/Hello_World_with_ESP32_Explained. Accessed Nov 2018
5. mitmproxy is a free and open source interactive https proxy. https://mitmproxy.org/. Accessed Nov 2018
6. Open on-chip debugger. http://openocd.org/. Accessed Nov 2018
7. Readme for mbed tls. https://github.com/ARMmbed/mbedtls/tree/master. Accessed Nov 2018
8. WolfSSL introduction. https://github.com/espressif/esp-wolfssl. Accessed Nov 2018
9. The secretary of commerce and the secretary of homeland security, a report to the president on enhancing the resilience of the Internet and communications ecosystem against botnets and other automated, distributed threats (January 2018). https://www.ntia.doc.gov/files/ntia/publications/eo_13800_botnct_report_for_public_comment.pdf
10. Amazon Web Services Inc.: AWS IoT. https://aws.amazon.com/iot/. Accessed Nov 2018
11. Antonakakis, M., et al.: Understanding the Mirai botnet. In: Proceedings of the 26th USENIX Security Symposium (Security) (2017)
12. Brand Media, Inc.: Where is geolocation of an IP address? https://www.iplocation.net/. Accessed Nov 2018
13. Columbus, L.: IoT market predicted to double by 2021, reaching $520b (August 2018). https://www.forbes.com/sites/louiscolumbus/2018/08/16/iot-market-predicted-to-double-by-2021-reaching-520b/
14. Cortesi, A., Hils, M., Kriechbaumer, T.: mitmproxy: A free and open source interactive https proxy. https://mitmproxy.org/. Accessed Nov 2018
15. Dhanjani, N.: Security evaluation of the philips hue personal wireless lighting system (2013). http://www.dhanjani.com/docs/HackingLighbulbsHueDhanjani202013.pdf
16. Espressif: Arduino core for ESP32 WiFi chip. https://github.com/espressif/arduino-esp32. Accessed Nov 2018
17. Espressif: Build and flash with Eclipse IDE. https://dl.espressif.com/doc/esp-idf/latest/get-started/eclipse-setup.html. Accessed Nov 2018
18. Espressif: ESP-IDF programming guide. https://docs.espressif.com/projects/esp-idf/en/latest/. Accessed Nov 2018
19. Espressif: ESP-TLS. https://docs.espressif.com/projects/esp-idf/en/latest/api-reference/protocols/esp_tls.html. Accessed Nov 2018
20. Espressif: ESP32 overview. https://www.espressif.com/en/products/hardware/esp32/overview. Accessed Nov 2018

21. Espressif: JTAG debugging. https://docs.espressif.com/projects/esp-idf/en/latest/api-guides/jtag-debugging/. Accessed Nov 2018
22. Espressif: Secure boot. https://docs.espressif.com/projects/esp-idf/en/latest/security/secure-boot.html. Accessed Nov 2018
23. Jin, Y., Hernandez, G., Buentello, D.: Smart nest thermostat: a smart spy in your home. In: Proceedings of the Black Hat USA (2014)
24. Ling, Z., Luo, J., Xu, Y., Gao, C., Wu, K., Fu, X.: Security vulnerabilities of Internet of Things: a case study of the smart plug system. IEEE Internet Things J (IoT-J) 4(6), 1899–1909 (2017)
25. Ling, Z., Liu, K., Xu, Y., Jin, Y., Fu, X.: An end-to-end view of IoT security and privacy. In: Proceedings of the 60th IEEE Global Communications Conference (Globecom) (December 2017)
26. Lohrke, H., Tajik, S., Boit, C., Seifert, J.-P.: No place to hide: contactless probing of secret data on FPGAs. In: Gierlichs, B., Poschmann, A.Y. (eds.) CHES 2016. LNCS, vol. 9813, pp. 147–167. Springer, Heidelberg (2016). https://doi.org/10.1007/978-3-662-53140-2_8
27. Lohrke, H., Tajik, S., Krachenfels, T., Boit, C., Seifert, J.P.: Key extraction using thermal laser stimulation. Proc. IACR Trans. Cryptogr. Hardw. Embed. Syst. 3, 573–595 (2018)
28. Luo, L., Zhang, Y., Pearson, B., Ling, Z., Yu, H., Fu, X.: On the security and data integrity of low-cost sensor networks for air quality monitoring. Sensors 18(12), 4451 (2018)
29. martinius96: ESP32-eduroam. https://github.com/martinius96/ESP32-Eduroam. Accessed Nov 2018
30. Microchip Technology Inc.: ATECC608A. https://www.microchip.com/wwwproducts/en/ATECC608A. Accessed Nov 2018
31. Molina, J.: Learn how to control every room at a luxury hotel remotely. In: Proceedings of DEFCON (2014)
32. Obermaier, J., Hutle, M.: Analyzing the security and privacy of cloud-based video surveillance systems. In: Proceedings of the 2nd ACM International Workshop on IoT Privacy, Trust, and Security (IoTPTS) (2016)
33. Park, J., Xu, X., Jin, Y., Forte, D., Tehranipoor, M.: Power-based side-channel instruction-level disassembler. In: Proceedings of the 55th ACM/ESDA/IEEE Design Automation Conference (DAC) (2018)
34. sylvainpelissier: JTAG debugging with bus pirate and OpenOCD (May 2014). https://research.kudelskisecurity.com/2014/05/01/jtag-debugging-made-easy-with-bus-pirate-and-openocd/
35. tedwood: Using eclipse with OpenOCD to build and debug ESP32 (Apr 2017). https://www.esp32.com/viewtopic.php?t=336&start=10
36. Vasile, M.J., Niu, Z., Nassar, R., Zhang, W., Liu, S.: Focused ion beam milling: depth control for three-dimensional microfabrication. J. Vac. Sci. Technol. B Microelectron. Nanometer Struct. Process. Meas. Phenom. 15(6), 2350–2354 (1997)
37. Williams, K.C., Williams, C.C.: Five key ingredients for improving student motivation. Res. High. Educ. J. 18(12), 104–122 (2011)

Curriculum Design Requirements and Challenges for the First Bachelor's Degree on IoT in the US

Kemal Akkaya[✉]

Department of Electrical and Computer Engineering,
Florida International University, Miami, FL 33174, USA
kakkaya@fiu.edu

Abstract. Internet of Things (IoT) devices have become part of our lives through their roles in smart and connected living. As they are increasingly deployed in various industries and residential areas, they are now readily accessible to the end users who need to manage them on a daily basis. However, management of these devices includes many aspects such as hardware troubleshooting, operating systems updates, security configuration, connectivity maintenance and scripting, etc. Given the complexities of these tasks, there is a need to educate and train technical people who will eventually form a new workforce to handle these issues on behalf of the ordinary users. This brings the need for a new IoT related curriculum that will serve to undergraduate students to acquire the above skills. In this paper, we present the first undergrad IoT curriculum in the US offered by Florida International University (FIU) by discussing the requirements and challenges. We explain how this new curriculum addresses the key aspects of IoT technologies and opportunities that come with the proposed IoT degree. We also highlight other related issues regarding the focus of this type of degrees and interdisciplinary aspects with other academic units and industry.

Keywords: IoT · IoT curriculum · IoT education · IoT challenges

1 Introduction

Motivated with the proliferation of smart, low-cost and small devices, there is a growing trend towards the development of smart buildings, cities, and infrastructures in order to make our lives more efficient, cleaner, safer and less costly than before [1–5]. These devices are now widely referred to as Internet of things (IoT), which became part of our lives. Examples of these IoT devices include smart sensors, thermostats, meters, phones, tablets, cameras, wearable technologies (e.g., glasses, watches), and cars that are currently ubiquitous [6–8]. These IoT devices have typically computation, communication, sensing, and storage capabilities and have been the focus of a great deal of research in the last several

© IFIP International Federation for Information Processing 2020
Published by Springer Nature Switzerland AG 2020
A. Casaca et al. (Eds.): IFIPIoT 2019, IFIP AICT 574, pp. 307–318, 2020.
https://doi.org/10.1007/978-3-030-43605-6_18

years. Such research activities range from the hardware/software characteristics [9,10] of these individual devices to their deployment challenges in the development of smart spaces and infrastructures [11,12].

With such developments, IoT applications started to dominate our lives in our homes, schools, workplaces. It can be said that while the term IoT was coined in 1999 by Ashton [13], we have started to witness the IoT era only after 2010s with the maturation of the IoT technology. Specifically, with the introduction of smart home devices such as Nest thermostat, Apple HomeKit, Amazon Alexa, etc. as well as the penetration of smart phones, we have seen a dramatic increase in IoT device deployment in every domain and hence the number of IoT devices that are deployed worldwide surpassed the number of people connected to Internet. According to a new Gartner report, almost 5 billion IoT devices are in use worldwide as of Dec. 2019 [14]. The application categories of these devices are listed in Table 1. The table indicates that there are numerous market segments where IoT devices are increasingly used. In fact, it is predicted that "the combined markets of IoT will grow to about \$520 billion in 2021, more than double the \$235 billion spent in 2017 [15]".

Table 1. IoT device count by billions in various segments (Source Gartner).

Segment	2019	2020
Utilities	1.17	1.37
Government	0.53	0.70
Building automation	0.31	0.44
Physical security	0.95	1.09
Manufacturing	0.40	0.49
Automotive	0.36	0.47
Healthcare providers	0.28	0.36
Retail & wholesale trade	0.36	0.44
Information	0.37	0.37
Transportation	0.07	0.08
Total	4.81	5.81

These developments indicate that the demand for the deployment of IoT will only grove further in the upcoming decade which will eventually require creating a new workforce to manage these devices. This is because, from their maintenance/updates to integration with IT, and from their security to programming, there will be a lot of technical tasks to be handled when IoT devices are used. This ultimately means, millions of new jobs will be created in the upcoming decade to fill the gap in the market. Indeed, International Data Corporation has predicted that IoT will be a \$7 trillion industry by 2020 [16]. Currently, there is already a growing job market in IoT in regards to managing IoT data on the cloud, analyzing security and privacy issues, understanding networking issues surrounding IoT systems (i.e., 4/5G, WiFi, Zigbee, Bluetooth), programming server side for IoT using *Node.js* and using machine learning to do predictions with IoT data [17].

We argue that most of the aforementioned jobs and skills are specific to IoT domain and independent from IT or computer science/engineer related jobs. This means they will require special training in the domain of IoT. Therefore, current curriculum in computer science or engineering will not be able to address this need given that their focus is not on IoT. While some of the jobs can still be done using general computer science or engineering skills, there is a need to design specific courses that will get into the realm of IoT to understand the context, requirements and challenges. Given the increasing demand and broad concepts under IoT, addressing this need with one or more elective courses will not be the ideal solution. While it is certainly helpful to have certificates or training programs such as Intel's IoT curriculum [18] or Stanford's IoT certificate for graduates [19], the training and education should be made more accessible to a broader audience including college students and professionals. Otherwise, companies will still need to train their employees in IoT domain to equip them with the emerging skills which may cost them more money.

In this paper, we present the first IoT Bachelor's degree in the US to address the above needs and challenges. We first motivate the specific need and thus the required type of curriculum and then we explain the details of the curriculum structure created in the Department of Electrical and Computer Engineering at Florida International University (FIU). We share our challenges when the degree is to be offered as a technology degree rather than engineering. We provide discussions on how and where to create such type of degrees in the future depending on the need.

This paper is organized as follows: In the next section, we motivate the need for a new IoT technology degree at the undergraduate level. Section 3 explains the pillars of the proposed IoT degree. Section 4 is dedicated to overall IoT map in the proposed curriculum. Section 5 presents other related issues and Sect. 6 concludes the paper.

2 Where Is the Need?

One of the challenges that comes with proposing a new degree is whether it is different than the existing degrees and it will survive in the long run. This was very much true for IoT since it includes many components that are already being taught under Computer Science or Engineering programs. In this section, we explain how the proposed IoT degree is different and what kind of gap it would fill.

2.1 IoT vs Computer Science/Engineering

IoT is mainly about engineering so a new engineering degree on IoT would be a special case of either Computer Science or Computer Engineering depending on the focus of the degree. For instance, if software is the main focus, then Computer Science courses could be expanded to cover IoT software development. Indeed, there is already courses on various universities that teach Android programming, iOS programming, IoT data collection via Cloud Computing, IoT data analytics, IoT security, etc. On the other hand, if the focus is more on hardware level, then Computer Engineering courses can be expanded to focus on microcontrollers for IoT, embedded programming, sensors for IoT, IoT communications, etc.

Nevertheless, current jobs in IoT domain require a comprehensive skill set that forces companies to train their computer science or computer engineering workforce in one of the above aspects of IoT as their training is not comprehensive enough to cover all of the desirable IoT skills. Thus, a new IoT Engineering degree would address these needs which would be a mix of computer science or engineering programs with some special IoT courses. Such IoT undergrad programs are indeed emerging in China [20–22] and becoming popular among the new college students.

2.2   IoT vs IT

Even if there is a justification for a new engineering degree, the booming applications of IoT showed that the need is not just at the engineering level. This is because, these devices are now used in many domains by non-technical people as a lot of homes/companies/cities are maintaining IoT devices and infrastructure. Thus, there is a different need in terms of their maintenance and management. Specifically, we need technical people to deploy, manage, secure, update, troubleshoot IoT devices and networks for sustainable operations.

This need is similar to the case with Information Technology (IT) related jobs in early 2000s. Basically, as Internet was penetrating through every domain, industries, organizations and schools started to deploy computers and a network infrastructure to manage their websites and store their data. However, this necessitated technical specialists who can manage these computers and networks which basically included maintenance, software updates, security, troubleshooting, upgrades, configuration, etc. Obviously, Computer Science graduates were capable of handling these tasks but they would be considered over-qualified for these tasks and thus they were not able to fill this gap. Therefore, a lot of Computer Science departments started to offer a new degree called IT or Information Systems (IS) which aimed at producing workforces that can handle IT maintenance/management. These programs spread to every College in the US and eventually attracted many students who were not necessarily strong in Math and programming but still have a genuine interest in technology. IT graduates filled the gap in the workforce and are still in high demand today.

This led us to think in the same way and offer IoT as a technology degree that will fill an important gap in the IoT workforce. In this way, the engineers or scientists who came out of computer science or engineering programs can still be employed in engineering related jobs for IoT (i.e., design and development of IoT devices or IoT networks) but there will be a separate pipeline for IoT management/maintenance jobs that will suit the students who are interested in technology.

3   IoT Technology Degree Curriculum

With the given motivation for a technology degree in IoT, under the Electrical and Computer Engineering at FIU, a new IoT BS degree is designed [23] in 2018. This is known to be the first IoT degree at the undergraduate level in the US. In this section, we explain the core elements of this proposed IoT degree and provide examples for the new courses.

3.1   University Core Requirements

Before discussing the IoT-related core courses, we first briefly mention the university core requirements for our degree. As the core courses that will be taken mainly within the first two years, we ensured that the prerequisites are different than engineering programs in terms of Math requirements. Specifically, Calculus or Discrete Math are not required as part of this new degree since it focuses less on Math but more on technology. However, we expect students to take some basic programming and data analysis courses which are widely available in many colleges.

3.2   Four Pillars of IoT

We consider 4 major pillars to base the proposed degree after the university core classes are completed. Basically, this corresponds to roughly the last two years of the program. These pillars are based on the main elements of an IoT device as shown in Fig. 1. We discuss each in details below.

Hardware. Hardware components are very critical for understanding IoT. Basically, these components refer to microprocessor/controller, sensors and memory which are very different than traditional ones used in computers due to resource constraints in IoT devices. Specifically, due to their size and cost requirements, the hardware is specially designed for IoT and it is a constant area of research that evolves every year. The hardware classes should cover all these aspects in a comprehensive manner. For instance, there needs to be a course focusing on IoT microprocessors or microcontrollers and teach their features within a comparative framework with others. Memory and storage units could be under another separate course. Finally, sensors augmented to IoT devices forms a whole different world that includes their design, calibration and management. A course on sensors should teach how these sensors are built and what their features are.

Obviously, in order to teach these courses, the students should first acquire a background on digital electronics and computer design. Therefore, we also introduce new courses on these topics that need to be crafted in such a way

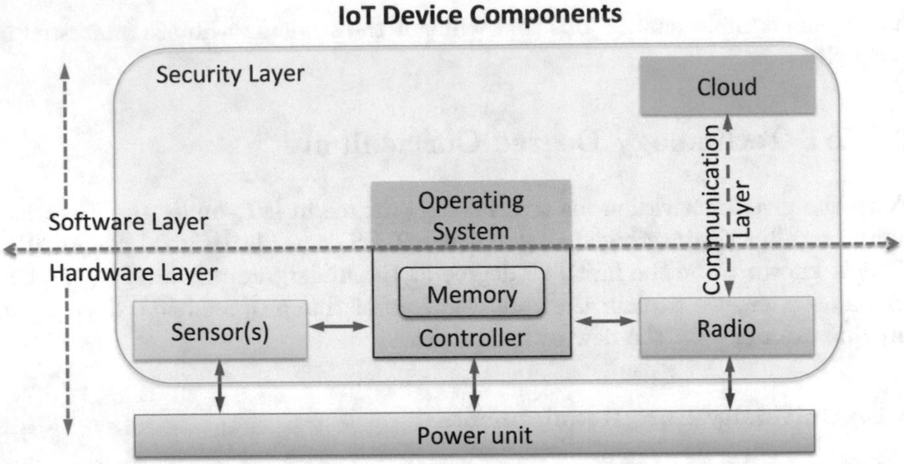

IoT Device Components

Fig. 1. Main components and related layers of an IoT device.

that they will not require Calculus. This is one of the challenges as most of the existing computer engineering courses require Calculus and Circuits courses as prerequisites. To this end, we propose two new courses that offers such a background: First, we designed a new course on Digital Electronics and Circuits which focuses solely on digital aspects and eliminates any analog elements which require more advanced Math. Second, we designed a course that will teach basic computer architecture by considering the IoT device architectures. These two courses are kept as mandatory before any other hardware related courses could be taken.

Software. The software aspects of IoT is pretty broad that spans from programming languages, operating systems to data management via cloud computing. Depending on the program's focus, the set of the software related courses could be adjusted. The major component is programming with IoT devices. To this end, we consider two major programming languages, namely Android Programming and C. As Java is already expected as part of the university core Math requirements, building Android skills on top of Java will be easier. Most of the Computer Science programs offer mobile programming courses and they can be easily adapted for the IoT degree. In our proposed program, since it was under Electrical and Computer Engineering, we offered only C programming which is instrumental in many embedded programming environments. For programs where Python is also offered, this can also be a good match for the Software component of IoT degree.

Apart from programming, there are other elements such as Operating Systems and data management. In our degree, we included an Operating Systems course as part of the curriculum although it is generic Operating Systems class. This will enable understanding the underlying operating systems for IoT devices such as Linux, Android, and other specialized real-time operating systems. For instance, widely used Raspberry PI devices [24] utilize Linux which makes it convenient to run many applications written in diverse programming languages.

Per the data management, there is a huge space that relates to cloud management as most of the IoT data is stored in cloud servers through special platforms. Teaching tools to store, retrieve and process IoT data would definitely be relevant. In our proposed curriculum, there is no mandatory course on it but we plan to offer electives as the program becomes more mature.

Communications. Another important aspect of IoT is their ability to communicate their data via a communication environment. In many cases, this communication is done via wireless channel so it is imperative to teach the wireless concepts before explaining how special IoT data collection protocols work. Current IoT applications heavily utilize WiFi, Bluetooth, Zigbee, Zwave, LoRa and 4/5G standards. Therefore, the students first need to understand the wireless communication basics. To this end, we designed a new course that will teach Wireless Communications which is a simplified version of Digital Communications course in Computer Engineering departments. This course explain the nature of radio signals, communication propagation, channel interference and modulation techniques without getting into their design principles.

Once these concepts are taught, the next step is to give some background on networking, mainly TCP/IP. As IoT devices heavily rely on IP, it is necessary to teach the students how these devices get connected to Internet and what services each layer of the TCP/IP protocol stack provides. Finally, with all of these background, we offer how the existing wireless standards work briefly in another course on IoT Protocols and Standards. This course aims to show the configuration for these protocols and weighs the different options to be deployed under various application requirements. It also offers a layered network architecture which introduces gateways and their communication protocols with the cloud through widely used communication standards for IoT such as Message Queue Telemetry Transport (MQTT) [25] or Constrained Application Protocol (CoAP) [26].

Cybersecurity. The final aspect of an IoT curriculum would be to focus on the security and privacy aspects of these technologies as they pose several critical issues that are probably the most important for the consumers and other stakeholders. To this end, our proposed curriculum first offers a fundamentals course on security which teaches very basics of cybersecurity elements and services. This course does not have any prerequisites other than College Algebra and is typically offered as soon as the students enter the program.

After this introduction, the students are offered a new course on Security of IoT. This course focuses on the threats and vulnerabilities of various IoT devices and networks and includes hands-on activities to be applied on actual IoT devices. This is one of the most attractive courses of the program given that it is new and providing hands-on learning experience.

Under this pillar, there are other aspects that can be taught under elective courses. For instance, we designed another new course on IoT Privacy which solely focuses on privacy of the users and shows how these devices may become vulnerable to privacy leakage. Another course, we designed was on IoT Forensics. This course is also elective but focuses on the forensics tools on various IoT hardware. Another potential course on this pillar could be IoT Ethics and Compliance that trains students on compliance issues when data are collected from IoT devices.

4 Proposed IoT Program Map

After providing the main elements of the proposed IoT curriculum, in this section we outline a sample map of the courses and prerequisites as well as providing other related information.

4.1 Prerequisites

Our degree is a 120 credits hours degree with 40 credits as part of the core IoT while the remaining are allocated for the university core courses and electives. Specifically, 50 credits are coming from university core requirements while 40 credits will be IoT core courses. The remaining 30 credits are electives. Among these 30 credits, 9 credits should be from the home department, 9 credits from other engineering electives while the remaining 12 credits can be from any other college. These credits can be adjusted depending on the needs and availability of electives. A sample flow chart for all courses in the curriculum is shown in Fig. 2.

4.2 Online vs Onsite

One of the other challenge in designing such a new IoT degree is whether to offer it online. This comes from the motivation that most of the students who will be attracted to the program are from professionals in other disciplines or college dropouts who would like to come back to a STEM degree. An online degree would be more flexible for their schedules. Therefore, we considered offering the degree online. However, this brought additional challenges in terms of hands-on learning. Some of the IoT courses require working with IoT devices in the lab to program or access them. When the course is offered online, such opportunities will decrease as the students may not have access to these devices.

To mitigate this situation, we designed the courses in such a way that the students can purchase IoT kits or devices to conduct their assignments as if this is replacing the textbooks. For instance, most of the assignments could be done on Raspberry PIs and a Raspberry PI costs about $30–$40 which is even cheaper than a book. Depending on the course, the instructor needs to plan the needed devices as a kit and ask students to buy them. If the assignment requires any demo, such demos could be recorded and submitted along with the assignment.

Internet of Things Flowchart

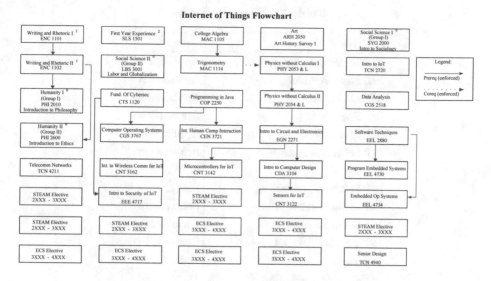

Fig. 2. A sample flowchart for the courses in the proposed IoT program at FIU.

Nevertheless, for group projects this might be a barrier. For instance, for Senior Projects the students will not be able to work as a team unless they live close to each other. For minimizing the impact, we currently offer Senior Design projects that are individual. Obviously, there needs to be more research on how IoT course assignments and projects could be offered online.

5 Other Related Issues

In this section, we discuss other related issues with the new degree.

5.1 Potential Jobs

The graduates of the program can seek employment in any area related to the tech industry including smart homes, smart grid, smart transportation and smart medical devices. The current growth and demand for professionals with the skill sets for developing and implementing IoT will have significant potential for employment locally, statewide, nationally and internationally. In Table 2, we list a categorization of these existing and potential job titles.

5.2 Tracks or Other Joint Programs

Currently, at FIU, we do not offer any tracks or concentrations under the proposed degree but this can be possible in the future as we see more developments and needs. For instance, data analytics with cloud can be a concentration as it has huge potential. Similarly, IoT programming, security and privacy and

Table 2. Potential IoT jobs.

Job title	Category
IoT Technical Architect	Application
IoT Fog Architect	Application
IoT Consultant	Application
IoT Specialist	Application
IoT Manager	Application
IoT Solutions Architect	Application
IoT Developer	Software
IoT Software Architect	Software
IoT Cloud Architect	Software
IoT Security Analyst	Security/Privacy
IoT Privacy Analyst	Security/Privacy
IoT Data Analyst	Data
IoT Machine Learning Specialist	Data
IoT Policy Advisor	Policy
IoT Compliance Manager	Policy

machine learning could easily become new tracks with the availability of new elective courses.

The other possibility is to consider joint certificates with other majors as IoT is being heavily used in certain areas under non-engineering degrees. For instance, at FIU, we currently started a certificate with School of Hospitality in IoT with a funding from Cisco Silicon Valley Foundation. This program targets up or re-skilling the workforce in Hospitality domain with IoT skills so that they can catch up with the technology. We offer IoT courses in relation to hospitality with applications, compliance and analytics. Some of the courses are offered by School of Hospitality while some more technical courses are used from our own IoT program in Engineering. Similar tracks could be offered in other departments such as Agriculture, Logistics/Supply Chain, Public Administration, Public Health, and Law School. For each of these joint certificates, new courses could be designed.

Finally, the question of where to host the IoT technology degree is relevant. We believe that either Computer Science or Engineering can offer this type of degrees. However, they need to focus on different aspects of IoT. For instance, Computer Science may focus on programming, cloud management, privacy, and machine learning aspects while Computer Engineering may focus on hardware/wireless, low level programming and security. It is important to note that these degrees can be designed either as a technology or engineering degree. In the case of latter, there will be Math and/or Discrete Math requirements and the aim will be on the designing and creation of IoT systems or devices.

6   Conclusion

IoT domain became very mature with a wide range of applications and it is ready to become a dedicated degree. An IoT undergraduate degree can be offered as an engineering or a technology degree as both are needed with the given projections of IoT applications, devices and jobs. The curriculum choices and requirements will be different depending on the objectives and directions. In addition, IoT degrees can also be tuned to have a flavor in one of the core areas such as hardware, software, etc. depending on where the degree is hosted.

In this paper, we shared our experience in designing the first technology degree in IoT which aimed to attract students who are not necessarily interested in Math/Engineering but still have a passion in technology. The proposed degree not only fills the gap in the changing job market which is being heavily dominated with IoT applications but also to help increase enrollment in STEM areas. The degree can also have a major impact on research by enabling collaboration with IoT industry and other disciplines where fresh students equipped with IoT-related skills could be involved. The online version of the program can also attract non-traditional and international students. We believe that upcoming years will witness an increased number of such IoT degrees and certificates at the undergraduate level.

References

1. Qiu, T., Chen, N., Li, K., Atiquzzaman, M., Zhao, W.: How can heterogeneous internet of things build our future: a survey. IEEE Commun. Surv. Tutorials **20**(3), 2011–2027 (2018)
2. Da Xu, L., He, W., Li, S.: Internet of things in industries: a survey. IEEE Trans. Ind. Inform. **10**(4), 2233–2243 (2014)
3. Lee, I., Lee, K.: The internet of things (IoT): applications, investments, and challenges for enterprises. Bus. Horiz. **58**(4), 431–440 (2015)
4. Bikmetov, R., Raja, M.Y.A., Sane, T.U.: Infrastructure and applications of internet of things in smart grids: a survey. In: 2017 North American Power Symposium (NAPS), pp. 1–6. IEEE (2017)
5. Mekala, M.S., Viswanathan, P.: A survey: smart agriculture IoT with cloud computing. In: 2017 International Conference on Microelectronic Devices, Circuits and Systems (ICMDCS), pp. 1–7. IEEE (2017)
6. Internet of things (IoT) examples. https://www.postscapes.com/internet-of-things-examples
7. 18 most popular IoT devices in 2019. https://www.softwaretestinghelp.com/iot-devices
8. Overview of the most popular smart home devices. http://iotlineup.com
9. Samie, F., Bauer, L., Henkel, J.: IoT technologies for embedded computing: a survey. In: Proceedings of the Eleventh IEEE/ACM/IFIP International Conference on Hardware/Software Codesign and System Synthesis, p. 8. ACM (2016)
10. Hejazi, H., Rajab, H., Cinkler, T., Lengyel, L.: Survey of platforms for massive IoT. In: 2018 IEEE International Conference on Future IoT Technologies (Future IoT), pp. 1–8. IEEE (2018)

11. Vermesan, O., Friess, P., et al.: Internet of Things-from Research and Innovation to Market Deployment, vol. 29. River Publishers, Aalborg (2014)
12. Ahmed, E., Yaqoob, I., Gani, A., Imran, M., Guizani, M.: Internet-of-things-based smart environments: state of the art, taxonomy, and open research challenges. IEEE Wirel. Commun. **23**(5), 10–16 (2016)
13. Ashton, K., Montgomery, L.R.: How to fly a horse (2015)
14. Gartner says 5.8 billion enterprise and automotive IoT endpoints will be in use in 2020. https://www.gartner.com/en/newsroom/press-releases/2019-08-29-gartner-says-5-8-billion-enterprise-and-automotive-io
15. Unlocking opportunities in the internet of things. https://www.bain.com/insights/unlocking-opportunities-in-the-internet-of-things/
16. The IoT job market: Who's getting hired, and why?. https://internetofthingsrecruiting.com/the-iot-job-market-whos-getting-hired-and-why
17. IoT jobs: Get a red-hot career by learning this red-hot skills. http://techgenix.com/hot-iot-jobs
18. Intel academic IoT course. https://www.youtube.com/playlist?list=PLFBM-eCNdj6A5VSmOEjpn8XoiM88398B7
19. Stanford internet of things graduate certificate. https://online.stanford.edu/programs/internet-things-graduate-certificate
20. School of internet of things engineering of Jiangnan university. http://iot.jiangnan.edu.cn/English/About1/About_us.htm
21. College of internet of things engineering of Hohai university. http://en.hhu.edu.cn/_t4/2012/1018/c357a606/page.htm
22. School of internet of things engineering of XJTLU entrepreneur college. https://www.xjtlu.edu.cn/en/find-a-programme/undergraduate/internet-of-things-engineering
23. IoT bachelor's degree at FIU. https://internetofthings.fiu.edu
24. Raspberry pi device. https://www.raspberrypi.org/
25. OASIS Standard: MQTT version 3.1. 1, vol. 1 (2014). http://docs.oasis-open.org/mqtt/mqtt/v3
26. Bormann, C., Castellani, A.P., Shelby, Z.: CoAP: an application protocol for billions of tiny internet nodes. IEEE Internet Comput. **2**, 62–67 (2012)

IoT in Smart Grid: Energy Management Opportunities and Security Challenges

Motahareh Pourbehzadi[1,2]([⊠]) [iD], Taher Niknam[1] [iD],
Abdollah Kavousi-Fard[1] [iD], and Yasin Yilmaz[2] [iD]

[1] Department of Electrical Engineering, Shiraz University of Technology,
71557-13876 Shiraz, Iran
{m.pourbehzadi, Niknam, Kavousi}@sutech.ac.ir
[2] Department of Electrical Engineering, University of South Florida,
Tampa, FL 33620, USA
mpourbehzadi@mail.usf.edu, yasiny@usf.edu

Abstract. This study is focusing on presenting an online machine learning algorithm that benefits from sequential data of IoT devices in the smart grid. This method provides the smart grid operator with the historical data of generation units of a smart grid that is connected to the IEEE 33-bus test system. The proposed smart grid consists of two photovoltaic cells, two wind turbines, a microturbine, a fuel cell and an electric car the behaviour of which is considered similar to that of a storage unit. In the training phase, the optimized generation units' data is used to form a regressive model of every unit's behaviour. Afterwards, the model is used to predict the behaviour of every unit in the next 24 h. The optimized operation data is used to solve the optimal power flow (OPF) problem. The output of OPF is useful in monitoring the stability of the smart grid, calculating power losses and locating possible faults. Moreover, the proposed framework benefits from the online discrepancy test (ODIT) method, which uses the data of the machine learning method to form a baseline for anomaly detection. The advantage of this method is that it minimizes false alarms and it eliminates false data in anomaly detection. The implementation of the proposed solution methodology has proven to be effective in regards with execution-time reduction and accuracy.

Keywords: Energy management · IoT · Machine learning · Microgrid · Security

1 Introduction

1.1 Background

Since the 21st century, the advancements in electronic communication technology have resolved most of the technical and economic limitations of the electric grid. This is the distinction between an electric grid and a smart grid. A smart grid is an electric grid that benefits from a communication infrastructure among its constituting units; i.e. smart meters, smart appliances and renewable energy resources [1]. Thus, finding the optimal energy dispatch of the generation units is a great matter of concern. Several studies

© IFIP International Federation for Information Processing 2020
Published by Springer Nature Switzerland AG 2020
A. Casaca et al. (Eds.): IFIPIoT 2019, IFIP AICT 574, pp. 319–327, 2020.
https://doi.org/10.1007/978-3-030-43605-6_19

have introduced different solution methodologies in this regard. It is a known fact that meteorological phenomena i.e. wind speed and solar irradiation have a sequential pattern. Historical analysis of other smart grid components such as electric load and market price show that they also have sequential behavior. Therefore, machine learning algorithms have turned into a popular choice for predicting the behaviour of the aforementioned units/ aspects of the smart grid. Figure 1 present the increasing trend in the popularity of addressing IoT-related security issues in smart grids.

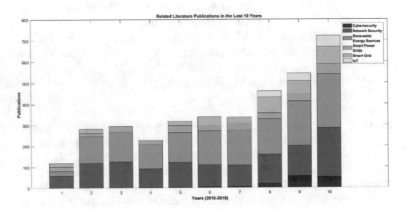

Fig. 1. Related Literature Publications in the Last 10 Years

A smart IoT-based grid is subject to various security challenges such as impersonation, eavesdropping, data tampering, availability and denial of service issues, etc. [2]. Since IoT devices are vulnerable to cyber-attacks the main problem that needs to be addressed is: "what if the IoT devices' data in the smart grid is hacked/ manipulated?" This justifies the existence of adversarial machine learning algorithms. If the manipulated data is not detected through a reliable and quick mechanism, the repercussions can inflict economic and technical cost to the smart grid. That is why addressing security issues in smart grids have been a popular topic in recent years. In [3] the authors used wide and deep convolutional neural networks to analyze the periodicity and non-periodicity in electrical energy consumption. The findings of this study have been used in anomaly detection (electricity theft) of a smart grid. In the study presented in [4] the availability of fine-grained time series data has been introduced as a game changer at the distribution systems level. This issue has prevented effective application of complex machine learning algorithms on grid operation. In this paper, the deep generative adversarial network (GAN) is introduced for learning the conditional probability distribution of real datasets. Article [5] presents adversarial machine learning, whereby models are fooled through malicious input, either for financial gain or to cause system disruption. This paper has presented simulation results that show the effect of adversarial machine learning on the operation of smart energy systems and has proposed directions for future research related to detection and defense mechanisms for such attacks. In [6] it is described that detecting False Data Injection (FDI) attacks by current bad data detection systems is impossible. Ergo, three various supervised learning techniques are presented, the accuracy of which are tested on the IEEE 14-bus, IEEE 57-bus and IEEE 118-bus test systems. The authors of [7] have proposed a new metric for the smart grid that is called the entropic state. This metric has two main purposes. First, it provides an indication of the grid's health on cycle-to-cycle basis. Second, it can be used to detect FDI attacks. The idea of this paper comes from the mentality of addressing state estimation in smart grids and cognitive dynamic systems at the same time.

The aforementioned literature review along with other studies lead us to the conclusion that in regards to adversarial machine learning you can take two main approaches. (1) Designing a robust machine learning algorithm and (2) Detecting attacks and mitigating them. The latter provides us from benefiting current machine learning techniques and is the general approach that has been taken into account. In this study, a regressive model has been introduced to substitute the time-consuming and off-line optimization method that is widely used for energy management in smart grids. Afterwards, the output of this model is given to the OPF solver to gain the power loss and voltage diagram of the main network. The security of the proposed framework is guaranteed using the online discrepancy test (ODIT). The distinction of this method lies within the fact that it eliminates false data, thus avoiding adversarial machine learning while minimizing false alarms.

1.2   Contributions

The present study has major contributions in regards to optimized operation and the OPF of smart grids. The outline of the contributions can be mentioned as follows:

- Presenting an online machine learning regressive method to find the optimized energy dispatch of a microgrid
- Presenting a machine learning based method for addressing the OPF problem
- Avoiding adversarial machine learning using the ODIT

The rest of the paper is organized as follows. In Sect. 2, the problem formulation is stated. Section 3 covers the solution framework implementation. Finally, the concluding remarks can be found in Sect. 4.

2   Problem Formulation

This section presents the operation cost minimization formulation and its associated constraints. The formulation is valid for a 24-h period and the proposed MG is consisted of a MT, a FC, two PVs, two WTs, a BAT and the main grid.

2.1   Cost Function

The cost function of the proposed MG is formulated as described in Eq. (1). Equations (1a–1j) express the detailed value of each term in Eq. (1):

$$F(X) = M(\sum_{t=1}^{T} Cost) = \sum_{t=1}^{T} \begin{array}{c} (Cost^t_{Winds} + Cost^t_{PVs} + Cost^t_{FC} + \\ Cost^t_{MT} + Cost^t_{BAT} + Cost^t_{Grid}) \end{array}$$

$$= M(\sum_{t=1}^{T}([\sum_{a=1}^{N_{WTs}} P^t_{WTs_a} \times Bid^t_{WTs_a}] + [\sum_{b=1}^{N_{PVs}} P^t_{PVs_b} \times Bid^t_{PVs_b}] +$$

$$[\sum_{c=1}^{N_{FC}} u^t_c \times P^t_{FC_c} \times Bid^t_{FC_c} + SU_{FC_c} \times u^t_c \times (1 - u^{t-1}_c) + SD_{FC_c} \times u^{t-1}_c \times (1 - u^t_c)] + \quad (1)$$

$$[\sum_{d=1}^{N_{MT}} u^t_d \times P^t_{MT_d} \times Bid^t_{MT_d} + SU_{MT_d} \times u^t_d \times (1 - u^{t-1}_d) + SD_{MT_d} \times u^{t-1}_d \times (1 - u^t_d)] +$$

$$[\sum_{e=1}^{N_{Bat}} Max(u^t_e, 0) \times P^t_{BAT_e} \times Bid^t_{BAT_e}] + P^t_{Grid} \times Bid^t_{Grid}))$$

$$X = [P_g, U_g]_{1 \times n} \tag{1a}$$

$$n = [2 \times (N_{MT} + N_{FC}) + N_{BAT} + 1] \tag{1b}$$

$$P_g = [P_{Grid}, P_{BAT}, P_{FC}, P_{MT}] \tag{1c}$$

$$U_g = [U_{FC}, U_{MT}] \tag{1d}$$

$$P_{Grid} = [P^1_{Grid}, \ldots, P^T_{Grid}] \quad T \in \{1, \ldots, 24\} \tag{1e}$$

$$P_{BAT} = [P_{BAT_1}, \ldots, P_{BAT_e}]$$
$$P_{BAT_e} = [P^1_{BAT_e}, \ldots, P^T_{BAT_e}] \quad e \in \{1, \ldots, N_{BAT}\} \tag{1f}$$

$$P_{FC} = [P_{FC_1}, \ldots, P_{FC_c}]$$
$$P_{FC_c} = [P^1_{FC_c}, \ldots, P^T_{FC_c}] \quad c \in \{1, \ldots, N_{FC}\} \tag{1g}$$

$$P_{MT} = [P_{MT_1}, \ldots, P_{MT_d}]$$
$$P_{MT_d} = [P^1_{MT_d}, \ldots, P^T_{MT_d}] \quad d \in \{1, \ldots, N_{MT}\} \tag{1h}$$

$$U_g = [u^1_{c_1}, u^2_{c_1}, \ldots, u^T_{c_1}, \ldots, u^1_{c_{N_{FC}}}, \ldots, u^T_{c_{N_{FC}}}, u^1_{d_1}, u^2_{d_1},$$
$$\ldots, u^T_{d_1}, \ldots, u^1_{d_{N_{MT}}}, \ldots, u^T_{d_{N_{MT}}}] \in \{0, 1\} \tag{1i}$$

$$U_E = [u^1_{e_1}, u^2_{e_1}, \ldots, u^T_{e_1}, \ldots, u^1_{e_{N_{BAT}}}, \ldots, u^T_{e_{N_{BAT}}}] \in \{-1, 0, 1\} \tag{1j}$$

2.2 Constraints

Considering the above formulation, X denotes the decision variables' vector, which is mainly consisted of two elements. The first element is that is constituted from the grid, battery, fuel cell and micro turbine's power. Note that since the renewable energy sources are not dispatchable; meaning that the main aim is to benefit their output power the most, they are not being considered as decision variables. The next element of the decision variable vector is Ug specifying the ON/OFF status of the fuel cell and micro turbine. One of the other coefficients in (1) is Uet, defining the battery charge status. This variable is equal to −1, when the battery is discharging and it equals 1 during the charging process. In order to demonstrate the battery state when the battery is neither being charged nor discharged, Uet equals zero. Note that the term SU/SD denotes the startup/shutdown cost of the MT or FC depending on the index. Also here, "a" denotes number of WTs, "b" is for number of PVs, "c" denotes number of FCs, "d" is for MTs and "e" stands for BAT numerator.

The main constraints that are associated with the proposed MG optimized operation are analyzed in this section. The most important constraint in this problem is the power balance constraint as described below:

- **Power/Load Balance Constraint**

The load and supply balance equation is considered as the major constraint that must be fulfilled. This constraint is formulated as Eq. (2):

$$
\begin{aligned}
&\sum_{a=1}^{N_{WTs}} P_{WTs_a}^t + \sum_{b=1}^{N_{PVs}} P_{PVs_b}^t + \sum_{c=1}^{N_{FC}} u_c^t \times P_{FC_c}^t + \\
&\sum_{d=1}^{N_{MT}} u_d^t \times P_{MT_d}^t + \sum_{e=1}^{N_{Bat}} Max(u_e^t, 0) \times P_{BAT_e}^t + P_{Grid}^t = \\
&\sum_{f=1}^{N_{LOAD}} P_{Load}^t - \sum_{e=1}^{N_{Bat}} Min(u_e^t, 0) \times P_{BAT_e}^t
\end{aligned}
\tag{2}
$$

- **Battery Constraint**

The utilization of energy storage systems in the proposed MG leads to some constraints that are mainly associated with the batteries' state of charge (WtBAT), the charge/discharge rate (Pch/dch), their corresponding boundaries and the batteries' efficiency (η). These constraints are described in Eqs. (3–8):

$$
W_{BAT}^t = W_{BAT}^{t-1} + \eta_{ch} \times P_{ch}^t \times time - \frac{1}{\eta_{dch}} \times P_{dch}^t \times time
\tag{3}
$$

$$
W_{BAT_{e,\min}} \leq W_{BAT_e}^t \leq W_{BAT_{e,\max}}
\tag{4}
$$

$$
P_{ch}^t \leq P_{ch,\max}
\tag{5}
$$

$$P^t_{dch} \leq P_{dch,\max} \tag{6}$$

$$P^t_{ch} = Max\left(u^t_e, 0\right) \times P^t_{BAT_e} \tag{7}$$

$$P^t_{dch} = -Min\left(u^t_e, 0\right) \times P^t_{BAT_e} \tag{8}$$

The limitations on the maximum and minimum levels of output powers of the fuel cell, the micro turbine, the grid and the battery must be taken into account, as described in Eqs. (9)–(12).

$$u^t_c \times P^t_{FC_{c,\min}} \leq P^t_{FC_c} \leq u^t_c \times P^t_{FC_{c,\max}} \tag{9}$$

$$u^t_d \times P^t_{MT_{d,\min}} \leq P^t_{FC_c} \leq u^t_d \times P^t_{MT_{d,\max}} \tag{10}$$

$$P^t_{Grid,\min} \leq P_{Grid} \leq P^t_{Grid,\max} \tag{11}$$

$$u^t_e \times P^t_{BAT_{e,\min}} \leq P^t_{BAT_e} \leq u^t_e \times P^t_{BAT_{e,\max}} \tag{12}$$

3 Solution Implementation

3.1 Machine Learning Substitution for Optimization Algorithm

Classical operation of microgrids is usually performed via solving the optimal dispatch of the system whilst considering the constraints explained in Sect. 2. Figure 2 illustrates the traditional chronology of microgrid operation.

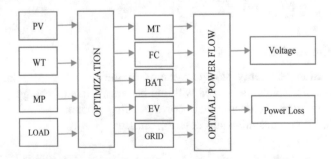

Fig. 2. Traditional microgrid operation

In this study, we have utilized the output of a solution methodology called the bird mating optimization (BMO) algorithm. The fundamental of this algorithm is based on the mating of birds. Male or female birds choose their elite mate or mates based on a series of preferences. This mating behaviour is scored in a descending order and it will be considered as the fitness function of the algorithm of the initial population. Detailed description of the BMO algorithm can be found in [8]. After implementing the BMO algorithm on the proposed microgrid and analyzing the results, it came to the authors' attention that the temporal behaviour of different units can be considered as training data for a regression-based supervised machine learning algorithm. Therefore, the optimization section in Fig. 2 was substituted with the machine learning algorithm.

The distribution of various constituting units of the microgrid on the IEEE 33-bus test system is illustrated in Fig. 3.

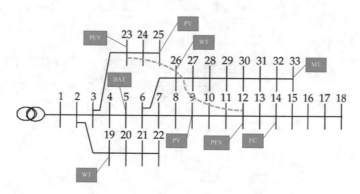

Fig. 3. Proposed microgrid topography

Considering the constraints of buses and lines in Fig. 3, it is obligatory that the OPF problem be solved for the IEEE 33-bus test system. Note that the dotted line illustrates the traveling path of the electric vehicle. Similar to the observations of the BMO algorithm, the OPF output has a temporal response as well. Ergo, the output data can be used to train another supervised machine learning algorithm to substitute the OPF calculations. It must be noted that the main motive for such substitutions lies within the fact that the traditional methods have two main deficiencies: (1) their performance is dependent on the initial population and (2) The computational complexity of these solutions is very high.

3.2   Online Discrepancy Test

It is a known fact that IoT devices are vulnerable to cyber attacks. The main question is: how can we avoid the manipulated data in machine learning? two main approaches can be taken: (1) Designing a robust machine learning algorithm and (2) Detecting attacks and mitigating them. The latter provides us from benefiting current machine learning techniques and is the general approach that has been taken into account. In this study, a regressive model has been introduced to substitute the time-consuming and off-line optimization method that is widely used for energy management in smart grids. Afterwards, the output of this model is given to the OPF solver to gain the power loss and voltage diagram of the main network. The security of the proposed framework is guaranteed using the online discrepancy test (ODIT). Detailed description of the ODIT can be found in [9]. The distinction of this method lies within the fact that it eliminates false data, thus avoiding adversarial machine learning while minimizing false alarms. The final scheme of the proposed operational framework is illustrated in Fig. 4.

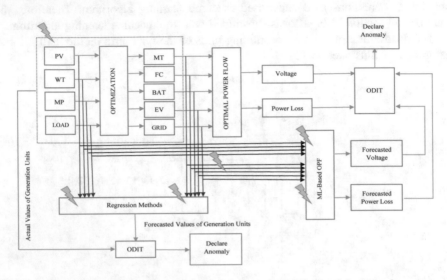

Fig. 4. Final operation scheme of the proposed ML-based framework

There are two important factors in regards to the final scheme of the system as illustrated in Fig. 4. (1) Both the optimization and OPF sections have substituted via regression methods. (2) The ODIT is used to declare any possible anomalies. The yellow surge signs in Fig. 4 show the possible parts of the scheme that can be subject to cyber attacks. The attack can occur in the optimization or OPF section, which supplies the training data for the regression method or it can occur on the system after the machine learning substitution. In either case, the ODIT's strategy is to get constant feedbacks from the actual values and the forecasted values and make a decision on the existence of anomalous activities using a cumulative criterion [9].

4   Conclusion

With the emergence and development of telecommunication technologies, a new generation of electric grid has been born; i.e. "the smart grid". Smart grids have facilitated several energy management limitations of classic grids. In this regard, two main points must be taken into consideration:

- The repetitive patterns of renewable energy resources such as solar irradiation and wind speed can be modeled using a regressive machine learning technique. Furthermore, other aspects that form the energy management of smart grid have a sequential pattern. For example the energy price and load demand are lower in the beginning and at the end of the day while they both have peaks sometime around noon. This justifies the usage of machine learning algorithms as a substitute for current off-line meta-heuristic algorithms that require high number of iterations to converge to the global optimal operation point.

- The security aspects of machine learning- based models in IoT systems. If the machine learning algorithm is fooled with false or manipulated data, then the final output of the computations will be false. This can lead to serious financial or even life-threatening consequences. In order to address this issue it is necessary to provide an anomaly detection method that is both quick and reliable.

Finally, The findings of this work can be summarized as follows:

We presented an online machine learning algorithm to substitute the optimized operation and optimized power flow of a smart grid. The benefits of using machine learning algorithms in energy management of smart grids can be reflected in addressing computational complexities in: (1) Time: Reducing the operation time and anomaly detection time. (2) Space: Real-life systems are large-scaled and solving the optimization problem for a grid-connected smart grid is mathematically complex.

We introduced an online anomaly detection method to detect and mitigate cyber attacks to IoT devices in smart grid so that: (1) the false alarms are minimized. (2) The false data is eliminated.

References

1. Sakhnini, J., Karimipour, H., Dehghantanha, A., Parizi, R.M., Srivastava, G.: Security aspects of Internet of Things aided smart grids: a bibliometric survey. Internet Things, 100111 (2019, in press)
2. Bekara, C.: Security issues and challenges for the IoT-based smart grid. Procedia Comput. Sci. **34**, 532–537 (2014)
3. Zheng, Z., Yang, Y., Niu, X., Dai, H.N., Zhou, Y.: Wide and deep convolutional neural networks for electricity-theft detection to secure smart grids. IEEE Trans. Ind. Inform. **14**(4), 1606–1615 (2017)
4. Zhang, C., Kuppannagari, S.R., Kannan, R., Prasanna, V.K.: Generative adversarial network for synthetic time series data generation in smart grids. In: 2018 IEEE International Conference on Communications, Control, and Computing Technologies for Smart Grids (SmartGridComm), pp. 1–6. IEEE, October 2018
5. Bor, M., Marnerides, A., Molineux, A., Wattam, S., Roedig, U.: Adversarial machine learning in smart energy systems (2019)
6. Sakhnini, J., Karimipour, H., Dehghantanha, A.: Smart grid cyber attacks detection using supervised learning and heuristic feature selection. arXiv preprint arXiv:1907.03313 (2019)
7. Oozeer, M.I., Haykin, S.: Cognitive dynamic system for control and cyber-attack detection in smart grid. IEEE Access **7**, 78320–78335 (2019)
8. Askarzadeh, A.: Parameter estimation of fuel cell polarization curve using BMO algorithm. Int. J. Hydrog. Energy **38**(35), 15405–15413 (2013)
9. Mozaffari, M., Yilmaz, Y.: Online anomaly detection in multivariate settings. In: 2019 IEEE 29th International Workshop on Machine Learning for Signal Processing (MLSP), pp. 1–6. IEEE, October 2019

Author Index

Aakur, Sathyanarayanan N. 142
Akkaya, Kemal 307
Albandes, Rogério 53, 71, 86
Almeida, Ricardo 86

Barbosa, Jorge 53, 71
Batista, Thais 21
Boddupalli, Srivalli 105

Cavalcante, Everton 21
Chen, Kwang-Cheng 219
Coutinho, Emanuel Ferreira 36
Crain, Jacob 289
Cui, Qimei 219

Dantas, Lucas Cristiano 21
de Souza, José Neuman 36

Fernandes, Alan 21
Ferreira, Samela 21
Fu, Xinwen 289

Jao, Nicholas Anton 197
Jin, Yier 289

Karam, Robert 252
Kasarabada, Yasaswy 123
Katkoori, Srinivas 142, 159
Kavousi-Fard, Abdollah 319
Khan, Md Fahim Faysal 197
Kougianos, Elias 273

Lewandowski, Matthew 159
Lopes, João L. B. 71
Luo, Lan 289
Luria, David 123

Machado, Roger 53, 71, 86
Mahdavi, Mehrdad 197

Mähler, Viktor 235
Mahmud, Shakil 252
Mohanty, Saraju P. 273
Moreira Neto, Maurício 36
Moreira, Leonardo Oliveira 36

Narayanan, Vijaykrishnan 197
Nie, Zixiang 219
Niknam, Taher 319

Olney, Brooks 252
Oquendo, Flavio 3

Pearson, Bryan 289
Pernas, Ana Marilza 86
Pourbehzadi, Motahareh 319

Qiu, Keni 197

Rachakonda, Laavanya 273
Ramnath, Vishalini Laguduva 142
Ray, Sandip 105
Reis, Ricardo 179
Rocha, Felipe 21

Santos, Luis Felipe 21
Sharma, Akshay 273
Shuai, Changchi 197
Soares, Bruna 21

Vemuri, Ranga 123

Wang, Yingze 219

Yamin, Adenauer 53, 71, 86
Yilmaz, Yasin 319

Zou, Cliff 289

Printed in the United States
by Baker & Taylor Publisher Services